LITERATURE AND THE ART
OF CREATION

LITERATURE AND THE ART OF CREATION

Essays and Poems in honour of
A. Norman Jeffares

edited by

Robert Welch
Suheil Badi Bushrui

1988
COLIN SMYTHE
Gerrards Cross Bucks
BARNES & NOBLE BOOKS
Totowa, New Jersey

First published in 1988 by Colin Smythe Limited
Gerrards Cross, Buckinghamshire

British Library Cataloging-in-Publication Data

Literature and the art of creation
  1. Literature —— History and criticism
  I. Welch, Robert, *1947-*   II.Bushru'i,
  Suheil Badi'
  809   PN523

ISBN 0–86140–252–9

First published in the United States of America in 1988
by Barnes and Noble Books, Totowa, N.J. 07512

Library of Congress Cataloging-in-Publication Data

Literature and the art of creation.
  Bibliography: p.
  Includes index.
  1. Literature – History and criticism. 2. Creation
(Artistic, literary, etc.) I. Welch, Robert,
1947–   . II. Bushrui, Suheil B.
PN56.C69L5 1988   809   88–3396
ISBN 0–389–20783–7

Produced in Great Britain
Set by Action Typesetting Limited, Gloucester
and printed and bound by Billing & Sons Limited
Worcester

For
Derry Jeffares

ACKNOWLEDGEMENTS

The works by W. B. Yeats that are quoted in this volume are published by kind permission of Michael B. Yeats and Macmillan London, Ltd., and for North America by kind permission of Anne Yeats and the Macmillan Publishing Co. Inc., New York.

CONTENTS

Contents

INTRODUCTION

ROBERT WELCH

One of the chief functions of effective criticism is to show how works of art originate in the human instinct for creativity. Criticism remains a sane activity when its questions and judgements are held in balance by a tactful sense that the objects of criticism, the works of art, accomplish acts of creation. 'Tact' is a word that is useful to bear in mind when engaged upon criticism or thinking about criticism. If a work of art originates in the human instinct for creativity, then to speak of the act of creation is to speak of a profound movement of human consciousness as it seeks coherence, definition and self-expression. It seeks, in other words, significant order. The accomplishment of such a significant order is a compound of delight and awe. The work of art shows us life, evolving, out of an impulse rooted in itself, more abundant forms for it to take. And as such the work of art originates in the complex, delightful and awesome laboratory of being, where new forms, including those of the intellect, take shape. Criticism should be content to be 'liminal', to be on the threshold of this powerful and lovely ordering. It should cultivate the old virtue of tact.

Whatever its programme, criticism should remain conscious of its duties, and the restraints within which it should operate. It can inform, instruct, contextualize. It may theorize and classify; adduce order where there had been apparent chaos, define or redefine tradition; but it should retain a tactful sense of the supremacy of the creative act itself, by which its own discipline is informed from time to time.

With literature one is dealing with the arts of language. Language itself, its existence, shows us the inevitability of the creative impulse in man. By the very fact that language came into being we can see an instinct in life towards articulation, order and coherence. Language is the interrelationship of physiology,

1

the locomotor and nervous systems, the brain and all its faculties, including memory, genetic inheritance, all deployed towards the act of expression. Language, we should try to realise continuously, is an astonishing achievement. And literature, which re-searches language ceaselessly, to see how its resources can be refined to speak of our felt existence in time, is language stretched to its utmost. Literature continually speaks of the heights and the depths ('heaven blazing into the head', and 'the foul rag and bone shop of the heart') and each extreme involves the other. Language is our most awesome technology, and literature is the exercise of that technology for understanding. To say that writers lie when they conceive fictions is to miss the point of the exercise, which is to stay in touch with the creative instinct, by means of which we invented language and became man.

Literature and creativity are closely related. The creative potential of language itself, which is the means, the material and the preoccupation of literature, and our most human technology, is brought before our minds in the forms and perceptions of literature. Literary criticism, which studies the works and achievements of language in literature, should be tactful, but it should be conscious too of the dignity of its calling. It is no mean thing to be an interpreter. It is a delightful and proud thing to make clear the relationship between a writer's life and his work, between the traditions a writer inherits and his own individual character and temperament, between imaginative work and its social context. All of these activities, and more, serve literature and creativity. The essays gathered in this volume are evidence of the variety of ways in which good criticism can interpret the relationship between literature and the art of creation.

What are the qualities of a really excellent critic or interpreter? that he care deeply about the creative instinct; that he care about accuracy, and in particular about the accurate use of language; that he be honest; that he be modest. The man to whom this volume of essays is dedicated has all of these qualities in abundance. He gives of himself freely because he cares. He hates sloppiness in language because he is totally aware of what language is. He knows there are no short cuts to anything that matters, and that once truth has begun to obey the student's call personal vanity disappears. Derry Jeffares is a man who has built and who encouraged others to build, not like him, but how they might wish to build for themselves. He was and is the easiest of masters and the hardest.

Derry Jeffares is a man who, as Brendan Kennelly puts it in his contribution to this volume, has had many lives. An Irishman first, he has become a citizen of the world. At the High School in Dublin he held the Erasmus Smith Scholarship and was Head Boy. At Trinity College, Dublin, he read Classics before proceeding to the Ph.D. there and the D.Phil. at Oriel College, Oxford, where he worked under Nicoll Smith. He taught Classics at Trinity and from there went to the University of Gronigen in Holland, where he was a Lector in English until 1948. In 1947 he married Jeanne, daughter of Emile Calembert of Brussels. *W.B. Yeats: Man and Poet* first appeared in 1949, and this book still remains one of the standard works on the relationship between Yeats's life and his work. Derry Jeffares showed great tact and discernment in the selection he made of the autobiographical writings to illuminate the poetry. Yeats is often a difficult and challenging writer. Our understanding of him grows all the time, but Yeats scholarship owes a profound debt to the judgement, balance and understanding that manifests itself throughout that serious, searching and still indispensable volume of 1949.

He lectured at the University of Edinburgh for a time, but the wider world had begun to call. In 1951, at the age of thirty-one, he became Jury Professor of English Language and Literature at the University of Adelaide, Australia. He was made Vice-President of the Film and Television Council of South Australia, displaying an understanding of and interest in the media, natural when one considers that one of Derry's main efforts in life has been and is to improve the lines of communication between individuals and peoples. He was made Secretary of the Australian Humanities Research Council in 1954.

While teaching and doing administration at Adelaide he edited Disraeli and worked on a large anthology of English poetry. In 1957 he was made Professor of English literature at the University of Leeds. He proceeded to build the English Department at Leeds into one of the finest and one of the most diversified in the United Kingdom. Furthermore, he helped to establish Leeds as an internationally known University by using it as a base to launch various projects which connected with the Commonwealth and the rest of the world. He was founding Chairman of the Association for Commonwealth Literature and Language Studies (ACLALS) in 1966; and was also founding Chairman of the International Association for the Study of Anglo-Irish Literature (IASAIL) in 1968. All of this while he was writing and editing: he worked on Goldsmith, George Moore, Yeats, Cowper, Whitman, Congreve, Richard Brinsley Sheridan; on the scientific background to literature; and on the new literatures in English, from Australia, India, Africa, the West Indies. This list shows the catholicity of his taste and his receptivity to new ideas, forms and styles. From Leeds also, he edited, from 1960–67, *A Review of English Literature*, one of the most stimulating of the academic literary journals of the 1960s.

At Leeds he established a Chair of American Literature, with the help of outside funding from the U.S., at a time when this kind of enterprise was virtually unknown in the Universities. Outside funding also helped him to establish: the Chair of Contemporary English; a visiting fellowship in Commonwealth Literature; the Bruern Fellowship in American Literature (set up with Professor Douglas Grant). Under him the School of English at Leeds established: the Institute of Bibliography and Textual Criticism; the Institute of Modern English Language Studies; and the Institute of Dialectology and Folk Life Studies. Each attracted graduate students (often from overseas) of a very high calibre; each produced outstanding research and scholarship; each gave individuals the freedom to develop their interests and potential as far as they wished. Not least of the achievements of the Institutes was the fact that the research work in which they engaged was reflected in the undergraduate syllabuses the School offered, thereby realising effectively Lord Edward Boyle's view that teaching should proceed in an atmosphere of research. Again, with the help of outside funding, he set up the *Journal of Commonwealth Literature*, which was edited from Leeds by Arthur Ravenscraft for many years. He organized the setting up of a University T.V. Studio, which expanded from a house into a potato store and a garage. It is now a prestigious centre, which is both a University facility and a teaching resource. He invited poets from all over the world to Leeds, and made recordings of them reading their work. Within the School of English he set up a Poetry Room to house the collection of recorded material with Arts Council of Great Britain funding. He created the post of Administrative Officer within the School of English. The School also acquired its own technician. He helped to establish the Workshop Theatre at Leeds, now one of the outstanding places for the study of drama in the United Kingdom. In the early days students of English would attend G. Wilson Knight's lectures on Shakespeare and act in productions in which Wilson Knight himself was an enthusiastic and thoughtful participant. The

Workshop Theatre developed from these beginnings and is now a prestigious postgraduate training school which attracts students from all over the world.

Throughout the sixties and into the seventies the School of English at Leeds was a warm, lively place, with an international reputation for excellence and innovation. Scholars, writers, artists, from all over the world came to the School. There was an atmosphere of seriousness and of fun.

Derry's own scholarship continued throughout this extraordinarily busy phase. The massive Commentary on the *Collected Poems of W.B. Yeats*, drawing on an unrivalled knowledge of Yeats and his sources, appeared in 1968; while the Yeats centenary was marked in 1965 by *In Excited Reverie: A Centenary Tribute to W.B. Yeats, 1865–1939*, edited by Derry. The Swift Tercentenary in 1967 was marked by *Fair Liberty Was All His Cry: A Tercentenary Tribute to Jonathan Swift*. He edited a volume of essays on Scott and another on Swift. He ceased to edit *A Review of English Literature* in 1967 and in 1970 was founding editor of *Ariel: A Review of International English Literature*. He was general editor of that very influential series from Oliver and Boyd in the sixties and seventies, the Writers and Critics series, in their attractive orange, white and black format. Those volumes were models of concision and clarity. He was general editor of the New Oxford English Series, the Irish Novels Series, Macmillan Commonwealth Writers, Macmillan New Literature Handbooks, Macmillan Histories of Literature, and literary editor of the Fountainwell Drama Texts.

The mammoth four volume edition, *Restoration Drama*, edited by Derry with an introduction and notes on each play, appeared in 1974. In that year he moved from Leeds to Stirling University, where he became Professor of English Studies. By now he was F.R.S.A. (1963), F.R.S.L. (1965), F.A.H.A. (1970), F.A.C.L.A.L.S. (1971).

At Stirling he worked with renewed energy. He and Jeanne and their daughter Bo set about turning Westermoss near Rumbling Bridge into a haven of peace and hospitality for travellers, friends, writers and scholars from all parts of the globe. A pottery was established by Jeanne, with a huge kiln that radiated warmth and creativity; next to it was the library, converted from the old barn, with long elegant carpet runners on the newly established concrete floor, laid, under Derry's watchful eye, over great sheets of thick polythene to keep the room snug and dry. Walls were built, by Derry, and visitors would willingly hump stone, mix concrete, talk and think, and sit down to conversation, wine, laughter and lashings of food that always tasted delicious. Industry combined with peace, laughter with kindness, excitement with ease. It was and is a special place.

With A.S.Knowland he published, in 1975, *A Commentary on the Collected Plays of W.B. Yeats*. In 1977 he was given an Honorary Doctorate by the University of Lille and in that year the edition of *Yeats: The Critical Heritage* appeared. In 1977 also he became a member of the Scottish Arts Council and Chairman of its Literature Committee. In 1978 he was made an Honorary Fellow of Trinity College, Dublin. In 1980 he became a member of the Arts Council of Great Britain and Vice-Chairman of the Scottish Arts Council in 1981. In 1982 appeared his *History of Anglo-Irish Literature*. *A New Commentary on the Poems of W.B. Yeats* appeared in 1984 and a volume of *Essays on Anglo-Irish Literature* will appear in 1988.

He has been a consultant and advisor to the British Council. He revised *British Book News* in the early sixties and helped to make it the influential reviewing medium it has become. He has been an assessor and an interviewer for many chairs in English literature throughout the U.K., Ireland and overseas. He has participated in and helped shape degree schemes, higher degree programmes, and academic planning generally. He has lectured and acted as external examiner throughout the world. He is a member of the Final Selection Board of the Civil Service Commission.

At the time of writing Derry and Jeanne are to move to Crail, to begin yet another phase of building and renewal. They will live by the sea, on the east Scottish coast. Derry has, for many years, been writing and publishing poetry. The verse is laughing, vigorous and satiric, a recreation of his spirit, which will expand even more in the new place.

We salute him, in the words of the poet whom he has so well served, and which seem appropriate to this world-traveller who is always at home:

> What motion of the sun or stream
> Or eyelid shot the gleam
> That pierced my body through?
> What made me live like these that seem
> Self-born, born anew?

CANON SHEEHAN AND THE CATHOLIC INTELLECTUAL

TERENCE BROWN

In December 1903 Canon Sheehan, the popular Irish novelist, addressed the students of his own *alma mater* in the *Aula Maxima* of St. Patrick's College, Maynooth. His lecture, stirringly entitled 'The Dawn of the Century', challenged his audience in a way to which they were not, by all accounts, accustomed:

> One safe principle may be laid down — that the Irish priest must be in advance of his people, educationally by at least fifty years. The priests have the lead, and they must keep it. But the right of leadership, now so often questioned, must be supported by tangible and repeated proofs; and these proofs must concern not only your spiritual authority, but your intellectual superiority. The young priest who has lectured on 'Hamlet' in the Town Hall on Thursday night is listened to with deeper respect on Sunday morning. The priest who conducts a long and laborious experiment before a literary and scientific society in any of our cities is, henceforward, an acknowledged and unquestioned guide in his village. And the priest who, quietly and without temper, overthrows one of those carping critics at a dinner-party, may confirm, without the possibility of its being disturbed again, the faith of many who are present, and whose beliefs, perhaps, were rudely shaken by the impertinence of the shallow criticism to which they had just been listening. [1]

The educational deficiencies of Maynooth, whatever its success as the clerical powerhouse of the increasingly dynamic Catholicism of later-nineteenth-century Ireland, were a recurrent complaint of Victorian social commentators. In 1850 those prolific scribblers Mr and Mrs S.C. Hall had written disparagingly in their vast compendium on all things Irish of the narrow and illiberal education offered there to a socially undistinguished studentry, lamenting its location in a cultural backwater: 'the

7

college should be, undoubtedly, removed from the miserable village where it at present stands to the immediate neighbourhood of some city; where, while the students are subjected to wholesome and sufficient restraints, they may be permitted occasional intercourse with mankind'.[2] A Royal Commission of 1854–55 tended to confirm these jaundiced opinions, and subsequent literary and autobiographical reminiscence of Maynooth life suggests that few improvements were effected in the following decades. Sheehan himself entered Maynooth in 1869. His memories were less than enthusiastic.

I think it was on the 25th August, 1869, I passed through the Sphinx guarded gates of Maynooth College, and stood near what was then the Senior chapel, and saw, with a certain melancholy feeling, the old keep of the Geraldine castle lighted up by the rays of the sinking sun. I remember well that the impression made upon me by Maynooth College then, and afterwards, when I saw its long stone corridors, its immense bare stony halls, the huge massive tables, etc., was one of rude, Cyclopean strength, without one single aspect or feature of refinement. So too with its studies. Relentless logic, with its formidable chevaux-de-frise of syllogisms, propositions, scholia; metaphysics, sublime, but hardened into slabs of theories, congealed in medieval Latin ... The Graces were nowhere. Even in the English literature or Belles Lettres class, as it was called, the course seemed to be limited to hard grinding Grammar and nothing more. [3]

Upon ordination Sheehan quickly realised how little his Maynooth career had prepared him for what he increasingly felt was required in modern pastoral life, intellectual as well as spiritual leadership of the kind he commended in his lecture of 1903. Accordingly almost all of his published work affords us a fascinating opportunity to observe the complex relations between a committed Catholic intellectual and Irish society in the period when modern Irish nationalism was forming itself into the force which would shape a new Ireland in the first two decades of the twentieth century. For throughout his career as essayist, novelist and priest Sheehan remained vigorously engaged in the project of establishing an intellectual Catholic presence in a country he believed was in dire need of such. Indeed the almost obsessional way in which the topic recurs in his writings suggests how desperate in his opinion was the lack of that leaven.

In Sheehan's writings the Irish Catholic of intellectual and cultural aspiration is confronted at the outset by a terrible awareness — that is of the comparative impoverishment of the country in almost every sphere of humanistic achievement. An early veneration at the shrine of Carlyle had given Sheehan an appreciation of all things German and amongst his first literary and cultural exploits had been a series of essays on the German university system beside which Ireland's halls of higher learning seemed pitiably inadequate. In modern Germany it seemed to him, as had not been the case since the days of the Greek Academy, an 'aristocracy of talent' held sway in a climate where 'chief prominence is given to religious science'.[4] And of the country he could claim 'infidelity is making no headway amongst any class in Germany'.[5] In his novel *Luke Delmege* (1901) we are introduced to a priest, one of the many interesting minor characters in the work, who has spent two years studying in Germany. His experience there compares sadly with the hero's period of cultural deprivation at Maynooth and the generally depressed quality of life in Ireland. Of this character Sheehan informs us: 'And when by degrees he began to realize that this country, which but a few years back had been cursed by a foreign tongue, had now, by a supreme effort, created its own language, and a literature unsurpassed for richness and sweetness, he saturated himself with the poetry and philosophy of the country, which gave a new colour and embellishment to life'. But it is in Sheehan's last novel *The Graves at Kilmorna* (1915) that the romance of Europe, and of Germany in particular, receives its fullest expression. Sheehan had himself holidayed in Germany in 1904 and in *The Graves At Kilmorna*, written in 1911, he has an ageing Fenian, depressed and discouraged by developments in Ireland, discover a world more headily attractive than any he has hitherto encountered. But the experience is no unalloyed pleasure:

As they advanced, and new worlds of wonder opened up to his view, and he saw what education and civilization had wrought; and how human life and its surroundings were lifted up and on to a high plane of refinement and culture; how literature and the arts sweetened toil . . . he became moody and silent and abstracted. He was thinking of the motherland; and how far she was in the rear of all modern civilization . . . . He would not admit for a moment that Nature had done less for Ireland than for the favoured countries of Europe; but oh! when it came to human effort and human genius, what a deplorable contrast.

Sheehan had in fact good reason to praise the quality of German civilization for in that country his own work was much esteemed.

In particular his fine semi-autobiographical account of the intellectual pilgrimage of a priest in *Luke Delmege* was admired by German readers. In that work the hero had conceived an ambition to engraft 'German ideas and German habits and manners on the peasantry at home', which improbable enterprise must have commended him to his German audience. But a more compelling aspect of *Luke Delmege* is its exploration of a sensitive and intelligent Irishman's encounter with the riches of Victorian English culture. Sheehan's enamourment of German life and letters was a matter of books and the romanticism of the distant — he presents Germany in his novels in terms of fictional tourism. His relationship with England was the fruit of his two years service on the English mission. As a consequence his study of Luke Delmege's complex and varying responses to England amounts to one of the most subtle, psychologically developed portraits in all his fiction.

Luke Delmege has graduated with high academic honours from Maynooth and is plunged into the priesthood in a land he cannot easily comprehend. His initial response is in terms of an Irish nationalist stereotype whereby England is apprehended in all its vast materialism in contrast to the spirituality of Ireland:

Everywhere it was the same. Whilst all around the splendid materialism of England asserted and showed itself; whilst shops were packed full of every kind of luxury and necessary, and the victuallers and pork-butchers vied with the fruit-sellers in exhibiting every form of human food; whilst public baths were springing up in all directions, and everything ministering to human wants was exhibited in super-abundance, whilst a perfect system of police and detective supervision guarded human life and safety, each solitary individual walked alone.

The English state seems to Luke 'a huge piece of perfect and polished mechanism — cold, clean, shining, smooth, and regular; but with no more of a soul than a steam engine'. Slowly however he finds himself penetrating the cold surfaces of English personality: 'he got used to it, and his nerves were gradually toned down into the silky smoothness that reigned everywhere around him. And he began to see great deeps of affection and love far down beneath the icy surface, and every day he was made aware of genuine kindness, gentle, undemonstrative, unobtrusive, until he grew to love these grave, pleasant people, and they loved him in return'. Furthermore he is transferred to a curacy where he has the opportuntiy to preach to an educated, urbane congregation and begins to make a mark as a Catholic apologist. A liberal cultivated social circle introduces him to the range of contemporary English intellectual life:

The beautiful, smooth mechanism was affecting Luke unconsciously. He no longer heard the whir and jar of machinery, or saw the mighty monster flinging out its refuse of slime and filth in the alleys and courts of southwest London; but the same smooth regularity, the same quiet, invincible energy was manifest here in the sleepy Cathedral town. Here was the beautiful tapestry, pushed out from the horrid jaws of the great mill; beautiful, perfect, with all fair colours of cultured men and stately women, and woven through with gold and crimson threads of art and science and literature. And Luke felt the glamour wrapping him around with an atmosphere of song and light and he felt it a duty to fit himself to his environment.

England has seduced an Irish intellect and sensibility. A visit back to his home village confirms his national disenchantment: 'As they drove along, the aspect of the landscape seemed intolerably melancholy and dull. The grey fields, that had not yet sprung into green, the thatched cottages, the ruined walls, the broken hedges, the ragged bushes all seemed to Luke, fresh from the prim civilization of Aylesburgh, unspeakably old and wretched. Ruin and delapidation were everywhere'.

Sheehan of course is not satisfied to show us in his fiction only the effects on the culturally starved of the rich diet of English and European civilization. He is perhaps even more absorbed as an artist with the problems confronting the Irish Catholic intellectual who wishes to influence his country through the broader cultural perspectives provided by English and European experience. The latter half of *Luke Delmege* therefore has Luke back in Ireland engaged in a vain attempt to teach his Irish charges the ways of English punctuality, self-improvement and personal independence. The result is catastrophic for Luke. But in a more muted, less schematic fashion Canon Sheehan's best known and most popular work *My New Curate* (1900) is preoccupied with precisely this theme. The degree to which this work revolves about this major concern of Sheehan's own intellectual life may surprise the reader who comes to this book in the knowledge of its Irish reputation as a benevolent, humorous, engaging series of scenes from Irish clerical life. In fact the work, for all its occasional drollery of tone and urbanity of manner, is a study in failure. The genial humour of the book derives from its central character, the quizzical, good-tempered, elderly classicist Father Dan, one of Sheehan's most attractive

and credible creations. His new curate is the impetuous, culturally ambitious, energetic social improver, Father Lethenby.
Father Lethenby's enterprises, however, come to grief. His
efforts to establish a factory and a fishing industry prove
disastrously ineffective and almost bring him to financial and
personal ruin. But the novel makes clear too that Father Dan,
now the repository of the calm wisdom of the aged, had once
nurtured similar ambitions until the years taught him sense:

I remember what magnificent ideas I had. I would build factories, I
would pave the streets, I would establish a fishing-station and make
Kilronan the favourite bathing resort on the western coast, I would write
books and be, all round, a model of push, energy, and enterprise. And
I did try. I might as well have tried to remove yonder mountain with a
pitchfork, or stop the roll of the Atlantic with a rope of sand. Nothing on
earth can cure the inertia of Ireland. It weighs down like the sweeping
clouds on the damp, heavy earth and there's no lifting it, nor
disburthening of the souls of men of this intolerable weight ... It was a
land of the lotus. The people were narcotized.

We know from Sheehan's biographer[6] that he himself had
experienced something of the same frustration when he returned
from the English mission to a curacy in Mallow. Accordingly it is
hard not to read in Sheehan's fiction a kind of intellectual and
spiritual autobiography in which he sought to come to terms
with difficulty, frustration and even failure. In each of his novels
in which he explores the dilemma of the priest as intellectual, *My
New Curate, Luke Delmege* and *The Blindness of Dr Gray* (1909), he
makes his heroes learn the hard lesson of the inadequacies of
intellect unless it is warmed by the fires of faith and feeling. Luke
Delmege is brought to acknowledge that the spirituality of the
Irish will never be satisfied by any philosophy rooted in the
materialism of English ideas of progress. Father Lethenby comes
to understand the role of suffering in the truly beneficent life and
Dr Gray must learn that the letter of an abstract and perfect law
is what kills the spirit, where love gives life. The fact that these
profound Christian apprehensions are mediated by Sheehan in
his novels through scenes and events reminiscent of the most
tendentious and propagandist of Victorian evangelical fiction is
probably the principal aspect of his work that has sent his once
bright literary reputation into eclipse. Too much, far too much is
made of fallen women, sacrificial sisters, miraculously heroic acts
of piety. As spiritual resolutions to sensitively explored psychological dilemmas, these Victorian motifs seem inadequate and

aesthetically unsatisfying. In relation to Sheehan's own biography it is hard not to entertain the suspicion that these pietistic dénouements represent some kind of wish-fulfilment. Be that as it may what is even more telling is the fact that at no point in any of these three intriguing if flawed novels does Sheehan give more than a hint of how the spiritually humbled Catholic intellectual should relate to his society, the error of his earlier ways reckoned with and cast aside. Father Lethenby's financial and personal survival is what is at stake at the end of *My New Curate*; Dr Gray in *The Blindness of Dr Gray* is close to death when his spiritual re-birth takes place; and, most significantly, *Luke Delmege* begins with the death of its hero. In this latter work it is as if Sheehan has taken Luke to the point of transformation but then cannot conceive of what to do with him. So he opens the work with Luke's death as a lonely, slightly eccentric figure who has apparently found no significant social role in the Irish priesthood despite the spiritual chastening, we learn by the novel's end, he has experienced.

Indeed, sounding as a bass-note through much of Canon Sheehan's fiction, deeper even than the prevailing *pietas*, is a sense of the intense solitude of priestly life, particularly as experienced by those of intellectual and cultural distinction. A passage such as the following, where Luke Delmege is set against the Irish landscape, is typical. Furthermore it gives some sense of the power which Sheehan can release in his work, and gives some hint of the very real strengths of this extraordinarily uneven, but under-estimated novelist:

The very solitude, which had oppressed him with such lonely and melancholy feelings, began to assume a strange and singular charm. There was a mysterious light over everything that gave an aspect of dreamland and enchantment, or of old, far-off times, even to the long, lonely fields, or the dark, sullen bogland. He could not well define it. There was some association haunting everything, inexpressibly sweet, but so vague, so elusive, he could not define what it was. The fields in the twilight had a curious colour or cloudland hanging over them, that reminded him of something sweet and beautiful and far away; but this memory or imagination could never seize and hold. And when, on one of those grey days, which are so lovely in Ireland, as the light falls sombre and neutral on all things, a plover would shriek across the moorland, or a curlew would rise up and beat his lonely way, complaining and afraid, across the ashen sky, Luke would feel that he had seen it all before in some waking dream of childhood; but all associations had vanished.

Throughout his career Sheehan had indicated in his fiction that nationalism as a social and cultural movement of high idealism could provide an intellectually aware priesthood with the means whereby it might achieve the leadership of the people in a worthwhile, ennobling cause. Novels like *Lishheen* (1907) and *Miriam Lucas* (1912) had made clear his views on the social evils of landlordism (the motif of absentee landlordism plays a part too in *Luke Delmege*) while *Glenanaar*, with its vivid story of O'Connell and the Doneraile conspiracy, had firmly nailed Sheehan's colours to the mast of Irish national aspiration. But the subtle-minded, vigorous imagination of the novelist could not observe the developments of late-nineteenth-century Irish nationalism without serious reservations. His novel *The Graves at Kilmorna* (1915) therefore, written when Sheehan knew of his own terminal illness, is a work of remarkable interest as an analysis of the varying strands of modern Irish nationalism about which Sheehan clearly felt less than happy. Late in his life the force that once might have allowed the Catholic intellectual to participate in Irish society as an enthusiastic leader is viewed with anxious concern.

The *Graves at Kilmorna* recounts a tale of the Fenian rising and tells the life story of one of the activists, Myles Cogan, who survives into a period of unheroic disillusionment. In this respect the novel is curiously anticipatory of a later work of revolutionary frustration by that other Cork writer, the Seán O'Faoláin of *Bird Alone* (1936).

Sheehan was a student in St Colman's College in Fermoy, Co. Cork when the incidents of 1867 took place, which form the basis of his novel. He would probably have known of the antagonism of many in his Church towards the Fenian martyrs but was clearly impressed, as his own record tells us, by the brave death of Peter O'Neill-Crowley, leader of the East Cork Fenians in Kilcloony-wood, holding at bay an entire British regiment and a posse of police. He remembered too how the curate of Mitchelstown ran to give the dying hero the last rites and how as a boy he himself had watched the huge funeral procession that bore O'Neill-Crowley to his patriot grave: 'the dark masses of men swaying over the bridge, the yellow coffin conspicuous in their midst'.

Fenianism in *The Graves at Kilmorna* is associated with high idealism, spirituality, an inclusive national vision derived from Thomas Davis, John Mitchel and the Young Irelanders. It opposes the acquisitive, degenerate corruption of conventional political and economic life. The Fenians are drawn from the most honourable, the most educated (the martyr Halpin is a school teacher), the most religiously scrupulous of the populace. Its soldiers are dominated by a vision of Ireland's heroic past, her physical beauty and her cruel subjugation. They combine pride, honour and duty with chivalric intensity. What Sheehan seems to be doing in this work of 1911 (it was published posthumously) is proposing a theory in which the corrupt materialism of an Ireland adapting itself to the modern world of commerce, power politics and pragmatism, will always stimulate a minority to acts of what they believe to be redemptive violence. In so doing he is interpreting the Fenian Rising less in its own terms than in terms of what he feared might occur in twentieth-century Ireland. This is quite clear when we consider the following extraordinarily percipient conversation in the novel. Myles Cogan is consulting with his leader, James Halpin, on the prospects for the Rising. He is told the outcome can only be disaster in military terms, but,

'The country has become plethoric and therefore indifferent to everything but bread and cheese. It needs bloodletting a little. The country is sinking into the sleep of death; and nothing can awake it but the crack of the rifle ... You and I will be shot. Our bodies will be stretched out on the Irish heather; our blood will have soaked back into our mother's breasts ... and the political degradation of the people which we shall have preached with our gaping wounds will shame the nation into at least a paroxysm of patriotism once again'.
'That means', said Myles Cogan after a long pause, 'that we, Fenians, are not soldiers, but preachers'.

Such an interpretation of the Fenians' purposes is of course something of an historic anachronism but one charged with accurate premonition. The full sense of Fenian martyrdom only came after the execution of the Manchester martyrs but it was such a reading of the past and the future which was to spur a new generation to rebellion a few years after Canon Sheehan's death. The revolutionary sermon was to be preached once more.

The personal consequences of a sacrificial role are explored in the second half of Sheehan's novel where we see Myles, released from prison in England, attempting to come to terms with the Ireland he has so despised in the past. He cannot do so. He makes efforts to promote social improvement in his hometown but holds himself apart from the new political nationalism of the Land League and Parnellism. He becomes isolated, politically uninvolved and remote from reality: 'He seemed to be drifting further and further from public life. He read the morning paper, watched with languid interest the course of that wretched gamble, called politics, then went back to his poets and philosophers, and grew absorbed in the serenity of their ideas and their lives'. On a holiday in Germany he is highly attracted by the anti-democratic, elitist fantasizing of a German aristocrat whom he encounters. The Thuringean counsels a form of authoritarian nostalgia:

Democracy has but one logical end — socialism. Socialism is cosmopolitanism — no distinction of nationalities any longer; but one common race. That means anti-militarism, the abolition of all stimulus and rivalry. And who is going to work or fight, my friends, for that abstraction, called Humanity? Not I. But, thank God, we have the Past to live in. They cannot take that from us.

Myles's nostalgia is for the revolutionary absolutism of the Fenians which draws him, towards the end of his life, to an extremism of religious renunciation, to a fiercely puritan vision of Irish Christianity. His contempt for the new materialism of the country together with a sense of ideals frustrated, revolutionary hope disappointed, has bred in him a kind of life-denying zeal — he seems finally satisfied when his Cistercian spiritual confessor assures him of the nation's ascetic destiny:

The nation will go on; grow fat like Jeshurun, and kick. And then, it will grow supremely disgusted with itself; it will take its wealth, and build a monastery on every hilltop in Ireland. The island will become another Thebaid — and that will be its final destiny!

Sheehan seems to be saying in the novel that he fears the narrow, zealous, ascetic and self-destructive nationalism that must be the outcome when the noble idealism of a minority encounters the prudent, cautious, self-interested national feeling of an increasingly materialistic even socialist majority.[7] That there might be another way is suggested in the book by the figure of Father James, a wise older priest, who tries to save Myles from himself. In him is embodied Sheehan's own sense, which *was* his despite admiration for the nobility of the Fenians' chivalric gesture, that a more fruitful nationalism must be rooted in intellectual renewal. 'It is not', he advises Myles, 'by the pike and the gun, but with the voice and the pen that Ireland's salvation can be worked out'. Education must inform the majority's nationalism so that the fatal dialectic between nobility and pragmatism can be transcended in a new national order.[8]

The tragic conclusion to the book suggests that Sheehan feared events had gone too far in his own day to permit of any such new departure. Myles is in the end prevailed upon to speak on behalf of a parliamentary candidate who has Father James's support and who seems to represent something of the cultivated generosity of mind that a true Irish nationalism should represent. Speaking before an audience who find his evident contempt for them wholly inflaming he is struck down by a stone and dies. Sheehan seemed incapable of showing how his intellectual clerical heroes might relate in any creative way with their own society. Similarly, he seems at the end of this dark and prescient work to prophesy, in the death of its hero at the hands of his own people, a period when the role of the Catholic intellectual in Ireland, and of a clergy culturally as well as spiritually endowed, would be overshadowed by the kind of cruel dialectic of revolutionary violence and reaction which destroyed Myles Cogan. Canon Sheehan had spent much of his life in the encouragement of a cultural leavening of Irish life. That the twentieth century was, he sensed, to make many of his labours irrelevant perhaps accounts for the sombre words with which this strange but compelling book concludes. Father James speaks the oration over the graves at Kilmorna which contain both Halpin and Myles Cogan:

There lie two Irish martyrs — one, pierced by an English bullet on the field of battle; the other after spending the best ten years of life in English dungeons, done to death by his own countrymen. There they lie; and with them is buried the Ireland of our dreams, our hopes, our ambitions, our love. There is no more to be said. Let us go hence!

W.B.YEATS: TONES OF VOICE

DAVID DAICHES

At the head of his poem 'Reflections on Having Left a Place of Retirement' Coleridge put a quotation from Horace, *sermoni propriora*, 'more appropriate to conversation'. Many poets have sought to bring a conversational style into their poetry. Robert Frost once said to me that all great poetry has the accent of conversation, which was surely an exaggeration; but he was making the point that the colloquial note is found in the most unexpected places. Frost actually quoted from Milton's *Lycidas*, 'Begin then, Sisters of the sacred well,' reciting the line in a friendly colloquial manner, to illustrate his point. One would not, at first sight, expect Yeats to adopt such an accent, either in his early dreamy style or in his later tough metaphysical-cum-symbolic phase. The fact is, however, that Yeats was the master of a conversational tone which he could introduce into his poetry at a particular stage and modulate out of it and back into it again with remarkable skill. This is particularly true of those poems of personal reminiscence which punctuate his poetic output from a fairly early stage.

Consider the poem *Adam's Curse*, written in 1902, recalling a conversation with Maud Gonne and her sister Kathleen. It begins as an impromptu reminiscence, the impromptu effect achieved by going back to the subject 'we' and defining it more explicitly in the second line:

> We sat together at the summer's end,
> That beautiful mild woman, your close friend,
> And you and I, . . .

The poet is remembering something in the imagined presence of one of those who shared the experience that he is remembering. '*That* beautiful mild woman' is a conversational pointing, implying 'you know who I mean, of course'. So colloquial is the run of the lines and the tone of voice that we are surprised to find the lines rhyming, 'end' and 'friend'. The rhyme introduces a note of unexpected formality, which henceforth is balanced against the colloquial tone. The poet goes on to quote what he said:

> I said, 'A line will take us hours maybe;
> Yet if it does not seem a moment's thought,
> Our stitching and unstitching has been naught . . . '

'I said' and 'maybe' are easy colloquial expressions; 'naught', which is a rhyme word, is more formal, giving an air of authority to what has been described as 'an exact definition of *sprezzatura*'. But note how the tone then changes, with the reversal of the opening iambic beat in the next line and the shift of movement away from end-stopped verse:

> Better go down upon your marow-bones
> And scrub a kitchen pavement, or break stones
> Like an old pauper, in all kinds of weather . . .

The explosive contempt in the first two of these lines is colloquial in a different way from what we find in the opening lines of the poem. Then, after this outburst of b's and t's and k's, we get a shift into a slower, quieter, more self-consciously artful line

> For to articulate sweet sounds together . . .

'Articulate sweet sounds' is a deliberately 'poetic' evocation of a deliberately poetic activity. But the poem continues

> Is to work harder than all these, and yet
> Be thought an idler by the noisy set
> Of bankers, schoolmasters, and clergymen
> The martyrs call the world.

'Work harder', 'idler', 'noisy set' are again colloquial expressions, and though the word 'martyrs' brings us up suddenly against a more posed kind of image, the ending of this verse paragraph before the end of the verse line gives the effect of spontaneous talk.

The poem goes on to alternate the posed and the spontaneous in the reporting of the conversation: this is *talk* about *poetry*, with the talk represented by such colloquial phrases as 'they do not talk of it at school' and 'it seems an idle trade enough', and the poetry represented by such phrases as 'find out all heartache' and 'compounded of high courtesy'. The way Yeats moves in and out between these two tones of voice is itself, of course, a high form of art.

After the report of the conversation is over, 'we sat grown quiet at the name of love' and the colloquial tone is dismissed:

> We sat grown quiet at the name of love;
> We saw the last embers of daylight die,
> And in the trembling blue-green of the sky
> A moon, worn as if it had been a shell
> Washed by time's waters as they rose and fell
> About the stars and broke in days and years.
>
> I had a thought for no one's but your ears:
> That you were beautiful, and that I strove
> To love you in the old high way of love;
> That it had all seemed happy, and yet we'd grown
> As weary-hearted as that hollow moon.

The record of the talk is over, and we now have the poet's presentation of his own sensibility. This is in Yeats's early dreamy style, but in its context, as a postscript to the account of a conversation, it seems almost quizzical, almost ironic, a sad shrugging-off of romantic possibilities.

Fourteen years later we find Yeats writing a very different kind of poem in *The Wild Swans at Coole*. It is the rhythms, and the spontaneous-seeming (but in fact highly artful) variation in the line-lengths, that arrest us here:

> The woods are in their autumn beauty,
> The woodland paths are dry,
> Under the October twilight the water
> Mirrors a still sky;
> Upon the brimming water among the stones
> Are nine-and-fifty swans.

The swelling out of the fifth line, while returning to the opening iambic beat, not only seems to imitate the actual 'brimming water among the stones', but suggests that the poet is carried away by the reality of what he says into constructing a longer line than he intended. Yet all the other stanzas have this same extended fifth line, which seems originally determined by the impact of the scene described and then accepted into the formal scheme of the poem. (This is reminiscent of many of Donne's love poems, where the opening stanza seems to have been carved out by the urgency of the feeling expressed, and the succeeding stanzas follow the channel dug by the emotion of the first.) The point I want to make here, however, is that the variations in line-length in the opening stanza, and the alternation of iambic and trochaic beats (compare, for example, the first and the third lines of the stanza quoted), set a note of what might be called descriptive spontaneity, as though the requirements of the scene were forcing the poet into a mould of their own. This is not exactly *sermoni propriora*, but something like it.

The poem moves into reminiscence and self-pity, but the alternating line-lengths, though more or less echoing the pattern set by the first stanza, continue to give an impression of form giving way to the imperatives of expression, that is, of a tone of voice rather than a pattern of art. This may be called an illusion, but it would seem to be a willed illusion.

Two years later in 'In Memory of Major Robert Gregory', we find Yeats in full command of his informal conversational tone, using it in a complex poem of reminiscence and reflection that appears to move in a totally spontaneous unpremeditated way, even to the point of expressing surprise at where he has got to in the end, yet which in fact is cunningly constructed to go just where it appears to go accidentally. The opening lines are positively chatty:

> Now that we're almost settled in our house
> I'll name the friends that cannot sup with us . . .

It is remarkable that without changing this tone Yeats can throw out a line such as

> Climb up the narrow winding stair to bed

which combines a quite literal statement of how he and his guests go up to bed with a haunting evocation of the meaning of the winding stair in his own developing pattern of image and symbol. (The winding stair is the road through life; as you proceed up the narrowing spiral staircase you both retrace your steps and go further upward, circling in an ever smaller circle in an endeavour to reach the stage where all points of the circumference are one, the circumference being contracted to a single point, the top of the tower, where you are in all phases of your life simultaneously, in a unity outside time and change; as you circle upward you look down on your former selves, measuring your progress by the increased number of your absences; but the point at the top, where all your different selves are united, is not attainable, for the tower is ruined at the top: when you get there, you are dead, or you are in Byzantium, which is 'death-in-life and life-in-death'. But such a summary of Yeats's developing imagination in relation to one of his central preoccupations is impossibly brief and inadequate.)

'In Memory of Major Robert Gregory' is ostensibly about his dead friends, Lionel Johnson, John Synge, his maternal uncle George Pollexfen, until he comes to the main subject of the poem, Major Gregory, 'Our Sidney and our perfect man'. There are colloquialisms, sly literary references (as in 'Lionel Johnson comes the first to mind / That loved his learning better than mankind', where the lines suddenly sound like an eighteenth-century couplet and there is an echo of Goldsmith's lines on Burke), half-ironic use of astrological language to indicate George Pollexfen's interest in 'the outrageous stars' as well as in horses, and then we come to Robert Gregory, and the language changes. 'Our Sidney and our perfect man' suggests a language more appropriate to Renaissance man, an ideal represented by the fifteenth phase of the moon in the system Yeats developed. The phrase 'that discourtesy of death' gives notice of the change in tone. Yet it is not a simple change from the colloquial to the formal. Renaissance man was many-sided, and the language of picturesque landscape description (stanza VII), practical horsemanship (stanza VIII: we remember the discussion of horsemanship at the beginning of Sidney's *Defence of Poesie* and Yeats's later use of the horseman), Elizabethan poetry ('Soldier, scholar, horseman, he / And all he did done perfectly'), John Donne ('Some burn damp faggots, others may consume / The entire combustible world in one small room'), Elizabethan poetry again ('As 'twere all life's epitome')—all these come into the poem before the concluding stanza:

> I had thought, seeing how bitter is that wind
> That shakes the shutter, to have brought to mind
> All those than manhood tried, or childhood loved,
> Or boyish intellect approved,
> With some appropriate commentary on each;
> Until imagination brought
> A fitter welcome; but a thought
> Of that late death took all my heart for speech.

The pressure of Gregory's death drove out the romantic desire to use the wind that shakes the shutter to launch a reverie about old friends, both of his childhood and his manhood, as well as the pedantic aim of providing 'some appropriate commentary on each'. That phrase is ironic and even dismissive; it is the language of examination papers, of 'bald heads forgetful of their sins, / Old, learned, respectable bald heads' of his poem 'The Scholars'. The pretence—if that is not too strong a word—that the memory of Gregory struck him dumb ('took all my heart for speech') is clearly a device to end the poem on a paradox: it was Gregory's death that produced the most inspired and many-faceted stanzas of the poem, and it is *sprezzatura* indeed to claim that it stopped his mouth. The paradox is a tribute to Gregory's Renaissance-like versatility.

Yeats's later poems of reminiscence, reverie or hope develop a remarkable richness and variety of tone and vocabulary, which include and subsume the colloquial. The grave and steady movement of the lines in the opening stanza of 'A Prayer for My Daughter' (1919) anchor the poem in both a scene and a mood with compelling precision, ending in two simple lines consisting entirely of monosyllabic words except for the word 'because':

> And for an hour I have walked and prayed
> Because of the great gloom that is in my mind.

One can hear an Irish conversational voice here. But the second stanza, while beginning in the same conversational way, soon leaps away into such phrases as 'excited reverie', 'frenzied drum', 'the murderous innocence of the sea'. The third stanza slows down to a grave prayer, yet this tone soon modulates into one of philosophical qualification:

> May she be granted beauty and yet not
> Beauty to make a stranger's eye distraught
> Or hers before a looking-glass, for such,
> Being made beautiful overmuch,
> Consider beauty a sufficient end,
> Lose natural kindness, . . .

The phrase 'a sufficient end' is precisely philosophical, while 'natural kindness' comes from the realm of ethical discourse.

The next stanza moves into an oddly quizzical use of Greek mythology, very Yeatsian in its phrasing and its amusedly reductive treatment of the characters:

> Helen being chosen found life flat and dull
> And later had much trouble from a fool,
> While that great Queen, that rose out of the spray,
> Being fatherless could have her way
> Yet chose a bandy-leggéd smith for man.

So much for mere beauty, runs the implication. The stanza ends on three lines showing a characteristic bringing together of two kinds of imagery:

> It's certain that fine women eat
> A crazy salad with their meat
> Whereby the Horn of Plenty is undone.

To suggest that behaving oddly is to eat a crazy salad with one's meat is curiously colloquial, yet provocatively strange: 'crazy' and 'salad' are both words found in ordinary speech, but it is far from ordinary to bring them together in such a context. The Horn of Plenty is of course a traditional poetic image, wholly different from a crazy salad, and it is given a new force by being juxtaposed with the crazy salad.

The controlled gravity of the succeeding stanzas is beautifully done, with its movement between personal preference ('In courtesy I'd have her chiefly learned') and benedictory prayer ('May she become a flourishing hidden tree'), while phrases such as 'magnanimities of sound', 'rooted in one dear perpetual place', 'radical innocence' soar up out of the even flow of the poem to arrest and provoke. The often quoted final stanza begins in benedictory prayer and ends in a quiet throwaway couplet of explanatory lines moving in a characteristic Yeatsian cadence and very colloquial in feeling if not in imagery. After the great and culminating rhetorical question

> How but in custom and in ceremony
> Are innocence and beauty born?

comes the schoolmasterly addendum

> Ceremony's a name for the rich horn,
> And custom for the spreading laurel tree.

This is not a climax, but a sort of pedagogical coda, and I can think of no poet other than Yeats who would have ended a poem on this note.

How different is the end of 'Coole Park and Ballylee ,1931'. It opens colloquially enough:

> Under my window-ledge the waters race,
> Otters below and moor-hens on the top,

but as the description of natural features develops everything becomes emblem ('Another emblem there!'); Robert Gregory appears, but this time as 'a last inheritor', a symbolic figure; and in the end the poem comes to a climax with a confession of faith and a sense of foreboding:

> We were the last romantics—chose for theme
> Traditional sanctity and loveliness;
> Whatever's written in what poets name
> The book of the people; whatever most can bless
> The mind of man or elevate a rhyme;
> But all is changed, that high horse riderless,
> Though mounted in that saddle Homer rode
> Where the swan drifts upon a darkening flood.

The ending is fine, but not peculiarly Yeatsian: the last line always reminds me of the last lines of Wallace Stevens' *Sunday Morning:*

> At evening, casual flocks of pigeons make
> Ambiguous undulations as they sink,
> Downward to darkness, on extended wings.

THE IMPERIAL BAWD

T.A. DUNN

The great, later plays of Shakespeare all deal in varying measure and in different ways with the theme of Human Love. While it is only in *King Lear* that Shakespeare's treatment attains to the level of the transcendental, in the popular imagination the one tragedy that deals directly with this theme, the one true 'love-story', seems to be *Antony and Cleopatra*. It is matter for reflection, however, that the mind that created *Lear* could not possibly have been content with the simplicities implied by the label 'love-story'. Another look at the play might reveal further subtleties in the way Shakespeare deals with love between a man and a woman.

No one, of course, would suggest that all that is important in the play is the relationship between the lovers and their tragic deaths at the ends of Acts IV and V respectively. *Antony and Cleopatra* is, after all, at base a rendering into dramatic form of history, and well-known history at that, which Shakespeare presents superbly, compressing the incidents of over ten years by a judicious selection of events and by reportage. Since history does not necessarily adjust itself to a shapely story, it is the playwright's business to shape his raw material into a dramatic plot. And in this respect, in this play Shakespeare is at the absolute height of his craft.

Surprisingly, there is almost nothing in the nature of 'dramatic' incident right up to the end of Act III. By the end of Act II we have reached the settlement (temporary as it turns out) between Octavius and Antony and the settlement (also temporary as it turns out) with Pompey. In Act III we find the marriage and the split with Octavia, the defeat at Actium, the passage with Thidias the messenger and the brawl and reconciliation between Antony and Cleopatra. Almost all this is the mere stuff of chronicle, but it is a skeleton that is fleshed out with an exhibition of the relationship between Antony and Cleopatra—of his doting upon her and losing the name of action, and of her quicksilver character in motion. Our interest is being focused upon this relationship against a *background* of the major political circumstances of the known world. In all of this, and perhaps in its brightest bits, Shakespeare is hardly dependent upon his source at all, at most merely drawing upon it for hints. There is a sense in which this part of the play is merely a preparation for the double-barrelled tragedy which follows, the part which Dryden seized upon when he came to write *All For Love*.

As Shakespeare took over the story, it was purely the tragedy of Antony. That is the story as Plutarch told it and as historians had handed it down. The defeated and conquered, in older and simpler days, always got a raw deal; their names were blackened in the record. So it was with the names of Antony and Cleopatra—with Cleopatra in particular. The story was of a great and noble general reduced to impotence in affairs by a trollop: brought to a tragic end by his own folly and madness. According to this version, Cleopatra was a scheming and worthless hussy, an imperial bawd, a woman who had already ensnared and seduced in near-fatal fascination two great Romans—Julius Caesar and Pompey the Great—and was now at work upon a third, Antony, for the gratification of her own purely selfish ends. This indeed, could, have been the play; but it isn't.

Nor, indeed, is this view the real, the historical Cleopatra. A woman who could seduce in succession, seduce three such men as Caesar, Pompey and Antony, who could maintain sway and rule over such a kingdom as Egypt, could be no mere strumpet. And, sure enough, research shows us just such a woman—a capable, highly-intelligent, well-educated woman-of-affairs; a live, magnetic and compelling personality; a fine linguist and student of literature, absolutely tireless, determined and resolute, with her abilities by no means confined to the bedroom.

For three-fifths of the play Cleopatra is the traditional strumpet, and it is interesting to note the clear-eyed way in which Shakespeare presents her as such. And we do indeed see Antony, 'the triple pillar of the world transform'd into a strumpet's fool'. Yet both seem much more than this. It is she who operates by reason and policy, and only occasionally—and further into the play— by whim and caprice. Moreover, she is given increased magnitude and majesty and power largely by what Antony says of her:

> Let Rome in Tiber melt, and the wide arch
> Of the rang'd empire fall! Here is my space,
> Kingdoms are clay: our dungy earth alike
> Feeds beast as man; the nobleness of life
> Is to do thus: when such a mutual pair,
> And such a twain can do't, in which I bind,
> On pain of punishment, the world to weet
> We stand up peerless.   I,i,33—39

On their very first entrance Cleopatra is asking how much he loves her. When he replies that love ought not to be measured, she responds with a bawdy joke in which she says that she knows exactly how far his love stretches, but he takes her up literally in replying, 'Then must thou needs find out new heaven, new earth'. The contrast here is between Cleopatra's realism in the bawdy joke and Antony's exaggerated imagery, and on this first entrance he is giving utterance to the imagery of the world, the sky, the sea and of vastness generally which interpenetrates the play. In his every thought, even in his loving, Antony is the one-third ruler of the known world. Can such a man be a strumpet's fool? It is difficult to think so when in the very next scene we see him disentangling himself from her fairly easily when more important affairs are toward. We wonder if this can really be considered as one of the great romantic love-affairs of the world, and we wonder if Shakespeare really considered it as such. If this is love between two human beings, then it is love that is rather different—more realistic and less romantic—than we see in the rest of Shakespeare.

Coleridge asks us to peruse this play in mental contrast to *Romeo and Juliet*. The couple can indeed be usefully compared with Romeo and Juliet, since the centre of the play is the relationship of two lovers. In that sense it is a love-story. Antony and Cleopatra are not so completely involved the one with the other that external events hardly impinge upon them, but they are at the centre of the play. This relationship is, however, far from the calm centre of a hurricane, such as we find in that complete relationship between the tragic couple of *Romeo and Juliet*. On the contrary, it is a tempestuous affair; with its ups and its downs, its quarrels, its vagaries and its frequent extravagances of temperament. It is not the ethereal, other-worldly, idealised and romantic love of a young man for a maid. It is the love of a man of the world, a soldier and a general, one of the triumvirate who ruled the Roman Empire, that of a man in his fifties, for a woman of the world and a queen, a royal courtesan. It takes, that is to say, a realistic view of life and an adult view of love and the problems connected with sex. The outer world may take a ribald or a bawdy view of this love-affair, but we have it from the lips of the lovers themselves how all-encompassing, how tremendous, this love is—when they allow themselves to indulge it. And it is significant that it is not something described in purely physical or sensual terms, but the occasion for flights into what, in accord with the extravagance of their positions, are the uppermost regions of the spirit and the human soul.

Here is Romeo taking farewell of the lifeless Juliet:

>   O here
> Will I set up my everlasting rest
> And shake the yoke of inauspicious stars
> From this world-wearied flesh. Eyes, look your last.
> Arms, take your last embrace! And lips, O you
> The doors of breath, seal with a righteous kiss
> A dateless bargain to engrossing Death.   V, iii, 109–115

And here is Cleopatra on the death of Antony:

> Hast thou no care of me? Shall I abide
> In this dull world, which in thy absence is
> No better than a sty? O! see my women,
> The crown o' the earth doth melt. My lord!
> O! withered is the garland of the war,
> The soldier's pole is fall'n; young boys and girls
> Are level now with men; the odds is gone,
> And there is nothing left remarkable
> Beneath the visiting moon.   IV, xiii, 60–68

Her first cry is—how humanly—for self: 'Hast thou no care of me?' But all the reference thereafter broadens out to the wide world and the effect of Antony's death upon it. When we come to her later lament for him we find that it is hyperbolic:

> His face was as the heavens, and therein stuck
> A sun and moon, which kept their course and lighted
> The little O, the earth. . . .
> His legs bestrid the ocean, his rear'd arm
> Crested the world: his voice was propertied
> As all the tuned spheres, and that to friends:
> But when he meant to quail, and shake the orb,
> He was as rattling thunder. For his bounty,
> There was no winter in't: an autumn 'twas

> That grew the more by reaping: his delights
> Were dolphin-like, they show'd his back above
> The element they lived in: in his livery
> Walked crowns and crownets: realms and islands were
> As plates dropp'd from his pocket. . . .
> Think you there was, or might be, such a man
> As this I dreamt of?   V,ii, 79–94

Cast in the very tone of voice of Antony himself, this is indeed hyperbolic—and also elaborately metaphysical. It has poetic force rather than that genuine expression of personal grief we find in, say, Lear's last speech—the rage, the simplicity, the absolute surrender to misery. Yet Cleopatra is a queen—and never more so than in her end.

This end has long been determined. As Octavius says: 'She hath pursued conclusions infinite of easy ways to die': and, of course, history has told the audience that she will kill herself. As early as Act I, scene ii, Enobarbus says:

> Cleopatra, catching but the least noise of this, dies instantly. I
> have seen her die twenty times upon far poorer moment: I do
> think there is mettle in death, which commits some loving act
> upon her, she hath such a celerity in dying.   I,ii,137–142

And in the next scene, Cleopatra herself says, 'Now I see, I see, in Fulvia's death how mine received shall be'. After Antony's death the matter is never far from her mind: 'Shall I abide in this dull world, which in thy absence is no better than a sty?'; while, later in the same speech, she asks: 'Then is it sin to rush into the secret house of death ere death dare come to us?'; and: 'Then, what's brave, what's noble, let's do it after the high Roman fashion and make death proud to take us.' In Act V, scene i, Octavius gives special instructions to prevent her suicide, recalling the long passage in North on her experiments with poison; while in the next scene Cleopatra remarks that 'it is great to do that thing that ends all other deeds.' In that scene too she draws a dagger to kill herself and calls on death to take her; but that this is a mere gesture is made plain when she has still enough care for life to attempt to swindle Octavius over the extent of her possessions.

Does a woman who has abandoned life and intends to kill herself go to such lengths to secure her financial future? Perhaps she does, but it is, in fact, the discovery that Caesar intends to take her away as a triumphal prisoner that precipitates her suicide. Though, it is true, she is going to die like Antony, she is

not going to die *for* Antony, but for her honour, like a Queen.
While, in the ending, Shakespeare follows North's *Plutarch*
closely in detail, he alters the emphasis ever so slightly in that he
ignores the squalor and ugliness of her last days and stresses the
courage and majesty described in the final passage of North's
account. Thus Cleopatra is not diminished into merely a mourning woman but is elevated into the nobility of a great queen,
dying by her own choice. One reason why Shakespeare does this
is so that there should be no diminution, no falling-off, in the
scale of the tragedy. This is, after all, a double tragedy. To the
end of Act IV the tragedy has been Antony's, but the tragic
movement must sweep on, without lessening in intensity, to the
end of Act V. This is not difficult for Shakespeare to do, since his
interest in Cleopatra as a character has been developing
throughout the play, and his deep appreciation of her as a
woman, and his total realisation of her, is one of the play's
significant features.

Within a hundred lines of her death Shakespeare has
Cleopatra say,

> I shall see
> Some squeaking Cleopatra boy my greatness
> I' the posture of a whore.

Was this an act of daring on Shakespeare's part—or an
expression of irritation that his mouthpiece should be inadequate
to a creation that, almost for the first time, held the centre of the
stage by virtue of her womanhood and her sexuality alone?
Certainly the drama of sexual danger that followed Shakespeare
showed an increasing interest in women.

But, of course, Cleopatra is not only a woman. She is also a
Queen. If a bawd, then she is an Imperial bawd. In Act V she
takes on Antony's role, and with his role, his nobility. Her 'voice'
and the matter of her speech, undistinguished in the earlier acts
(in which, indeed, she has remarkably few lines to say), become
the voice and matter of Antony, an imperial ruler. Had she been
only a woman, deprived of hope for life by the death of her lover,
then her dying speeches would have been very different. She
dies amidst a sparkling shower of tropes and conceits and
imperial imagery. Within six lines of her death she is even
making a joke. Addressing the asp, she says, 'O, couldst thou
take her away as a triumphal prisoner that precipitates her
suicide. Though, it is true, she is going to die like Antony, she is

naught, that appeals most to her in conjuring up the sound of the
asp jeering at him.

If *Antony and Cleopatra* is a 'love-story' then it is a very Roman
love-story, of political liaisons, divorces and widowings for
power. Its real theme is Honour, as the real theme of *Lear* is
Human Love, and Honour is a very Roman virtue. Its opposite is
Betrayal, and it is his belief in Cleopatra's betrayal of him and,
particularly, its accompanying political disaster, that initiates
Antony's suicide. He has been dishonoured by what he
supposes to be her death:

> I . . . condemn myself, to lack
> The courage of a woman, less noble mind
> Than she which by her death our Caesar tells
> 'I am conqueror of myself.'   IV,xiv, 56–62

When he dies on the Monument, whither he has been borne,
since Cleopatra dare not come down to him lest she be taken,
their last words are of policy and honour, not of love.

The tone of the play is Roman—but not solely Roman. It is not
so coldly Roman as, say, *Julius Caesar*. For Rome is counter-
balanced by Egypt, Antony by Cleopatra, the calculations of
policy and power by the passions, by the sensual, the sensuous.
Yet it is Cleopatra at the end who dies a Roman death and
becomes—uniquely in Shakespeare—a heroine, and far from the
imperial strumpet of legend. In every way her death matches her
queenliness and assorts well with the death of Antony.

Why, then, do we feel this play is not on a level with the
greatest of the tragedies? It has the noblest protagonists of the
world, with which it deals. Its canvas is the whole known world
and its politics. The language is of the highest and its imagery of
the most spacious. Yet, as A.C. Bradley said, 'We are saddened
by the fact that the catastrophe saddens us so little.'

The reason, I think, is that it is too specific, too much tied to the
literal matter of the chronicles, of history. Thus it is unable to
move from the world of specifics into the world of myth. Antony
is an 'exemplary' hero; his story brings the lessons of history.
When he has gone, Cleopatra steps into his role. It is, in its epic
construction, its masterly reworking and adaptation of complex
material, the apotheosis of the Chronicle Play, and, try as he
might, Shakespeare cannot make it touch the raw nerve of
humanity, as *Lear* does, as *Othello* does.

PANGUR BAN AND THE SCHOLAR CRITIC[1]

MAURICE HARMON

Since modern Irish literature in the English language draws upon two separate cultures, the Irish and the English, it is inevitable that the scholarship connected with it should also take into account the effects of this dual heritage. The degree and the nature of the interaction between the two cultures vary from time to time and from one writer to the next, but its presence is undeniable. Our scholarship reflects our sense of the overlapping and mutually supportive nature of the various disciplines that are involved in the dual heritage, particularly on the Irish side, as do the composition of our scholarly journals and our educational programmes. My impression, however, is that we have as yet not marked out a clearly defined critical method or system for dealing with the literature. We seem to be moved this way and that in response to what we find in this writer and that, in one work or another. We stretch contexts and perspectives backwards and sideways, as we try to provide the right kind of critical awareness and to satisfy our feeling that the literature somehow requires method and flexibility.

The fact is we are hampered not alone by the complexity of the task, but by the absence on all sides of basic scholarly supports in both cultures. Our task is quite different from the scholar who works in English studies because much of the groundwork has still to be done and because the back-up reference systems have still to be prepared. We also lack established critical procedures that have shown themselves to be fully adequate to the literature. So little has been defined that we have almost nothing to work from or to build upon. The absence of generations of critics before us, or of critical schools that have emerged in response to the achievements and special characteristics of the literature, means that we still need to define, to develop and to operate a critical method or set of critical guidelines that are adequate to the literature.

An interdisciplinary approach is crucial. Our inquiry is dictated by the writers themselves, whose work we study. If they draw upon mythology, folklore, history, the literature of the Irish language, Hiberno-English, and so on, we have no alternative but to follow in their footsteps. This principle is fundamental to the development of a critical response that is adequate to the literature and able to meet it on its own terms. And that, after all, is essential: that we allow ourselves to be guided by the literature rather than insisting that the literature stay in line with our own notion of what it should be doing or not doing. Increasingly among the writers themselves there is the impulse to explore, to understand and to re-interpret the roots from which they come, the traditions that lie behind them, the culture that has shaped their imaginations. There is the habitual need on the part of the Irish writer to compensate for deficiencies within the heritage or within a particular environment by drawing widely from cultures outside of Ireland. Both of these impulses lead to the production of a literature that draws deeply and widely from the whole spectrum of the Irish past and that ranges well beyond the boundaries of the two major traditions of the Irish and the English. There is a need to develop a critical approach that will serve to interpret and evaluate this assimilative and chthonic literature.

It is not easy to cope with a literature that is rooted in tradition and wide ranging in its affinities. The difficulties are compounded by the lack of specific supporting reference, bibliographical and scholarly material. Those available for English literature are seriously deficient for Irish literature in English and quite inadequate for an interdisciplinary Irish studies approach. Most students of modern Irish literature, since they have been trained in English literary studies, are able to cope reasonably well with those areas of the literature that parallel or play against the English tradition. That dimension is always there, although its field of influence has not been worked as well as it could be.

For example, it has been a matter of regret to me for many years that we have not been able to see what the reaction was in English journals to the work of nineteenth-century Irish writers. They wrote with the idea that London was the literary centre, the place where their work would be judged, yet even now we have not systematically examined the reviews or critical articles. Historians, however, have not been slack in noting the reactions in English newspapers and periodicals to events in Ireland. I regret, too, in more general terms, that we have not explored systematically the differences and similarities between English and modern Irish literature in, for example, the area of genre. Why is it that Irish fiction seems to express itself predominantly in the romance rather than in the novel? Why is it that dramatists like Wilde and Shaw work happily enough in accepted modes, such as the comedy of manners, but that dramatists like Synge and O'Casey produce a mixture of comedy and tragedy, mock pastoral, melodrama and so on? Why is it that Irish literature on the whole, and not just the drama, is anti-naturalistic?

It is, however, the other dimension, that of the Irish tradition—complex, foreign to many, of distant and even obscure origin, of a split culture—that causes most difficulties. The Irish Literary Revival was founded on a belief in the integrity of the heritage; the nineteenth-century poets, novelists and scholars prepared the groundwork, made the 'matter of Ireland' available in much the same way as Tudor historians, translators and editors made the matter of England, the romance literatures and those of the classical past available to Shakespeare and his contemporaries. Throughout the present century Irish writers have turned to myth and legend, to folk custom and belief, to topography, to early Irish literature, to the distinguishing linguistic features of English as it is spoken in Ireland. There is a continuity of intent and with it an evolutionary progression, so that we can take all or any one of these and see how they emerge in the work of successive writers.

When we consider the beginnings of Irish fiction, in William Carleton and Maria Edgeworth, the presence of the two traditions is evident. Carleton's roots go deep into the Gaelic world of seventeenth- and eighteenth-century Ireland and this ancestral source gives authority to his account of folk custom and belief, family relationships, the hedgeschool culture, and to his visions of the idiom of a people for whom Irish was a dominant linguistic influence. The oral tradition lives on in his language, in the structure of some of his stories, in his notion of what is effective in narrative, indeed in some of those elements of his work that we may find most strange. At the same time he tried to learn from the traditions of English literature. He began by writing by essays in imitation of Addison in the *Spectator*, including one on Goldsmith. That attempt is threatened, however, by the enormous gap between the civilised persona of eighteenth-century English literature and the turbulent conditions

,of rural Ireland. The problem is illustrated in his story, 'The Party Fight and Funeral', where he tries to tell the story of sectarian feud and trial by funeral through the eyes of an educated narrator and has to change gears downward through two other personae before he finds one whose knowledge of such matters can be conveyed through the natural authority of an idiom linked to the social background. That problem is to be expected in a writer of Carleton's peasant background, with little formal education, a vivid imagination and a determination to make a name for himself in the world of letters by means of the best available models, which were mainly English. When the differences between eighteenth-century London, with its coffee shops, theatre, Samuel Johnson, Pope, *The Spectator* and life in the Clogher valley at the end of the same century are brought to mind, we can see how difficult his task was. But what does it do to our sense of these matters to remember that a contemporary poet, Richard Murphy, with an Ascendancy background and an almost entirely British education, also struggles with the task of reconciling that education and that background with his experience and understanding of west of Ireland life? Virtually his whole poetic career is an example of that attempt to find a place somewhere between the two or a mode of expression that will be faithful to the formality and sense of order of his Ascendancy experience and the wildness and intensity of life on the western shore. It would be possible to move backwards and forwards through the literature, using Carleton and Murphy as points of reference, in an investigation of this problem of the relationships between one tradition and the other.

But, for now, let us look back again to the other major figure at the beginning of Irish fiction in English, Maria Edgeworth. We may find her easier to cope with than Carleton, since her fictive procedures in the awareness of form, the uses of persona, the rational handling of a subject are all familiar to us. I am not a great believer in *Castle Rackrent* as a realistic novel, but let us assume that she does attempt an inclusive view of Irish life and tries to bridge the gap between Big House and peasant cottage. The oral narrator, Thady, is an attempt at this. The Glossary is another. She tries to make the strangeness of Irish life understandable to the English reader. The notes are quite good on linguistic points, on customs at wakes and funerals, and on fairy lore. We can verify them from other sources. The apparent inaccuracies—that belief in fairies is a thing of the past, that the *beansidhe* was heard in the old days but not at the time of writing — are normal in the records of early folklorists. Informants almost always say that such practices belonged to the past, not to their own times. Maria Edgeworth's account of the man waking up after he has met the fairies is a genuine piece of folklore, one of the migratory legends passed into popular tradition, and hers, so far as we know, is the first version to have been written down from oral recital in Ireland. Her skill as an observer of Irish life is even more in evidence when she records the speech of the man who tells about meeting the fairies in the convoluted and digressive account he gives to the justice of the peace. Her ear is tuned to the rhythms of Hiberno-English, to its syntax, idiom and power of characterisation; and she knows that habits of mind are revealed in the way a man uses language. Folklore confirms the accuracy of some of Maria Edgeworth's observations but it also suggests that her knowledge was often superficial. Her comments on the *beansidhe* are at best general; she shows no knowledge of the folklore of the Big House which to the folk mind was an otherworld place, outside the realm of ordinary people, a place to which haunted coaches travelled at night. A proverb says '*is sleamhain iad leacacha an tí mhóir*', 'the flagstones of the Big House are treacherous'.

The whole question of the Big House in Irish literature needs to be handled with caution. How people felt about the Ascendancy varied form one part of the country to another, depending on the nature of the family and their relationship to the people and of course it varies from period to period. But Carolan, for example, wrote nationalistic kinds of verse yet lived off the Big House; Liam Dall Ó hIfiernáin took his meals in the landlord's kitchen yet wrote a mock lament about him.

Their dual heritage is an issue for both Carleton and Edgeworth. Both wanted to reach across the divide, to encompass something of the other culture. For critics the sobering fact is that we are ill-equipped even yet to cope with this dual heritage as it operates in their work. They raise questions of language, of form, of the effects of the two traditions, of the problem of audience, of the nature of contemporary taste. When we view them in their context, they challenge us to find a critical procedure that is adequate to them.

There are historical and ideological aspects to the interdisciplinary approach, such as the connections between the Easter Rising and the literature; or the changing nature of Irish nationalism as reflected in the literature over the years; or how social and political aspirations and circumstances have affected the literature. Many of these matters have been documented and we have benefited from the work of the historians. There are key dates and events and defining circumstances which are important, if only as landmarks to help us to see the literature in relation to particular periods. We need history all the time. Historical research can confirm the accuracy or inaccuracy of the literature. Imaginative reconstructions of the past have to be checked: Richard Murphy's *The Battle of Aughrim*, Austin Clarke's *The Singing Men at Cashel*; such works impose an historical investigation upon us. Our trust in work which makes use of history is strengthened when we find that it is accurate. It shakes our faith, however, when we discover that Austin Clarke's account of the killing of Cormac of Cashel is not correct. Cormac was not struck down in his chapel, as Clarke's poem says, but beheaded at the Battle of Belamoon, as several sources tell us. When Seamus Heaney announces that someday he will go to Aarhus to see the Tollund Man, we know he cannot, unless the Danes oblige him by moving their famous relic from Silkeborg. Too many inaccuracies affect our judgment of a work. We expect the literary imagination to base itself on accurate use of material. Thomas Kinsella once thought of going downstream to Durrow but wisely suppressed that notion later.

The uses of places and of localities is another aspect of the literature that we have not sufficiently stressed. Patrick Kavanagh's claim for the validity of the parish, so richly realised, is confirmed by marking in the place names of his work on the map. The area in a tight radius around Inniskeen quickly becomes dotted. To say that the naming of place in his poetry is an act of imaginative possession is thus supported by a straightforward exercise that works well also for some other writers. It is but a short step from that simple task to a study of the use and function of landscape. There are holy places of the imagination: Nephin, Slieve Gullion, Clonmacnoise, Glenasmole. Whole regions have particular associations, retaining distinctive associations drawn from history, myth, or culture. Writers in turn revivify localities, often by drawing upon these associations. A northern painter, Colin Middleton, has argued passionately for the importance of place. 'Place', he said, 'is everything . . . You've got to go to a place until it does something to you . . . There's got to be some sort of place, particular places, holy places. Once you get there you know you're kith and kin. The stones start to talk.' That sort of credo, when manifested in works of art, confirms and strengthens our belief in the importance of place in the literature. In his poem, 'In

Small Townlands', Seamus Heaney responded to Middleton's striated form and texture.

A sophisticated awareness of context may extend to the other arts where the trends and emphases resemble and parallel those we find in the literature. In music there is the outstanding impact of Seán Ó Riada evident in the work of a number of poets. Even a casual glance through the recent catalogues of contemporary Irish composers reveals thematic similarities in the work of writers and composers like Gerard Victory, Seoirse Bodley and John Kinsella. Relationships can also be plotted between the work of contemporary writers and painters like Gerard Dillon, Michael Farrell, Oisín Kelly, Anne Madden and Louis Le Brocquy. All this suggests the fruitfulness of a comparative study of the arts. We have, too, comments by writers on painters: Thomas Kinsella on Louis Le Brocquy; Seamus Heaney on T.P. Flanagan; John Montague on Barrie Cooke; Pearse Hutchinson on Nano Reid; and so on. If we say, for example, that Irish writing is closely identified with place and with landscape, it is also true of Irish art. T.P. Flanagan, for example, has long been haunted by the interaction of sky and bogland. His painting, 'Gortahork 2' (1972) is the subject of Heaney's poem, 'Bogland, which is both a gloss on the poem and a statement of common identity and common response to landscape and homeland.

Irish life is more integrated than one might realise and this is more true today than ever before when there is more opportunity for the writer or artist to see, hear and read what one's fellow-practitioners are doing. There is a considerable amount of interaction within the artistic community. There is also the bonding sense of generation which has always been a strong feature of the Irish psyche. There are unifying figures and movements now as in the past, creative movements of aspiration and of feeling. The example of Seán Ó Riada in recent years is well known and there is the creative energy in literary studies associated with Thomas Kinsella.

I would like to look at the influence of archaeology on contemporary Irish artistic life. This can be demonstrated over and over: in Kinsella's *Finistère* and *Notes from the Land of the Dead*; in Montague's *A Slow Dance*. Many literary works have evoked the associations of archaeological sites. It is amazing that no one seems to have studied the connections between Yeats and archaeology. But now I want to look briefly at the excitement generated by the uncovering of Viking Dublin.

That excitement spread through the community, involving

archaeologists, historians, conservationists, city planners, musicians, artists and the general public. In 1969 Richard Ryan, then a university student, published a poem on Viking Dublin. In that year you could visit High Street, where Breandán Ó Riordáin had uncovered 10,000 Danish artifacts, and walk along a twelfth century split-log street between wattle houses. In 1973 the Seventh International Viking Congress was held in Dublin and its Proceedings were published. In 1975 the National Museum, which was carrying out the excavations, mounted an exhibition of the findings and issued a catalogue. In 1976 the Dublin Arts Festival concentrated on Viking Dublin, and published a booklet that included a reproduction of Speed's 1611 map of the city, articles by medieval historians, accounts of the old city and its churches, and a walking tour of its main sites. From this developed the organisation known as the Friends of Medieval Dublin, who began to fight for time to do a more extensive 'dig' before the city fathers plunged the Wood Quay area forever under an office block. In 1977 12,000 people visited Wood Quay in a few months. The Dublin Arts Festival put on a medieval festival that included morality plays, medieval music and other relevant attractions. There was, in short, a surge of public interest and response and a revised perception of the Vikings, not as murdering marauders but as a civilised people who had greatly contributed to Irish life and culture. There was also the impact of these events and discoveries in the poetry of Seamus Heaney and Thomas Kinsella and in the drama of Brian Friel.

It would be possible to illustrate the value of the interdisciplinary approach in many other examples drawn from different periods, but its validity hardly needs to be demonstrated further. What is of greater relevance is a more general question of the status and the directions of scholarship.

I have in mind an approach to the literature that sees it as an organic subject in which certain issues and events, and certain emphases and responses are prominent characteristics. There was a time when such an approach would have made little sense, because the idea that there existed a separate and distinctive literature in English produced by Irishmen would have been hard to establish convincingly. But once the Irish Literary Revival had run its course, and once major and distinctive work had been done in all the major genres, there was no longer any doubt about it. Increasingly, too, there is the evidence that the writers themselves feel comfortable within a tradition which they can follow or rebel against as they wish. There is this sense within the literature, of perceptions by writers of their predecessors. We can see this in broad terms, as for example in the lines that connect Kavanagh to Montague to Heaney, or in the links between Joyce, Clarke and Kinsella. We recognise in the two generations of poets since the time of Yeats a whole range of attempts that indicate both the determination to be different from him in idiom and subject matter, as in Clarke, Kavanagh, MacNeice, Coffey, Hewitt, Devlin, Fallon, and in the uses of language by Heaney, Kinsella, Montague, Murphy, Mahon, not to mention their quite different sense of the past, of history and, of myth. Discontinuity is also a form of continuity. These are brief notations on a complex and rich area, but one that will become increasingly fruitful as we produce scholars in sufficient numbers, whose sense of an indigenous Irish literature extends well back beyond Yeats, Joyce, Beckett and the fixation on major figures. There is a section in Kinsella's *Nightwalker* volume that lends itself readily to an illustration of this: there is a poem in which he raises the figure of Keats; another in which he echoes and imitates Yeats; another in which he acknowledges the rhythms and emphases of Clarke; and yet another in which he absorbs the imagery and situation of Aogán Ó Rathille in the seventeenth century.

Our perceptions of certain works are affected when we place them in an inter-disciplinary context. *At Swim Two Birds* may be a modernist novel with an innovative assertion that a good book may have three openings, but that notion comes as no surprise to anyone familiar with early Irish prose. The narrator's retirement into the privacy of his own mind for creative purposes also reminds one of the training of bardic poets. Our view of the Sweeney material should at least be based on the fact that while O'Brien's translation is incomplete it does include material from all stages of the original. Similarly, when dealing with Kinsella's later poetry the parallels with and echoes from *The Divine Comedy* can hardly be missed, but the allusions to the *Book of Invasions* can. Austin Clarke's poetry makes a lot more sense if we follow up his allusions to Eriugena, Cumian, or the Goddess of Sovereignty, and stop skipping over the 'hard bits'.

These are selective observations on one area of Irish Studies. Anyone who is involved with Irish Studies in a broad and interdisciplinary manner knows how many opportunities there are for research. Even within the context of the literature itself as it has developed from the earliest times the scholarly opportunities are many. More particularly the literature of the modern period has enough opportunities for scholarship to satisfy a whole generation of scholars. Until we tackle the basic tasks our thinking and teaching run the risk of being superficial and of giving inadequate guidance to those coming after us. All the basic tasks remain. We lack works of reference, we lack bibliographies, we have no *Dictionary of National Biography*, no definitive history, no history of ideas, no series of reliable monographs, too few biographies (and most of these are amateurish). On all sides and in every period there is a need for scholarly, annotated editions of novels, poems and plays. Surely the work of annotation, indexing and editing is a worthwhile task for the trainee scholar. Surely the preparation of a definitive bibliography is also rewarding. Or are we going to ask no more than the usual exercise in literary criticsm, one more thesis on a minor writer, one more industrious analysis of some portion of a major writer's work? Because so many Irish periodicals and newspapers have not been indexed and are not included in standard indexes, every bibliography published is deficient, every critical study of an Irish writer is incomplete, every account of the literature is suspect. And because the basic work has not been done our research is needlessly repetitive as we make successive investigations of the contents of particular periodicals. Yet we have not come together in any planned, systematic programme. The institutions and organisations exist; there are enough scholars at work, enough universities with programmes in Irish Studies. All that is required is our determination to plan a sustained programme that is practical, unglamorous and essential.

LAFCADIO HEARN, W.B. YEATS AND JAPAN

BARBARA HAYLEY

Though Lafcadio Hearn and W.B. Yeats approached Japan in very different ways and by very different routes, that country was a source of vitality and inspiration to both, and both writers are of lasting interest to the Japanese. Yeats, like many late-nineteenth-century Westerners, was fascinated from a distance by Japanese art and artefacts. He never visited Japan, and what he took from its culture was specific and individual—more to do with the art of W.B. Yeats than with that of Japan. He quickly found in the Noh plays, via Ezra Pound and Ernest Fenollosa, what he needed, seeing the possibilities for his own work in an imaginative vision of an art that he had not experienced. The artistic use that Yeats made of his idea of Japan is paradoxically disproportionate to his first-hand knowledge of it. The scholarly interest that the Japanese take in Yeats had its beginnings in the fact that when Japan opened its gates to Western culture, a conscious decision had to be taken whether to begin to study contemporary Western literature and keep abreast of it, or to start at its beginnings and work forwards. The former course was decided upon; and the profusion of Irish writers in the last decades of the nineteenth century occasioned an enduring interest in Anglo-Irish writing.

Whereas Yeats, like many artists, stayed at home and received Japanese influence from afar, Hearn was unique. He was a solitary explorer who brought the East to the West, not by returning with travellers' tales but by staying in the East and sending back both his first lively impressions and the osmotic orientalism of one who worked and settled in Japan, married a Japanese wife, lived a Japanese life. He became Japanese by naturalisation, by adoption, by affinity. He wrote from a deep affection for the Japanese people as well as from an interest in their country.

There is a paradox in Hearn's Japanese-Irish connection too: to the Japanese, Hearn is seen as an Irish writer, whereas in Ireland he is only beginning to be claimed as such, and in fact he lived for only a few years in that country as a boy. The circumstances of Hearn's youth, even of his name and family, are somewhat obscure.[1] The Irish connection started with the first Hearn to come to Ireland in the seventeenth century as chaplain to the Lord Lieutenant; he became Bishop of Cashel and settled in County Westmeath. His descendant, Surgeon Major Charles Bush Hearn of the Seventy-Sixth Foot, was Lafcadio Hearn's father. He went to the Ionian Islands on garrison duty when they were still British possessions, and married a local girl; their son was born on the Island of Santa Maura, in Modern Greek Lefcada, in ancient Greek Leucada. (The island's other claim to literary fame was that Sappho was supposed to have leapt to her death from the Leucadian rock.) Hearn always prided himself on his classical and mediterranean frame of mind, detesting all that was cold, Anglo-Saxon, northern. The family returned to Dublin when Britain ceded the Ionian Islands; the parents separated, both remarrying; the sons were left with the father, and then taken in by various relatives, Hearn by an aunt, Mrs Brenane, who lived in Wales and, being a Catholic convert, sent him to a number of harsh Jesuit schools in France and England. He quarrelled with his aunt, left home, went to London and then to America, and drifted into journalism and travel writing. He never returned to Ireland, and seems to have kept in touch with only one member of his family, his brother Daniel. His movement towards Japan was slow yet inexorable; his letters show him moving closer and closer to the Orient in his interests, his reading and his undefined yearnings. He loved Japan and its people from his first days there; and in return he is still widely studied not as 'English literature' but as the first folklorist of Japan.

To Hearn and to Yeats, Japan offered a way out of a tired literary tradition: to Hearn a permanent and single way, to Yeats one of many interconnecting paths. They had much in common beyond an attraction to the East. Both were late Romantics, *déracinés*, who reached out towards the inaccessible. One of them found it and found himself—that one not being Yeats. Whether finding oneself as a man and as a thinker creates the finer literature is another question: it is the tension of reaching out and not grasping that makes Yeats's poetry great. But the freshness and sense of fulfilment in Hearn's Japanese writings convey one aspect of the late romantic spirit shared by these near-contemporaries (Hearn was born fifteen years before Yeats in 1850).

Neither was a true *fin de siècle* decadent willing to push literary or other experience to the limit, although Yeats's years in Paris and Hearn's in New Orleans, where he had a brief illegal marriage to a mulatto woman, suggest a certain breaching of frontiers. Both wished to go beyond jaded conventional material and belief. Hearn found his new world already existing and hallowed by tradition; Yeats had to invent or resurrect his. When each searched beyond Christianity, Hearn found a philosophy living all around him in Japan, in priests, in shrines, in temples, expressed in gardens and houses and in Japanese people; Yeats had to create his own philosophy and had to invent the rituals of the Golden Dawn with his confrères as they went along. (Hearn is scathing about esoteric Buddhism, 'which is damnable charlatanism'.[2]) Hearn did not need to revivify the Japanese myths and legends as Yeats did the Celtic; they were alive in the minds of the Japanese.

Hearn was interested in many of the same things as Yeats: folklore, myth, legend, the dance, dreams, the occult, the genius of the race, Buddhism. In these materials each found a rich symbolism. Here again, Yeats had to construct his own symbols or at least to reinterpret such symbols as the Rose and Cross, the Platonic skein, the Hermetic path. He had to build his own Byzantium. But Hearn's objects were already symbols; his Byzantium was all around him. One might think that the forging of the symbol would make for the greater literature: but is the found symbol any less potent than the forged one?

Yeats regretted 'the romantic movement with its turbulent heroism, its self-assertion'. In 'The Autumn of the Body' (1897), he analyses the idealism of the 'old romanticism', and warily acknowledges decadence:

I see, indeed, in the arts of every country those faint lights and faint colours and faint outlines and faint energies which many call 'the decadence', and which I, because I believe that the arts lie dreaming of things to come, prefer to call the autumn of the body.[3]

One way out of this autumnal vapour was by way of the East: 'Europe is very old and has seen many arts run through the circle and has learnt the fruit of every flower and knows what this fruit sends up, and it is now time to copy the East and live deliberately'.[4] This sense that the fruit of Eastern philosophy was both new and restorative had much to do with Yeats's interest in Japan. He received the Noh drama circuitously through Pound and Fenollosa (whom Hearn knew and quarrelled with). He wrote in 1927 that he had read some Japanese literature including D.T. Suzuki's *Essays in Zen Buddhism*, Arthur Waley's translation of *Genji Monogatari*, Lady Murasaki's tenth-century novel of aristocratic life; and Toyohiko Kagawa's *Shisen O Koete (Before the Dawn)* which he expounds in *Explorations* and recalls at the end of *A Vision*: 'I remember the Apocalyptic dreams of the Japanese saint and labour leader Kagawa, whose books were lent me by a Galway clergyman'.[6] He wrote in 1928 to Kazumi Yano:

I do not think my interest in your country will ever slacken, especially now that I have found this new interest— its philosophy. Whether I shall ever see Japan is another matter ... Since I have met you I have felt a door open into Japan; you have told me so much, and given to me the means of further knowledge.[7]

One tends to think of Hearn only as the Japanese Hearn; but it is easy with hindsight to see him moving towards Japan throughout his early life and literary career, pushed by an undirected romanticism. In 1869, having left Ireland and Europe behind for ever, he turned up in New York. He wrote later in 'Intuition':

I was nineteen year old, and a stranger in the great strange world of America, and grievously tormented by grim realities. As I did not know how to face these realities, I tried to forget them as much as possible; and romantic dreams, daily nourished at a public library, helped me to forget.[8]

Here are the two main axes of Hearn's existence: the 'grim realities' are often there in his letters, but Romanticism is there as well; not, always as here, escapist, but idealistic and literary. The letters[9] and articles[10] written before his arrival in Japan show a nostalgia for romanticism, a loathing for realism, and a wary admiration for the decadents: 'What our age really needs is not more realism, but more of that pure idealism which is founded on a perfect knowledge of the essential facts of human life', and 'the most imminent danger ... lies in the loss of idealism', through 'debauching realism' ('Realism and Idealism'). In 'Decadence as a Fine Art', he sees the *décadents* as the 'jewel in a dung hill' (that is, the 'enormous putrid mass of realistic rhyme and fiction which has been created by the pessimistic philosophy and morbid feeling of certain French writers'). The decadent writers 'affect to worship only the crumbling, the effete, the ruined, the medieval, the Byzantine', but are admirable in having an ideal, even if it is still 'spectral'. He detests Zola's 'revolting realism', despises Matthew Arnold, has no patience with Emerson or with Whitman's 'Calibanish shagginess'. He praises John Addington Symonds and Algernon Charles Swinburne in 'Eclecticism in Literature'; Gustave Flaubert, especially for *Salammbo*; Gerard de Nerval (for his *Voyage en Orient* and his Abyssinian wife); Charles Baudelaire (for his 'intense passion for exotic singularity' and the black madonna figure of his 'savage mistress') in 'Idol of a Great Eccentric'. He admires Edgar Allen Poe, Dante Gabriel Rossetti, George Borrow, Ernst Hoffman; Thomas De Quincey's *Spanish Nun* and Théophile Gautier's *Mademoiselle de Maupin*. The author he most reveres is Pierre Loti, for his 'elegance of tinted words', and for 'reflecting the romance of an Oriental country' ('A New Romantic').

From his earliest criticism onwards, he seeks out 'the new, the strange, the exotic, the amorphous, the bizarre'. He is physically and intellectually restless in the West, writing in 1883: 'Surely all mysteries seem to issue from the womb of nations—from the heart of Asia'. In 1887, he writes: 'I am trying to find the Orient at home,—to apply the same methods of poetical-prose treatment to modern local and living themes'. By 1889 he has 'a library of Oriental books'. In 'A Peep at Japanese Poetry' he says 'The more the Western world learns of the extreme East, the more are the antiquated notions of Oriental inferiority weakened'. These were the interests that drew him Eastwards.

When Hearn arrived in Japan in 1890, he had feared that his literary career might end 'without a single flash of brightness or a solitary result worthy of preservation'. He had made his way up from typesetter to journalist in Cincinatti on a variety of *Enquirers*, *Gazettes* and *Commercials*; then in New Orleans had worked on the cheap *Daily Item*, and from 1881 on the 'quality' *Times-Democrat*, to which he had contributed a weekly translation from the French, and literary articles in which he displayed romantic idealism and exotic reading.[11] He had published *One of Cleopatra's Nights* (six translations of Théophile Gautier, 1883); *Chita: a story of Last Island* (1884); travel sketches from the Windward Islands for *Harper's Magazine*; and, as a result of living in Martinique, *Two Years in the French West Indies*; a small output for one who had had high literary aspirations.

He was forty, and had fourteen more years to live. He had accomplished little so far, but he was now about to produce a distinctive body of work, perceptive, reflective and full of integrity. In those fourteen years he was to produce twelve books about Japan and the Japanese which would make a bridge between East and West. His openness to Oriental tradition, religion and philososphy made them accessible to him. He was no detached observer; he had an affinity with and love for the Japanese people.

His first Japanese book, *Glimpses of Unfamiliar Japan*, penetrating gazes rather than glimpses, established his way of looking at the country.[12] Anyone familiar with his work will remember 'My First Day in the Orient'; but for Hearn it is not just the first impression that is important, it is the reflection afterwards, the movement outwards from the immediate shrine to its history, to present beliefs surrounding it, to the lives of its thousands of worshippers. 'In a Japanese Garden' moves from Hearn's own garden to the philosophy of the garden and the relationship of landscaping to Buddhism; to the legends and literature of Japanese gardens; to plants and trees, butterflies, lizards and toads; concluding that 'the art that made the beauty of this place was the art, also, of that faith to which belongs the all consoling text, "Verily, even plants and trees, rocks and stones, all shall enter into Nirvana" '.[13] The early 'Pilgrimage to Enoshima' gives some idea of the number of associations encompassed in each object that Hearn looks at:

'And this,' the reader may say,— 'this is all that you went forth to see: a torii, some shells, a small damask snake, some stones?' It is true. And nevertheless I know that I am bewitched. There is a charm indefinable about the place,— that sort of charm which comes with a little ghostly thrill never to be forgotten. Not of strange sights alone is this charm made, but of numberless subtle sensations and ideas interwoven and interblended: the sweet sharp scents of grove and sea; the blood-brightening, vivifying touch of the free wind; the dumb appeal of ancient mystic mossy things; vague reverence evoked by knowledge of treading soil called holy for a thousand years; and a sense of sympathy, as a human duty, compelled by the vision of steps of rock worn down into shapelessness by the pilgrim feet of vanished generations. And other memories ineffaceable: the first sight of the sea-girt City of Pearl through a fairy veil of haze; the windy approach to the lovely island over the velvety soundless brown stretch of sand; the weird majesty of the giant gate of bronze; the queer, high-sloping, fantastic, quaintly gabled street, flinging down sharp shadows of aerial balconies; the flutter of colored draperies in the sea wind, and of flags with their riddles of lettering; the pearly glimmering of the astonishing shops. And impressions of the enormous day,— the day of the Land of the Gods,—a loftier day than ever our summers know; and the glory of the view from those green sacred silent heights between sea and sun; and the remembrance of the sky, a sky spiritual as holiness, a sky with clouds ghost-pure and white as the light itself,—seeming, indeed, not clouds but dreams, or souls of Bodhisattvas about to melt forever into some blue Nirvana. [14]

Glimpses of Unfamiliar Japan was the product of a happy year at Matsue, a remote town almost unchanged since the fourteenth century, where Hearn taught in the Middle School, married Setsu Koizumi, a girl from an impoverished Samurai family, and took her family name, becoming Yakumo Koizumi ('many clouds', 'little spring'). Matsue was the formative influence of his life in Japan, but ill-health forced him to move. His next book, *Out of the East*, written in Kumamoto, a more modern, less sympathetic town, shows a fiercer race than the gentle, smiling people of Matsue. Later books included *Kokoro* and *Gleanings in Buddha-Fields*, written when he lived in the open port of Kobe. As Professor of English at the Imperial University of Tokyo he wrote *In Ghostly Japan, A Japanese Miscellany, Kotto, Kwaidan* and *Japan: An Attempt at Interpretation.*

Hearn's minute observation in describing the Japanese is one of the most attractive features of these books. 'From the Diary of an English Teacher', for example, lovingly scrutinizes each of his pupils. But it is in his generalised observations that he is most remarkable. He vividly conveys specific features of the Japanese: their complexion, their musculature, their 'small, symmetrical, tilted feet'. He devotes an entire essay ('Of Women's Hair') to ways of washing, dressing, oiling, cutting and combing the hair, and to the conventions underlying each degree of elaboration. He considers the subtlety of Japanese etiquette, and his conclusions are much the same as Yeats's: 'How but in custom and in ceremony/Are innocence and beauty born?' His sensitive attitude to the Japanese can be seen in the essay 'The Japanese Smile', in which he explains the stoicism, politeness, sensibility and self-abnegation behind the smile, which shows 'the difficulty of mutual comprehension between the Eastern and Western races'. Westerners, suspecting insincerity, often misinterpret, say, the smile that masks pain.

Hearn often reverts to the smile, never suspecting, never resenting:

The country-folk gaze wonderingly at the foreigner. At various places where we halt, old men approach to touch my clothes, apologizing with humble bows and winning smiles for their very natural curiosity, and asking my interpreter all sorts of odd questions. Gentler and kindlier faces I never beheld; and they reflect the souls behind them; never yet have I heard a voice raised in anger, nor observed an unkindly act. [15]

The sympathy and openness of this passage give some idea of Hearn's attitude as observer and observed; always, one senses an affection for the people of Japan and not merely an interest in their country, their beliefs and their customs:

Regret for a single individual smile is something common to normal human nature; but regret for the smile of a population, for a smile considered as an abstract quality, is certainly a rare sensation, and one to be obtained, I fancy, only in this Orient land whose people smile forever like their own gods of stone. And this precious experience is already mine. [16]

Such love of 'a population' is never evident in the work of Yeats, who loves the peasantry and the aristocracy but not many in between.

It is in their collecting of folklore that Hearn and Yeats correspond most closely, though even here their purposes differ. Yeats mentions in 1893 the 'noteless Gaelic poet' who made a bird-story into 'a forgotten ballad, some odd verses of which my white-capped friend remembered and sang for me', but comments in a footnote in 1924: 'There is a ballad in my *Wind Among the Reeds* on this theme' ('The Host of the Air'). [17] Myth and legend to Hearn were to be absorbed, re-told, and thus preserved: to Yeats they were a source for his own creative work. In religion the two writers held similar beliefs but had different aims. In Yeats's exploration of the occult, of Rosicrucian, Hermetic, Kabbalistic and finally Buddhist doctrine, he was looking for a personal experience, a moment of revelation which he never achieved (hence the panic and fury of the late poetry). Hearn sought no personal revelation; his own faith was a modified Spencerian Evolutionism which he reconciled happily with the Buddhism he saw around him. The Yeats of 'The Mandukya Upanishad', or of *The Holy Mountain* is almost wistful as he describes the bump on the swami's forehead; Hearn observes, explains, but never envies. The region in which Hearn and Yeats converge yet markedly diverge is that of Japanese art and artefacts, dance and drama: that is where they use the same symbol-laden material but look for and find something quite different in it.

Hearn's studies of folk legends, dream traditions, stories and ballads can be likened to those of the affectionate early Yeats of *The Celtic Twilight* who shows a world where peasant and ghost mingle familiarly:

> The house ghost is usually a harmless and well-meaning creature . . . these spirits have a gloomy, matter-of-fact way with them. They come to announce a death, to fulfil some obligation, to revenge a wrong, to pay their bills even—as did a fisherman's daughter the other day—and then hasten to their rest. All things they do decently and in order. It is demons, and not ghosts, that transform themselves into white cats or black dogs. [18]

Hearn's demons and *gaki* of Buddhist belief have much in common with Yeats's fairies and *sidhe*; they are like the beautiful 'gentry' of 'Kidnappers' or 'Dust hath closed Helen's eye', who need humans, who desire and spirit away husbands, babies and brides, thus imparting a value to the humanity of the poor peasant.

In many essays Hearn systematically retails folk legends, often beautiful, often grisly. Many have to do with the dead returning, as Yeats's do, to finish the business of their earthly lives. 'A Promise Kept' tells of a man whose only way to keep a promise to return is to kill himself so that his spirit can keep the appointment. 'Of a Promise Broken' tells of a husband who breaks his promise to his first wife by marrying another when she dies, with horrible consequences to the new bride, whose head is torn off. A Buddhist invocation demolishes the avenging spirit, 'but the fleshless right hand, though parted from the wrist, still writhed;—and its fingers still gripped at the bleeding head,—and tore, and mangled,—as the claws of the yellow crab cling fast to a fallen fruit'. [19] Not all revenants are so bloodthirsty: a mysterious pale woman begs for food and is found in the cemetery feeding a living infant, 'for the mother had been prematurely buried; the child was born in the tomb, and the ghost of the mother had thus provided for it,—love being stranger than death'. [20] Hearn notes numerous variations of such comings and goings between this world and the next, including the macabre joke of a woman who apparently eats corpses, thus frightening away all her suitors until one is brave enough to eat the proffered arm fresh from the coffin and it turns out to be made of the best Kwashi confectionery.

Many legends tell of spirit transference, the spirit of one girl transferred to the body of another and leading an everyday life whilst her original dead or comatose body is watched over by her family (as in 'Before the Supreme Court'). Not only humans change magically: 'The Story of Kwashin Koji' tells of a wonderfully painted kakemono or religious painting whose scroll goes blank when the artist is cheated and killed; his headless body comes to life (and drinks a good many bowls of wine) and the painting comes back to more than life:

all saw the boat suddenly turn, and begin to move toward the foreground of the picture. It grew rapidly larger and larger . . . And, all of a sudden, the water of the lake seemed to overflow,—out of the picture into the room,—and the room was flooded; and the spectators girded up their robes in haste, as the water rose above their knees. In the same moment the boat appeared to glide out of the screen, —a real fishing-boat; and the creaking of the single oar could be heard. [21]

But it is difficult to separate legend from all other kinds of Japanese folk belief, nor did Hearn wish to do so. 'Of Ghosts and Goblins', like many other pieces, is partly folklore but partly religion. 'Folklore Gleanings' in *A Japanese Miscellany* include 'Song of Japanese Children' and 'Buddhist Names of Plants and Animals', which encompass natural history and religion: 'Many names of plants or living creatures refer to Buddhist customs, legends, rites, or beliefs . . . '. 'Dragonflies' considers Japan as 'The Island of the Dragon-fly' and describes the names, etymology and entomology of dragonflies, children's dragonfly games, and dragonfly literature including sixty dragonfly 'picture poems'. These are subdivided into 'Dragonflies and Sunshine', 'Flight of Dragonflies', 'Lightness of Dragon-flies', and glossed as follows:

In the form *hokku*—limited to seventeen syllables— . . . almost the only rule . . . not at all a rigid one,—is that the poem shall be a little word-picture,—that it shall appeal to some experience of sense . . . the reader will find that they are really pictures,—tiny colour-prints in the manner of the Ukiyo-ye schools.

Nagare-yuku
Awa ni yume miru
Tombo kana!

· Lo! the dragon-fly dreams a dream above the flowing of the foam-bubbles.[22]

This translation brings irresistibly (and I suppose coincidentally) to mind Yeats's seventeen syllables:

> Like a long legged fly upon the stream
> His mind moves upon silence.

Folklore and legend are part of Japan's life, its scenery, its nature, its literature; both are imbued with Buddhism and inseparable from visionary belief. Folklore for Hearn, as for Yeats, was a stage in a journey away from Christianity. In 'An Indian Monk', Yeats describes Shri Purohit Swami's book as 'something I have waited for since I was seventeen years old. About that age, bored by an Irish Protestant point of view that suggested by its blank abstraction chloride of lime, I began to question the country people about apparitions'.[23] Hearn too moves from his boyhood religion, this time Catholicism, towards Buddhist belief; the following passage from the essay 'Of Moon Desire' also seems to express his successfully achieved yearning to become part of Japan:

I remember when a boy lying on my back in the grass, gazing into the summer blue above me, and wishing that I could melt into it—become a part of it. For these fancies I believe that a religious tutor was innocently responsible: he had tried to explain to me, because of certain dreamy questions, what he termed 'the folly and wickedness of pantheism' — with the result that I immediately became a pantheist, at the tender age of fifteen. And my imaginings presently led me not only to want the sky for a playground, but also to become the sky! Now I think that in those days I was really close to a great truth—touching it, in fact without the faintest suspicion of its existence. I mean the truth that the wish *to become* is reasonable in direct ratio to its largeness—or, in other words, that the more you wish to be, the wiser you are; while the wish *to have* is apt to be foolish in proportion to its largeness.[24]

Like Yeats, Hearn starts from 'the country people'. In 'Otokichi's Daruma', the little clay household god, which is blind until an offering is made, is treated with sympathy and humour: 'The blind Daruma can be expected to do wonderful things, because he has to work for his eyes. There are many such funny little deities in Japan. . . . Faith in very small gods—toy gods—belongs to that simplicity of heart which, in this wicked world, makes the nearest possible approach to pure goodness'. [25] In 'Gaki' we see gods that come from hell but can take part in human life, and Hearn, with typical thoroughness, classifies the thirty-six kinds of Gaki recognised by Japanese Buddhism, which form two divisions, the 'Gaki-World-Dwellers (Gaki-Sekai-Ju)', that is, 'all Hungry Spirits who remain in the Gakido proper, and are, therefore, never seen by mankind'. The other division contains 'Nin-chu-Ju (Dwellers-among-men)', who 'remain always in this world, and are sometimes seen'.

There is yet another classification of gaki, according to the character of their penitential torment. All gaki suffer hunger and thirst; but there are three degrees of this suffering. The Muzai-gaki represent the first degree: they must hunger and thirst uninterruptedly, without obtaining any nourishment whatever. The Shozai- gaki suffer only in the second degree: they are able to feed occasionally upon impure substances. The Usai-gaki are more fortunate: they can eat such remains of food as are thrown away by men, and also the offerings of food set before the images of the gods, or before the tablets of the ancestors. The last two classes of gaki are especially interesting because they are supposed to meddle with human affairs. [26]

He examines Buddhism as it affects the common people: in 'Dust', children playing at funerals with cicadas bring him to a neo-Buddhist understanding:

These little boys and girls, being Japanese and Buddhists, will never, in any event, feel about death just as you or I do ... In the strangely penetrant light of their creed, teaching the ghostliness of all substance, granite or gossamer ... this their present world, with its bigger mountains and rivers and rice-fields, will not appear to them much more real than the mud landscapes which they made in childhood. And much more real it probably is not. At which thought I am conscious of a sudden soft shock, a familiar shock, and know myself seized by the idea of substance as Non-Reality. [27]

In 'The Stone Buddha' he fuses the higher Buddhism and simple faith, illustrating the result by a typical ghost story of a haunted house. 'Anger, secretly indulged, can have ghostly consequences,' he observes. This is a Yeatsian, purgatorial notion which he debates throughout the essay, concluding:

We may have to learn that the infinite whirl of death and birth, out of which we cannot escape, is of our own creation, of our own seeking; that the forces integrating worlds are the errors of the Past; that the eternal sorrow is but the eternal hunger of insatiable desire; and that the burnt-out suns are rekindled only by the inextinguishable passions of vanished lives. [28]

But he also examines the less 'popular' essence of Buddhism in 'The Higher Buddhism', to which he relates his own Oriental-Occidental Spencerianism: 'I venture to call myself a student of Herbert Spencer and it was because of my acquaintance with the Synthetic Philosophy that I came to find in Buddhist philosophy a more than romantic interest. For Buddhism is also a theory of evolution'. Spencer's highest point of development, 'Equilibration', corresponds with the supreme point of development in Buddhist evolution, except that in Buddhism 'this supreme point vanishes into Nirvana'. [29] The universe of Matter and the universe of 'conditioned Mind . . . represent in their evolution a strictly moral order'. The 'most remarkable teachings of the Higher Buddhism' are:

That there is but one Reality: That the consciousness is not the real Self: That matter is an aggregate of phenomena created by the force of acts and thoughts: That all objective and subjective existence is made by Karma—the present being the creation of the past, and the actions of the present and the past, in combination, determining the conditions of the future . . . All things having form or name—Buddhas, gods, men, and all living creatures—suns, worlds, moons, the whole visible cosmos— are transitory phenomena . . . Assuming, with Herbert Spencer, that the test of reality is permanence, one can scarcely question this position. [30]

He tackles the complex notion, alien to Westerners but much dwelt on by Yeats, of Nirvana. As always, his aim is to help Westerners overcome their misunderstandings of Eastern thought. There is an idea, he writes,

that still widely prevails in Europe and America, the idea that Nirvana signifies, to Buddhist minds, neither more nor less than absolute nothingness—complete annihilation. Nirvana, indeed, signifies an extinction. But if by this extinction of individual being we understand soul-death, our conception of Nirvana is wrong. Or if we take Nirvana to mean such re-absorption of the finite into the infinite as that predicted by Indian pantheism, again our idea is foreign to Buddhism. Nevertheless, if we declare that Nirvana means the extinction of individual sensation, emotion, thought— the final disintegration of conscious personality—the annihilation of everything that can be included under the term 'I'—then we rightly express one side of the Buddhist teaching. [31]

In religious matters he sees himself as a guide, not a guru. Yeats on the other hand sees himself as the guided, the disciple.

Whatever the veneration Hearn felt for religion, his heart was always with the worshippers, the people. In religion Yeats wishes to de-personalise, to see the symbol. Hearn is moved at the shrines he visits by their religious symbolism, but also by the people he finds there: bereaved women hanging up tiny kimonos in memory of dead children, or sending little paper boats out for them. He sees too the poor priest beneath the holy garment, and is sensitive to his human feelings, as when he visits a very poor shrine and is overwhelmed at his own vulgarity in assuming that the priest's offered gift of hot water is a begging bowl.

What Yeats admired in Buddhism was its mystical and contemplative elements. As Alex Zwerdling points out in *Yeats and the Heroic Ideal*: 'what attracted Yeats was the idea of the eternal return, the cyclical view of history, which stressed the recurrence of life in perpetual reincarnation ... Nirvana is the release from the cycles', which Yeats does not want, desiring 'Conflict, more conflict'. [32] He does admire those qualities that Hearn ascribes to Shinto, the indigenous religion of Japan, a mixture of nature-worship and loyalty to the reigning dynasty as descendants of the sun-goddess:

For Shinto signifies character in the higher sense,—courage, courtesy, honour, and above all things, loyalty. The spirit of Shinto is the spirit of filial piety, the zest of duty, the readiness to surrender life for a principle without a thought of where-fore. It is the docility of the child; it is the sweetness of the Japanese woman. It is conservatism likewise; the wholesome check upon the national tendency to cast away the worth of the entire past in rash eagerness to assimilate too much of the foreign present. It is religion,—but religion transformed into hereditary moral impulse,—religion transmuted into ethical instinct. It is the whole emotional life of the race,
—the Soul of Japan. [33]

In writing about Sato's sword Yeats stresses what the gift symbolised: continuity, hereditary impulses, loyalty:

The consecrated blade upon my knees Is Sato's ancient blade, still as it was, Still razor-keen, still like a looking-glass Unspotted by the centuries; That flowering, silken, old embroidery, torn From some court-lady's dress and round The wooden scabbard bound and wound, Can, tattered, still protect, faded adorn. ('A Dialogue of Self and Soul')

The sword that Hearn receives from his pupils (in 'Sayonara'), 'that beautiful sword with the silver karashishi ramping upon its sheath, or crawling through the silken cording of its wonderful hilt', is a symbol both of duty, ritual sacrifice and military dedication ('The sword is the Soul of the Samurai') and of the friendship, affection and loyalty of those who gave it to him. [34] Hearn stresses the personal background to the gift.

This different perspective affects the way in which the two writers approach art. Yeats was obsessed with the dance as a means of abstracting the performer from humanity. His dancer fuses with and is lost in the dance. Art takes over until we can no longer tell the dancer from the dance. Hearn, too, is responsive to classic art, admires it and is moved by it. In 'Kitsuki' he describes the 'Dance of the Miko, the Divineress' performed with what sounds like Yeats's bell-branch, 'a queer instrument . . . somewhat like a branch with the twigs bent downward, from each of which hangs a little bell':

Her every movement is a poem, because she is very graceful; and yet her performance could scarcely be called a dance, as we understand the word; it is rather a light swift walk within a circle, during which she shakes the instrument at regular intervals, making all the little bells ring. Her face remains impassive as a beautiful mask, placid and sweet as the face of a dreaming Kwannon; and her white feet are pure of line as the feet of a marble nymph. Altogether, with her snowy raiment and white flesh and passionless face, she seems rather a beautiful living statue than a Japanese maiden. [35]

Hearn always looks at the dancer beneath the costume and ceremony. In 'Of a Dancing-girl' he describes the geisha's role, her training, the rigours she endures to achieve her elegant accomplishments. He sees the ironic contrast between the beauty and decorum of her dances, songs and music-making and the cruel discipline behind it:

Her voice may be flexible enough, but lacks the requisite strength. In the iciest hours of winter nights, she must ascend to the roof of her dwelling-house, and there sing and play till the blood oozes from her fingers and the voice dies in her throat. The desired result is an atrocious cold. After a period of hoarse whispering, her voice changes its tone and strengthens. She is ready to become a public singer and dancer.[36]

In 'Bon-Odori' he describes a dance that 'suggests some fancy of Somnambulism,—dreamers, who dream themselves flying, dreaming upon their feet':

And always the white hands sinuously wave together, as if weaving spells, alternately without and within the round, now with palms upward, now with palms downward; and all the elfish sleeves hover duskily together, with a shadowing as of wings; and all the feet poise together with such a rhythm of complex motion, that, in watching it, one feels a sensation of hypnotism—as while striving to watch a flowing and shimmering of water.[37]

There comes to him 'the thought that I am looking at something immemorially old, something belonging to the unrecorded beginnings of this Oriental life, perhaps to the crepuscular Kamiyo itself, to the magical Age of the Gods; a symbolism of motion whereof the meaning has been forgotten for innumerable years'. This 'Dance of Souls' is reminiscent of the mystic dance in Yeats's 'Rosa Alchemica':

The dance wound in and out, tracing upon the floor the shapes of petals that copied the petals in the rose overhead, and to the sound of hidden instruments which were perhaps of an antique pattern, for I have never heard the like; and every moment the dance was more passionate, until all the winds of the world seemed to have awakened under our feet.[38]

To yield to the 'immortal august woman' with whom he dances this supernatural dance would be fatal:

Suddenly I remembered that her eyelids had never quivered, and that her lilies had not dropped a black petal, nor shaken from their places, and understood with a great horror that I danced with one who was more or less than human, and who was drinking up my soul as an ox drinks up a wayside pool; and I fell, and darkness passed over me.[39]

But the rejection cannot dispel the terror.

After their Dance of Souls, on the other hand, Hearn's supernatural dancers turn into ordinary girls:

Instantly the witchcraft ends, like the wonder of some dream broken by a sound; the chanting ceases; the round dissolves in an outburst of happy laughter, and chatting, and softly-vowelled callings of flower-names

which are names of girls, and farewell cries of 'Sayonara!' as dancers
and spectators alike betake themselves homeward, with a great koro-
koro of getas. And I, moving with the throng, in the bewildered manner
of one suddenly roused from sleep, know myself ungrateful. These
silvery-laughing folk who now toddle along beside me upon their noisy
little clogs, stepping very fast to get a peep at my foreign face, these but
a moment ago were visions of archaic grace, illusions of necromancy,
delightful phantoms; and I feel a vague resentment against them for
thus materializing into simple country-girls.[40]

If, then, Hearn always sees the dancer beneath the robe, the
country girl beneath the witchcraft, the actor beneath the mask,
Yeats does not. The elements of the Noh plays as 'translated by
Ernest Fenollosa and finished by Ezra Pound' that attracted him
were precisely those that eliminate actor and public as far as
inhumanly possible. The Noh plays suggested to Yeats 'a form of
drama, distinguished, indirect and symbolic, and having no
need of mob or Press to pay its way—an aristoctatic form'. For
Yeats, 'all imaginative art remains at a distance and this distance,
once chosen, must be firmly held against a pushing world'. In
'Certain Noble Plays of Japan', he expounds the necessity for art
to detach itself from life and by stylisation to free itself from
suspect realism. The mask is the perfection of this freedom—not
only from realism but from the unworthy actor:

A mask will enable me to substitute for the face of some commonplace
player, or for that face repainted to suit his own vulgar fancy, the fine
invention of a sculptor and to bring the audience close enough to the
play to hear every inflection of the voice. A mask never seems but a dirty
face, and no matter how close you go is yet a work of art; nor shall we
lose by stilling the movement of the features, for deep feeling is
expressed by a movement of the whole body. In poetical painting and in
sculpture the face seems the nobler for lacking curiosity, alert attention,
all that we sum up under the famous word of the realists, 'vitality.' It is
even possible that being is only possessed completely by the dead, and
that it is some knowledge of this that makes us gaze with so much
emotion upon the face of the Sphinx or of Buddha.[41]

It is in this inhuman dimension that the outreaching Yeats is
magnificent. His unachieved and unachievable notion of Japan is
only one of the ideas to which he reached out in his determination not to let life substitute itself for art. For Yeats, Japan, like
Sato's sword, was emblematic:

> ... Sato's gift, a changeless sword,
> By pen and paper lies,
> That it may moralise
> My days out of their aimlessness.
> A bit of an embroidered dress
> Covers its wooden sheath.
> ... In Sato's house
> Curved like new moon, moon-luminous,
> It lay five hundred years.
> Yet if no change appears
> No moon; only an aching heart
> Conceives a changeless work of art.
>
> ('My Table', 'Meditations in Time of Civil War')

The sword's permanence is not consoling: individual father and son are lost; art remains. It is in reaching out to this abstraction from the human that Yeats is magnificent.

Hearn's Japan, in contrast, is one in which the abstract, the artistic and the mythological are encompassed by the human:

To have studied and loved an ancient faith only through the labours of palaeographers and archaeologists, and as a something astronomically remote from one's own existence, and then suddenly in after years to find the same faith a part of one's human environment,—to feel that its mythology, though senescent, is alive all around you,—is almost to realize the dream of the Romantics, to have the sensation of returning through twenty centuries into the life of a happier world.[42]

If there is grandeur in Yeats's unfulfilled reaching is there not also a magnificence in Hearn's sense of arrival?

RENAISSANCE EMBLEM BOOKS: A COMMENT ON TERMINOLOGY

JOHN HORDEN

It is now fifty-three years since Mario Praz's pioneering *Studi sul concettismo* first appeared, thirty-nine years since Rosemary Freeman's admirable *English Emblem Books*, and twenty years since Arthur Henkel and Albrecht Schöne's majestic, but selective, *Emblemata: Handbuch zur Sinnbildkunst des XVI und XVII Jahrhunderts*. More recent times have, of course, witnessed the publication both of major works and of numerous specialist papers. Potentially most massive of all is the Index Emblematicus projected by Peter Daly of McGill University. When completed—work on it seems to be in abeyance—the Index would record on computer a detailed linguistic, thematic, and iconographical analysis of, effectively, every emblem book.

Although there is no longer any need to establish the emblem book's credentials to serious consideration as an unusual and significant literary genre, emblem studies surprisingly lack a full vocabulary of generally accepted descriptive and analytical terms. It is not feasible to require a terminology as authoritative as, say, the language of heraldry. Indeed, elaborate taxonomy can become a weariness of the flesh. But in certain areas of emblem studies the need for a more searching vocabulary is very real, and with the creation of Professor Daly's Index, which is to be the product of an international team of scholars working independently, the need is urgent. What is wanted is a set of terms that are exact, adaptable, and generally acknowledged, and that lend themselves, especially, to recording the grouping of symbols and their qualifying influence upon each other. A glance at a few areas of particular difficulty may indicate the nature of the task.

Fundamentally, the emblem book is a picture book consisting of symbolical pictures accompanied by passages of explanatory prose or verse interpreting the picture and pointing its moral lesson. In style and in degree of complexity, the pictures differ widely; in some books the text is very brief. And only the more successful emblems fulfil the prescription suggested by Scipioni Bargagli, a sixteenth-century commentator, that picture and interpretation should be 'so strictly united together, that being considered apart, they cannot explicate themselves distinctly the one without the other'. Emblem theory is convoluted, and the exact nature of the emblem is still debated. But it is generally the relationship between idea, picture, and text that is still exercising critics.

Most aspects of the problem which calls for fresh terminology may be found in pictures from emblem books belonging to the category which Rosemary Freeman named 'diagrammatic'. This is the more complicated type in which several symbols are juxtaposed to present a single idea. In his *A Collection of Emblemes* (1635) George Wither has an emblem (Bk. 1, XXII) devoted to a close version of the fabled debate, recorded by Xenophon, between Hercules, Virtue and Pleasure (here Vice). The emblematic plate, which was borrowed from Gabriel Rollenhagen's *Nucleus Emblematum Selectissimorum* (1611–13), depicts the semi-nude figure of the youthful Hercules. To the left (Hercules' right) sits the bearded figure of an old man representing Virtue; to the right, Vice, also seated, is depicted as a hideous naked semi-human female with wings, horns, and tail. Again on the left, there is a caduceus resting against Virtue's knees, and behind both him and Hercules a sunflower grows. On Vice's side of the plate are a lute and scorpion, a vase of lilies, and a skull and crossed bones. Both personifications also bear their own personal accoutrements. Virtue has a large book on his knees, while Vice holds up a mask simulating human features without wholly concealing her own, and her left hand holds a whip. It is also to be remarked that Hercules is standing above the two seated figures, and that he is looking at Vice. Both his hands are raised: the right in a beckoning gesture to Virtue, the left, and the lower of the two, extended repressively at Vice. It is, of course, not coincidental that Vice is on his sinister (left) side.

Wither interprets this plate (or, in contemporary terms, 'moralizes' it) in verse which explains that at eighteen years of age he went 'into the World alone' to seek his fortune. He was apt in both mind and body to pursue either vice or virtue. Vice offered pleasures, the satisfactions of the flesh and 'all those Achievements which [Vice's] Service brings'; Virtue gave promise of wisdom and 'those brave things, which noblest

Mindes doe crave'. Wither, undecided, noticed both that Death attended Vice and that her face was 'but a painted Vizard' which hid the foulest deformity. He concludes by asking the Lord to give him the grace always to see the ugliness of Vice and so eschew her falsehoods and vain allurements. His final plea is that his affections shall be directed to virtue, whose beauties he shall contemplate and whose love he shall embrace, and that his life may be conducted according to virtue's dictates.

Most emblem books have affinities, near or remote, with the methods exemplified here by Wither. Some characteristics may be readily observed. To begin with, the plate—as in many emblem books—has been borrowed and, again as so often happens, it does not precisely suit Wither's use of it. In the closing reference to the personification of Virtue (who is described as 'faire'), Wither arbitrarily follows tradition rather than his eye and mentions 'her' beauty, 'her' love, and 'her' safe direction. (In classical mythology Virtue is personified as a woman, but is often depicted as a man in the seventeenth century.) Also, certain symbols are left to make their impact on the reader undirected by the emblem-writer. As far as Vice is concerned, Wither specifically alludes only to her ugliness, her mask and her deformity. With her he also links Death, represented by the skull and bones, though Death is in the far background and could readily have been associated with Virtue as well. Yet the grave and venerable appearance of Virtue, a protagonist after all, is not described. No allusion is made to the book (learning), the caduceus (wisdom), and the sunflower (constancy in pursuit of an ideal), which reinforce Virtue's merits; and similarly there are no references to the lute (worldly gaity), the whip (punishment), the scorpion (the sting of conscience), and the—presumably festering—lilies (corruption) by which the nature of Vice would be emphasized.

It will be seen that, with emblems of some complexity, there are two essential aspects to the correct interpretation of the picture and to a full understanding of the emblem's theme: first, identifying the individual symbols precisely; second, relating the symbols both to one another and to the text—recognizing a structure that is at once visual and literary. (One other factor that may exert a modifying influence is the presence in some emblems of a motto, epigram or quotation, and the like.)

The identification of symbols, to treat that first, is fundamentally an exercise—simple or extensive—in literary and historical research. Nevertheless it is essential that the modern commentator does not underestimate the inherent awareness of symbolism among the people of the Renaissance. The taste for symbolism was so pervasive that, as has often been said, virtually no object was without meaning and none had only a single meaning. This is doubly true of even the most apparently trivial component of an emblem. A brief comparison of two paintings may indicate something of what can so easily be missed.

Even the most unsophisticated of present-day observers would recognize that the famous 'Rainbow' portrait of Queen Elizabeth I, painted by an unknown artist about 1600, is manifestly heavy with symbolism. There is the rainbow (peace) and the motto 'non sine sole iris' ('no rainbow without the sun'), the cloak decoratively embroidered with eyes, ears and mouths (fame), and the bodice and sleeves covered with flowers (eternal spring), all calling attention to the Queen's fame and wisdom and to the coming of a new age. An ornament of serpent and armillary sphere (wisdom and understanding) on the left sleeve has a red, heart-shaped, jewel hanging from the serpent's mouth (wise choice), and these, like the great head-dress of pearls, Imperial Crown, and crescent moon (virginity and majesty) continue the message. In an age as alert as the Renaissance to symbolic implication, the nature of the message would be understood even if its precise terms were not clear to all.

By the side of this portrait, the painting attributed to John de Critz of Henry Wriothesley, third Earl of Southampton, imprisoned in the Tower of London seems unadorned. Apart from the motto 'in Vinculis Invictus' behind Wriothesley's shoulder, and his arms displayed on the cover of a book, there is no obvious message. Wriothesley is plainly dressed in black (melancholy?) and the pattern on his gloves is black and white (grief?). He is alone but for a cat—his pet, might it be presumed? To Renaissance eyes, however, the cat would surely offer a sardonic comment on Wriothesley's situation: enduring life imprisonment for treason. It is black with a white nose and chest, and it sits demurely in the window place, behind Wriothesley, like him looking toward the artist. But its yellow staring eyes and fierce gaze carry the reminder that here is not only the usual companion of the personification of Melancholy but also the sinister familiar spirit of witches. This is the animal that so many people regarded as, to borrow terms from the emblematist Henry Peacham, 'light-loathing', 'hateful', and 'ominous'. Alas, poor Wriothesley.

The same unobtrusiveness of symbolism in the context of emblem pictures is often to be found in accoutrements used to enhance a personification. The familiar figure of the shepherd— the symbol of loving care—offers an immediate example.

The traditional accoutrements of the shepherd are tar-box and crook. The latter has been persistently misunderstood by modern commentators. From Theocritan times shepherds have been described and depicted as carrying one of several similar implements. These, to oversimplify, are either a plain staff, a staff with a spud (or small trowel) on one end, a club rather like a modern hockey-stick, or a staff with a crook. The forms of these vary, and the crook and spud are often depicted on different ends of the same staff. The matter has been well-documented as an item of agricultural history. In herding, the staff with the spud was used for digging up a stone or turf and hurling it beyond a straying flock to turn it back. (Pepys attempted this when, on 14 July 1667, he met a shepherd on Epsom Down: 'I tried to cast stones with his Horne Crooke'.) The club—like the staff—was thrown with similar intent. But the crook was an implement of a different order, since it was used for gently restraining a sheep by holding one of its legs. Symbolically, the club and the staff with a spud represent a forceful, even violent, method of *driving*; the crook suggests caring *restraint*. Is it surprising that Anglican bishops (and other such dignitaries) carry a crook as symbol of their pastoral office? Yet the most recent commentators on the emblematic woodcut title-page border of Sir Philip Sidney's *Arcadia* (1593) have contentedly described as a crook the shepherd's staff with a spud that is clearly delineated—an indifference to the exact interpretation of a symbol that runs quite contrary to Renaissance instinct.

Modern commentators, it must be allowed, are at some disadvantage in the understanding of accoutrements. Small, but significant, features of familiar instruments have naturally changed in three hundred years. One of the pictures—once again from a borrowed plate—in Francis Quarles' *Emblemes* (1635) depicts the Human Spirit observing the figure of Death in the distance with the Heavenly Host immediately above it (Bk. 3,XIV). The text refers to these as consequently being brought into closer view. But the Human Spirit is looking through the larger end of the telescope, which would, with the modern instrument, present a diminished image. Commentators have been misled into thinking that Quarles was careless or unobservant. An examination of seventeenth-century telescopes in, say, the Ashmolean Science Museum, Oxford, confirms that the eye-piece was at that time placed at what would today be regarded as the wrong end. Some Renaissance paintings also illustrate the practice, but other documentary evidence is hard to find.

The significance of individual symbols established, the critic has then to consider the pattern of their grouping. What immediately catches the attention in Wither's picture is the unit formed by Hercules, Virtue, and Vice. The other symbols only modify, or interpret—according to their own meaning and positioning—the significance of the group. Many commentators would refer to this group as the 'motif' of the emblem. As a critical term this seems altogether too imprecise, especially as many emblems clearly have more than one such motif. These can often, it is true, adequately be described as 'central' and 'secondary' motifs. But sometimes their order of importance is hard to decide, and sometimes there are more than two. Also the term 'motif' permits the arbitrary inclusion of quite unrelated and subsidiary elements. These figures are what first attract the eye, and what focus the attention. 'Focus of attention' or, perhaps better, 'focus' might well serve as a term. Another plate from Wither provides an opportunity to consider this further.

What is at once presented to the view is a heap of earth, newly-turned as the emerging worms declare, surmounted by a skull and against which rest a crossed sceptre and mattock (Bk. 1, XLVIII). The immediate message seems plain: both high and low are subject to mortality. But this is modified by a background in which are depicted (to the left) a great house and a majestic tomb and (to the right) a humble funeral procession issuing from a village, with the body being carried uncoffined. The message thus seems changed. It now proposes that although both high and low are subject to mortality, even after death social distinctions are still made, in funeral ceremonies and the splendour of tombs. But Wither, endorsing this point, then moralizes in an unexpected way, by declaring that what he wishes 'to preach' is that men of each degree should cultivate thoughts and behaviour suitable to their station in life. The rich should remember that they are certain to die and should embrace virtue; the poor, equally assured of death, should take comfort from the fact that, although afflicted in this life, death will make them as happy as a king.

In comparison with the other plate the elements of this are more clearly defined. A symbol of universal mortality is in the foreground with two substantially realistic scenes, giving it particular application, lying behind. It is significant that the grand tomb is placed in the immediate background on the right of the focus (viewer's left) and that the sceptre points toward it. The humble funeral is more distant, and on the other (sinister) side. To describe the skull and implements as the 'central motif' and the tomb and funeral merely as 'secondary motifs' is surely less satisfactory than to use, say, terms like 'focus' and 'interpretative scenes'? That they are 'interpretative' rather than merely 'illustrative' is conveyed by the text. In this way, weight is given to the primary aspect of the plate, and its position, both symbolically and iconographically, is more adequately indicated.

By an extension of the principle, terms such as 'modifying', 'reinforcing', 'exemplifying', even 'contradicting', could be used to describe subsidiary themes and show their relationship to the 'focus'. With this in mind, a critic could be led to make a more orderly analysis of an emblem picture than would otherwise occur. A picture from Francis Quarles' *Hieroglyphikes of the Life of Man* (1638) can be taken by way of illustration (no. VI).

In the foreground are depicted the figures of Death (a skeleton) and Time (the traditionally bearded figure with wings and a long forelock) and a large, steadily-burning candle representing man's life. Behind them the sun, high in the sky, blazes down and a sundial marks the hour. Both Death and Time carry traditional accoutrements: in his left hand Death has his arrow and in the other, slightly less commonplace, an extinguisher, while Time has an hourglass. Time's right hand, which might normally carry a sickle, is empty and is being used to restrain Death from extinguishing the candle's flame. The accompanying text is a verse dialogue between Death and Time. The moral can be anticipated: all men will die, but Death cannot come until Time permits. So man should use his days well.

In present parlance the plate might be said to have the Candle of Man's Life with the figures of Death and Time as its motif. It is quite possible that a sundial might be considered so much another expression of the passage of time as to be without special significance. But if it were thought important, then the triple group would become the central motif, and the sundial—with or without mention of the sun—would become the secondary motif. How much more informative to regard the candle as the focus. (That it is, indeed, intended to be the focus is confirmed by its appearing, with different supporting symbols, in each of the other fourteen emblems of *Hieroglyphikes*.) The candle is still far from consumed and the flame burns brightly, indicating that, at this moment, life is still in full vigour. That theme is then 'reinforced' by the fact that Time is restraining Death. And the situation is exactly 'interpreted' by the position of the sun, still high in the sky, and by the sundial's consequently showing the hour to be four o'clock in the afternoon. Man, here, is still far from the evening of his life.

It happens that in each plate of *Hieroglyphikes* the symbol that is the focus lies in the foreground. But it should not be inferred that the terms 'focus' and 'foreground' are synonymous. Indeed, in many emblems the focus may lie manifestly elsewhere. In a plate from Robert Farlie's *Lychnocausia* (1638)—an emblem book which relies on the same dominant symbol as *Hieroglyphikes*—the candle that is Hero's light, toward which Leander swims, is obscurely in the far background. So, too, is the focus in the picture from Quarles' *Emblemes* which has the misleading telescope already described.

The emblematic use of the pelican and its young provides yet a further example—and introduces a new difficulty. There is a tradition dating at least from late antiquity that when the pelican is no longer able to find food for its young it will, in its great love, peck open its breast and feed them on its own blood. The Pelican in her Piety (to use the heraldic term) has become an acknowledged symbol of self-sacrifice and love, and, because of the obvious parallel with Christ's death on the Cross, also of the Redemption. The Pelican in her Piety has been widely used in Christian art, often just to emphasize the meaning of the Crucifixion. (It is to be seen in that function, for instance, on the top of the Cross in Francesco Pesellino's 'The Crucifixion with St Jerome and St Francis'.) Again, Wither provides the emblematic example (Bk.3,XX).

In this picture the Pelican is seen in her Piety, but in the background (to the left; that is, the Pelican's right) the Crucifixion is depicted with a throng of the redeemed around the foot of the Cross catching the Blood in goblets. The question to be answered here is whether the focus (the Pelican) is to be regarded simply as a general symbol of self-sacrifice, but given Christian application by an 'interpretative' background, or whether it is inescapably a Christian symbol merely 'reinforced'. Most commentators, without much analysis, accept the latter view. At least one has opted for the former. It could be argued that, in view of the arbitrary nature of emblem writing, it is theoretically possible that such a manifest symbol of self-sacrifice as the Pelican in her

Piety might be shown with, say, the Star of David on one side and the Crescent Moon of Islam on the other, and moralized to declare that self-sacrifice is common to both faiths.

An earlier emblem-writer than Wither, Geoffrey Whitney, also moralizes this symbol. In his *A Choice of Emblemes* (1586) Whitney addresses an emblem to Dr Alexander Nowell, Dean of St Paul's, urging him to emulate the Pelican, and search his breast to convey from it his zeal and his learning (p. 87). Then, by using his pen as he has already used his celebrated preacher's tongue, he is to 'proceede to doe our countrie good'. With the example of the Pelican before him he is thus being asked similarly to share himself. It has to be considered whether the Pelican is being used by both Wither and Whitney merely as a symbol of self-sacrifice (and of sharing) and can indeed be shorn of its Christian connotations, or, alternatively, whether it is by now virtually a traditional, and inescapably Christian, symbol. To decide the matter here is not important. But the need to recognize that symbols may have variable, as well as inherent and unavoidable, connotations is pressing. It presents the commentator with the necessity of making fine distinctions, and always of assessing the extent to which the emblem-writer has selected particular facets of his chosen symbols to satisfy highly personal ends.

It may be conceded that the terms 'central motif' and 'secondary motif' are inadequate. The force in many elements of what, in this terminology, is merely secondary can be great, and can entirely transform what might otherwise seem to be the most powerful and unambiguous symbolic statements. It is astonishing that at the second conference of scholars of several nations assembled at the Herzog August Bibliothek at Wolfenbüttel to advise Professor Daly it was seriously proposed that 'secondary motifs' need not be included in the Index Emblematicus.

Throughout, the main factor that complicates the task of arriving at an appropriate vocabulary of descriptive and analytical terms is the overriding authority of the emblem-writer's personal vision as it affects each and every element in the picture. Wittgenstein's stipulation that the meaning of a term is to be sought in its use applies even more cogently to emblem symbolism than to language. The emblematist may be unorthodox, arbitrary, even perverse in what aspects of a picture he moralizes. Even the symbols he leaves unmentioned in his text may not retain their full traditional connotations. They too may be modified by their context. Any terms devised to reflect the iconographical structure of an emblem picture must, as perhaps demonstrated, be sufficiently flexible to accommodate without ambiguity the vagaries of context and of textual prescription. With emblems, as with any other genre, exact vocabulary is a prerequisite for making valid judgements about literature and the art of creation.

MY LIFE'S WORK, WITH A
DISCUSSION OF FRANCIS BERRY'S
POETRY

G. WILSON KNIGHT

I

This essay is an expansion of a talk I was asked to give on my life's record in literature and acting at the Cheltenham Festival of Literature in 1984, held in the Town Hall. It was a pleasure to revisit the Cheltenham Town Hall, redolent of happy memories: for it was here that, while a master at Dean Close School, I performed in the British Empire Shakespeare Society's presentation in 1928 of *As You Like It* and *Hamlet*; and later, in 1940, on my return from Canada, gave the first performance of my dramatic recital, *This Sceptred Isle*, subsequently repeated at other centres and finally, in 1941, for a week at The Westminster Theatre in London.

My expanded essay has been accepted by Professor Robert Welch for inclusion in his collection compiled to honour my good friend Professor A. Norman Jeffares, who was appointed Head of the Leeds Department of English Literature on the retirement of Bonamy Dobrée. As myself an older member of the staff I was keenly aware of his tact and consideration in regard to my departmental way of life. My *Ibsen* was composed in response to his invitation as Editor of the Writers and Critics series of literary studies. I was always happy to visit his home and meet his charming and so gifted wife, Jeanne. His own work on Irish literature, and especially Yeats, is widely acclaimed; less well-known is his editorship of Disraeli's novels, which I would probably not have read had he not presented me with copies of *Sybil* and *Lothair*. I must also mention his drawings, among them his admirable views of Trinity College, Dublin, still vivid in my memory.

I am honoured by the welcome accorded my mainly personal

and autobiographical contribution for inclusion in this important collection.

II

My own main tendency both in commentary and on stage I should define as characterised by an emphasis on *positive* directions. By this I mean that it has always been in sharp distinction from the prevailing negatives of satire and despair that have been so prevalent in modern literature. This positive approach does not involve the shirking of evils and terrors: it is an approach to them. My term 'positive' may appear inept, but I can find nothing else so suitable.

The definition is easiest to explain with examples from my Shakespearian acting, where it took the form of a reliance always on the *poetry* as my guide; in Hart House Theatre, Toronto, and The University of Leeds, and elsewhere. I recall speaking of love in my Silvius (in *As You Like It*, produced in Cheltenham in 1928) like this:

> It is to be all made of fantasy,
> All made of passion, and all made of wishes,
> All adoration, duty and observance;
> All humbleness, all patience and impatience;
> All purity, all trial, all endurance;
> And so am I for Phebe.

(V. ii. 101)

The repetition of 'observance' in the fifth line is clearly impossible. I accept the emendation 'endurance' as a natural Shakespearian climax.

A modern producer would probably discount the poetry, smothering it by a reading of Silvius' character as a rough yokel, though how such lines can be adequately so spoken appears highly questionable. No doubt my own early speaking (which I have tried in this talk to recapture) was too lyrical; I subsequently developed more tonal variation. My speaking has often been called 'old style'; why I do not know, unless poetry itself is old style.

Here are two examples from my performance of 'Shakespeare's Dramatic Challenge' as given at the Northcott Theatre, Exeter, in 1975 and at various colleges and universities in England, with five tours in Canada and the United States, from 1975 to 1983. My first example is Macbeth's words on hearing of his wife's death. The hearing of his wife's death. The speech appears grim, even nihilistic. Where, then, is my 'positive'? I follow the poetry and find it develops from distress to a bold *challenge*, like Romeo's 'Then I defy you stars' (V. i. 24). Here it is:

> She should have died hereafter.
> There would have been a time for such a word.
> Tomorrow, and tomorrow, and tomorrow,
> Creeps in this petty pace from day to day,
> To the last syllable of recorded time,
> And all our yesterdays have lighted fools
> The way to dusty death. Out, out, brief candle!
> Life's but a walking shadow, a poor player
> That struts and frets his hour upon the stage
> And then is heard no more; it is a tale
> Told by an idiot, full of sound and fury
> Signifying nothing.
>
> (V. v.17)

In scorning life Macbeth has, as it were, taken a stand beyond life; the poetry suggests a perception beyond negations. My second example derives more directly from an extra-sensory suggestion. It is Caliban's lines in *The Tempest* on the music he is, as a primitive being, aware of as permeating his universe.

> Be not afeard; the isle is full of noises,
> Sounds and sweet airs that give delight and hurt not.
> Sometimes a thousand twangling instruments
> Will hum about mine ears; and sometime voices
> That, if I then had wak'd after long sleep,
> Will make me sleep again; and then, in dreaming,
> The clouds methought would open and show riches
> Ready to drop upon me: that, when I wak'd
> I cried to dream again.
>
> (III. ii. 147)

A full performance would give more emphasis to Caliban's personality; a degree of characterisation may always be in place, but the poetry should direct. We may observe that Caliban is near to being the 'villain' of the drama. He has even been equated with the Devil. Yet he speaks perhaps the most cosmically revealing lines in Shakespeare. Our reading of poetry must often be morally ambivalent.

The positive, which is the symbolic and spiritualistic, even mystical, approach in my well-known literary commentaries will not, at this hour, be questioned. For this reason, I tend to reject the name 'criticism' to define it: the term by derivation implies judging, and I seldom judge.

This spiritual quality was eminent in my early reading in 1929 of Shakespeare's Final Plays, in *Myth and Miracle* (reprinted in *The Crown of Life*). T.S. Eliot was deeply interested in its treatment of *Pericles*, and soon after composed *Marina*, in part, as I have good reason to believe, under the influence of *Myth and Miracle*.[1] In all his poetry this exquisite poem stands out as the only creation, both in subject and in matter, wholly optimistic; in my present term 'positive'.

III

While a master at Dean Close School, I met Francis Berry, as a boy, and from then on a central contribution of my life's work has been my support of his poetry, of which a new volume, *From the Red Fort*, has just been published by The Redcliffe Press, Bristol (October, 1984).

I was from the first struck by the care with which he handled both the troubles of our existence and the raising of them to a higher positive dimension. This I was aware of in his early poem, *The Beggar's Soul* (1933), showing a mutilated organ-grinder looking back on his handsome youth and bitter present: yet, we are told, 'external things don't count' and he accordingly feels his romantic heart-self as driving a triumphal chariot to heavenly splendours above mortality.

This sets the tone of three long and important poems that followed. The first is historically authentic: *The Iron Christ* (1938) is about a war threatened between Chile and the Argentine. Berry heard of the events, if I remember correctly, during a conversation with the poetess Dallas Kenmare.

The causes of war are here subtly diagnosed:

> Agony, frustrations, lonely hours,
> Drowned hope, the many omens shouting Yield,
> Withered understandings, throat-sob at night,
> Unforgiving tortures, need resolve.
> So wars come.
> No other way than this? With lighted eyes
> Be dishonest, be the virile child,
> Drug disappointment with a warrior poise ...

Then the resolution, prompted by a Sermon, as the Christ statue is planned, to be set high on the Andes. Its making involves a grim process, carefully described, as the guns are melted down, until

> Horny torso set in place
> Dripping with its natal grease
> Bit by bit emerges It,
> Gun, Iron, Man, Christ.

In the guns we watch *the war-instinct itself* making the Christ. This suggests that we cannot transcend the long history of wars without honouring the instinct and using it for a nobler purpose, following the doctrine of Nietzsche's *Thus Spake Zarathustra*. We have to forgive, not only the sinner, but the sin. There is no short cut.

How to attain such sublimation? Two ways are open to us. One is through tragic poetry. In re-reading lately Stephen Spender's *Trial of a Judge* (1938), an astute and prophetic pre-war document, my horror was vividly aroused by the hated Black Shirts as villains of the drama; and yet what lingers most powerfully with me is their well-defined force and their prophetic threat to 'burst like a bomb across Europe'. Our reaction is likely to be ambivalent. Intellectually we may reject essences while we are simultaneously gripped by our aesthetic response; and this is true of all tragic poetry from Homer and Aeschylus on.[2] Compacted within this poetic ambivalence is a training towards sublimation. Indeed, that may be what such poetry is for.

Our other way is by enlisting assistance from higher dimensional powers: the Christ is set on heights. I am here reminded of Margot Davies' poem 'March, 1941' in *Calling Newfoundland* (Edited and Introduced by G. Wilson Knight, published by Memorial University, St. John's, Newfoundland, 1981, and Warren House Press, North Walsham, 1982) on man's futile efforts to break the seemingly self-made bonds that bind his instincts to their terrible courses. Man's reason is here useless. We must look elsewhere:

> Do not attempt to break the bonds, saith God;
> If you use weapons on an earth-bound scale,
> Success or failure, both will surely fail;
> Rise above earth—attack with heavenly might,
> Teach them in shackles, when they feel the Light,
> The chains will snap, the blind receive their sight

As night breaks through the dawning into morn:
And running blood will harry out the thorn.

We may have reticences about any direct approach to 'God'; but we can surely get in touch with beneficent spirits.

Our next two Berry poems, though without exactly stating it, suggest a transition to a higher, spiritual, order; as did *The Beggar's Soul*, envisioning a chariot-drive to other higher spheres. There is a sharp contrast in the poems that follow between nightmare and a waking to splendours. Such a transition has good authority, established by the ancients, Plato and others, and spiritualistically asserted today. [3]

The second of the three poems which we are considering, *Fall of a Tower* (1943), is not on war, but on personal and social violence . These two, war and violence, are both major anxieties today. We are shown a neurotic youth, Edmund, suffering torments by night, to whom the nearby church, with sunken crypts and its square squat tower, ugly gargoyles and jangling bells, acts as a repressive, bullying power which he would destroy. Through an underworld agent, not explicitly I.R.A. but of similar kind, he gets an explosive; descends into the foundations and ignites it, bringing the whole fabric down on himself.

The poem ends with what might be supposed Edmund's spiritual vision, an extended poem of praise celebrating a new order in nature and in man, bright instincts all active beyond our present religious habitude, addressed to the Sun, though with Christian reference included, ending:

Thus sang all the men and women to the Sun, and as they stood in groups on promontories by the sea, or on hills, and celebrated, their eyes glistened, and their faces were radiant in the Sun. And they resolved to rear a true temple to the Sun, one that would rise high and receive his rays; a new Heliopolis.

It is a wondrous temple, domed and made to music and of ever-changing colours. So they will

worship there the Sun: O Jesus, wise
Compassionate, strong and gentle, there will rise
Between the matin east and farewell west
A glistening phane in honour of the Sun,
Tall and stately in a rainbow trance.
Beneath its various Dome will violins play

> Their fountain music while we humans love—
> Boys and girls their love-bliss will profess
> And kiss beneath this Dome of rich Christnéss.

This Domed up-reaching excellence, the violin music and various colouring, contrasts with the deep-sunk 'bull-black' Tower and its iron bells. I recall that I used to criticise the last word, but I now regard it as well designed, the stress falling on the Christ-quality rather than the personality.

Our third narrative, *Murdock* (1947; reprinted in Berry's new volume) penetrates further. Based on dark village folklore, it appears to penetrate atavistic origins. We have rumours of two ghostly brothers, always fighting by night in the woodland depths, but never coming out to daylight vision, as though locked deep in our subconscious instinct. The fighting brothers are as mankind. Will they ever emerge? We fear it.

After superstitious terror is piled on terror, we are told not to fear. They 'can not come out'. But it is better to be fully conscious of these antagonists who have been contesting since 'long Time before the Flood'; it will be better to know the worst since 'There's Mastery in that but none in Doubt'. So suppose they could come out, what then?

They would charge across the world, becoming gigantic in their release from prison. They are man's inmost potentiality at present imprisoned, bottled up, but, like the atom, of vast possibility. So they ascend, still fighting, higher and higher, disturbing nature and man, until they reach the heights. And now, at height, they change miraculously. Their age-old feud is stilled:

> The Fighting still. In Snow They stand like Flame,
> Haughty yet calm, and their quiescent Eyes—
> Like Martyrs'—shine from mastered Mysteries.

They sing, resolving

> All fears, from bleeding Womb to bloodied Hearse,
> Endured by Man or by the Universe.

That is what might be supposed to happen, if they were to break free; this is what they truly *are*. Note that here—as once in *The Iron Christ* also—the whole Universe is involved. Our acceptance cannot be limited to earthly life. Note too that *heights* are again emphasised, as in our other two poems. This is our summing up:

For Murdock's Brothers are the World's new Fame,
Its high unborn and glistering Renown,
Its present Dread resplendent in its future Crown.

The vision is Nietzschean.[4]

These three remarkable poems must be read *as* poems; they are not statements of fact, but gestures; attempts at the least to enlist, or call down, poetic inspiration to indicate, or adumbrate, what may be behind the terrifying instincts that drive men on.

They are there for us, collected in *The Galloping Centaur* (1952, 1970; temporarily out of print, though *Murdock* has also been included in *From the Red Fort*, noted above). That so much is out of print is symptomatic of our constricted literary intelligence, our near-total impercipience of the potential of 'romantic' tendencies, causing the rejection of all power-charged happy themes as disreputable. After the late war Berry's work developed more in tune with contemporary taste; his former sharp and well-defined resonances were, without being lost, dissolved into more normal narratives; as in the astute treatment of a Jamaican rebellion in *Morant Bay* (1961) and the harking back to the ancient world of *Ghosts of Greenland* (1966), also treated in his prose work *I Tell of Greenland* (1982). Berry's range of geographic insight and realisation in these narratives is remarkable: he has lately added Australia in his Australian broadcast *Eyre Remembers* (1983); to which we must now add India, on the Mogul Emperor Shah Jahan, and Africa in two gripping shorter narratives, recently published in *From the Red Fort* (1984). The whole Commonwealth, capped by a long and heavily compacted poem, *In Honour of London Town* (1947/51), has had notice in his narrative surveys. For these, and other, reasons I have pressed as forcefully as was in my power to advance his name for the Laureateship. In both bulk and detail his life's work deserves a far greater renown than it has as yet received. My extended study is given in my *Neglected Powers* (1971); and see the high value accorded Berry in Philip Hobsbaum's *Tradition and Experiment in English Poetry* (London, 1979).

IV

In conclusion I would say something about my recently published novel, *Klinton Top*. Written in 1926–7, it was thought by publishers too sombre for the average reader, and it was put aside. Now at long last, in 1984, it appears from The Redcliffe Press, Bristol.

Its story is simple. In a setting of nature alternately kind and ominous, the hero is initiated early into sudden death and grows up mentally disturbed. He comes near to suicide but is saved by a powerful love. Various ups-and-downs follow, troubled dreams and a near-murder, and the action drives towards a tragic conclusion. As tragedy closes down, the hero experiences a strange exaltation. Bound for suicide, he is happy, beyond time and enjoying a timeless state, the mystical 'now' which is 'eternity'; rather like Shakespeare's tragic heroes who have hints of an other-worldly insight at the end. These I have studied in *Shakespeare's Dramatic Challenge* (London, 1977; out of print and available now at Eurospan, 3 Henrietta Street, London) and in *Shakespearian Dimensions* (Brighton, 1984) and illustrated by performances at various universities and colleges in England and in America, from 1974 to 1983. *Klinton Top* may have attuned me to this enquiry and understanding. And there is more to say. Just as Shakespeare develops his semi-mystical approach in tragedy to the more full-blooded mysticism of the Final Plays, of which I wrote in *Myth and Miracle* soon after *Klinton Top*, so we find that our hero here, after his turmoil of suffering, is finally projected into a higher, and superlatively happy, state of being. Following his attempted suicide, he falls in a trance and when he returns to normal consciousness he describes his experience. Such accounts by people who have nearly died are normal.[5] I may in 1927 have heard something of such out-of-the-body experiences; I do not know. But it is all there and corresponds exactly to what is now so often spiritualistically recorded. It should at least be clear why I regard the reading of *Klinton Top* as a necessary preliminary to any description of my life's work. Religious thought was further developed in *The Christian Renaissance* (1933) and Spiritualism in the as yet unpublished *Caroline, Life and After-Life*. Much of more personal concern is also included in *Atlantic Crossing* (1936) and *Jackson Knight: a Biography* (1975).

If I were to sum up what my total accomplishment might be supposed, at the limit, to have been, I might quote the third quatrain of an early sonnet to me by Francis Berry:

> Herald of a wild-eyed Easter singing,
> Bugler of the blasts of purple death,
> Unwinder of the Python's coils, which, clinging,
> Snap our ribs, and violate our breath ...

I realise that these lines, in what Eliot in 'East Coker' called 'a worn-out poetical fashion', may be used as a criticism of Berry and mockery of myself. But they are, if excessive, so apt a description of the positive nature of my attempts that I let them stand. 'Attempts' is however an inapposite word. My course was not planned, but came naturally: meanwhile I have always, whatever the optimism carried by my unveilings, been well aware of the turmoils and terrors of existence. My writings do not spring from any settled theology; nor do I make any assertions regarding Berry's personal beliefs. We must always allow for a degree of instinct, if not inspiration. For myself, I am doubtful, even at 87, what my theological beliefs are, though I accept trance addresses from higher spirits. What I trust to is more likely to have been drawn from my books than inserted into them. And there we must leave it.

Looking back on my past life I am at least gratified by the support I have been privileged to give to the poetry of Francis Berry, Margot Davies, and many others: and by the apparent influence of my investigations on T.S. Eliot at a significant point in his literary career.

Now, if my present ruminations appear extravagant, I fall back on a striking mystical passage by Masefield; such visions as he describes are usual to mystics, but rarely so exquisitely expressed as by this master of narrative prose. The passage occurs in *Lost Endeavour*:

My dream was not like common dreaming, in which the dream dominates the personality; but wonderful and kingly, my own self, awake and strong, directing my own actions. When I say that I dreamed I express myself badly. I should say that I woke up into a new and vivid life, more splendid than this, a life of intenser colour and finer ecstasy, in a world conducted by another intelligence and governed by other laws. It was, as I suppose, the real world, of which this world is nothing but the passing shadow. I woke up, then, in the cave where I had fallen asleep, but I woke up into its reality. The walls of hewn stone were changed to opal in which fire burned. The fire on the hearth was like visible music. I cannot describe the beauty of the flame in any other way. The trees outside stood like an array of knights in mail. Their fruits were like lamps, their leaves like jewels. The plaques which lay beside me coloured and took life. [6]

There is more, as the experience develops, before the return to normality.

Such mystical visions may be regarded as possible pointers to cosmic truth.

DION BOUCICAULT'S 'AMERICAN' PLAYS: CONSIDERATIONS ON DEFINING NATIONAL LITERATURES IN ENGLISH

HEINZ KOSOK

The year 1940 saw the publication of the first volume of a new series of plays, programmatically entitled *America's Lost Plays*, a series that was eventually to run into no less than 26 volumes. Edited by Allardyce Nicoll and F. Theodore Cloak, it contained six unpublished plays by Dion Boucicault: *Forbidden Fruit, Louis XI, Dot, Flying Scud; Or, A Four-Legged Fortune, Mercy Dodd; Or, Presumptive Evidence* and *Robert Emmet*. The selection came somewhat as a surprise. Only two of these plays (*Forbidden Fruit* and *Dot*) had been premièred in America; four of them (*Louis XI, Dot, Mercy Dodd* and *Robert Emmet*) were adaptations of English or French sources; not a single one was set in America; and none of them dealt with specifically American subject matter or themes. Moreover, they were the works of a writer who had been born, and grown up, in Ireland, had had his first great successes on the English stage, had lived for several years in France, had travelled the world as an actor, and had spent less than a quarter of his life in America. If these plays were nevertheless used to introduce a new series devoted to the lost plays of the *American* stage, this can be taken as a measure of the difficulties with which everyone is confronted who attempts to differentiate between the various national literatures in English.[1]

These difficulties are underlined by the criteria for selection which are given by the general editor of the series, Barrett H. Clark:

As for the term 'American', it is used in the broad sense of plays, regardless of authorship, using American themes; plays, regardless of theme, written by residents of the United States or enjoying wide

81

popularity in America; as well as plays of various sorts written by native-born writers whether actually produced in this country or not.[2]

This is an exceptionally comprehensive catalogue that would allow one to include even *Hamlet* or *The School for Scandal* ('enjoying wide popularity in America'). It is, however, useful as a checklist of those criteria that are normally drawn upon to establish the canon of a national literature. Listed systematically, these criteria are, then: (1) the author's place of birth, (2) the author's country of residence, (3) the play's place of origin, (4) the play's place of production, (5) the play's theme, (6) the play's reception. Probably Clark considered (7) the play's setting as too obvious a feature to require separate mention.

The present paper will discuss the suitability of these criteria for demarcating various national literatures in English. At the same time, it will suggest certain additional categories, such as (8) the influence from literary traditions, and (9) the impact of individual sources and models, (10) the author's purpose, (11) his intended reading public or audience, (12) the actual conditions of writing, and also (13) the play's influence on later works. To do so, it will draw upon the life and works of Dion Boucicault who, it will be argued, is an exceptionally suitable subject for such a study precisely because he has been claimed by critics for the literatures of at least three countries, Ireland, England, and the United States. In this respect he is typical of those numerous writers who are controversially regarded as belonging to more than one national literature: Jonathan Swift between English and Anglo-Irish, Henry James between English and American, Katherine Mansfield between English and New Zealand, Brian Moore between Anglo-Irish and Anglo-Canadian literature, to name only a few well-known examples of an ever-increasing group of writers who make it more and more difficult to maintain the traditional demarcations of national literatures. It should be added that this is not entirely a matter of critical hair-splitting, because it has immediate consequences for a writer's evaluation, this depending to a large extent on the national context in which his work is seen. Someone who may be regarded merely as continuing long-established traditions in one literature may be hailed as a great innovator in another.

Boucicault was, of course, one of the most successful drama-tists of the nineteenth century.[3] He produced an enormous series of plays, the exact number still being a matter of debate (surveys of his output vary between 135 and 400 titles), and he also exerted a considerable influence on the international theatre scene, ranging from the invention of fire-proof scenery to the introduction of touring companies for West-End successes. He was born in Dublin sometime between 1810 and 1822. His full name, Dionysius Lardner Boursiquot, indicates that he came from a family of French Huguenots who had settled in Ireland, but also that he may well have been the illegitimate son of the scientist Dr Dionysius Lardner who later became his foster-father. Many other events of his life are equally shrouded in mystery. He seems to have resisted quite successfully Dr Lardner's well-meant attempts at education. In the late eighteen-thirties he appeared with touring companies in the English provinces, where he apparently received a rough apprenticeship in the theatre. He did, however, retain his emotional ties to Ireland. When, decades later, someone tried to provoke him with the question whether he was an Irishman, he replied: 'Sir, nature did me that honor.'[4]

The sudden success of his comedy *London Assurance* (1841) catapulted him into the theatrical world of London; the years from 1842 to 1846 saw no less than 22 of his plays on London stages. From 1845, after marrying a rich French widow, he spent approximately four years in France where he studied the theatre life of Paris and laid the foundation for many of his future stage successes, in which he exploited French models. The mysterious death of his rich wife did not prevent him from going bankrupt, but he re-emerged to bless the English stage with numerous melodramatic adaptations. When the great Charles Kean took over the Princess' Theatre in 1850, he made Boucicault his literary adviser. Moreover, Boucicault began a second career as an actor. These activities introduced him to his future wife, the actress Agnes Robertson, whose stage successes became the immediate reason for his first journey to America.

Agnes Robertson attempted, as was indeed becoming standard practice around the middle of the century, to exploit her London successes on an American tour. Boucicault arrived in New York on 18 September, 1853, and spent the following years as her impresario, receiving at first only a modest share of her popularity, which soon began to take on 'American' dimensions. However, he also started writing plays of his own for her, such as *The Young Actress* (1853), *Andy Blake; or, the Irish Diamond* (1854), *The Fairy Star* (1854), *Agnes Robertson at Home* (1855), *The Cat Changed into a Woman* (1855) and *Rachel is Coming* (1855). And from autumn 1855 onwards he also appeared as an actor, his successes in character parts (especially his 'Irish' roles, written for himself) soon rivalling those of his wife. It is important for a correct evaluation of his attitude to America to realize that his first years on the other side of the Atlantic were spent almost exclusively on tour, in the role of the adored visitor who nevertheless remained a stranger and was not in a position to develop emotional ties with any one city or region. He must have been confirmed in his position as an outsider by the fact that three attempts to manage a theatre of his own in America (the Gaiety in New Orleans, 1855, the Washington Theatre in the capital, 1857, and the Winter Garden in New York, 1859) all turned into miserable failures. It is significant, too, that his greatest success in the United States, the New York première of *The Colleen Bawn* in 1860, led to his decision to return to London, because he wanted to reap the fruits of his popular play in the capital of world theatre.

The following twelve years were again spent in England, with occasional excursions to Ireland. Although he undertook various risky enterprises which regularly ended in financial catastrophe, he knew how to compensate for these with a series of stage successes. Not until 1872 did he return to America. He assembled his own company, with which he toured all the larger cities in the United States and Canada, usually with his own plays and frequently as his own star actor. Again it is significant, however, that his greatest successes caused him to return to England where, for instance, he produced *The Shaughraun* both in 1875 and in 1880. To what extent he saw himself as a cosmopolitan of world theatre can be gathered from the fact that in 1885 he led his company on a tour to Australia (where, incidentally, he married a youthful member of his company without having been divorced from Agnes!). Not until 1888 did he dissolve his company; the last years of his life were spent as the impoverished director of a school for actors in New York, where he died in 1890.

This brief survey of Boucicault's life may be justified if it illustrates that the 'biographical criterion', still the most frequent if also the most naive of all criteria for defining national literatures ('Milton's works are part of the literature of England, because the author was born in England, lived in England and wrote his works in England'), is next to useless when applied to Boucicault or, for that matter, to numerous other writers. Just as his French descent or his Irish birthplace are not sufficient to include him in the canon of French or Irish literature, so his American sojourns alone do not make him an American writer. If the writer's biography is accepted at all as a viable criterion, it could rather be argued that Boucicault's plays are part of the literature of England, where he spent approximately forty years (more than half his total life), where he received the decisive impulses for his career, where he had the majority of his stage successes, and where almost two-thirds of his plays, as far as they can still be identified, were premièred.[5]

Yet it is much more important to realize how unreliable the 'biographical criterion' as such can be. One could cite numerous cases where, like Boucicault's, the author's birthplace and life history are not sufficiently satisfactory criteria to determine whether his works be regarded as the products of one national literature rather than another. Biographical data become relevant only when it can be shown that they have a direct bearing on the author's works. One has to turn to the works themselves if a clearer view of the criteria for including them in one national literature or another is to be gained.

The decision as to whether the plays of Boucicault should be included in a history of American literature could perhaps be advanced by a discussion of four of his plays, all of them, for various reasons, far more likely to be considered as 'American' than the ones in the *America's Lost Plays* series: *Jessie Brown, The Poor of New York, Belle Lamar* and *The Octoroon*. All of these plays were written during the second half of the author's life (between 1857 and 1874), and after his arrival in America. All of them deal with contemporary events, and they show very clear traces of the tradition of American melodrama, which had in fact been largely influenced by Boucicault. Each of these plays was premièred in New York, and three of them—*The Poor of New York, Belle Lamar* and *The Octoroon*—were probably the only ones among his American productions to have an American setting, which renders them especially likely to be classified as 'American'. A discussion of these plays may also lead to certain insights as to the viability and completeness of the criteria suggested above.

Jessie Brown; or, The Relief of Lucknow had its première on 22 February, 1858, in Wallack's Theatre, New York. Apart from the place of production, however, there is little to justify its inclusion in a history of American drama. Boucicault used a highly topical subject, the Indian Mutiny, in the course of which the British garrison of the town of Lucknow was besieged for three months and finally relieved by a regiment of Highlanders.

Through a small group of characters, Boucicault dramatises the highly sensational events, from the first rumours of an imminent danger, through the various stages of the siege, to the garrison's total exhaustion and the arrival of the relief troops in the nick of time. He presents the British defenders of Lucknow as super-humanly brave, self-sacrificing, unselfish, dignified and patriotic. His *leitmotiv* is the natural superiority of the white conquerors which gives them the unassailable right to rule over the natives. The image of the natives as the 'scum of the earth' is established with the first scene and is never called in question in the course of the play:

MRS.C. . . . tell me, what news from Delhi? (*they sit*)
GEORDIE. Oh, the siege continues; but it will be taken, of course—
    these black rascals are mere scum.
    (ACHMET, C., *who is serving* GEORDIE, R.C. *looks round*)
ALICE. *There* is one who disagrees with you on that point.
GEORDIE. Does he?
ACHMET. No, sahib, Allah Akbar! it is so—we are scum. Lady, in
    Hindoostan there are one hundred millions such as I am, and there
    are one hundred thousand such as you; yet for a century you have
    had your foot on our necks; we are to you a thousand to one—a
    thousand black necks to one white foot. Allah is great, and
    Mohammed is his prophet. We are scum!
GEORDIE. I can't answer for the truth of your calculation, but I agree in
    the sentiment—you *are* scum. (*drinks*)
ACHMET. Sometimes the scum rises.
GEORDIE. Yes, Dusky, and when it does, the pot boils over and puts
    the fire out; so the scum extinguishes the element that made it rise.
ACHMET. I cannot reason with a European.
GEORDIE. No, nor fight with one; by your own calculation, it takes one
    thousand of you to do either one or the other. [6]

In the course of the play, the elaborated 'scum metaphor' is not, as might be expected, ironically qualified to question the arrogance of the British position but is confirmed by the developing plot. The leader of the rising is assigned the role of the typical villain of melodrama who has personal designs on the (British) heroine and wants to send her to his harem, which makes him even more despicable than the fact that he is also responsible for the murder of helpless women and children. The British defenders, by contrast, prove their superiority through their courage in the face of death, their moral integrity and their willingness to sacrifice themselves for each other and for the common cause: in the final Act, the starving soldiers refuse to eat their last rations and distribute them to the women and children, although ten of them are expected to repel the attack of thousands of natives, while the women would rather be shot than left to the mercy of the enemy, and their worthy children are busy rolling in the last few cannon balls.

Jessie Brown, in other words, is an example of the worst type of British Colonial literature, serving to justify the occupation and exploitation of foreign countries through the presentation of the enemy's cruelties and the irreproachable behaviour of the British troops. It is somewhat surprising that Boucicault should have yielded to the melodramatic potential of this subject-matter, because in his 'Irish' plays he tended to be quite critical of British colonial attitudes in his native country. His version of 'The Wearing of the Green' ('They are hanging men and women / For the wearing of the green') aroused the joint anger of Queen Victoria and the British censor. It is even more surprising that he should have produced such a play for an American audience. It can only be assumed that neither the writer nor his audience were aware of the parallels between the situation in India and in America: there is nothing in the text to suggest any similarities between the colonial present of India and the colonial past of America, which after all had been shaken off less than seventy years before, nor is there any indication that the attitude of white Americans to the Red Indians might be just as questionable as that of the white master-race in India.

Consequently, *Jessie Brown* is not difficult to assign to a specific national literature. The place of the original production is the only feature that could be used to argue the play's inclusion in the canon of American literature. Neither the setting—India—nor the subject matter—a rising in a British colony—nor the theme— the superiority of British colonisers over the natives—nor the author's purpose—a justification of British colonial behaviour in Asia—would confirm such an inclusion. Little is known of the play's reception; it is significant, however, that only a few months elapsed after the American production before it was acted in England (at first in Plymouth) where it really belonged.

The play immediately preceding *Jessie Brown*, *The Poor of New York*, which opened in Wallack's Theatre on 8 December, 1857, seems a much more likely candidate for an inclusion in a history of American drama. The setting as established by the title indicates that the play is immediately concerned with conditions in present-day America. Boucicault uses the background of the economic crisis of 1857 to draw a picture, sometimes quite moving in the individual scenes, of human solidarity and unselfishness on the lowest level of existence. The sharp confrontation between good and evil that is demanded by the melodramatic structure runs in this case between the poor and the rich. The play's villain is a rich banker, revealingly named Gideon Bloodgood, who during the slump of 1837 cheats an honourable sea-captain of his money and leaves him to die of a heart attack in the street. Twenty years later Bloodgood has succeeded in amassing immense riches with the help of the captain's money, while the captain's family live in degrading poverty. Boucicault utilizes this promising situation to develop a complex plot, shot through with sensational events and the typical motifs of melodrama. The climax is the 'sensation scene' (V,ii) where the villain sets fire to an apartment building in Cross Street, Five Points, while the courageous Badger succeeds in salvaging, from the collapsing building, the decisive document that will eventually prove the villain's machinations and will reinstate the virtuous family. Badger arrives on the scene of the fire in time because he has spotted it from his lookout on Brooklyn Heights. There are approximately fifty such references to New York localities: streets, squares, buildings etc.; this wealth of local references—unusual in any drama—appears at first to underline the specifically 'American' nature of the play.

Boucicault's concept of poverty, too, seems to confirm this impression. It is the 'shabby genteel', the lower middle-classes and those who have descended the social scale without any fault of their own, who are poor in this play. The moral code of their previous status forces them to pretend to a respectability that has long been lost, as Boucicault has one of his characters explain in a programmatic speech:

The poor!—whom do you call the poor? Do you know them? do you see them? they are more frequently found under a black coat than under a red shirt. The poor man is the clerk with a family, forced to maintain a decent suit of clothes, paid for out of the hunger of his children. The poor man is the artist who is obliged to pledge the tools of his trade to buy medicines for his sick wife. The lawyer who, craving for employment, buttons up his thin paletot to hide his shirtless breast. These needy wretches are poorer than the poor, for they are obliged to conceal their poverty with the false mask of content—smoking a cigar to disguise their hunger—they drag from their pockets their last quarter, to cast it with studied carelessness, to the begger (*sic*), whose mattress at home is lined with gold. These are the most miserable of the Poor of New York. [7]

This specific image of poverty encouraged the New York audience to identify themselves with the 'virtuous' among the stage characters, because they either must have felt that the play concerned them directly, or that it was by no means unlikely that one day they would find themselves in a similar position as that of the characters on the stage. Such a skilfully manipulated identification then justified the play's final words, which succeeded, in a master stroke of P.R. appeal, in combining the call for charity in the street with the call for applause in the theatre:

Bad. You have seen the dark side of life—you can appreciate your fortune, for you have learned the value of wealth.

Mrs.F. No, we have learned the value of poverty. (*Gives her hand to* PUFFY.) It opens the heart.

Paul. (*To the public.*) Is this true? Have the sufferings we have depicted in this mimic scene, touched your hearts, and caused a tear of sympathy to fill your eyes? If so, extend to us your hands.

Mrs.F. No, not to us—but when you leave this place, as you return to your homes, should you see some poor creatures, extend your hands to them, and the blessings that will follow you on your way will be the most grateful tribute you can pay to the
POOR OF NEW YORK. [8]

The actress's apparent unselfishness, denying herself the sympathies of the audience in order to see them turned to the beggars, undoubtedly contributed to the play's stage success.

At a first glance, *The Poor of New York* therefore appears as a play specifically designed to dramatise the topographical as well as the social realities of the contemporary scene in New York, an American play if ever there was such a thing. This impression, however, clouds somewhat when one realises that Boucicault produced the play not only under the alternative titles *The Streets of Philadelphia* and *The Money Panic of '57*, but also under such un-American titles as *The Poor of Liverpool*, *The Poor of Leeds*, *The Poor of Manchester*, *The Streets of London*, *The Streets of Islington*, *The Poor of the London Streets* and even *The Streets of Dublin*.[9] Looked at more closely, it soon becomes clear that the numerous place-names in the play are mere ciphers, interchangeable at will without necessitating any further alterations and in no way part of a unified topographical structure. Boucicault's sociological commentaries, too, his definition of poverty and the final appeal to the audience, can be transferred without the slightest difficulty to any other city, because, as a second glance at the text confirms, Boucicault has carefully avoided all references to specific conditions in New York.

The stage history of *The Poor of New York* shows, therefore, that Boucicault has created a multi-purpose melodrama that could be successfully acted wherever a predominantly lower middle-class audience delighted in witnessing on stage its own situation and the ever-present threat to its precarious existence. This impression is confirmed by Boucicault's subject matter, characters, language, and theme. There is, for instance, not a single character who is influenced in any way by specific living conditions or the unique historical situation in America, or who gives the slightest indication in his speech of being an American. The theme, the moral superiority of those who have been deprived of their rights in the world, and their claim to be reinstated in their original position, is equally independent of national associations. The restoration of social and moral order through punishing the 'evil' ones and rewarding the 'virtuous' is one of the basice constituents of international nineteenth-century melodrama; this type of play is characterised by creating a dream-world as an alternative to a reality dominated by injustice, a world into which the audience could escape when it felt too greatly oppressed by reality.

This sceptical view of *The Poor of New York* can be further confirmed by reference to the genesis of the play. It is not, as might have been supposed, an original play at all, but a skilful adaptation of a contemporary French model, *Les Pauvres de Paris* by Edouard Louis Alexander Brisebarre and Eugène Nus.[10] The international character of this seemingly 'American' play could hardly be made more explicit. This was observed by at least one early reviewer:

[The play] purports to be local, and should therefore be original, but it really has been taken from one of those curious melodramas which so delight the frequenters of the theatres on the Boulevards.

He then goes on to criticise various errors in the presentation of conditions in New York.[11] *The Poor of New York* is nothing less than a model of international melodrama with its typical constellation of characters, its stereotyped plot motifs like love, flight and pursuit, its preference for sensational events, its culminating sensation scene, and its harmonizing morality. [12]

The third play to be discussed here, *Belle Lamar* with the significant subtitle *An Episode of the Civil War* (first produced at Booth's Theatre, New York, on 10 August, 1874) can lay much stronger claim to being included in the canon of American literature. [13] In this case, it is possible not only to muster the criteria of 'origin' and 'production', but also those of 'setting' and 'subject matter'. *Belle Lamar* is set in the Shenandoah Valley, fought over in 1862 by both sides in the Civil War. The military events take up a large part of the play, and General Thomas J. Jackson ('Stonewall Jackson') is even brought on stage in person.

The individual action is closely interwoven with the historical events. Belle Lamar, mistress of Mount Lamar Estate and a strong supporter of the Southern cause, has been married to Colonel Bligh. When, at the outbreak of the war, he refused to join the Confederate army, she divorced him. Another Northern officer, Marston Pike, provides her with information about the movements of the Union troops on condition that she marries him when the war is over. Belle is caught as a spy and brought in front of Bligh (of all people), who is expected to sentence her to death, which leads him to discover the actions of Pike, too. When Bligh, in an apparently hopeless situation, defends White Stone Gap, Belle confesses her continuing love for him. After he has rejected General Jackson's offer of an honourable retreat, Pike at the last moment brings relief, and the two lovers—Bligh and Belle— remain alive as well as united.

As this brief sketch may indicate, Boucicault aims to a certain extent at historical authenticity. Moreover he adds a specifically American element in the character of Old Sam, a negro who even after the abolition of slavery still feels responsible for his old masters and sacrifices himself for them—one of those naive, faithful and humorous characters from the tradition of Uncle Tom, idealized and romanticized of course almost to the point of absurdity, but a 'national' character all the same as no character in *The Poor of New York* had been 'American'. In Sam, Boucicault also created a character who speaks a specific and unmistakable American dialect, which again adds to the aura of authenticity which without doubt surrounds the play.

Despite such an approximation to American reality the play preserves, however, the typical ingredients of English melo-drama—sentimentality, danger, romantic love, sensation scene, last-minute reprieve etc. And the play's theme is, despite its American background, almost entirely independent of the historical events. The theme is not, as one would expect, the conflict between North and South but the purely private conflict of love and honour. In the last analysis, *Belle Lamar* is a play about a few individuals who can prove their worth in the face of a difficult military situation. Once each of them, against all initial appearances, has saved his honour, love can triumph between the hero and the heroine; the outcome of the larger, historical conflict remains without interest as long as the lovers are given the chance to return to each other and, against all probability, to survive. In other words, a traditional theme of English drama has been dressed up in a costume of American reality. The author's purpose in writing the play, as can be gathered from the text, remains to enlist the audience's sympathy for the private difficulties of his central characters, not to analyse a specifically American political conflict.

None of the reservations that have been voiced so far against the inclusion of Boucicault's plays in a canon of American drama hold for *The Octoroon; or, Life in Louisiana*. This play fulfils all the criteria that—explicitly or implicitly—have been marshalled for defining such a canon. This is not, of course, a question of literary quality; *The Octoroon* is just as much a commercial piece for public consumption as Boucicault's other plays, but it achieves its object with the help of ingredients that can be classified as typically American.

It is a matter of debate whether Boucicault, in writing this play, utilized certain sources like Mayne Reid's novel *The Quadroon; or, A Lover's Adventures in Louisiana* (1856); in any case he relied to a large extent on his own impressions, gathered during various sojourns in New Orleans where in May 1855 his eldest son was born and where he managed the Gaiety Theatre during the winter season of 1855/56. The play's genesis therefore points to its American background, as does its stage history (it was first produced at the New York Winter Garden on 6 December, 1859).

The same is true of the subject-matter: the actual events on a typical Southern plantation in Louisiana. Boucicault created an exciting situation to begin with, a situation that was not too far removed from similar situations in nineteenth-century melodrama but was equally close to real conditions in mid-century Louisiana. Terrebonne Plantation on the banks of the Mississippi is to be sold by auction because its owner was heavily in debt when he died. This is due not only to his financial carelessness but also the evil and fraudulent machinations of M'Closky the estate manager, a typical stage villain. George Peyton, the owner's nephew, just returned from Paris, falls in love with Zoe (the octoroon), the illegitimate daughter of the deceased, one of whose great-grandparents, however, was black and who therefore technically counts as a slave. This initial situation develops into a far-reaching, entertaining plot that provides ample room both for exciting and for sentimental scenes. As is to be expected of a stage villain, M'Closky persecutes Zoe, and he also kills a negro boy who carries an important letter. A Red Indian is mistaken for the murderer and is about to be lynched, but a photographic camera that was stationed accidentally on the very spot (!) has recorded the real murderer. M'Closky escapes by setting fire to a river steamer (this develops into the sensation scene) but is tracked down by the Red Indian and finally killed in a swamp. In the meantime the slaves of the plantation are auctioned off; Zoe, who has been bought by the villain, takes her own life before the letter arrives that clears the plantation of all debt.

This brief (and incomplete) plot summary indicates that the play is dominated by four groups of characters whose specifically American identity has been developed by Boucicault with considerable attention to detail. The society of plantation owners is characterised as aristocratic, arrogant, easy-going and sexually irresponsible, but also as just, understanding, compassionate and in the last resort sympathetic. It is diametrically opposed to M'Closky who is significantly depicted as a Yankee from the North, and who is distinguished by his brutality, his calculating materialism, and his vindictiveness. Considerable attention has been devoted to the presentation of the third group, the slaves. They are, of course, stereotyped stage characters, idealized to an incredible degree when they propose, for instance, not to cry during the auction so that their previous owners will not take the separation too much to heart; nevertheless it is remarkable that they are shown to be more humane—unselfish, helpful, humorous—than the whites. And finally there is Wahnotee the Red Indian (a role that Boucicault wrote for himself) who proves unshakable in his friendship as well as in his revenge.

Each of these four groups owes its existence to specific conditions that prevail only in America and cannot be transferred into any other milieu. This is confirmed by the language they use. Boucicault provides each group with specific linguistic features derived from observed reality. This is how old Pete admonishes his fellow slaves during the auction:

Dar, do ye hear dat, ye mis'able darkies; dem gals is worth a boat load of kinder men dem is. Cum, for de pride of de family, let every darky look his best for the judge's sake—dat ole man so good to us and dat ole woman—so dem strangers from New Orleans shall say, Dem's happy darkies, dem's a fine set of niggers; every one say when he's sold, 'Lor' bless dis yer family I'm gwine out of, and send me as good a home.'[14]

It is not essential to decide whether Boucicault's transcription of dialect is absolutely correct. He did not write for the printer but for the actor; and he could be sure that every American theatre would find actors who specialised in such roles. The linguistic authenticity would be taken care of as long as he provided, in his text, the requirements for differentiated American dialects and sociolects.

The theme of the play could be defined as the conflicts resulting from the existence of a planter society in Southern states with its basic dichotomy of pseudo-aristocracy and slave population. Each individual scene contributes to a varied illumination of this situation. Boucicault intended neither to glorify nor to denigrate such a society. He carefully balanced the weights so that, in an explosive political situation, shortly before the outbreak of the Civil War, both sides found themselves confirmed in his play. The abolitionists saw their views endorsed when the happy ending that an audience had a right to expect in a melodrama was made impossible by the fact that hero and heroine were not allowed to marry, and the heroine was even driven to suicide, because she counted as a slave. Conversely, the adherents to slavery pointed out how humanely the slaves in this play are treated by the planters, that their relationship actually is a highly harmonious one, and that the real slave-driver comes from the North, so that the responsibility for Zoe's suicide rests, in effect, with a Yankee.

Boucicault's purpose in *The Octoroon*, in other words, was specifically directed towards an *American* audience. This was confirmed by the reception and the stage history of the play. That he was correct in gauging the expectations of a politically divided American audience can be deduced from the fact that *The Octoroon* became one of his greatest successes in the theatre.[15] That he had written it with an *American* audience in mind became even clearer when the play was transferred to England. The London audience, which was less immediately involved with the burning issue of slavery, and less familiar with its terrible consequences, protested against the death of Zoe and insisted on its right to a happy ending. Boucicault, after hesitating for a few days, saw himself eventually forced to alter his text: in London, Zoe was every evening happily united to her lover. [16] However doubtful a light such a compromise may cast on Boucicault as a serious dramatist, it underlines the fact that the original version had been explicitly designed for an American audience.

The Octoroon, therefore, is the only one among these plays that can be seen, without a shadow of a doubt, as an American play. All the individual criteria of categorisation—both those expressed by Clark in his preface to the *America's Lost Plays* series and the additional ones that have been evolved in the present paper—point to such a decision: it was written and produced in America, its setting, plot and subject-matter are American, it has specifically American linguistic features, its theme is an American one, and the author had an American audience in mind when writing it—characteristics that were confirmed by its reception on stage both in America and in England.

Such a categorisation has certain consequences for the evaluation of the play. Seen in the context of English melodrama, *The Octoroon* would be merely one of numerous examples, superior to the average play perhaps in its handling of plot and character, and slightly unusual in the original ending, but part of a long tradition of popular entertainment all the same. In the context of American drama, however, it is much more important: not because of its 'literary qualities' in an abstract and unhistorical sense, but because of its influence on the further development of drama in America. Plays like *The Octoroon* formed the basis for the 'Americanisation' of American drama after the Civil War had come to an end.

These remarks, however incomplete and sketchy they may be, enable one to draw certain conclusions concerning the demarcation of national literatures in English, conclusions that may be relevant not only for Boucicault and not only for American literature but for the whole range of English-language literatures in England, Ireland, the United States, Canada, Australia and New Zealand as well as in numerous countries in Africa and Asia. The case of Boucicault is particularly suitable for such a purpose, not only because both his person and his work are exceptionally difficult to classify, but also because they can be seen in an historical perspective.

The most obvious conclusion is that of the unsuitability of the 'biographical criterion'. As the example of Boucicault shows, the author's birthplace as well as his place of residence at the time of writing his works are not safe indications for his inclusion in any one national literature. Boucicault in America wrote in three successive years plays that have to be classified as British (*Jessie Brown*), American (*The Octoroon*) and Irish (*The Colleen Bawn*). The 'biographical criterion' is next to useless except in cases where no doubt is possible anyway.

Instead, one should turn to an author's work rather than to his person, and preferably to the individual work, because it is quite often the individual work alone that reveals those national features that permit of classification. It would be practically impossible to make general statements about the national character of Boucicault's dramatic output, but it is possible, if not always easy, to categorise his individual plays. Such an approach would lead to a literary history of works rather than of writers, where the author's private experience is less important than the reflections of this experience in his writings. Such an approach would not, of course, deliver us from all problems; there would still be a number of works that would be difficult enough to classify, but they would be the exception instead of the rule, and could be treated as such.

Next, it is important to realize that the 'national' classification of any individual work should not be based on any one criterion alone, but that there is a whole range of such criteria. Subject-matter, setting, plot, characters and theme are the most obvious of these. If all these in a given literary work, in a very general sense, are American, as in *The Octoroon*, this is a fairly safe indication that it belongs to the context of American literature.

There is, however, a certain danger inherent in this approach; if, that is, these features are seen as the one and only criterion. Such an approach would ignore all those works that transcend the narrow limitations of time and locality; the more 'universal' they are the less easy would they be to classify. Or, conversely, this approach could easily be used to argue the case for the provincialism of any one literature, because all the 'universal' works would drop out of it.

It is, therefore, necessary to consider additional criteria. One ought not to ignore all that occurs before a literary work is finished; the influence from literary traditions of genre and theme as well as the influence of individual models and sources; the author's purpose in writing it, and his intended audience; and also the genesis, the actual process of creation. It is important to realize that the 'national' characteristics of a given work may be further identified by such questions as: under what conditions was it written?, where did the author find his models and suggestions?, what kind of reading public or theatre audience did he envisage?, and what purpose did he try to convey?

Equally, it would be wise to consider the 'after-effects' of a literary work, its critical and popular reception and the repercussions these may have had on the work itself. One would have to ask: how was the work received by the reviewers and the general audience? What does the reception say about its national characteristics? And what kind of influence did it exert on later works? Did it perhaps initiate a new tradition which would give it a firm position in the national literature of one particular country? It is true, of course, that these criteria may suggest diverse and even contradictory conclusions. An author's purpose may, for instance, have been far removed from the actual impact his work had. Also, it will not always be possible to apply the full range of criteria that have been suggested above. And frequently it will be difficult to decide which of the various criteria is to be given special emphasis.

Despite these difficulties, however, the demarcation of national literatures is an important object of literary scholarship, because it has immediate consequences for literary evaluation. A certain work that, in the context of the literature of England, would do nothing more than confirm a long-established tradition, may, in the context of a more recent literature, have contributed to the beginnings of a new tradition. Literary evaluation cannot be completely separated from historical conditions, and these may differ widely from one literature to another. Critics who propose to ignore altogether the matter of nationality in literature, who argue for a general concept of 'world literature' where the questions that have been discussed in this paper become redundant, can usually be shown to argue subconsciously from the point of view of one particular national literature whose standards and traditions they generalize into a fake universality. It may be more honest, if more difficult, to distinguish between various national literatures. The case of Boucicault may help to sharpen our awareness of such distinctions.

JULIA CAHILL, FATHER McTURNAN, AND THE GEOGRAPHY OF NOWHERE

AUGUSTINE MARTIN

'Julia Cahill's Curse' is deservedly the most famous and anthologised story in George Moore's *Untilled Field*. In the first edition of the book it is placed between two of the most neglected pieces, 'A Letter to Rome' and 'A Play-House in the Waste,' forming with them a coherent triptych centred upon Moore's vision of the two most desolate parishes in Mayo, one managed by the puritan Father Madden, the other by the saintly Father McTurnan. Their themes of social and spiritual bleakness, of religion, magic and agrarian decay also interweave to reveal a strange human drama on a landscape that must be the epicentre of the 'untilled field' in the author's imagination. Together they reveal the quintessence of the book's vision and the most refined application of its narrative technique.

Julia Cahill's story is archetypal both in its characters and its central fable; and it expresses the innermost tensions of Moore's social, ethical and artistic concern. Of all his short stories it employs, beneath its apparently simple structure, the greatest variety of his rhetorical resource. From the outset it is clear that the author is determined to subdue his own personal voice, control his polemic and allow the action to speak for itself. In order to achieve this aesthetic distance he employs a narrator, a travelling representative of the co-operative movement, who sets the scene and provides a background of action and discourse against which the central fable—which is related by the young driver—can be measured and judged. That fable is to be about a struggle that had taken place twenty years before between Julia Cahill and the repressive Father Madden. The framing story, therefore, begins with a casual eulogy of the priest whose parish the travellers have just left, and continues in a disarming, mandarin idiom:

But, perhaps because of his many admirable qualities, Father O'Hara is not the subject of this story. We find stories in the lives of the weak and foolish, and the improvident, and his name occurs here because he is typical of not a few priests I have met in Ireland.[1]

The remark has a triple effect, establishing an easy, conversational tone for the story, assuring us of the narrator's fairmindedness, and finally putting us quite off guard as to what the present story will be about—a vehement and archetypal clash of wills symbolizing massive cultural tragedy.

The theme is faded in slowly, the narrator musing to himself in rhythm with the horse's movement as he approaches what he has been told is 'the loneliest parish in Ireland':

'The land has made them', I said, 'according to its own image and likeness', and I tried to find words to define the yearning that I read in their eyes as we drove past. But I could find no words that satisfied me. 'Only music can express their yearning, and they have written it themselves in their folk tunes'.

The story he is telling will be *his* attempt to express it. The landscape becomes increasingly desolate with evidence of wholesale and recent emigration. With a passing reference to the 'untilled fields' it becomes clear that we are approaching the heart of George Moore country. Before the young man sets the narrator down he mentions the local belief that 'there's a curse on the parish'. There is no time just yet to pursue the question, but as he is to pick up his passenger in half an hour the matter can wait.

The narrator as he kneels at Father Madden's Mass notices that the only communicant in the sparse congregation is a blind woman:

'This blind woman', I said to myself, 'will be the priest's last parishioner', and I saw the priest saying Mass in a waste church for the blind woman, everyone else dead or gone.

The remark is a natural extension of the narrator's earlier musings on Ireland's depopulation: the imagined scene is a sort of prophetic symbol for Catholic Ireland—an old, blind woman bereft of her children, being ministered to by a sullen, life-denying priesthood. As such it has clear affinities with Joyce's symbolism in a story like 'The Sisters'. The symbolic old woman is to return. When the narrator has left Father Madden, having received at first hand an idea of his autocracy and puritanism, he takes up again with his young driver the question of the curse. He is told the story of Julia Cahill who had been driven from the parish by Father Madden twenty years before.

The driver's story—which I call the fable to distinguish it from the larger story which contains it—is delivered in lively colloquial idiom, and as it concerns events of twenty years before it has the archetypal quality of a folk-tale. Julia's beauty, liveliness and independence are legendary and absolute. Her refusal to be party to a made marriage and her defiance of the priest prompts the latter to denounce her from the altar and declare her 'the evil spirit that sets men mad'. Her father's attempts to subdue her are seen as an effort 'to tie up the winds'. Her seeking sanctuary with the blind old woman— whose acknowledged sanctity makes her immune to the priestly thunderbolt—gives her story an added dimension of symbolism, and of irony. Only the true saint defends beauty and freedom; but the saint in question is blind and cannot feel the full force of Julia's beauty and its threat.

The viewpoints of the two narrators subtly interlock; each finds in the story his own meaning. In the driver's view, informed by the folk imagination, a beautiful, headstrong girl had opposed the priest, received his curse, sought aid from the fairies and, through their power, laid her curse on the parish before departing. Her curse would come to pass, Father Madden would minister to a congregation made up of one blind woman. The boy does not adjudicate between the two mysterious forces of institutional religion on the one hand and demonic beauty on the other. But it is the latter that has the greater hold on his imagination.

His listener, from his rationalist viewpoint, sees the same consummation, but from a different sequence of causes. In his previous discussion with Father Madden he had, in a different language, foreshadowed the fable's import:

'In every country', I said, 'boys and girls walk together, and the only idealism that comes into the lives of peasants is between the ages of eighteen and twenty, when young people meet in the lanes and linger by the stiles'.[2]

And when he leaves the priest he reflects that in Ireland 'religion is hunting life to the death'. When, therefore, the young man has told him the story of Julia Cahill he concludes:

'He had sent away Life', I said to myself, 'and now they are following Life. It is Life they are seeking'.

There is a consequent irony in the exchange that immediately follows:

'It is said, your honour, that she's been seen in America, and I am going there this autumn. You may be sure I will keep a look out for her'.
'But all this is twenty years ago. You will not know her. A woman changes a good deal in twenty years'.
'There will be no change in her, your honour. She has been with the fairies'.

The story ends with the two approaching the town with its great cathedral wall rising above

dirty and broken cottages ... the nunnery, its schools and laundry; altogether they seemed like one great cloud.
'When,' I said , 'will a ray from the antique sun break forth and light up this country again?'

The final image is superbly ambiguous: is the antique sun that of true Christianity smothered within the masonry of the church's structure, or is it the ancient paganism against which Father Madden had earlier inveighed? It is a rare moment of balance in the rhetoric of Moore's fiction in his investigations of the untilled field of Irish Catholic experience.

Certainly, 'Julia Cahill's Curse' is one of those Moore stories where one feels that the author's obsessions about Ireland, love, religion, art and social reality, are brought within the control of an artistic vision. In it he manages to portray his least attractive cleric without yielding to his predominant urge for polemic. Madden emerges from the story as puritan, authoritarian, misguided and formidable, but he is not inhuman. He is allowed to argue his case with intelligence and force; he is even shown as willing to yield, despite genuine misgivings, on the matter of the looms. Indeed it is one of the story's better effects that Moore refuses to show him as the haunted man, suggested by the folk melodrama of the driver's tale—'saying Masses for the last ten years, that the curse be taken from the parish'. Julia resides in the area of poetical myth, powerfully suggesting the triumph of all the imponderable and elemental forces which the priest would abolish. In between are the two narrators, one a rationalist and a reformer, attempting to bring life again to an apparently doomed culture, the other an imaginative young story-teller, poised for flight in pursuit of the spirit of Julia Cahill. In one sentence towards the end the viewpoints of these two meet in a moment which summarizes the curious success of a story which deftly blends and counterpoints two versions of lived reality and two conventions of fictional narrative:

There was no doubt that the boy believed what he had told me; I could see that he liked to believe the story, that it was natural and sympathetic to him to believe in it; and for a moment I, too, believed in a dancing girl becoming the evil spirit of a village that would not accept her delight.

At the end of 'A Play-House in the Waste' the narrator says to his driver: 'I don't like your story. I liked the story about Julia Cahill better'. It is not hard to see why: the desolation of Father Madden's parish could be linked to a clear human cause—the failure of the priest himself; also it had given birth to a life-affirming myth in the defiance and beauty of Julia. 'A Play-House in the Waste' issues in no such clarity; it is at once a plaintive and a brutal story: Father McTurnan's parish is the poorest in Ireland in spite of his efforts to improve it and to keep his people at home; his positive exertion to bring joy and imagination to his community is crushed by a malevolent and ambiguous providence. The story's plaintiveness arises from the portrait of a priest who is gentle, compassionate and indomitable, the credible portrait of a saint who fails. Its power derives from the counterpoint of that glowering providence and doomed landscape with the priest's tireless patience and optimism. As in 'Julia Cahill's Curse' the counterpoint is managed by a subtle blend of narrative modes and the shrewd alternation of different viewpoints.

Again the story begins on the side-car. The young driver has by now lost his reticence. His first remark about the horse taking fright introduces the motif of folk superstition that acts as a frame of irony around an action that is in itself ironic on several levels:

'It was Christmas Day and I was driving the doctor; he saw something, a small white thing gliding along the road, and he was that scared that the hair rose up and went through his cap.

The boy's quaint volubility prompts the narrator to the thought that 'he is a legitimate descendent of the old bards'. In their early dialogue the theme of the story is swiftly, obliquely exposed:

'It is the poorest parish in Ireland, and every third year there's a famine, and they would have died long ago if it had not been for Father James'.
'And how does he help them?'
'Isn't he always writing letters to the Government asking for relief works. Do you see those bits of roads? They are the relief works'.
'Where do those roads lead to?'
'Nowhere. The road stops in the middle of the bog when the money is out'.

As they proceed they discuss the various possibilities of keeping the people at home, a road to the sea, a harbour—'the engineer said it would be cheaper to send the people to America'—home industries. Then the driver mentions the priest's most remarkable scheme and its failure—the play-house on the hill which the parishioners had built for the performance of a miracle play, and which had, at the last minute, been damaged by a storm. The viewpoints of the driver and narrator—of folk myth and modern rationalism—again cross tentatively when the latter asks why the play-house was not repaired and is told: 'where would be the use when there was no luck in it'. The appearance of Father McTurnan suspends further discussion, and the story moves into its second phase.

Here Moore's narrational strategy of counterpoint and juxtaposition is developed and complicated. The narrator's voice is that of the practical reformer, the man of the world outside. As he converses with the priest by the fire and penetrates further into the world of his strange parish he speaks and reflects in an idiom of increasing fatalism, yielding to a tone of lyrical nostalgia. Looking back over the centuries of Irish history, sensing the tragic decline of Gaelic culture since its last great flowering in the medieval Celtic-Romanesque, he concludes that:

'The Celt is melting like snow, he lingers a little in the corners of the field, and hands are stretched from every side, for it is human to stretch hands to fleeting things, but as well might we try to retain the snow'.

The priest remains stubbornly optimistic. As they talk he knits socks. It is a symbolic activity. He has taken up the habit because there is no woman in the parish who could turn a heel. He persists with it—adding to a pile of unneeded socks in the corner—because it is a pastime that he can easily suspend if called suddenly to visit the sick. It symbolises at once charity, persistence and futility. It is another version of his famine roads that lead nowhere. When he goes out on a sick call the narrator imagines him in a symbolic tableau—reminiscent of the blind woman receiving communion from Father Madden—which further extends the theme:

There was a pool of green water about this hovel, and all the hovels of the district were the same—one-roomed hovels, full of peat smoke, and on the hearth a black iron pot, with traces of some yellow meal or stirabout in it. The dying man or woman would lie in a corner on some straw, and the priest would speak a little Irish to these outcast Celts, 'to those dim people who wander like animals through the waste', I said.

The priest recalls his work on the play-house as an exertion of foolish optimism. He had hoped to create an Irish Oberammergau, but he now accepts, for reasons not yet clear to his listener, that he had been mistaken. The latter feels impelled to pluck out the heart of his mystery, to understand the failure of his dream and the secret of his present resignation. So far he has only the driver's cryptic folk judgment—'there was no luck in it'. In his mood of sympathy and nostalgia for the vanishing race he tries to revive the priest's enthusiasm:

'Yet it was as well to build this play-house as to make a useless road—a road leading nowhere. While they were building this play-house they thought they were accomplishing something. Never before did these people do anything except for bare life. Do you know, Father McTurnan, your play-house touches me to the heart' and I turned and looked. 'Once pleasure hovered over your parish, but the bird did not alight. Let me start a subscription for you'.

But the priest is no longer interested. In partial explanation he remarks that the people may have seen in the storm 'a manifestation of God's disapproval', and proceeds with the reflection that men are on earth 'not to make life successful and triumphant, but to gain heaven'. Even if the race disappears in America,—'the saddest thing in the world'—it will mean the spread of Catholicism. The great secret, he argues, is 'to acquiesce in the will of God'.

It is in the third and last movement of the story, with the return of the driver's voice, that the brutal idiom of the folk imagination closes in around the experience. As they leave Father McTurnan's parish behind he relates casually how the pretty girl who had been cast as Good Deeds in the miracle play had become pregnant during rehearsals:

'She had been 'wake' going home one evening, and when the signs of her 'wakeness' began to show upon her, her mother took the halter off the cow and tied the girl to the wall and kept her there until the child was born. And Mrs. Sheridan put a bit of string round its throat and buried it one night near the play-house. And it was three nights after that the storm rose and the child was seen pulling the thatch off the roof'.

The three voices within the story, narrator, priest and driver,—a triple balance of forces—conspire to make the experience at once eloquent and inscrutable. The strangled child—'the only bastard that was ever born in the parish'—powerfully symbolizes the strangulation of 'joy' and creativity—'the bird of pleasure' that had tried to alight—which the opening of the play-house had promised to release. The pretty girl, like Julia Cahill, had fled to America. The priest has learned that 'amusement' is an extravagance that he and his parish must not hope for. The lesson is implicit in the fact that for pastime, instead of reading which he had once enjoyed, he resigns himself to the knitting of unneeded socks.

The rhetorical counterpoint persists on other levels in the story's close. For the priest's orthodox reading of the events—'a manifestation of God's disapproval'—the people, through their spokesman, the driver, have their older and grimmer folk version of the failure, 'there was no luck in it'. Present also is the voice of the engineer, the social pragmatist, that 'it would be cheaper to send the people to America'. Yet the final mystery is that of Father McTurnan and the miraculous source of his 'good deeds': Moore wisely leaves him intelligible but still mysterious, presiding patiently over his own dismal acre of the untilled field as the story closes:

'He has always been thinking of something to do good, and it is said he thinks too much. Father James is a very queer man, your honour'.

'A Play-House in the Waste' registers its charge of social comment by virtue of Moore's scrupulous concentration of the human action, his refusal to remark on the spiritual, cultural and agrarian nightmare except in so far as it bears on the characters and their predicament. In this respect it resembles more than most of his stories do Joyce's presentation of Dublin's 'hemiplegia' in such stories as 'Two Gallants' or 'Counterparts'. 'A Letter to Rome' is an even more chilling portrait of social despair, and it too achieves much of its power by a steady insistence on the demands of plot and character. It too concerns a 'folly' of Father McTurnan's. Alarmed by the poverty of rural Catholics, the advance of Protestantism and the emigration of his parishioners to America he writes a letter to the Pope proposing that Irish priests be allowed to marry.

This strange plan is born out of the priest's isolation, his struggle with a remote and hopeless agrarian system and a human predicament which even in modern terms could be described as cosmically absurd. The absurdity is starkly presented in an argument between the priest and the Government inspector over the relief works; the inspector wants to apply the grant to building a useless road parallel to the existing one:

'I don't agree with you, I don't agree with you', said the priest. 'Better go in the opposite direction and make a road to the sea'.
'Well, your reverence, the Government do not wish to engage upon any work that will benefit any special class. These are my instructions'.
'A road to the sea will benefit no one ... I see you are thinking of the landlord. But there is no harbour; no boat ever comes to that flat, waste sea'.
'Well, your reverence, one of these days a harbour may be made, whereas an arch would look well in the middle of the bog, and the people would not have to go far to work'. 'No, no. A road to the sea will be quite useless; but its futility will not be apparent—and the people's hearts will not be broken'.
The inspector seemed a little doubtful, but the priest assured him that the futility of the road would satisfy English ministers.

The absurdity which the dialogue reveals is extreme, and its satiric force within the story is considerable. But the irony is employed in the service of plot and character. If the world is mad, the system grotesque, then only one of God's fools can survive with hope within it. Father McTurnan's response to his predicament, and that of his characters, has its own mad grandeur. Father Meehan, when he hears of the letter to Rome, attempts to dissuade his friend from sending it: 'You've been living too long in the waste. You've lost yourself in a dream,' and though his point is well taken, there is a sense in which Father McTurnan is closer to reality, *because* he is so isolated from the world of social convention. From his vantage point the world in which decisions are made is radically unreal:

Father McTurnan began to think of the cardinals and the transaction of business in the Vatican; cardinals and ministers alike are the dupes of convention. Only those who are estranged from habits and customs can think straightforward.

The passage is typical of Moore's tone in the story. The irony is affectionate: the priest, his eagerness and his folly, is caught in a benign conspiracy of understanding between author and reader. We realize that his plaintive letter from nowhere will have no success—that it will probably be misinterpreted by natures less simple than his; that the Vatican officials will misunderstand his intentions just as the English ministers will continue to thwart his schemes. But we also feel the pressure of human reality under which his earnest imagination conceives his plan, and this reality is rendered in images of remarkable strength, as in the picture of James Murdock who has built a house for his intended wife at the end of a famine road, a road going nowhere:

There was a wild look in his eyes, and he seemed to the priest like some lonely animal just come out of its burrow. His mud cabin was full of peat smoke, there were pools of green water all about it, but it had been dry, he said, in the summer; and he intended to make a drain. 'It's hard luck, your reverence, and after building a house for her. There's a bit of smoke in the house now, but if I get Catherine I wouldn't be long making a chimney. I told Mike he should give Catherine a pig for her fortune, but he said he would give her a calf when I bought the pig, and I said, 'Haven't I built a fine house and wouldn't it be a fine one to rear her in'.

When set against the irony of James Murdock's schemes for happiness the irony with which we view Father McTurnan's scheme is considerably modified. And the grotesquerie of the social panorama is further sharpened when we realize that beyond James Murdock's present squalor is an even bleaker alternative mode of being, the poor-house from which he has recently emerged. Looking after his retreating form the priest wonders whether 'he would give up life as a bad job and go back to the poor-house'. If his present condition is 'life' then beyond it is clearly a living death, the existence of the animal robbed even of the dignity of its own burrow.

This is the background against which the *contretemps* with his superiors may be seen; all of it is presented incidentally, without auctorial comment. The emphasis remains on the priest through whose eyes the reader perceives landscape and action. The priest's zeal is so unselfconscious that our sympathy with him is total. We feel the extremity of discomfiture when he finds himself looking in a new way at Norah Flynn and trying to adjust his celibate nature to the possible consequences of his scheme. There is a subtle tact in Moore's choice of detail when he points the humour of the priest's apprehensions, his distressed vision of Norah Flynn 'sitting opposite to him in his arm-chair', the moment when 'his face flushed deeper when he looked towards the bedroom door, and he fell on his knees and prayed that God's will might be made known to him'.

The same steady but playful irony controls his interview with the Bishop:

'I hope your Grace doesn't think for a moment that—' 'I only want to know if there is anyone—if your thoughts ever went in a certain direction, if your thoughts ever said, "Well, if the decree is revoked"' 'No, your Grace, no. Celibacy has been no burden to me—far from it. Sometimes I feared that it was celibacy that attracted me to the priesthood. Celibacy was a gratification rather than a sacrifice'.

It is altogether consistent with Father McTurnan's character that when the talk turns on his parish and on the problem facing James Murdock that he forgets his scheme. He leaves the Bishop's palace with five pounds for the latter's pig and does not recall the letter till he is well on the way home. Even then it has diminished in the light of 'the happiness he was bringing to two poor people'. In the final sentence he is back in the middle of his impossible parish: the social horror of the untilled field and the mysterious goodness of the priest who tries to make it fertile are caught in a single, vivid tableau:

... he drove down the famine road, and he and the driver called till they awoke James Murdock. The poor man came stumbling across the bog, and the priest told him the news.

In the great central stories of *The Untilled Field* we find Moore's remarkable power to create characters who are not only arresting in themselves, but also vividly representative, symbolic, archetypal: James Bryden, Father Maguire, Kate Kavanagh, Biddy M'Hale. Father McTurnan belongs to their company. He is Moore's attempt to create a saint, and perhaps the only attempt by an Irish short story writer to present a priest in the light of sanctity. It is by any standards a successful characterization: Father McTurnan's gentleness, simplicity, tenacity and resignation

resignation are as powerfully dramatized as the clumsy, overbearing zeal that marks Father Maguire's character and ministry. One has only to compare Father McTurnan to Daniel Corkery's sentimental hero in 'The Child Saint' to realize what a feat of fictional creation the Father McTurnan stories represent. It is interesting, therefore, to examine the means, the rhetorical techniques, by which the portrait is made at once so attractive and convincing.

Moore's primary insurance against a sentimental characterization is the aesthetic distance he achieves by a flexible use of irony. In 'A Play-House' this irony operates, as we saw, through his alternation of three voices, each speaking from a distinct view of the world. The driver is a product of that old, half-pagan folk tradition that insists on shaping the stuff of daily life into simple but coherent myths, splendid and exotic like that of Julia Cahill, macabre and ugly like that of the murdered child taking its revenge on its begetters amid the thatch of the play-house. The narrator is worldly-wise and rational; he probes for natural explanations, though he has a poetic flair that makes him sensitive to other versions of reality. But most important, he is not himself involved; his life is not organically part of the experience around which the story is shaped. Between the priest and the driver he is subtly undermined, condemned to an almost impertinent curiosity. He departs with the wry, evasive, almost defeated remark—the last line of the story—that his driver is 'the legitimate descendent of the ancient bards'. Certainly, he has not penetrated the secret of the priest's spiritual stamina. Indeed *his* sudden desire to revive the play-house is, within the rhetorical field of the story, very close to sentimental. Measured against the priest's earned resignation it is made to seem somehow idle and dilettantish. The priest, on the other hand, resides in a world of mysterious certainties, and these are tactfully presented as deriving from a transcendant source; they have the strength and dignity of a realistic and indestructible religious faith which permits him to learn, revise, tirelessly cut his earthly losses and begin again: 'Whether God sent the storm or whether it was an accident must remain a matter for conjecture, but it is not a matter for conjecture that one is doing certain good by devoting oneself to one's daily tasks . . . the people are entirely dependent on me, and when I'm attending to their wants I know I'm doing right. All the rest is conjecture'. The most active visionary is at the same time the greatest realist of the three. This is an old Christian paradox, and there are other traditional Christian patterns behind the figure of Father McTurnan which I shall, in a moment, attempt to expose.

In 'A Letter to Rome' the same quality of Christian realism is evident in his argument with the relief inspector and in his care for James Murdock. There the controlling irony operates through the author's carefully judged distance from the character. The narrating voice is close enough to the priest to allow us to see the world from his viewpoint, removed enough to show us where his zealous imagination is leading him. The ardour of his idealism and the radical extravagance of his vision make us smile, even make us fear for him in his inevitable collision with the power structures that govern his parish from afar. But his mastery of the reality within his parish creates a balance in our response, convinces us that his work, drawing its strength from the mysterious source of his faith, is good, and that the faith itself makes him ultimately invulnerable to the world.

It is from these patterns of irony and also from a consistent use of Christian imagery that Moore gives Father McTurnan such a densely real existence on the landscape of his untilled field. He constantly reminds us of earlier Christian prototypes, Christ himself in the desert, St Francis of Assisi, the early Irish ascetics; and a recurrence of waste and desert imagery creates an archetypal sense of Christian renunciation. We find him reflecting that 'men who live in the world accept the conventions as truths', and 'the world' in that context carries its full biblical resonance. He is solidly on the earth, but he is beyond the world, beside 'a waste mountain' against which 'a rose could only seem incongruous', in the middle of 'a waste bog', 'mud hovels' and 'green pools of water', on the edge of 'a waste sea' where no boat comes, amid the 'whins and heather' of 'dismal distant mountains', ministering to 'these outcast Celts' who 'wander like animals through the waste', and in a world of 'roads leading nowhere'. The symbolism of waste, desert and desolation is cumulative, and it accumulates a Christian resonance as it builds. It is within this symbolic landscape that the lonely, persevering priest takes on his weight of archetypal saintliness.

We can conceive of the three stories then as presenting an imagined territory in desperate need of redemption. The forces that might work that salvation are locked in conflict while the people perish. Julia's beauty is denied fulfilment and fertility, so she is driven from the country leaving the black magic of her curse upon the parish. Against that curse Father Madden's Christian magic of ban and interdict proves helpless. Art in the form of the elegiac folk-tune, the driver's story-telling and Father McTurnan's Christian drama are equally unavailing. The driver will follow Julia into exile and the dark magic of the strangled child is too strong for the priest's good deeds. The wasteful relief works of the engineer underline the distant cynicism of Ministries in London, just as the remote theorising of the Vatican entirely misconstrues the import of Father McTurnan's letter. The only manifestations of hope amid the damp and gloom are a lonely traveller trying to promote the use of hand looms and an indefatigable priest who writes letters to the great, plans impossible schemes, but finds a bedrock of consolation in humbly doing what he knows is God's will. This is the imaginative field of force with which Moore gives light and energy to his geography of nowhere.

THE POET AND BARABBAS: KEATS, HIS PUBLISHERS AND EDITORS

J.E. MORPURGO

Genius is not an irresistible force propelling whosoever possesses it upward to the peak of Parnassus. Chance plays its part, and Chance must have alert and active servitors. Had Keats not gone to school to the father of Charles Cowden Clarke, had Cowden Clarke not been a friend of James Henry Leigh Hunt, had Hunt not been gifted with rare editorial percipience, would we have had as 'light unto eternity' the poetry of John Keats?

The Keats who lives still in our minds and in our gratitude is resplendent, Leigh Hunt a footnote in literary history, if remembered at all then for two poems 'Jenny Kissed Me' and 'Abu Ben Adhem'; for a fine autobiography; and, monstrously, for that vicious caricature, Harold Skimpole in *Bleak House*, 'a sentimentalist, vivacious and engaging, but thoroughly selfish and unprincipled.'

Eleven years older than Keats, Hunt outlived him by thirty-eight years and

by living too long . . . lost the attention of accidental contemporaries and slipped the plaudits of posterity.

Yet, for his centrality to the literature of his time and for his influence upon it, Hunt's call upon fame is strident. Keats, Shelley, Byron, Coleridge, Lamb, Hazlitt, Carlyle, Macaulay, Cobbett, Scott, de Quincey, Tennyson, Dickens, Thackeray, Southey: editor to some, friend and ally to many, linking them all was Leigh Hunt.

He helped, first, Southey and then Tennyson to the office of Poet Laureate, though he coveted—and needed desperately—the honour for himself and though there were powerful voices raised for his election. In that is sufficient refutation of Dickens's libel. But Hunt's most vigorous claim to a place in the pantheon is that he recognised genius in its infancy and encouraged genius in its adolescence.

Keats was a few weeks short of his twenty-first birthday when he passed his examination at Apothecaries Hall. He had versi-fied, privily, throughout his boyhood but only one of his poems, 'O Solitude', had been published, and that recently in Hunt's *Examiner*. Then it was that he announced to his amazed guardian, Richard Abbey, the fateful decision:

Not be Surgeon! (so runs the seemingly authoritative record of that encounter) Why what do you mean to be?—I mean to rely on my Abilities as a Poet—John, you are either Mad or a Fool to talk in so Absurd a Manner—My Mind is made up, said the youngster, very quietly. I know that I possess Abilities greater than most Men, and therefore I am determined to gain my living by exercising them.—Seeing nothing could be done Abbey called him a Silly Boy, and prophesied a speedy Terminus to his inconsiderate Enterprise.

History justifies Abbey's irascibility; few are they who have wrestled a livelihoood out of the whimsy of poetry; and so did the evidence of Keats's twenty-one years. One poem published, and for the rest he had not lisped in numbers. He was not, as was Hunt, the product of superb schooling, nor gifted, as was Coleridge, with formidable erudition and a mighty intellect. When compared to many of his contemporaries—Lamb, for example, 'tipped early into a library of great books'—he was not even notably well-read. The mermaids on the Celtic fringe did not sing for him as they sang for Scott and Moore. Wordsworth knew the benison of a blessedly poetic landscape; Keats only Clerkenwell and Enfield. Shelley and Byron had been touched at birth by the wand of aristocracy. Cobbett, Clare and Burns had been from boyhood battered into literature by poverty and peasant drudgery. Keats was an ordinary lower middle-class boy, destined, at best, to become an ordinary middle-class man, his shingle on a door in Edmonton.

A few weeks after that sensational confrontation with Abbey, Keats was presented to Hunt by Cowden Clarke.

The pretentious word is appropriate. This was the poet he had honoured by imitation in his fledgling verses. One of the most influential editors in England, here was the man who had given to him the accolade of print and, cause for awe beyond all else, this was the hero who had suffered imprisonment for his reforming zeal.

Twelve years later Hunt recalled that meeting. In his first

misbegotten essay into autobiography, *Lord Byron and some of his Contemporaries*, he wrote of

the impression made upon me by the exuberant specimens of genuine though young poetry that were laid before me, and the promise of which was seconded by the fervid countenance of the mind.

And of Keats himself he wrote:

We became intimate on the spot and I found the young poet's heart as warm as his imagination.

From the moment they met, and perhaps even from that day when Hunt accepted 'O Solitude', Keats was encouraged by Hunt's recognition to attempt poetry palpably independent of the Hunt model. It was Hunt's generous spirit and his energetic manipulation of the strings that were his to pull which set aside Abbey's prophecy. Had it not been for Hunt then, indeed, Keats's 'inconsiderate Enterprise' might well have come 'to a speedy Terminus' and he to an unsatisfactory career as a doctor, marking out his restlessness by verses scribbled on the back of his prescription pad.

Cowden Clarke has it writ plain: once Keats was absorbed into the Hunt family and into a literary circle which included Lamb, Wordsworth, Hazlitt and Godwin, he had no time to spare for his work as dresser at Guy's Hospital. Yet this is at once too dramatic and too prosaic. Keats had no vocation for medicine and for surgery some abhorrence. Hunt confirmed him in his true calling and conferred upon him the support, spiritual and practical, of his peers.

At the Hunt's house in the Vale of Health, Keats met another neophyte poet for whom Hunt was flexing his entrepreneurial muscles. In the popular imagination these two, Keats and Shelley, are inseparable; at the time their relationship was troubled:

Keats did not take to Shelley as kindly as Shelley did to him. (So wrote Hunt, sadly, in his *Autobiography*.) Shelley's only thoughts ... were such as regarded (Keats's) health, with which he sympathised, and his poetry, for which he has left such a monument of admiration in Adonais. Keats being a little too sensitive on the score of his origin, felt inclined to see in any man of birth an enemy.

There followed lines at once anguished and revealing:

I could not love him as deeply as I did Shelley. That was impossible. But my affection was only second to that I entertained for that heart of hearts.

Thirty years after the death of both poets, still Hunt did not comprehend how much this disparity in tenderness had fretted Keats's sensitive spirit.

There were other, and more mundane, reasons for the breach between Hunt and Keats which opened soon after their meeting: Keats's distaste for Marianne Hunt's slatternly ways: his impatience—made feverish by awareness of impending doom—to be on with an independent career; and mischievous meddling by the painter, Benjamin Haydon. The confidence which Hunt had fuelled fired soon in Keats the knowledge that he, the acolyte, was superior to his master.

Happily the friendship between Hunt and Keats did not shatter into acrimony as did that between Hunt and Byron. Amity returned and, though it was never again as intense as it had been in those early days, for all the tragically short time left to Keats and in all Hunt's long life thereafter, Hunt spared himself no effort in the cause of John Keats.

It was, however, in those months when Keats was a frequent visitor, and sometimes a resident, in Hunt's home, that Hunt added most to the huge debt owed to him by all who treasure Keats's poetry.

Already he had noted Keats's potential. He had opened for him the door to literary society. Now Hunt proclaimed his discovery to the world.

In an article, published in his *Examiner* in December 1816, Hunt heralded the three young poets, Keats, Shelley and J.H. Reynolds, he had picked as successors to leadership of the poetic revolution initiated by Wordsworth and Coleridge. (Two golds and an outer! No mean score for an archer shooting his arrows into the mists of the future!) The article was clumsily contrived, and in detail careless. Hunt was impatient to be on with the business of advertising genius; he could not wait even to release from the anarchy of Marianne's housekeeping the only copy of one of Shelley's poems. (Keats was more fortunate; just in time for quotation 'Chapman's Homer' was rescued from the clutter of children's toys, dirty linen, bills, bills and ever more bills.)

Hunt had sounded the trumpet. Next he must bring to the wall of Carnarvon Castle his young prince, armed with the authority of a volume.

Hunt considered publication by subscription. Only seventeen years earlier this, the last stuttering of patronage, had been whispered over Hunt himself, to magical effect. The subscription list for *Juvenilia: or a Collection of Poems, Written between the ages of Twelve and Sixteen by J.H.L. Hunt, Late of the Grammar School of Christ's Hospital* reads like a recension of *Burke's Peerage, Debrett* and *Crockford* with a few additions from the *Dictionary of American Biography*. It contains one resounding name which to this day makes recital of all the rest redundant, 'Right Hon. Lord Nelson, Duke of Bronte'.

That volume had sold four editions, but Hunt judged correctly that by 1816 publication by subscription was as out-moded as inscription on stone tablets. Keats must have his volume and for that volume a publisher.

The advance of publishing to a professional and social state almost as it is today had been engineered in the last years of the eighteenth century. A reference book, published in 1759, did not so much as include 'publisher' in its categorisation of London trades though it did ascribe to 'bookseller' some but not all of the functions which by 1817—as still today—were in the province of publishers. By 1817 most publishers must have resented inclusion in a work entitled *London Tradesmen*. In our times who would have dared to dismiss to the tradesmen's entrance Lord Stockton, Lord Weidenfeld, Sir Stanley Unwin, Sir Geoffrey Faber, Sir Robert Lusty, Sir Allen Lane or Sir John Murray? Only Sir Basil Blackwell interrupts that seigneurial roll-call as reminiscence of those times before publishers had sloughed off onto a lower order of bookmen the sordid business of retailing—and he a latter-day heir to the race of bookseller-publisher which was vanishing fast even when Hunt was delivering up Keats.

In 1817 not one publishing house in London had celebrated a centenary. And Longman, the oldest, like every other firm not still in the hands of its publisher founding-father, had emerged from the rude chrysalis of bookselling only in the previous fifty years.

So also Murray's. John Murray I, a half-pay Marine officer, had gone some way to respectability in London by excising from his name the provincial resonance of the prefix Mac but though, from 1768 when he opened in Fleet Street, he had toyed with publishing, he remained indisputably a shopkeeper, a tradesman. His son, John Murray II (the imperial enumeration persists; we are now at John Murray VII. Or is it VIII?) was irreproachably a gentleman, 'a rogue, of course', said Jane

Austen, 'but a civil one'. Another contemporary wrote of his 'classic establishment' in Albermarle Street:

To secure a passport to the table of Mr. Murray three things are necessary: first, that the party be an author of some celebrity; secondly, that he be an unexceptionable Tory; and thirdly, that he be patronised . . . by the artistocracy.

This gentrification and, with it, this enhanced professionalism of the publishing element in the commerce of books played some part in the coincident elevation of authorship from the gutters of Grub Street. It also encouraged into the business many newcomers. So it was that, in 1817, Hunt and Keats faced a plethora of possibilities. Between them Hunt and his friends knew almost every publisher who mattered. Unfortunately almost every publisher who mattered had marked against Hunt some sin, literary, political or religious.

John Murray II would have been the obvious choice. His imprint, declared the American publisher George Haven Putnam, 'was accepted as stamping a book with literary importance.' Murray had in his list many of the stars of that glittering Regency firmament, Jane Austen, Scott, Crabbe and, of most relevance, Byron, then the most dazzling planet in that galaxy and, then, still close to Hunt. But, to a Tory as perfervid as Murray, Hunt was the Devil's plenipotentiary. Murray published the *Quarterly Review* and the *Quarterly* detested all Cockney poets.

His selection thus inhibited by prejudice and by the antagonism he had aroused, Hunt settled on a newcomer, on the firm of Charles and James Ollier of Welbeck Street.

Cowden Clarke and Haydon supported him and, of all his acquaintances, only Shelley demurred and he, not because he was antipathetic to the Olliers—he was himself contracted to the firm for a political tract—and not because he feared Keats as rival, but because he questioned that Keats's achievement was as yet sufficient to justify a volume, and—in this wise beyond his years—because he sensed that Keats was not yet ready to endure the barbarities of the critics. Hunt had his way. On 7 March 1817 the Olliers announced:

This day is published, price 1s, A PROPOSAL for Putting REFORM to the VOTE, throughout the Kingdom. By the HERMIT OF MARLOW. Also in 1 vol., post 8vo, price 6s 6d, boards.
Poems by John Keats.

The Hermit of Marlow was, of course, Shelley. The conjunction was a coincidence but a happy postscript to Hunt's 'Young Poets' essay. Conjunction and coincidence would come at last to tragic finality 'in the English burying ground at Rome, near the monument of Caius Cestius'.

7 March 1817! Only three months after the first flutter of negotiation between Hunt and the Olliers! The calculation is awesome and all the more remarkable because, as is the dastardly habit of novices (and of many who should know better) at the proof stage Keats had made substantial amendments to his original text.

The proofs reached Keats (by hand of messenger) when he was at a party. Immediately he sat down and, his technical confidence no doubt sharpened by weeks of competitive cross-the-table sonneteering at the Hunts, tossed off, for the messenger to take back to the printer, the dedicatory sonnet to Leigh Hunt:

> I feel a free,
> A leafy luxury,
> Seeing I could please,
> With these small offerings
> A man like thee.

The Olliers' nimbleness in the processes of production adds a knife-thrust to the bruising suffered by modern authors under the leaden shoes of our contemporary publishers and printers. Keats's agility in composition springs amazement and admiration in all bookmen of all generations. What followed after publication was set to a pattern which is to this day hideously familiar.

Keats, Hunt and all their friends purred over the wonder they had wrought. The poet's genius, appropriately garlanded by a handsome grey binding, was now accessible to the public and to posterity. A few, a very few friends of friends joined the chorus of delight. The public ignored this six-and-sixpenny benison. Posterity could wait.

Already, before ever *Poems 1817* was put to bed, Keats had begun an affair with another publisher; the procurer: Benjamin Haydon.

Such fame as remains to Haydon stems from his autobiography, rich with recollections of his friendships with others greater than he. (His canvasses are happily and best forgotten; though, once seen, their scale makes forgetting difficult.) Yet it must have been because Haydon envied the influences exerted by his friend Leigh Hunt over his friend John Keats that, even whilst he was lauding the Olliers, this most clubbable of men set about luring the inexperienced Keats into committing a professional solecism.

Carried on the winds of book-world gossip—as brisk then as they are today—the news of Keats's ingratitude came swiftly to the Olliers and, just at that moment, George Keats stomped onto the scene.

No less than his brother George was sure of John's destiny but he lacked John's tact and his adroitness with words. The letter he wrote to the Olliers has vanished but its brazeness and harshness can be judged by the publishers' blistering reply: 'We regret that your brother ever asked us to publish his book'—this but a few weeks after publication—and then, insult, the few customers who had passed across 6/6d were unanimous in displeasure. One had told the publisher that he thought it 'no better than a take-in'. George Keats could have the many unsold copies to sell as he wished—and if he could.

The name of John Keats was en tered into the sad list of authors, great and unknown, who have experienced the ignominy of distribution by remainder-merchants. One Edward Stibbs bought up all the unbound sheets, at 1 1/2d a set, cased them in shoddy bindings, and sold them off—very slowly—at 1s 6d a copy.

Unpropitious though it was in its beginnings, and even unscrupulous, the choice of Taylor and Hessey as his second publisher was to serve Keats well. This was an established house which, settling the adventure on a solid, profitable 'educational' list, had but recently expanded into *belles-lettres*. It could afford Hazlitt, Coleridge, Clare, Keats and—if for a short and not altogether happy period then even so to its everlasting credit— the *London Magazine*, because its balance-sheet was nourished by titles like:

Practical Hints to Young Females (that sold twelve editions)
Reciprocal Duties of Parents and Children (five editions)
Correspondence between a Mother and her Daughter at School (seven editions)
The Present of a Mistress to a Young Servant (seven editions)

In the steely heart of many a publisher there is a gilded man of letters shrieking to be set free. Taylor had come to London brisk with ambition to establish himself as a poet, and throughout his publishing career he fancied himself to be capable of improving upon his author's work—a notion which authors regard as a disease endemic among publishers.

Taylor did publish several books of his own authorship but his mark upon the literature of that time—and of all time— was made by his confidence in his literary judgment. Admirably and unhesitatingly supported by his junior partner—himself a poet, of a sort—he cossetted his discoveries and persisted with them even when, as with Keats so often, they were anathematised by critics, even when, as with Keats too often, the buying public was as uncharitable as the critics.

In that same year when the firm took on Keats, Taylor and Hessey became distributors—though not yet publishers in the full sense—for an author whose work would have especial significance for Keats's poetry. They engaged to sell for Henry Cary the verse translation of Dante which he had published at his own expense in a limited edition. The intermediary was Samuel Taylor Coleridge.

As poet, as metaphysician and as critic rarely matched, few of his admirers, then or now, would deny that Coleridge was vague, his mind, when not dulled by opium, soaring so far into the clouds that it could not find its way back to earth and to mundane, practical affairs. Yet for all his notorious 'somnam-bulistic inefficiency' Coleridge's letters in the business of Cary's *Dante* make up a concise, precise and shrewd treatise on sound commerical publishing.

And with one letter to Cary, Coleridge earned more than a parenthesis in any record of Keats and his publishers, for this is a testimonial to the excellence of Taylor and Hessey, written by the noblest referee of the age. Coleridge even held up his own formidable reputation as mirror in which Cary could see the publisher's worthy image:

Mr. Chalmers and several other highly respectable men had congratu-lated me on having Taylor and Hessey in my Prospectuses . . . one of the most respectable Houses in London . . . of high estimation . . . really of very superior order as men . . . very honest and honourable.

Taylor had had his eye on Keats since reading Hunt's 'Young Poets' essay. Four weeks after the Olliers published *Poems 1817* he wrote triumphantly and with abundant confidence to his father:

We have agreed the next Edit. of Keats Poems and are to have the refusal of his future Works. I cannot think he will fail to become a Great Poet.

The manuscript of *Endymion*, Keats's first work for Taylor and Hessey, was with the firm very early in 1818. The advance paid seems to have been £20. (Longman paid 3500 guineas to Tom Moore for *Lalla Rookh* and Murray 2000 guineas to Byron for *Don Juan*—fortunes in the early years of the nineteenth century and by extrapolation to our own times sufficient to tempt into verse Len Deighton or Harold Robbins.) But there was, in the agreement with Keats, a hint that he might draw more than the original £20 and that hint became generous reality.

Even so the care which the publishers exercised for Keats was more significant than money. The firm's principals, and their trusted adviser, Richard Woodhouse, read the manuscript scrupulously. Taylor corrected Keats's punctuation—no easy task— and even suggested improvements to his versifying, an audacity repeated for later manuscripts but never again accepted by Keats, as he did with *Endymion*. More pleasing to Keats, and in that age more surprising, Taylor was as active in designing the format of the book as he was editorially energetic.

Endymion was published at the end of April 1818—another example of vanished publishing athleticism and one made all the more remarkable by the fact that two weeks before publication, at Taylor's insistence, Keats was still working on a revised Preface.

Speedy production did not engender speedy sales. Six months later Hessey in London wrote to Taylor in the country:

I have much pleasure in saying that Endymion begins to move at last—six copies have just been ordered by Simpkin and Marshall and one or two have been sold singly in the Shop . . . here and there a man of taste may be found to admire its beauties.

This just one year before *Don Juan* began to sell in thousands on both sides of the Atlantic.

The publishers persevered, with *Endymion* and with Keats's subsequent works, determined, as Hessey put it, 'to make a stir' for Keats's poetry. With Keats they suffered the contempt poured upon him by the Tory Press. Sometimes they spat back; more often they encouraged counter-attack by a friendly literary notable, a task taken on with relish by Hunt, eagerly by Hazlitt and with dexterity and vigour by Byron. As was the custom of the time they made for Keats at their office a place for literary conviviality. As was the custom of the time—a custom, alas, no longer followed by publishers—their premises became for Keats a kind of Social Security office, a sort of bank giving loans against no security save talent.

Whenever Keats needed funds he appealed to Taylor and Hessey. Always, though often hesitantly, Taylor and Hessey answered his plea. When, his body wracked with disease, his mind by obsessions and his heart by love, Keats thought of escaping to Italy it was to Taylor that he turned, Taylor who organised his passage, Taylor who found for him a doctor in Rome, Taylor who paid for all.

After *Endymion* Keats was never again a docile author and once at least, when *The Eve of St. Agnes* was in preparation, poetic arrogance clashed with editorial heavy-handedness. The earthquake which followed came close to separating forever poet and publisher and has left an indelible mark on the seismographs of Keats scholarship.

This Folly of Keats (wrote Taylor) is the most stupid Piece of Folly I can conceive ... It excites in me the strongest Sentiments of Disapprobation ... He does not bear the Opinion of the World Calmly and yet he will not allow it to form a good Opinion of him and his Writings ... He will again challenge Neglect and Censure ... if he will not so far concede to my wishes as to leave the Passage as it originally stood, I must be content to admire his Poems with some other imprint.

By Dr Bowdler out of Mrs Grundy? So it seems at first to one who sat in court throughout the trial of *Lady Chatterley* and who was there when the cases were heard against *Last Exit to Brooklyn* and *The Philanderer*. Taylor's squeamishness strikes discord even more shattering to twentieth-century ears when we read the offending passage (Barbara Cartland made elegant?):

See while she speaks his arms encroaching slow
Have zon'd her, heart to heart ...

So it is that we are tempted to applaud Keats's spluttering *riposte*:

I would despise any man who would be such an eunuch in sentiment as to leave any maid with that Character about her in such a situation.

And yet Taylor was fulfilling the publisher's prime responsibility; he understood the market.

Dispirited by frequent haemorrhages and thwarted love Keats gave up the fight. Taylor and Hessey continued as his publisher.

Keats's later works sold well enough, even in his lifetime, but none of them prodigiously. Long after his death and long after the death of John Taylor the publisher's heirs gathered some substantial financial return for Taylor's consistent and persistent loyalty to his young 'Great Poet'. In 1897 a relative sent to Sotheby's the manuscripts of *Endymion* and *Lamia*. The *Endymion* fetched £695, the twenty-six sheets of *Lamia* £395, sums described by the *Athenaeum* as 'almost startling'. Had the Taylors held their treasures for another ninety years only the University of Texas and the Getty Museum would have dared a representative at the auction.

John Taylor had his reward, in his lifetime but not in cash. Before he died even Tory critics had accepted the validity of his bold prophecy. All, then as now, were agreed that John Keats is one of the greatest of 'Great Poets'.

Authorship is a simulation of Hell endured on earth and, having paid this penance for forty years, I could expect some credit hereafter were it not that I have mortgaged remission against long service on this, the peacock-side of the professorial lectern and even longer on the bastard-side of the editorial desk. So, denied expectation of a placid hereafter, I console myself just a little with sublunary calculation of the fate of others.

There are more publishers below than 'vast Hell can hold'. Charles and James Ollier are there, damned for relegating Keats to the remainder-stall. But I like to think that, for their immediate recognition of John Keats, Barabbas will have secured for these, his fellow professionals, an occasional ticket-of-leave.

Keats is assuredly in 'the other place' to eternity, composing sonnets for angelic recitation, and with him Leigh Hunt, his place earned by his zeal as Keats's mentor, his little sins of omission all forgiven through the intercession of his schoolfellow (mine too, and there's my only hope) St Edmund Campion. Nor do I doubt that for the glories which, on earth, they strove so nobly to pass on to us, John Taylor and James Hessey are there in 'the realms of glory', or that St Edmund Campion, son of a bookseller and the Trade's patron-saint, will have negotiated with the Keeper of the Book to win for them the benefits from sempiternal long-runs.

SOUTH AFRICAN NOVELISTS AS PROPHETS

ARTHUR RAVENSCROFT

The simplest fact about life and literature in South Africa is that it is impossible for either to be non-political. While this statement may also be true of many other societies, indeed, in one way or another, of all societies, it applies most particularly to South Africa because of the multiplicity of laws that govern the ways in which South Africans may, or more frequently, may not behave. White South Africa often complains that it has become the whipping-boy of the western world and points indignantly to English class distinctions and the Hindu caste system to support its belief that apartheid is not unique. But nowhere else in the world is behaviour that dehumanizes people more blatantly inscribed on the pages of the statute book, more violently in contradiction of those humane values that the European Renaissance incubated and European colonization across the face of the globe almost immediately began to stifle. The crowning irony is that these humane values have been all but eradicated in South Africa by the very measures the apartheid state has taken, on the pretext of preserving them.

It is a truism that the laws of the apartheid state bear particularly brutally upon Black South Africans, but also seriously confine the lives and horizons of White South Africans, apart from steadily eroding their humanity. All South Africans are subject to a vast tangle of prohibitions affecting every action from the most deeply private to the most broadly social: how you are born, the quality of your education, the kind of job you get, where you work at it, how you travel and with whom, what you think, where you swim, where you lay your head down to sleep, whom you sleep with, where you are buried. There can have been few states that have rested on bulkier foundations of parchment bond and bureaucratic tape, kept from collapsing under the weight of its own imbecile perfectionism only by legalized intimidation and military force. Such societies come about when a segment of society so imagines its existence to be under threat that it will forge mechanisms for its own survival with a single-mindedness that not only denies life to all the other segments, but preys upon its own life-sustaining tissues, and thus creates the conditions for its own surer eradication. There is more in common between the Afrikaners of South Africa and the so-called Loyalists of Northern Ireland than a dislike of Roman Catholicism.

Non-rational as they are, religion and racism are seldom the causes of civic division, but are usually pressed into service to provide emotive rationales for the institution or continuation of inequalities that are economic.

The process began in South Africa with the arrival of white settlers and gunpowder technology in Table Bay in 1652, and the marvel is that it still continues. It is a tale that can be told as farce, as comedy, as satire, as irony, as history, as documentary, as tragedy, as horror, as melodrama, but seemingly without end. South African novels that evade the central political issues of South African life can hardly be regarded seriously, except to be branded as having made a political choice in turning away from what in one way or another the art of the novelist must face and come to terms with. It can probably be granted that, despite all its protean possibilities in the twentieth century, the novel is probably still characterized chiefly by story—whether sequential in pattern, or about internal events of mind and personality, or of myth or symbolism or parable. Consequently the political requirement of high seriousness and the need to make their narratives respond to a situation yet without end, place enormous demands upon the creative imagination and technical inventiveness of South African novelists. The object of this article is to examine how half a dozen writers of some stature in South Africa have addressed themselves to such problems. One way in which four of them have tried to grapple with 'the end of the story' has been to prophesy, to imagine 'the end', and to set their novels in the future. They also tend to prophesy in the other sense, that of proclaiming a faith, as do the other two novelsits discussed.

Karel Schoeman's *Na die Geliefde Land*[1] (literally, 'To the Beloved Country') is one of the most accomplished Afrikaans novels of the past quarter-century. Winner of the Afrikaans literary award, the Hertzog Prize, Schoeman was a journalist in

Northern Ireland in the early years of the present 'troubles', and it is typical of his predilection for ironic understatement that in *Na die Geliefde Land* he refers to the South African revolution of the future (after all, the great nightmare of Afrikaner history) as 'the troubles'. The fable is itself a literal revolution, in the sense that the Afrikaans characters, a generation after 'the troubles', are very much in the position that Black South Africans today are, under the present Afrikaner hegemony. They live in a distant, run-down corner of the country, where it is dangerous to be out of doors at night. They are fugitives from the cities, unhappily enduring an insipid existence on what are left of their ancestral farms. Land has been expropriated, people are taken away by the police and never heard of again. The elderly live only in their memories of past glories, the young plot ineffectually until arrested. Drabness, gracelessness, insecurity, a grinding life of left-overs without any vital purpose. All this is registered through the consciousness of the central character, George, though by means of third-person narration. The son of former South African diplomats, George has lived most of his life in Europe and works for a publisher in Switzerland. After his mother's death, he has come to visit the place of his birth and childhood. It is a hurried, indulgent journey in the whimsical hope of finding his own roots in the glowing gold landscape of his mother's talk, a search also for clues to the kind of person she really was. He finds nullity, a bleak and desolate land and others' reminiscences of a fun-loving young woman who bears no resemblance to the invalid he watched dying in her elegant Swiss home. He learns that his patrician grandparents had been driven, 'like kaffirs', from their farm, Rietvlei, that his uncle had died while in detention, that after a period of use as a secret arms dump and refuge for insurrectionists, Rietvlei was razed to the ground. Where there had been homestead, dams, orchards, pleasure-gardens, he finds only a few trees, some stone steps, part of a low wall, rose-bushes gone wild, a little moisture among some stones. For George, who has grown up in and into Europe, the discovery that nothing remains of the world of his earliest memories is poignant, but he briskly prepares for his return to Europe. But to his hosts, the Hattinghs, and their friends in the neighbourhood, the annihilation of Rietvlei was a representation of all that had befallen them as a people, and at the party in honour of George one of them asks complainingly:

What more could we have wanted? We had everything. What did we do to deserve this? Why did we have to be punished like this?' (p.150)

These may be the character's words of incomprehension, but it is difficult to believe that the novelist has not intended them also to be words of national self-examination.

The irony of approach that reverses the political fortunes of the Afrikaners and makes them the underdogs is done with great delicacy. When the police break in upon the party in the small hours and haul the young men off into detention, there is no physical description of them as people apart from the mention of boots, uniforms, holsters, guns; no hint of their race; nowhere in the novel any account of the 'new' rulers of the country, except for general complaints about the situation. The emphasis is entirely upon Afrikanerdom Defeated (and much more so than in 1902) and it is flavoured by the ingenious use of George as a visitor from abroad who is nevertheless an Afrikaner by birth and speaks their language. For him the visit ends in a *cul-de-sac* from which he can easily reverse; for the embattled people he meets, the visit from the grandson of the apparently extirpated Neethling family becomes an outward sign of their dream of the old Afrikanerdom resurrected, and causes Gerard Snyman, the most irreconcilable of the young men, to remark with grim comfort: 'Broom is a tough shrub ... You can't eradicate it so quickly' (p.87). It is this faith in their own toughness that links the post-revolution Afrikaner plight with the pioneering origins of Afrikanerdom and with its period of power and triumph.

It is just possible that *Na die Geliefde Land* can be read as a tribute to the courageous resoluteness of the Afrikaner national will, but the characters who treasure the past when their people wielded power are shown to be shuffling dreamers, while the new generation, however defiant their opposition, can only shadow-box, and get arrested for their pains. Schoeman does, however, include two young characters, Carla and Paultjie Hattingh, who will have no part in the prevailing worship of the past or the realities of their withdrawn present. Paultjie can think only of absolute escape, but Carla has developed a new mutation of toughness, a respect for reality, a spirit that makes her refuse George's offer of convenient marriage and flight abroad. She feels impelled to abandon the sterility of their laager-ed existence, and seek some place for herself in the mainstream of her country's new life, however difficult it might be. 'There is work to do, life must go on' she says (p.64). Through Carla, and through the many levels of ironic juxtaposition in the novel, Schoeman seems to be giving a sympathetic, deeply understanding, but very just assessment of his people's transition from determination into inflexibility and self-destroying obduracy.

But Schoeman's novel of the future is also very much about the present. In describing how Afrikaners could be treated in the future, he is reminding them also how they are treating others in the present, and diagnosing the national traits that have led them to wield power thus.

In *Na die Geliefde Land* people—their faces, gestures, voices, silences—are graphically detailed, the desolation of their obscure corner vividly delineated, but the story does not require that the locale itself should be precise, and it could be almost anywhere in South Africa. On the other hand, J.M. Coetzee's Booker-prize novel, *Life and Times of Michael K,* [2] gains much of its immediate impact from the firm precision of its Cape Province geography; almost every step the chief character takes over a vast area could be plotted on a map of adequate scale. This particularity of landscape and setting initially fills the reader with great confidence in the novelist's craft, and even well into the book, when it becomes difficult to gauge the solidity of the central character and the significance of his experiences. The novelist has set up expectations that Michael's story will bear a very precise relationship to an objective reality, even when Michael (with greater linguistic dexterity than his birth and estate make probable) thinks: 'His [i.e. Michael's own] was always a story with a hole in it: a wrong story, always wrong' (p.151).

Early in the novel a throw-away phrase reveals that there is a war on in South Africa, which steadily increases in intensity and involves insurgent activity over large areas of the country, and attacks on towns and villages. There are interrogation centres and internment camps. But there is nothing about the issues being fought over, the nature of the insurgent cause, or any indication of Michael's part in it all, except as an adventitious victim. And perhaps, in what is undoubtedly a post-Northrop Frye novel, that is the whole point of Coetzee's creation of a mythic figure disconcertingly placed in a very realist setting. As one follows Michael's attempts to get, first, his ailing mother, and after her death, her ashes, to the peaceful Karoo countryside of her childhood, as one observes him alone on a deserted farm growing a few vegetables for his subsistence, or sitting rock-still himself, more spirit than corporeal reality, on the highest reaches of the Swartberg Mountains, one is almost convinced of the sheer nobility of mankind's capacity for suffering, endurance, and bare survival. Everything that befalls him, including imprisonment, thirst, starvation, and houselessness, makes of him a larger-than-life figuring of human suffering that excites admiration for the boundlessness of the human spirit, until a niggling doubt asks whether it is not a romanticizing of what is unutterably ugly—the state of extreme deprivation. The disfigured and retarded Michael is pauper, war refugee, pariah, outcast, clown, invalid, suspected terrorist. Shakespeare's Tom o'Bedlam, without clothes, wits, shelter, friends, was Edgar of Gloucester in disguise. Michael is 'the thing itslf'. Coetzee makes him even less than Lear's unaccommodated man, for Michael learns 'That to live in times like these a man must be ready to live like a beast' (p.135).

Reading this novel raises afresh the question whether the extremes of experienced human suffering, as in the wholesale Nazi destruction of the Jews, can be conveyed in art, other than wholly symbolically, without appalling offence being done to the everyday dignity of human nature. At the lowest-pulsed phase of Michael's living, he is no more than a creature in hibernation in its burrow:

The first day passed when K did not come out of his burrow at all. He awoke in the afternoon feeling no hunger. There was a cold wind blowing, there was nothing that needed his attention, his work for the year was done. He turned over and went to sleep again. When next he knew, it was dawn and birds were singing.

He lost track of time. Sometimes, waking stifled under the black coat with his legs swaddled in the bag, he knew that it was day. There were long periods when he lay in a grey stupor too tired to kick himself free of sleep. He could feel the processes of his body slowing down. You are forgetting to breathe, he would say to himself, and yet lie without breathing. He raised a hand heavy as lead and put it over his heart: far away, as if in another country, he felt a languid stretching and closing. (pp.162–3)

This is magnificently imagined. Is it, however, what the reader is to make of Michael? Is he a latter-day noble savage? Is he a tribute to the human ability to survive beyond the human, beyond even the animal, into oneness with tree and soil and water? Or does the entirely different mode of Part II, narrated in the first person by a sceptical rehabilitation camp officer, suggest that human credulity is readily taken in by images that evoke pity? Here the officer imagines himself addressing Michael:

Extraordinary, though, that you should have survived thirty years in the
shadows of the city, followed by a season footloose in the war zone (if
one is to believe your story), and come out intact, when keeping you
alive is like keeping the weakest pet duckling alive, or the runt of the
cat's litter, or a fledgling expelled from the nest. No papers, no money;
no family, no friends, no sense of who you are. The obscurest of the
obscure, so obscure as to be a prodigy.(p.195)

Whatever view one takes of Michael's role, reading the novel can
be a stirring experience. It is very cleverly done and one of the
themes is itself the effect on the reader's sensibilities of the
sufferings portrayed. Its sophisticated consciousness of
manoeuvre, from the highly evocative rhetoric that releases
generalized pity for suffering humanity, to such symptoms of
decayed civilization as when Michael, without desire or
revulsion, is fellated, as an act of charity, by a woman casually
encountered, does, however, provoke some unease about the
author's performance. Does not one perhaps miss the conviction
that the novelist's knowledge and skill in mapping the
topography of his native land is matched by his knowledge and
skill in tracing out the topography of his fellows' mundane
miseries? The reader can't help wondering whether the
novelist's admiration of fortitude and resilience in the face of
poverty has not led him into presenting poverty almost as a god-
given moral nutrient, instead of the man-made social poison it is.
The novel begins and ends in a Cape Town suburb, but most of
it consists of Michael's adventure into the country,[3] which
facilitates his symbolic dehumanization. Though partly a plunge
into healing nature, it is also a sort of Darwinism in reverse, a
reduction of a man, in order to expand the reader's response of
pity for the human condition at large. But this Lazarus has few
sores.

Far from gazing into South Africa's future, Sheila Fugard's *A
Revolutionary Woman*[4] harks back to the 1920s, thus enabling her
to invent and use a character who was a disciple of Gandhi in
Natal and the Transvaal in the first decade of this century.
Christina Ransome, an Englishwoman, is the revolutionary of
the title, living in a small Karoo town under the Lootsberg
Mountains, which keep changing their appearance in line with
the heroine's changing moods. In addition to providing the
narrative voice, Christina Ransome is presented as a would-be
prophet, a seer proclaiming to the Afrikaners (whom she
nevertheless scorns as latter-day Goths and Vandals) Gandhi's
belief in the future of a classless South Africa:

[Gandhi] sows his sesame seeds. He is a father and also a creator. Gandhi's tears wet the world, and they will fall here as rain. Then, the drought in men's hearts will be over, and we will see a different story. There will be no Brahmins in their splendour, and no Untouchables in their poverty. I mean that we shall see no Boer enclaves, and no Coloured locations. (p.142)

The novel contains much political emotion of this kind. It's heady stuff, but the 1920s political language, (e.g. *Boer* for 'Afrikaaner', *Kaffir* for 'Black'), while lending radiance to the basic dream of a new, healed South Africa, carries no hint of political brass tacks, and is more evangelical than truly revolutionary. What is of more lasting interest, however, is Christina Ransome's awareness that however saintly Gandhi's life and teaching, his role as Kasturbai's husband may have left something to be desired. She apprehends very clearly the connection between political oppression and the subjugation of women in sex and marriage, but agonizes over the true nature of the Gandhis' man-and-wife relationship. The mystical notion of Gandhi as a king and Kasturbai as a regent hardly meets the case that Sheila Fugard has so perceptively put. Finally the near-hysteria of the narrating character, when she tries to relate the Gandhi ethic to avowed socialist European heritage, her sexuality, and ultimately her womanhood, indicates that the novelist has herself not been able to resolve the seeming contradictions.

Nadine Gordimer's *July's People*[5] also treats some of the fictional ingredients so far discussed: another woman under stress, revolutionary war, retreat to a distant corner of the country, reversal of White-Black roles. Though lacking the imaginative sweep of its two predecessors, *Burger's Daughter* and *The Conservationist,*[6] it is a very concentrated, and, as one would have expected, a very professional handling of the long-expected and unthinkable Black Revolution. With modern warfare raging in Johannesburg, Maureen and Bam Smales and their three young children accept the offer of their Black servant, July, of shelter among his remote people in a meagrely bucolic existence, with no modern conveniences whatever, but leaking, smoke-filled huts, elementary agriculture, pigs rooting for human excrement, flies crawling over the faces of sleeping children. No Arden or crypto-Eden for these fugitives from the carefree, pretty White suburbs of the Witwatersrand.

Nadine Gordimer's scenario for the possible events of a War of Liberation is securely founded on recent events in and around South Africa, and therefore as convincing a piece of prophecy as is likely to be thought up, but she has often urged that her fiction has never been primarily concerned with the political, but rather with human relationships. and so it clearly is with *July's People*. Fictionally, the war exists in order to examine the effects of physical and emotional disorientation upon Maureen Smales, and upon her relationships with her husband and with their former Black servant. The self-confident, liberal-minded woman, happily married, trusting in her husband's wider experience of the world, proud that he and she have for fifteen years treated their servant with decency and courtesy, gradually comes to two destructive realizations. First, as Bam finds himself no longer the master (which he never admitted to being but was), but the utter dependent of July, his masculine certainties dwindle into mere indecisiveness and fuss, and she despises him for it. Secondly, when July's new role becomes symbolized in his taking *de facto* possession of their light motor-truck (the lifeboat that should eventually take them back to civilization), and Maureen discovers that July holds them in his benevolent power as they formerly did him in theirs, then she sees that all the outward courtesies of their good 'working relationship' (p.66) had merely covered 'the meanness of something hidden under a stone' (p.68). It is this hard-headed, shrewd understanding of how the exercise of power, at whatever level, poisons the human heart, that makes Nadine Gordimer's psychological study of yet another unlovely white South African an enterprise that is also politically just and relevant. Mehring in *The Conservationist* was no liberal, and the exposure of his moral and political ugliness was disturbing but appropriate. But with Maureen Smales, Nadine Gordimer seems to have shifted to a more radical political position than ever before, by presenting White South African liberalism as but the smiling face of savage oppression. Without White privilege for a firm foothold, how could anyone dance the elaborate liberal minuet? When Maureen first feels the hope of the eventual resumption of their, probably modified, suburban life threatened, her reaction becomes self-centred: 'Not fear, but knowledge that the shock, the drop beneath the feet, happens to the self alone, and can be avoided only alone' (p.41). From this point on, the novel records Maureen's steady deterioration as a human being, through her refusal to prop her husband's sagging confidence, and through her attempt at the moral blackmail of July by reminding him that she could tell his rural wife about his city woman, Ellen. Her performing the sort of tasks in the wilderness that neither she nor her husband would have thought suited to a sensitive, civilized woman (such as drowning the superfluous litter of kittens) is not an index of courage or adaptability but a sign of her coarsening as a person, just as her casual peeling off of her T-shirt to shake out the fleas and exposing her breasts in daylight in Bam's company has nothing to do with sexuality but is a crass expunging of meaningful intimacy. Indeed she learns a new honesty, but it is the corrosive that is flung to disfigure others, as when she looks 'triumphantly' at Bam, 'expecting nothing of him' (p.129); as when she finally accuses July of having stolen their vehicle: 'You want the bakkie, to drive around in like a gangster, imagining yourself a *big man*, important ...' (p.153; novelist's italics). When, at the end, she dashes in blind panic through the bush towards the sound of the unidentified helicopter just landed, she is abandoning all the civilized values she used to think she possessed, running 'like a solitary animal at the season when animals neither seek a mate nor take care of young, existing only for their lone survival, the enemy of all that would make claims of responsibility' (p.160).

This is the kind of unflinching vision that has made Nadine Gordimer a powerful and incisive writer, for in pushing such investigations into the imagination to their limits, she is also throwing her own 'nerves in patterns on a screen', as an author living and working in the conditions of privilege she so honestly and unrelentingly shows up from within.

Also very much from within, but on the other side of the great social, racial, political, and economic divide is Sipho Sepamla's novel, *A Ride on the Whirlwind,*[7] an exhilarated tribute to the school-children who were the heroes and the victims of the June 1976 uprising in Soweto. Although the novel opens with the Black Resistance Movement beyond South Africa's borders exploiting the children's riots by sending in a trained guerrilla, Mzi, to assassinate a brutal and much-hated Black policeman, the novel does succeed in assimilating both Soweto 1976 and the Black Resistance abroad into the long and respectable history of Black South African resistance to oppression. But the main purpose of the book is to glorify and absorb into the national mythology the exploits of the 1976 schoolchildren, who taught all their people the lesson that Blacks could raise their heads again and that limbs of the system could be removed. By petrol-bombing (in the absence of ballot-boxes) the outward symbols of white rule in Soweto, by taunting the police on the streets, by leaping the myriad back-yard fences of Soweto, where police vehicles cannot follow them, the somewhat romanticized gang of youthful heroes inspires to new effort old campaigners like Uncle Ribs Mbambo, who had been lying low for fifteen years, numbed by the brutality of Sharpeville, and the former Communist Party member, Papa Duz, now a coal merchant. Despite its serious purpose of saluting the Soweto schoolchildren, and aligning them with past and present figures like Sikukune, Moshoeshoe, Luthuli, Mandela and Sisulu, *A Ride on the Whirlwind* has all the verve and pace of a competent thriller. Unfortunately Sepamla does falter in his characterization of the guerrilla, Mzi, and Mandla, the most active of the student-revolutionaries. Mzi's self-confidence, vanity, and arrogance are repeatedly underlined but to no apparent end in the development of plot or theme. Mandla, normally full of irrepressible enthusiasm, blows up the wrong policeman, falls into guilt and remorse, and decides to quit: 'I hate myself because I am dirty' (p.210). It does violence to Mandla's exemplary part in the book, but perhaps it is Sepamla's clumsy means of acknowledging that June 1976 did not actually become the Revolution. He makes Mandla continue in this vein: 'I thought we'd won. But the cops have come and we were left to pick up the dead; to wail with greying mothers and fathers' (p.210).

Yet just how spirited the students' stand was is conveyed by the teeming detail with which Sepamla fills in what life is like in the monstrous urban conglomerate of Soweto—the vast crowds of workers daily assembling before dawn to pour into white Johannesburg by train, bus, and shared taxi, and then streaming back wearily as darkness falls, not knowing what perils the night will bring. Police raids. Road blocks. Shootings. Interrogation. Vicious torture. Detainees murdered. The diabolical side of the South African reality that Sepamla justly caricatures in the crazed behaviour of the Black policeman Batata in the Club Siyagiya and when he tortures Roy during interrogation. What White South Africa regards as the normal operations of law and order, Black South Africa experiences as uniformed thuggery, legalized terrorism, often the mindless barbarity of violence for its own sake. On the one hand, Sepamla celebrates the vivacity of African living, the caring of Black humanism, as integral parts of life in Soweto, a constantly tested solidarity of the downtrodden; on the other, this huge, ill-equipped sprawl of a slum of one million is the product of White South African policy, and in it common criminals and police informers batten alike upon the lives of their fellows, allowing even less security of home or limb than in urban areas elsewhere in the world.

In setting his novel in the Soweto of 1976, Sepamla is, of course, dealing with the past, but trumpeting its importance for the future. His novelistic account of that historical moment is a declaration of how those events transformed the entire mood of Black political sentiment. For some intoxicating days Black schoolchildren showed their elders that all the resources of the apartheid state had to be called upon to contain Soweto, that (admittedly at the cost of great suffering) Blacks could exert power where they had hitherto assumed they could not. To judge from the thrust and groundswell of *A Ride on the Whirlwind*, as a writer Sepamla found in the events of June 1976 and the implications, material of importance to his people's future that needed to be commemorated as they receded into the past—and re-lived, as a novel can make a past event and its ethos glow in the minds of readers. Moreover, in the South African situation, no novelist (no artist) need seek justification for endowing his writing with a serious didactic purpose, in the hope of affecting wholesomely the outcome of his people's future. If the Soweto children dared to ride on the whirlwind, dared 'to take a leap into the unknown dark side of life' (p.211), they also showed Black South Africa when it was in despair that 'Freedom will come to us one day. God is no fool!' (p.211).

In contrast, Ma-Maria, an old woman in Mongane Serote's novel, *To Every Birth Its Blood*,[8] declares: 'If God isn't bringing any fire, we are going to make the fire' (p.158). These two gnomic references to the deity epitomise the differences in tone and tenor between Sepamla's and Serote's novels. They do, however, have much in common, since both are rooted in the dismal yet triumphant realities of Black life in Soweto and Alexandra and all the other sub-cities of South Africa. At the centre of both books are the ordinary daily activities, in an infinitude of variety, of city-dwellers anywhere, but here augmented to the highest degree by unpredictability, insecurity, and dangers. Both novels unambiguously honour the Soweto children of 1976. And there is a singular appropriateness in their doing so, for Serote and Sepamla were poets before they wrote novels, and in both periodical publication and public performance their poems were important strands in the Black Consciousness Movement that in part inspired the Soweto uprising.

In Serote's book the emphasis is rather more upon the enduring political value of the children's uprising. Though Serote doesn't shut his eyes to the shootings and imprisonments that ended the 1976 disturbances, and have continued ever since, he proudly asserts that the new South Africa or Azania will issue from the blood that flowed then. June 1976 he presents as the earliest phase in the expensive and demanding process by which Blacks will liberate themselves, against all odds, and without looking to others for help. Self-reliance and fortitude are the traits most strongly underlined in the mesh of tales of inter-related individual efforts that *To Every Birth Its Blood* consists of. Inspired by the children's actions (there are frequent references to 'the days of Power'), the characters are all engaged, in a post-1976 period that merges into the future, in resistance of one kind or another, from research and publication, through protest meetings and rallies, to the sabotage of airports and oil installations. The novel ends short of the full-scale war that happens in *July's People*, but there are massive public protests all over the country and guerrilla attacks from across the borders, to which White South Africa responds with air raids on neigh-bouring states. The novel makes an extension into the future of patterns of events familiar in the present or the immediate past.

To Every Birth Its Blood is a crusty, knobbed sort of novel. The technical relationship between the first-person narration by a character named Tsi Molope of Part I and the much brisker third-person narration of Part II is by no means clear. Perhaps Part I is intended to exemplify through a single, intelligent, sensitive individual the almost intolerable pressures bearing upon all who live in the Black townships, with Part II broadening the perspec-tive back in history, forward into the future, and across many different groupings of people. It is a pity, however, that in using a wide-angle lens in Part II, Serote doesn't succeed in differen-tiating his characters adequately; they do too many similar things and their voices sound very alike. Perhaps, after all, it isn't a serious blemish. The aim of *To Every Birth Its Blood* is to perform a utilitarian function, to use the novel genre to honour the newest heroes in the terrible beauty of a long drawn out struggle, so that the faithful may be encouraged and the waverers turned. Serote's strong sense of the history of his people, which was detectable in his earliest poetry, informs the events of present and future in the novel, Guerrilla strikes at the heart of White cities are seen as an extension of a pattern of Black endurance and resistance from the slave trade to today's detainee with trousers down being approached by an officer of the law holding a pair of pliers. From time to time the connections are made in passages of poetic intensity. Here Tsi meditates on a man he has just seen lying by the roadside, beaten to death by policemen:

The darkness, the moonless sky, the starless sky, the vastness of the empty patches running for miles and miles to the horizon, all were prepared to conspire against us, had presented themselves as conveniences, cloaking and encouraging the killers. I thought about how Africa once conspired and gave birth to a slave trade. And the sea too aided the insane adventurers. Everything, that time, had been against us. Those ships sailed for miles and miles and miles across the seas, to far and strange lands. Canned inside their guts was a terrible pain, a brutal pain, the worst results the human heart can produce.

When I looked ahead of us, I saw that there were police waving us to stop.

'Oh my God!' Boykie said in Setswana. The horror clung to me, erased my speech. We were lost in the night and the drama of our time was this time set again. It was not just another story to be written and submitted at some deadline. It was us who were the issue of the drama, of the vicious hatred white people have managed to have against black people. The car slowed down. It came to a standstill.   (p.52)

One of the most refreshing qualities of Serote's writing is his use of direct, simple, everyday English to convey in rapid, flexible rhythms extremely personal and private emotion without the embarrassment that many of the words used might be expected to create. Perhaps it is because the language is in the same idiom as that of the lyrics and jazz of the townships, which this novel constantly reminds us is the accompaniment of so much of Black urban life. This is how Serote describes Grace Ramono's feelings when she is back home after hearing her husband sentenced in a political trial:

'The boers have hit us hard indeed,' Grace said with a great sigh. Now it was as if she had not only to accept but to deal with what all this meant. Her Michael, her Mike, had been taken away from her, had been taken away from her, had been taken away from her. For fifteen years. The father of her children, Dikeledi, Mpho and Morolong, her husband, a father, brother, man of the house, her bed companion, her everything, her what else, was now gone. She knew now that she was going to cry.

She knew now that there was an enormous vacuum in her life and that for the next fifteen years she was going to have to live differently from the past that she had lived with her Mike. The three women of the house sitting side by side, silent, had their thought running this and that way, thinking about the man who had played all sorts of roles in their lives.

(p.136)

It is refreshing probably because it is so unliterary and seemingly unstudied. I suspect, though, that this directness and simplicity is nicely calculated, as so much of Serote's poetry is, to speak directly to an unliterary proletarian audience that will recognize and be stirred by the articulation of an experience widespread and frequent among them. Serote's skill lies in his ability to do this without sentimentalizing or falsifying the experience, for it is all held in check by the large-scale context of historical awareness in the very texture of the novel, which gives communal and shared significance to every personal grief. Such effects lead to another level of prophecy in *To Every Birth Its Blood*: the emergence, uncertainly and haltingly, of the novelist, not as the inventive individual of idiosyncratic orig- inality, but as a voice of corporate sensibility, speaking both to his people and for them, at a period in their history when they know at last that they can endure until the first light of dawn, but cannot be at all sure yet how many long hours must still elapse.

In discussing these six novels, and in some ways comparing them with one another, I have not been trying to establish any critical order of excellence among them, though my preferences no doubt show through, but have been trying simply to find out, and go a little way towards describing, the ways in which novelists from different segments of the South African population try to deal with the singularly intractable experience of being segmented. The first novel considered is about tiredness and defeat, the last about tribulation, boundless energy, and the first scent of victory in the distance. It is impossible to break off without remarking explicitly on what most distinguishes Sepamla's and Serote's novels from the others (again as a mere statement of difference, not as a qualitative judgment): the glorious love of life, the irrepressible energy, the movement and dance and song, the Africanness, that have been forced into but not destroyed by the sordidnesses and sufferings of existence in Alexandra and Soweto and all the rest. As one writes, at the twenty-fifth anniversary of Sharpeville, the true cost of apartheid, what living in the segregated ghettos, with the para-military presence in and around them, means for Black South Africa has yet again been demonstrated by the shootings at Langa and Kwanobuhle in the Eastern Cape.

Note: Since this article was written in 1985, a few of the prohibitions listed in the second paragraph on p.128 have been tinkered with, but draconian edicts and censorship have greatly aggravated living conditions in the townships. A.R.

STONE PEOPLE IN A STONE COUNTRY: ALAN PATON'S *TOO LATE THE PHALAROPE*

ANNA RUTHERFORD

It is by the failures and misfits of a civilization that one can best judge its weaknesses.
Epigraph to *The Grass is Singing* by Doris Lessing

Only by the most outrageous violation of ourselves have we achieved our capacity to live in relative adjustment to a civilization apparently driven to its own destruction.
R.D.Laing, *Politics of Experience*

I would like to examine *Too Late the Phalarope* in the light of the critical theory of the Guyanese novelist and critic Wilson Harris. [1] Harris is concerned with the role and function of the novel in heterogeneous societies. Anyone who has lived in such a society cannot fail to sense those features which characterize it: the sharp racial divisions; the creation of polarizations; the exploitation of one group by the other; the determination of the exploiter to maintain the status quo no matter what the cost or consequences; and the justification of exploitation by appealing to so-called objective truth, a truth believed to be embodied in the social, religious and historical institutions. Harris maintains that these so-called objective institutions are in fact animistic, that built into them are deep-rooted patterns of racism and exploitation, of codes of fear as well as codes of racial superiority. He points out that man is constantly in pursuit of certain concrete targets and that though these targets differ from one society to another, one could say with a great deal of justification that for most of Western civilization the target is a material one. And this of its very nature almost cerainly necessitates a racist target as well, for the prosperity of the so-called first world countries is

140

based on the exploitation of the third world peoples. As Eric Williams has pointed out, the origin of negro slavery was economic, not racial.[2]

Harris refers to one version of the Carib myth of the flute of bone in which the flute was actually fashioned out of the bones of the dead ancestors. The bone flute was essential to the religious life of the Caribs for it was the instrument used for evoking the dead spirits and involving them in an act of creation and recreation. It must be realized that the act of creation and re-creation necessarily involves ruin and origin, a death wish and a birth wish, both of which are basic concepts in the rites of initiation. The flute embodied both ruin and origin; ruin because it was made from the bones of the dead, origin because through the apertures of the flute, Carib man was capable of communicating with his past (his ancestors). Modern man can regard the flute of bone (and its capacity to break through the walls of time) as a means of re-assessing a relationship of contrasting spaces and horizons in the present and the future.

Closely connected to the bone flute are the skeleton walls of time. These are horizons or fortresses of culture, and the gaps in these walls of time as portrayed in the diagram are parallelled by the apertures in the bone flute.

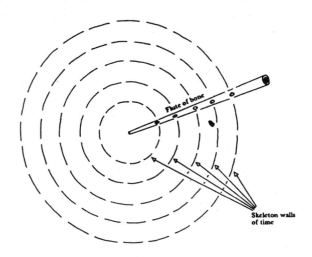

When these walls harden the gaps close into a specific horizon or character of space that conditions the responses of a culture. Thus these may consolidate into being a conviction of absolute order, and a lapse in the dialogue between strong inner and weak outer spaces (or strong outer and weak inner spaces) occurs, a lapse in the dialogue between contrasting themes and potentialities. In some degree this lapse is inevitable between besieging and besieged cultures as invading or retreating bodies reinforce their conquest of a safe place and idealize it into a timeless condition to govern the imagination.

The human mind has a hankering for order and continuity; in Wilson Harris's words, 'it finds that there is a beauty of conception in timeless orders'. This eagerness to accept and use already established patterns can however be dangerous. It can either give rise to complex self-deceptions where one mistakes one's own subjective viewpoint for timeless order, or it can become even more destructive as in the case of Nazi Germany, where the application of the past helped to engender the destruction of the current civilization.

Central to Harris's criticism is the theme of light. Light is traditionally connected with truth; therefore a quest for truth would also be a quest for light, but with each conscription of 'truth' in the name of 'homogeneity' light becomes an implacable tool to subdue, perhaps exterminate, others. This means that in order not to conscript truth / light one is forced to move back to darkness and to start one's journey all over again, to return to the 'womb of space' like the crew in Harris's novel *Palace of the Peacock* or Marlowe in *Heart of Darkness*. The whole truth comprises both light and darkness and in isolation either becomes a perversion of the truth.

The complexity of the creative challenge lies at the heart of the alchemical traditions wherein the dark/*nigredo* and light/*albedo* sides of life are viewed and fused together in an apotheosis of colours, representing the goal, the *cauda pavonis*. What one must remember is that the goal of the spiritual journey, which is the realization of one's vision, can never be final except in the beginning of something new. The possibility and necessity of beginning again is always inherent in it; true permanence is never static, it is an eternal process of becoming, susceptible to dialogue with otherness.

There are moments in history that may endure for a decade or a generation when a culture may 'rest' in its achievements. This is natural and desirable. When however such a pattern of 'rest' begins to assume an idolatrous function of 'changelessness' Wilson Harris suggests that the institutions and models of the day begin to conceal from the body politic itself a growth of catastrophe to which there has ceased to be a 'creative' or 'digestive' response. Then there seems to be no possibility of change except through the familiar patterns of violence and revenge.

South African society today provides an excellent illustration of some of the concepts that have just been discussed. The two alchemical dimensions, *albedo* and *nigredo* (not necessarily black and white but in this case they happen to be so) have become isolated in every way from one another. The white South Africans have locked themselves in their own apparently changeless fortresses of culture; *albedo* (white supremacy) has become a basis for an idolatrous self-sufficient feedback. The dialogue between opposites has been superseded by a totalitarian family of man.

After what I stress is a very brief and, of necessity, fairly simplistic introduction to some of Wilson Harris's ideas,[3] I would now like to turn to Alan Paton's *Too Late the Phalarope*[4] and see in what way Harris's critical theory may be applied to this novel.

The story tells of the struggle of a complex and sensitive man, Pieter van Vlaanderen, to conform to a racist, Calvinist society which will tolerate no deviation from its norms which have been elevated to religious status. Their homes are not just homes but 'holy home[s]' (p.93); in the eyes of Pieter's father, who epitomizes the men who rule South Africa, 'the words of the Book and of South Africa' (p. 59) are synonymous. The protection of both lies in the hands of the Afrikaners who are described by W.A.de Klerk in the following manner:

What bound them together in the deepest sense, was the Calvinist ethic. True enough they had long since ceased to find a free intellectual discussion going on around them concerning this matter. Yet rather strangely, the Calvinist tradition had remained.

Such was the isolation of these builders, who lived so distantly and self-sufficiently, that they knew next to nothing of Europe's tremendous Age of Enlightenment, nor could they have cared. The sixty-six books of the Bible were sufficient for all their educational purposes.

The word of God was the fountain of all knowledge, learning, morals and authority. The conclusion of the whole matter . . . was to fear God and keep his commandments. Subtleties of human interpretation played no part in it. Each patriarchal head was his own theologian, consistory and educationist.[5]

Compare Pieter's description of them as he looks out over the town of Venterspan:

The whole town was dark and silent, except for the barking of some dog, and the sound of ten o'clock striking from the tower of the church. The mist had gone, and the stars shone down on the grass country, on the farms of his nation and people, Buitenverwagting and Nooitgedacht, Weltevreden and Dankbaarheid, on the whole countryside that they had bought with years of blood and sacrifice; for they had trekked from the British Government with its officials and its missionaries and its laws that made a black man as good as his master, and had trekked into a continent, dangerous and trackless, where wild beasts and savage men, grim and waterless plains, had given way before their fierce will to be separate and survive. Then out of the harsh world of rock and stone they had come to the grass country, all green and smiling, and had given to it the names of peace and thankfulness. They had built their houses and their churches; and as God had chosen them for a people, so did they choose him for their God, cherishing their separateness that was now His Will. They set their conquered enemies apart, ruling them with unsmiling justice, declaring 'no equality in Church or State', and making the iron law that no white man might touch a black woman, nor might any white woman be touched by a black man. (p.18)

An analysis of this passage reveals how closely the society conforms to the polarized, self-destructive societies that Harris describes. We find a fierce desire to be separate—Pieter's father 'hated to be touched by a stranger' (p.72); a complete isolation of black from white; an animistic element in their institutions; and a religious justification for their position. The rock, stone, iron imagery which occurs again and again in the novel is a mark of the rigidity, and, as a consequence, the sterility of their society.

The irony, of which there are many instances in the book, lies in their belief that to be separate is to survive, whereas in actual fact the establishment of a society with the complete ostracization of all alien elements eliminates the possibility of change and development and must lead eventually to destruction.

The Afrikaner society of *Too Late the Phalarope* provides a perfect illustration of Wilson Harris's ideas about *albedo/nigredo* and a depiction of the consequences when either element is conscripted. Harris doesn't, of course, associate the black races with darkness and the white with light. Colour symbolism in the English language has been closely investigated, and it is a commonplace 'that by the Victorian period the word "black" had come to evoke evil, sin and treachery, ugliness, filth and degradation, night and funeral mourning, while "white", on the other hand, was associated with qualities like cleanliness, purity, beauty, virginity and peace'.[6] It is in these colour prejudices that the white racist society of South Africa and *Too Late the Phalarope* has invested so completely, and it is in its conscription of white in the name of truth that its destruction lies.

What must be emphasized is that *nigredo*/darkness is not in itself a negative. It is on the contrary a necessary component just as night is to day. In *Heart of Darkness* Kurtz is destroyed not because he chose to investigate the darkness but because of his total investment in one element, the dark. So too Austin Roxburgh in Patrick White's *A Fringe of Leaves*, only in his case he invests completely in the light. Both elements become destructive forces if either is conscripted; the opposing element will take its revenge if an attempt is made to isolate it and ignore its existence. What is needed is what Ellen Roxburgh achieves, 'a happy conjunction of light with nature'.[7] What Patrick White has done is what Joseph Conrad did before him, namely, use the native peoples and (for the white person) the unexplored land as objective correlatives of the *nigredo*/shadow/darkness to illustrate the reversal of light. The validity of using the native peoples and the so-called unknown continent in this way has of course been called into question.[8]

One image used to symbolize the Afrikaner society and its locked horizons is that of the house, which of course on another level is South Africa. No foreign element, in particular, no black element may enter. Nella's reaction, when she discovers that the Afrikaner boy who has just been in her house has been caught chasing a black girl, is one of shock and revulsion, 'to think he was in this house' (p. 20). Her instant demand is that he must be banned from the house, and when Pieter points out the impossibility of this she requests, significantly, that he can be in Pieter's study, 'not in our other rooms' (p. 20). The most obvious example of the house image in connection with the society occurs at the end of the novel after Pieter has been accused. The striking of his son's name from the Book, the elimination of all evidence of his existence, and the sealing of the house is a final attempt on the father's part to exclude the darkness. Ironically enough the so-called purification process achieves the opposite effect, for the drawing of blinds and sealing of doors create an even greater darkness. It is with an even more terrible and prophetic irony that the father reads the Hundred and Ninth Psalm, '*Let his posterity be cut off; and in the generation following let their names be blotted out*' (p.187). It is a logical consequence of the symbolic pattern that eight days later the old man, Jakob van Vlaanderen, is dead.

'The mind of man is capable of anything—because everything is in it, all the past as well as all the future.'[9] According to Jungian psychology this is the knowledge gained with the individuation process. This is the knowledge that Marlowe eventually gains, as does Voss; and with it comes a compassion and understanding. Marlowe understands Kurtz for, as he said, 'I had peeped over the edge myself'.[10] One could argue that Ellen Roxburgh reaches a similar state and that she reaches it because of her encounter with and participation in the life of the aborigines, a participation that reaches the ultimate climax in her act of cannibalism which assumes a sacramental function and which in Wilson Harris's terms would be described as the digestion and liberation of contrasting spaces. It shows the close and necessary relationship between ruin and origin, a relationship stressed in the ritual of the Mass in the words spoken after the consecration: 'Christ has died, Christ is risen, Christ will come again.'

Marlowe, like Martha Quest in Doris Lessing's *The Four Gated City*, sees the self as a microcosm, which like the world is divided between the state of victim and tormentor. Martha Quest is both 'the ragged bit of refuse (me) pushed into the gas chamber and the uniformed woman (me) who pushed'.[11] No such recognition of duality and of negative and positive capabilities exists in the Afrikaner mind and this in part accounts for its lack of compassion. What also accounts for it is its failure to recognize a common humanity, a theme Athol Fugard explores in *The Blood Knot*. This failure of course is intimately related to Afrikaners' closed society in which the past is conscripted and in which there is no dialogue with otherness.

Pieter's father is 'a stranger to compassion' (p. 9); Nella, Pieter's wife, reveals the same characteristic in her remark 'I'll not forgive him' (p. 20). This lack of compassion is related to one of the many and interconnecting polarizations which exist in the society, in this instance the division between Old and New Testament. The Afrikaners cling grimly to the God of the Old Testament who, like themselves, rules with 'unsmiling justice' and whose iron law of 'an eye for an eye and a tooth for a tooth' is one they can easily comprehend. The virtues they cherish are the Old Testament ones of Faith and Hope, the one they neglect is that of the New Testament, Charity. The division between the two books is brought into sharp relief by the sermon preached by the new Dominee. Appropriately enough the Dominee sees himself in the role of shepherd, not judge; the gospel he preaches is the gospel of love, of the power of love to transform. The Dominee sees the lack of love in the society and in yet another reversal of the darkness/light metaphor he courageously suggests that these people who regard themselves as people of light may in fact be sitting in darkness, recalling the whitened sepulchre of the New Testament and the city of Brussels in *Heart of Darkness*. He has sufficient psychological insight into the situation to see how the Boer's past, 'history, and war, and narrow parents, and poverty' (p. 58), has contributed to their present situation in the way that the past contributes to the present of any beleaguered group. But he also sees that they are chained by this past, they are manacled just as surely as is the accountant by his white celluloid collar in *Heart of Darkness*. In both cases there is an ironic reversal of light, both have conscripted one element and it has taken its revenge. Manacling and enslaving others in the name of white supremacy, they in turn are imprisoned themselves. [12] The one way to reverse the process, to transform them from destroyers to creators, is the gospel of love. The Dominee appropriately concludes his sermon with the words of the New Testament: 'I am come that ye might have life, and have it more abundantly' (p. 58).

It is not surprising that such a sermon falls on deaf ears as far as Pieter's father is concerned; for 'obedience was a word he understood, better than he understood the word of love' (p.65). He would prefer to do what St. Paul advised the Romans to do, to 'put himself under the magistrates, because there is no power that is not from God, and all powers are ordered by Him'. Likewise he seeks his consolation in Paul's assurance that 'rulers are not a cause of fear to the good but to the evil' (p. 35).

The Dominee is not the only person who queries the society's lack of compassion. Pieter's aunt does so also. In fact she suggests that one reason she tells the story is so that 'men may have more knowledge of compassion' (p. 10). Her musings about the relative merits of the laws of the Old and New Testaments are prompted by the incident in which a white farmer made his black servant pregnant and then killed her to hide evidence of the 'crime'. The reaction of the society to the incident is a typical one: it shuts out or ignores the unpalatable, the unspeakable:

His case was talked about privately, not before children or servants, not even before people in a room. If two men were talking about it in the street, they would do it in low voices; and if another joined them, even a friend, they might well talk at once of something else. A man might sit at his table with his grown-up family, and put down the newspaper angrily, and say in a strained voice, he must be hanged; they would all know what he meant, but they would not talk about it, they would let it rest. My brother would read about it, with a face of anger and revulsion, but he never talked about it to my sister-in-law or to me. Nella van Vlaanderen would neither read nor talk about it at all, and there were many women like her, as if by reading of it they would acknowledge that such things happened in the world. Others would read the newspaper in private, hiding their reading from others, attracted and repelled by its horror, ashamed of themselves and of a world where such things happened. (p. 33)

We are reminded of the reaction of the white community to Mary Turner's murder in *The Grass is Singing*. Pieter's aunt is uncertain whether the law of the Old or New Testament should be applied. Her mind is confused but eventually she resolves this dilemma for, as she remarks,

I am one of a people who in this matter of white and black suffer no confusion. Therefore I said to myself, what indeed many others said, what even I believe my brother would have said, let the man be hanged and the woman go free. For my brother believed as the Apostle Paulus, that the husband is the head of the wife, and that her true nature is to be obedient; which thing indeed he practised in his own house. Yet I grieved for the man in my heart, that did such evil because he was in terror. (p. 35)

This invites a discussion of the male/female relationship in the novel and the role of sex. It is not surprising in a white, Calvinist, racist society to find a strict division between the sexes with the male as the dominant partner and the woman as subservient to the male. As Simone de Beauvoir has pointed out, the nature of men is defined by men and the nature of women is defined as a complementarity to men; man is the subject, but woman is the 'other'. Feminist critics have pointed out that man has needed woman as a sort of negative standard so that the womanly qualities of passivity, timidity, docility, and so on, can point up the glory of the corresponding masculine qualities of aggression, assertion and initiative.[13] The society of *Too Late the Phalarope* provides an illustration of this situation. It also shows the close connection between sexist and racist prejudices and points up once more the black/white, darkness/light dichotomy.

In the society depicted by Paton there is a complete acceptance of the view that the male element is one of light, reason, etc. and is infinitely superior to the female element of darkness, emotion, etc. Hence the female dark element, like the native element, must be eradicated from male consciousness. There can be no tolerance of either in the superior, male, light element. This polarization creates a dilemma with regard to the role of the woman in the family and society at large, a dilemma solved by the male creation of the whore/madonna, darkness/light dichotomy, a dichotomy which excludes the possibility for either to participate in the other.

For the puritan, sex is an evil and therefore related to darkness. The sexual aspect of their women is ignored, and what is stressed is the madonna/light image. There must be no taint of darkness, the white boys may play with the black boys but 'not our girls with their girls' (p. 21).

Kenneth Parker remarked in *The South African Novel* that Peter van Vlaanderen was presented as having the stature of a tragic hero and that, like all tragic heroes, he was destroyed by a fatal flaw. Parker suggests that Pieter's flaw is lust, lust for a black woman. I cannot agree with this and would argue that Parker has missed the subtlety of a complex situation. Pieter's 'flaw' is that he is the one whole man in a maimed society, and in a novel riddled with irony, perhaps the greatest irony of all is that the one complete man is destroyed by the so-called forces of light. In a society that had completely separated one element from the other and eliminated what they considered to be all alien forces, Pieter van Vlaanderen stands apart. The aunt-narrator tells us how Jakob van Vlaanderen

had fathered a strange son, who had all his father's will and strength, and could outride and outshoot them all, yet had all the gentleness of a girl, and strange unusual thoughts in his mind, and a passion for books and learning, and a passion for the flowers of veld and kloof, so that he would bring them into the house and hold them in his hands, as though there were some deep meaning that he was finding in them. Had he been one or the other, I think his father would have understood him better, but he was both. (p. 8)

Part of the tragedy and irony lies in the fact that Pieter van

Vlaanderen never seriously questions his society and its values; he believes that it is he who is maimed and he resents it bitterly. This is brought out very clearly when he reminisces about the story told by Moffie.

Why Moffie's story should come back to me then I do not know, for I cannot remember that I had ever thought of it all these eleven years. But it came back to me now, and I thought of him, and of all those like him, with a deep envy, and a longing too, that I could have been like that myself.

How we laughed at Moffie's story, partly because of the way he told it, and partly, I suppose, because we were laughing at ourselves. I do not think we were laughing at the Malay woman, nor at the way he let her fall to the ground. And I suppose there was some shame in it too. But I would take the shame, and I would be like that myself, if I could; for to have such horror is to be safe. Therefore I envied him. (p.97)

Whilst he lacks a true understanding of the situation he has sufficient insight to realise that in attempting to eliminate what his society and he believe to be the alien, 'dark' element he is in fact doing terrible violence to himself.

It is significant that when he endeavours to conform he is described in the same imagery that characterizes his society, in particular, that of the house. For he, like his society, out of a sense of survival and also fear, 'shut the door of his soul' (p.7). He is on the point of speaking his innermost thoughts to the Dominee but at the last moment draws back so that 'the lights went out suddenly in the house of the soul, and its doors and windows were shut and its curtains were drawn' (p.61).

Given the person he is, we are not surprised that his attitude to sex runs contrary to that of the majority of the male population. It is unfortunate for him that just as his father epitomizes the male Afrikaner in its extreme so does Nella the female:

... she was the country girl, quiet and shy and chaste, as most of our country girls are. She was frightened of Johannesburg, and of the evil things that men and women do, even of staying in an hotel. She was frightened even of the laughter that came out of the Royal Bar, where men like her father and brothers were jesting a little coarse and rough. Therefore when he in his extremity asked for more of her love, she shrank from him, thinking it was the coarseness of a man. (p.39)

Pieter writes to her and tries to convince her that there is nothing evil or coarse about his love, that it 'is a love of everything about you, and not just a love of your body' (p.104). It is a desperate plea for understanding. Given the person she is, Nella's reply presents no surprises. One feels that Nella's idea of an ideal relationship would be the one offered by Morrie in *The Blood Knot*: 'a corresponding pen-pal of the opposite sex'.[14] Pieter has insufficient psychological insight to realise that it is sexual frustration that leads him to intercourse with Stephanie. Instead he attributes his act to a 'mad desire of a sick and twisted soul' (p.123). And as with the Moffie incident he wishes he could be other than he was. 'I thought of Nella and Martha and my mother, and my brother Fran's wife, with their simple chastity, and wished to God I had been made a woman' (p.155).

The demand that he be other than he is creates within him a deep resentment and leads to what is described as his dark, black mood which turns him momentarily, like his people, into a man of stone. On the plot level it is his over-zealous embracing of the role which leads to his downfall. It is when he most resembles his father that he triggers off the sergeant's revenge. This illustrates quite clearly how the alienated element will take revenge. He had attempted, like his father, to eradicate the so-called darkness, and the darkness, allegorized in the person of Stephanie, destroys him.

'And I write it all down here, the story of our destruction' (p.8). *Too Late the Phalarope* tells the story not only of Pieter's destruction, and that of his family, but of the eventual destruction of a whole society. In the lectures given in Aarhus in 1973, Wilson Harris illustrated his point about the self-destruction of modern society with a quotation from Werner Heisenberg:

With its seemingly unlimited growth of material power mankind finds itself in the situation of a skipper who had his boat built of such heavy concentrations of iron and steel that the boat's compass points constantly at herself and not North. With a boat of that kind no destination can be reached; she will go round in a circle, exposed to the hazards of the wind and the waves.[15]

If we can compare Pieter's dream:

Then he fell into sleep, and dreamed that he was at the top of a hollow tower, with no way up and no way down. And it was not like any other tower, for the walls were hollow too, from the bottom up, and the space between the walls was filled with knives and forks, and the handles of the knives were made of metal not of bone, like they use in a soldiers' camp. And he lay naked on the knives and forks, and they cut his flesh and drew the blood, and down below on the ground his cousin was shouting to him to come down, but he dared not look at her because of the dizzy height, and because the whole tower shook and quivered, as though it might at any moment crumble to destruction. (p. 122)

The gaps which should have existed in the skeleton walls of time to allow for an interaction between the races and between past, present and future have been filled with instruments of torture and destruction. The bone flute with its apertures has been replaced 'with knives and forks': 'the handles of the knives were made of metal not of bone . . . and they cut his flesh and drew the blood'. It is appropriate and suggestive that the people of iron should eventually be destroyed by instruments of their own torture. These 'people of rock and stone in a land of rock and stone' (p.18) are like Titus, 77th Lord Groan of Gormenghast, 'heirs to a crumbling summit: to a sea of nettles: to an empire of rust: to ritual's footprints ankle deep in stone'.[16]

THE THEATRICAL VOICE: *THE WORDS UPON THE WINDOW-PANE*

ANN SADDLEMYER

On 17 November 1930, in his sixty-fifth year, a new play by William Butler Yeats was produced at the Abbey Theatre in Dublin. Apart from a prose ballet version of his 1916 verse drama, *The Only Jealousy of Emer* (*Fighting the Waves*, 1928), and two translations from Sophocles (*King Oedipus* and *Oedipus at Colonus*, 1926 and 1927), it had been eleven years since Dublin audiences had seen a new work by Yeats, when his fantastic comedy *The Player Queen*—made even more inventive by Gordon Craig's screens—was produced. Yeats's new play, *The Words Upon the Window-Pane*, seemed, in contrast to these experiments, considerably different; in fact it strikes one at first glance as the cuckoo among his golden birds of Paradise.

True, other plays had been in prose, but *The Resurrection*, which was completed almost immediately afterwards, and the two *Oedipus* translations were heightened to heroic lyricism and interspersed with the choric verses his audience had come to expect from the author of *Plays for an Irish Theatre* and *Plays for Dancers*. Even those curiosities *The Cat and the Moon*, with its Kyogen-like comic shattering of decorum, and the multi-authored *Unicorn from the Stars*, share an exaggerated touch of Kiltartan dialect which lifts them out of this world. In contrast, *The Words Upon the Window-Pane* is thoroughly rooted in the tradition of realism. Indeed, some critics have gone so far as to suggest that this is one of the reasons for its success; for in embracing the methods of Ibsen and Shaw, Yeats departed even further from the select audience of no more than fifty in 'some great dining-room or drawing-room' he wished for the verse plays founded on the Noh. Instead of 'an audience like a secret society where admission is by favour and never to many', Yeats in this play has provided matter and manner for the public

153

theatre he had disparaged in his open letter to Lady Gregory in 1919, the year *The Player Queen* was produced and *Two Plays for Dancers* was published. Instead of 'the theatre's anti-self,' and 'a mysterious art ... doing its work by suggestion,' we seem here to have 'theatre of the head', 'direct statement', in fact 'the objective Popular Theatre' he claimed to have left behind.[1] In the following pages I intend to examine this apparent anomaly in the Yeats canon and in so doing to explore the many voices he has employed to create what I believe is a significant turning-point in the work of the older Yeats.

The Words upon the Window-Pane is the only play by Yeats which requires the reality of a sitting-room and its furnishings, middle-class characters, the vulgarities of common speech, the trappings of bourgeois contemporary life of the town. Drawing upon his own experience of séances in seedy areas of Soho or Holloway among naive servant girls and 'fat old mediums'[2], and upon his observations of the run-down tenement settings familiar to Dublin audiences through the plays of Sean O'Casey and Lennox Robinson[3], Yeats vividly re-creates the atmosphere and detail of a typical contemporary séance. The characters who seek assistance, advice, and consolation from those who have passed over are archetypal to the extent of parody, so intent and sincere are they in their expectations: Mrs Mallet, 'a very experienced spiritualist' who is 'utterly lost' if she cannot gain her dead husband's advice concerning her proposed teashop in Folkestone; old Cornelius Patterson, the punctual gambler who seeks confirmation of a world of racecourses and betting shops in perpetuity; irascible impatient Reverend Abraham Johnston, who demands consultation with the evangelist Moody in order to become even more effective singing and preaching among the poor and ignorant of Belfast; even the inevitable sceptic, John Corbet, doctoral candidate from Cambridge, who desires objectivity and fact for his thesis on Jonathan Swift and Esther (Stella) Johnson. Just as appropriate to a genuine séance are the medium herself, Mrs Henderson, 'a poor woman with the soul of an apostle'; Dr Trench, President of the Dublin Spiritualist Association and so comfortable in his hard-won conviction by way of Swedenburg and the weighty researches of F.W.H. Myers[4] that trance mediumship has nothing to show *him*; and the invaluable secretary Miss Mackenna, who 'does all the real work' serving as gate-keeper and protector of the sacred circle, and who herself reserves judgment, hovering between receptiveness to the mystery and rationalizations about thought-transference. The names of the two men have a certain personal resonance also, rooting them in Yeats's private reality, partly mischievous, partly with a sense of loss. Wilbraham FitzJohn Trench, described elsewhere by Yeats as 'a man of known sobriety of manner and of mind'[5], succeeded J.B. Yeats's old friend Edward Dowden in the chair of English at Trinity College, a chair Yeats in 1910 had himself hoped to occupy; Trench was a specialist in Shakespearean drama and Aristotle's *Poetics*. The Corbets of Sandymount were, of course, Yeats's relatives, and on 11 September 1930, while completing this play, Yeats had recorded in his diary recurring tragic dreams of 'a great house which I recognize as partly Coole and partly Sandymount Castle'.[6] Even Lulu, the experienced six-year old control who speaks through Mrs Henderson, is a likely candidate from Yeats's notebooks with her childish lisp and ready responses. 'All were people I had met or might have met in just such a séance', he tells us in his introduction to the play.

What we do not expect is the emergence of Dean Swift and Esther (Vanessa) Vanhomrigh as the 'hostile influence' which has disrupted Mrs Henderson's previous séances and soon shoves the distressed Lulu aside in this one. Nor, later still, the older Swift, suffering senile relict of all that was noble in eighteenth-century Ireland, who rapidly replaces his earlier, passionate self and with an anguished plea first to Stella, then to his God, sends both control and witnesses scurrying to escape. Yet even in these details Yeats has conscientiously laid down clues of a realistic nature: he uses the discovery of words carved upon the window of 'Fairfield', the house owned by Dr Oliver Gogarty in which Yeats lived for some time in 1910 while working on his first attempt at translating Sophocles, perhaps strengthening the fabric even further with Swift's known practice of scribbling little poems on windows at Inns in England during his travels.[7] Yeats has the Cambridge doctoral student recognize some lines carved in the window of the séance-room as being from Stella's poem to Swift on his birthday, 30 November, 1721. Finally, to allay any suspicion of fantasy, we are reminded in the play that such eighteenth-century houses, now reduced to penury like their owners before them, are common in Dublin to this day. Only fifty years before (1880, the year the Yeats family returned to Ireland, that Lady Gregory married, that Gladstone became Prime Minister), this house had been in private hands; then it became a boarding house and now a portion of it has become a spiritualist haven. Two hundred years ago, Stella had played cards in just such a room; during the same century, just such a house saw the births of Grattan and Curran, both of whom, like Swift, were lovers of human liberty. In such a house of intellect the spirit of Swift might well linger; in such architecture is reflected the grandeur of Ireland's Age of Reason. On such a night in Dublin in 1930, two men like Dr Trench and John Corbet, one all practised wisdom and the other full of youthful inquiry, might well discuss not only the finer points of spiritualism, but the tragic life and loves of the Dean of St Patrick's, and recall what Yeats was frequently to call 'the greatest epitaph in history'.

This naturalness sets the tone for the evening. The implied contrast between the two types of sitters—shopkeepers and evangelists, the materialistic spiritualists, versus scholars and humanists, the reasoned believers—is developed in the debate over a 'hostile influence' which has already spoiled two, if not three, séances since Mrs Henderson returned to her native Dublin from London. The Reverend Johnson, distressed as much by his wasted expenses travelling from Belfast as by the threat to the search for knowledge, seeks to eradicate this disturbance through an ancient ritual of exorcism, but Dr Trench pleads for charity and courtesy: 'The spirits are people like ourselves, we treat them as our guests and protect them from discourtesy and violence ... We do not admit that there are evil spirits.' His argument for acceptance continues: 'Some spirits are earth-bound—they think they are still living and go over and over some action of their past lives, just as we go over and over some painful thought'. There is only one difference between us and them, he claims, especially since we have acknowledged the séance ritual: 'where they are thought is reality.' And he concludes his brief Swedenborgian sermon with the few lines essential to our understanding of the plot of the play:

Sometimes a spirit re-lives not the pain of death but some passionate or tragic moment of life ... In vain do we write *requiescat in pace* upon the tomb, for they must suffer, and we in our turn must suffer until God gives peace. Such spirits do not often come to séances unless those séances are held in houses where those spirits lived, or where the event took place. This spirit which speaks these incomprehensible words and does not answer when spoken to is of such a nature. The more patient we are, the more quickly will it pass out of its passion and its remorse. [8]

After such sweet reasonableness, the stage is set, for both audience and performers, for the enactment of the ritual. Indeed, the séance itself is acknowledged as a performance: Mrs Henderson is upstairs resting, preparing for her role; when she enters, she takes centre stage in the large comfortable armchair around which the attendants seat themselves; she welcomes her visitors and explains that her responsibility is merely 'to make the right conditions' so that the spirits may come—a sort of superior Stage Manager. Even the disruptive spirits are described in theatrical terms—they have consistently behaved 'as if they were characters in some kind of horrible play', complains Mrs Mallet. The audience on stage, too, must perform with appropriate decorum: the door is locked against blundering latecomers; Miss Mackenna feels 'that something is going to happen'; the singing of a familiar hymn provides the prologue; and, on cue, Lulu enters through the body of the snoring medium.

From now on the audience on stage are helpless witnesses to a performance which goes awry. Mrs Henderson is taken over first by Lulu, who uses the medium's hands to aid her description of the first Spirit to be invoked, that of Mrs Mallet's husband; her body then becomes a battleground for Lulu and 'the bad man who spoilt everything last time', 'that horrible spirit' who 'would not let anybody speak but himself'; then Lulu is in turn audience to a young lady who, she thinks, must be 'at a fancy dress party'. Gradually the voice of Jonathan Swift's passion fills the room, taking possession of Mrs Henderson, calling forth as co-inhabitor the costumed young lady who, John Corbet informs Miss Mackenna in a whispered aside, is Vanessa.

The medium's actions punctuate the rapid give-and-take that follows, and I have taken the liberty of rearranging the stage directions to emphasize this accompanying physical action as Vanessa pleads, and Swift refuses, to accept her love in words made even more striking because we are intently listening in to a séance:

VANESSA: If you and she are not married, why should we not marry like other men and women? [. . .] It is not enough to look, to speak, to hear. Jonathan, Jonathan, I am a woman, the women Brutus and Cato loved were not different.
SWIFT: I have something in my blood that no child must inherit.I have constant attacks of dizziness; I pretend they come from a surfeit of fruit when I was a child. I had them in London . . . There was a great doctor there, Dr. Arbuthnot: I told him of those attacks of dizziness. I told him of worse things. It was he who explained. There is a line of Dryden's . . .
VANESSA: O, I know "Great wits are sure to madness near allied". If

you had children, Jonathan, my blood would make them healthy. I will take your hand, I will lay it upon my heart—upon the Vanhomrigh blood that has been healthy for generations.

Unwittingly, the medium performs as the voices speak through her by slowly raising her left hand.

VANESSA: That is the first time you have touched my body, Jonathan. *Mrs Henderson stands up and remains rigid.*

SWIFT: What do I care if it be healthy? What do I care if it could make mine healthy? Am I to add another to the healthy rascaldom and knavery of the world?

VANESSA: Look at me, Jonathan. Your arrogant intellect separates us. Give me both your hands. I will put them upon my breast. *Again, Mrs Henderson raises first her right hand to the level of her left, and then raises both to her breast.*

O, it is white—white as the gambler's dice—white ivory dice. Think of the uncertainty. Perhaps a mad child—perhaps a rascal—perhaps a knave—perhaps not, Jonathan. The dice of the intellect are loaded, but I am the common ivory dice. *Mrs Henderson's hands are stretched out as though drawing somebody towards her. Vanessa's voice continues, persuasive, seductive, passionate. Mrs Henderson's movements grow convulsive, matching the voice of Swift:*

SWIFT: O God, hear the prayer of Jonathan Swift, that afflicted man, and grant that he may leave to posterity nothing but his intellect that came to him from Heaven.

VANESSA: Can you face solitude with that mind, Jonathan?

The question is too penetrating, and Swift tries to escape out of the room:

SWIFT: My God, I am left alone with my enemy. Who locked the door, who locked me in with my enemy? *Mrs Henderson beats upon the door, sinks to the floor, and speaks as Lulu once more.*

The scene continues, with actions matching those unseen powerful voices. Led back to her chair by that 'experienced spiritualist' Mrs Mallet, Mrs Henderson as Lulu asks for a hymn to 'bring good influence'. Now Swift returns once more, calmer under the 'new influence' felt by all in the room. Sadly, regretfully, painfully, he questions not Vanessa, but Stella, providing his own answers from her poem for his last birthday, the words upon the window-pane:

> You taught how I might youth prolong
> By knowing what is right and wrong;
> How from my heart to bring supplies
> Of lustre to my fading eyes;

He takes comfort in a further verse where she promises to save him from that solitude threatened by Vanessa:

> Late dying may you cast a shred
> Of that rich mantle o'er my head;
> To bear with dignity my sorrow,
> Ond day alone, then die to-morrow.

'Yes,' he continues, 'you will close my eyes, Stella. O, you will live long after me, dear Stella, for you are still a young woman, but you will close my eyes.' With that self-delusion, Swift retires in favour of a weakened Lulu and, finally, an exhausted Mrs Henderson.

The séance over, all depart after leaving their tribute. (At first demurring, Mrs Henderson peeks through her fingers at what is paid as each leaves—a detail, Yeats tells us, suggested by his wife.[9]) All leave, that is, but the indefatigable, inquisitive student, who, paying a double tithe (one pound), congratulates the medium on her 'creation' as 'an accomplished actress and scholar'. His thesis is confirmed; the only plausible explanation for Swift's celibacy can be his fear of madness. But, as is the way with students, he is still not *entirely* satisfied:

But there is something I must ask you. Swift was the chief representative of the intellect of his epoch, that arrogant intellect free at last from superstition. He foresaw its collapse. He foresaw Democracy, he must have dreaded the future. Did he refuse to beget children because of that dread? Was Swift mad? Or was it the intellect itself that was mad?

The exhausted spiritualist looks at him in astonished bewilderment—what is the young man talking about? 'That dirty old man' surely cannot be Swift? 'I saw him very clearly just as I woke up. His clothes were dirty, his face covered with boils. Some disease had made one of his eyes swell up, it stood out from his face like a hen's egg.' Assured that Swift did indeed look like that in his last years, she comments ingenuously, 'Now they are old, now they are young. They change all in a moment as their thought changes. It is sometimes a terrible thing to be out of the body, God help us all'. Nor does this simple Dublin woman, who has just had her own body taken over, comprehend the irony of what she has just said.

Alone once more, Mrs Henderson crouches down by the hearth to brew some tea, but her hands once again become Swift's, Lulu's 'bad man' 'in that corner over there'. 'Five great Ministers that were my friends have gone', he intones. 'Ten great Ministers that were my friends are gone. I have not fingers enough to count the great Ministers that were my friends and that are gone'. In her own voice the medium looks for a tea cup, but it is Swift again who answers, 'Perish the day on which I was born!' With these horrible words from the Book of Job, the saucer falls to the floor; the curtain falls.

I have taken the liberty of so much quotation to illustrate how adroitly Yeats draws first the séance attendants, then the audience of the theatre, into his web of supernatural as normal, super-reality as realistic. From the still centre of the medium's trance as she sits in her comfortable armchair in the middle of the shabby gentility of her boarding-house drawing-room, the other world is evoked as we sit watching her, so clearly that we can see in our mind's eye the old man with glasses crouching in a corner, then the young lady kneeling, then the old man, while all we see on stage is an elderly Dublin woman by her hearth. Our world never disappears; it is heightened with a greater intensity while 'breathless mouths' summon further 'breathless mouths' 'out of a medium's mouth'. Yeats did not finish *The Words Upon the Window-Pane* until 4 October 1930; two weeks earlier Lady Gregory noted in her Journal, 'Yeats has been reading me his Swift play ... Very wild and terrible behind its simple setting, an *everyday* séance'.[10] That same month, September, he was clarifying the thought of 'Sailing to Byzantium' by creating 'Byzantium,' which also invokes the dead:

> The unpurged images of day recede;
> The Emperor's drunken soldiery are abed;
> Night resonance recedes, night-walkers' song
> After great cathedral gong;
> A starlit or a moonlit dome disdains
> All that man is,
> All mere complexities,
> The fury and the mire of human veins.
>
> Before me floats an image, man or shade,
> Shade more than man, more image than a shade;
> For Hades' bobbin bound in mummy-cloth
> May unwind the winding path;
> A mouth that has no moisture and no breath
>
> Breathless mouths may summon;
> I hail the superhuman;
> I call it death-in-life and life-in-death.[11]

The details of the poem comment on the details of the play; the implication in both is, of course, that the spirits are always within reach, requiring only to be summoned by place, emotion, or their own passionate need. To my knowledge no one has observed that at the beginning of *The Words Upon the Window-Pane*, when Miss Mackenna is welcoming the Reverend Johnson from Belfast, she urges him to cross the hallway into her room where 'old Patterson and some others are there already'. Yet she has only greeted Cornelius Patterson. 'Some others' are always there,

> The elemental things that go
> About my table, to and fro. [12]

In much that is said by the spiritualists in the play and in what is evoked through Mrs Henderson, we recognize Yeats's own theories as expressed in his private system, which he was actively revising between January 1926, the date of first publication of *A Vision*, and February 1931, when he wrote to Olivia Shakespear, 'I have really finished *A Vision*—I turn over the pages and find nothing to add . . . I have constructed a myth, but then one can believe in a myth—one only assents to philosophy'. [13] In that revised edition he at last confesses the role his wife, George Yeats, played as medium for the 'Instructors' who came offering him through their System 'metaphors for poetry'. They came first through automatic writing, then, to save her from exhaustion, as speech through her sleep; once she suffered a severe shock because someone 'blundered' in just as she was going under. There is little need to go into the entire doctrine of *A Vision* in detail here: suffice to say that for Yeats and his wife it affirms 'a Communion of the Living and the Dead', and 'much that has happened, much that has been said, suggests that the communicators are the personalities of a dream shared by my wife, by myself, occasionally by others . . . a dream that can take objective form in sounds, in hallucinations, in scents, in flashes of light, in movements of external objects'. [14] Perhaps here would be the most appropriate place to point out that George Yeats, according to her husband, 'urged' him to write the play. [15]

In *A Vision* we find a complex elaboration of the process Yeats called 'Dreaming Back', described more simply by Dr Trench in the play, where a Spirit

is compelled to live over and over again the events that had most moved it; there can be nothing new, but the old events stand forth in a light which is dim or bright according to the intensity of the passion that accompanied them. They occur in the order of their intensity or luminosity, the more intense first, and the painful are commonly the more intense, and repeat themselves again and again . . . All that keeps the Spirit from its freedom may be compared to a knot that has to be untied or to an oscillation or a violence that must end in a return to equilibrium.[16]

Of one who died a solitary death, Yeats comments, 'his *Dreaming Back* would be imperfect. He would lack not only physical but spiritual burial. The contents of his *Husk* (the incarnate body) being, as I suppose, too much himself, he would continue to look through a window-pane upon which he had breathed.'[17] Other passages further enlighten the situation in his play: 'After its imprisonment by some event in the *Dreaming Back*, the *Spirit* relives that event in the *Return* and turns it into knowledge, and then falls back into the *Dreaming Back* once more.' But, 'where the soul has great intensity and when those consequences affected great numbers, the *Dreaming Back* and the *Return* may last with diminishing pain and joy for centuries.' 'During the *Dreaming Back* the *Spirit* is alone with its dream; during the *Return* in the presence of those who had a part in the events explored in the *Dreaming Back*'.[18]

Clearly then, the soul of Jonathan Swift is caught in events that have not yet resolved themselves, either on earth or in the other world. I will speak of the events in Yeats's Ireland later; for the moment let us return to the play and trace the painful journey of Swift's spirit as it attempts to turn certain events into knowledge.

When the spirit of Swift is first perceived, he is quickly driven away at the instigation of the spirit of Mr Mallet; Lulu describes the incident for us: 'He says . . . he says, "Drive that man away!" He is pointing to somebody in the corner, that corner over there'. Mr Mallet then also disappears, and in his place Lulu reports: 'Young lady here—Lulu thinks she must be at a fancy dress party, such funny clothes, hair all in curls—all bent down on the floor near that old man with glasses'. But then, 'That bad man, that bad old man in the corner, they have let him come back', and following Lulu's scream, we hear the voice of Swift accusing Vanessa, who sits 'crouching there', of 'behaving like some common slut with her ear against the keyhole.' For this is 1719 and Vanessa has written to Stella demanding to know whether she and the Dean are married. The shift from the older Swift to the fifty-two year-old man is so sudden, only the spirit's own thought could have performed it. Is the senile seventy-eight year-old man watching himself and Vanessa in what is clearly the most intense of the passions he dreams back? Is this why he finds himself in Celbridge with Vanessa rather than in Dublin with Stella? The scene concludes with his pounding on the door 'locked in with [his] enemy'. During the singing of the hymn Mrs Henderson has been murmuring the name of Stella and simultaneously the séance attendants notice the 'new influence in the room'. When the spirit of Swift again speaks, he is three years older, and takes consolation in Stella's poem on his fifty-fourth birthday; we do not hear Stella, nor does she apparently respond to his anxious questions, 'Have I wronged you Stella? Are you unhappy?' Is she there, or is it merely her poem that is present and that has recalled him to this house in Dublin? Surely, as Peter Ure has suggested, 'her spirit has long ago proceeded to some purer stage of the discarnate life'.[19] Besides, the older Swift knows that Stella did indeed leave him to a solitary death. And so his next appearance, as Mrs Henderson awakens, is as the 'bad old man' of the opening scene of this play-within-a-play, the Swift of the deathbed.[20] But that is not the last we hear of him; tradition tells us that Swift habitually greeted his birthday with the quotation from Job III, 3: 'Let the day perish wherein I was born',[21] the phrase which concludes the play. The Swiftian image is a constant, even while we move rapidly through the last twenty-five years of its life on earth.

The play is a masterly piece of stagecraft that is consistent with Yeats's final spiritual system, his personal myth, while at the same time progressing naturally from the given situation. But it is consistent also with Yeats's philosophical beliefs throughout his life. As early as 1901 he wrote his well-known essay on Magic, the cardinal three points being that 1) the borders of our minds flow together; 2) our memories form one memory; and 3) the Great Mind and Great Memory can be invoked by symbols.[22] His 1914 essay, 'Swedenborg, Mediums and the Desolate Places', written to introduce the second volume of Lady Gregory's monumental *Visions and Beliefs in the West of Ireland* (1920), describes the 'absorbing drama' of the séance, and in particular the role of the medium who, he says,

has his gift from no heightening of all the emotions and intellectual faculties till they seem as it were to take fire, but commonly because they are altogether or in part extinguished while another mind controls his body. He is greatly subject to trance and awakes to remember nothing, whereas the mystic and the saint plead unbroken consciousness.

You will recall that Dr Trench describes Mrs Henderson as 'a poor woman with the soul of an apostle', but she recalls little of her trance. Even the fact that we hear voices and do not see spirits is consonant with his earlier essay: 'it seems plain from certain Polish sentiments that the intelligence of the communicators increases with their economy of substance and energy. Often now among these faint effects we will seem to speak with the very dead'.[23] And finally, in 1937, he dictated to his wife his last statement, the 'Seven Propositions', which begins, 'Reality is a timeless and spaceless *community* of Spirits which perceives each other. *Each Spirit is determined by and determines these it perceives*, and each Spirit is unique.'[24] Like Swift, Yeats remained constant to his basic principles. In his commentary Yeats himself remarks,

In my play, Swift and Vanessa are obviously dramatisations; the medium thinks and speaks what they say, and it seems natural for Dr. Trench to talk of them as condemned to re-enact the past. His explanations is traditional, one finds it in Japanese plays and in Swedenborg ... [25]

And, he might have added, one finds it in the younger Yeats.

But the play has an inner consistency also, a dense pattern of oppositions, themes, and voices to which one might apply Yeats's own description of the System dictated by the disembodied Instructors of *A Vision*: 'Stylistic arrangements of experience' which have 'helped me to hold in a simple thought reality and justice'.[26] I have already suggested the suitability of Yeats's choice of characters: none has complete knowledge; that can come only from the viewer who pieces together what is said on stage and through the play-within-a-play with his or her own inner convictions about the afterlife. The sitters leave with no more than they expected and for most of them considerably less than they had hoped for. Even the medium, despite her sensitivity to the conditions around her, is ignorant of the great debate that has ravaged Swift's mind and her body. Yet all in one way or another serve as spokes in the wheel of consciousness: the young student provides an intellectual link between the living and the dead as Mrs Henderson does an occult one[27]; through the conversation first of Dr Trench and John Corbet, and later Swift's own dialogue, we observe, in David Clark's words, 'a pattern of classical ideals, of traditional religion, of traditional literature and of Irish patriotism' set up against 'a pattern of

commonness, of commercialism and of abstract fanaticism'.[28]
Thus the decaying house represents an Ireland suitable only for
horse-racing, evangelism, and shopkeeping; Swift's great
cathedral has dwindled to a chapel or—in this case—a shabby
drawing room used as the spiritualists' church; the glory that
was Ireland's in the eighteenth century, a reflection in its turn of
the glory of ancient Rome, is past as surely as Swift's keen
intellect has descended into madness or senility. Swift refuses to
accept the gamble offered by Vanessa and bring children into the
world; Ireland in the twentieth century has become sterile. John
Corbet enthuses over his thesis on Swift,

His ideal order was the Roman Senate, his ideal men Brutus and Cato.
Such an order and such men had seemed possible once more, but the
movement passed and he foresaw the ruin to come. Democracy,
Rousseau, the French Revolution; that is why he hated the common run
of men,—'I hate lawyers, I hate doctors,' he said, 'though I love Dr. So-
and-so and Judge So-and-so'—that is why he wrote *Gulliver*, that is why
he wore out his brain, that is why he felt *saeva indignatio*, that is why he
sleeps under the greatest epitaph in history.

These large patterns are illuminated by the many smaller
parallels evident throughout the play. Vanessa's metaphor of
'white, ivory dice' and her challenge to Swift are reflected in the
references to Mrs Mallet's dead husband's tie-pin in the shape of
a horseshoe; Miss Mackenna takes the opportunity of getting a
few tips on the horses from old Corney Patterson who seeks
proof that the joys of the turf will not die with him; the séance
itself is a gamble which, for most on this particular evening, has
failed. Opposed to this emphasis on chance is that of choice,
reason and intellect combatting passion and body: Swift chooses
to reject a life of the body; Stella in her poem elects a platonic
relationship; John Corbet chooses to believe that Mrs Henderson
is an actress and a scholar. Choice in turn implies loss or
abandonment: loss of loved ones (Swift, Vanessa, Mrs Mallet)
and money (Stella at cards, Mrs Henderson through vocation);
loss of health (Stella), strength (Mrs Henderson), reason (Swift).
Related themes of innocence and childhood reverberate throughout: Lulu, Mrs Henderson's control, is a child of five or six; her
hymn, John Keble's 'Sun of my soul, thou saviour dear', two
verses of which are sung during the play, contains the line, 'If
some poor wandering child of thine'. Swift denies Vanessa
children, though the spectre of a possible mad child is reinforced
by the' mad old man in the play; he fends off guilt at having

encouraged Stella to settle for 'a cross and ageing man for friend—nothing but that'; Lulu's baby talk may remind us of the nonsense language Swift uses in his *Journal to Stella*, when he chaffs her for losing money at cards in this very room; one thinks also of that savage satire, *A Modest Proposal*. And finally, in contrast with the imagery of Swift's heroic world, we have the Lilliputians of present day Ireland reflected in those attending the séance; for most, even the dreams and hopes have shrunk.

Language and vision also provide parallels and contrast throughout the play. Accents range from the harsh northern tones of the Reverend Johnson to the Dublinese of Corney Patterson, from the educated class of Dr Trench and John Corbet to the more homely, comfortable notes of Mrs Henderson, from Mrs Mallet's southern English to Miss Mackenna's more formal Anglo-Irish; the voices of the living, separated by class, education, and geography, contrast even more sharply with the rhetorical passion of Swift and the simple, yet still eighteenth-century voice of Vanessa. Stella's heroic couplets are set against the loose rhymes of Keble's nineteenth-century hymn. Her words are carved upon the window-pane, but though Dr Trench has shown them to many and doubts whether Corbet will 'make them out in this light', the Cambridge student is the first to recognize them; we have truly lost sight of a more heroic vision. One of Swift's own window-scribblings begins,

> The glass, by lover's nonsense blurred,
> Dims and obscures our sight:
> So when our passions Love hath stirr'd,
> It darkens Reason's light. [26]

Not only do we see through a glass darkly, but where so many of the Abbey Theatre's early plays represented the beckoning spirit just outside the door of cottage or cabin, [30] here the entrance to the world of wonders has narrowed to a window which is closed to many, and the entrance to the sitting-room itself is through a long hallway, far from outdoors. Even the medium, unlike Yeats's earlier plays of possession, is no hawk-woman, no woman of the Sidhe, but a simple woman ignorant of the significance of the forces around and through her, entirely human. She lives in a smaller room above her 'church': is there a further reference here, to the half-dead tree Swift is said to have likened to himself in old age, to Yeats's tower, to a nation dead at the top and haunted twice over? [31] The structure is almost

Shavian in its triadic groupings: three Swifts (aged 51, 54, 78); three settings (the Dublin boarding-house where Stella once played cards, Celbridge where Vanessa waited hopelessly for Swift, the Deanery which becomes the dying Swift's prison); three mediums (Mrs Henderson, Lulu, Swift himself); even the characters on stage group conveniently into threes. This is indeed discussion drama.

From the realistic details of the séance we have constantly been enticed into speculations about the world of Swift in contrast with modern Ireland, and this, of course, has been Yeats's intention. In his last 'Introduction to the Essays', written in 1937, Yeats spoke of realism as 'always topical, it has for public theme the public itself', adding, 'But those themes we share and inherit, so long as they engage our emotions, come first'.[32] *The Words Upon the Window-Pane* manages to combine the qualities of both approaches, for just as the realistic details of a séance draw us into the mystery of the supernatural presence, so the inherited themes of government, freedom, and spiritual fulfilment sweep through a plot about two haunted ghosts. In his 1930 Diary Yeats wrote, 'I would found literature on the three things which Kant thought we must postulate to make life livable—Freedom, God, Immortality'. And elsewhere,

I cannot discover truth by logic unless that logic serve passion, and only then if the logic be ready to cut its own throat, tear out its own eyes ... I must not talk to myself [in abstractions] ... but see myself set in a drama where I struggle to exalt and overcome concrete realities perceived not with mind only but as with the roots of my hair.

And he reminds himself that Swift, among others, 'spoke as it were sword in hand, that they played their part in a unique drama, but played it, as a politician cannot though he stand in the same ranks, with the whole soul'.[33] The play seeks to express, itself a gesture 'sword in hand', what Yeats recognized as Swift's greatness and his failure. A later great play, *Purgatory*, would have in it all he knew about 'this world and the next'; *The Words Upon the Window-Pane* has in it all he cared about this world and the past.

'Swift haunts me; he is always just round the next corner', Yeats wrote in his Introduction to the play.[34] The 'half symbolic image of Jonathan Swift' and the image of Berkeley, he was to write a year later, must 'concern all those who feel a responsibility for the thought of modern Ireland that can take away their sleep'.[35] It had not always been so: an early draft of his autobiographies confesses that he 'knew little of Burke, Swift, Grattan, and nothing of history'.[36] But even then Swift the man intrigued him; an article of 1896 claims, 'he revealed in his writings and his life a more intense nature, a more living temperament than any of his contemporaries'[37], characteristics Yeats would continue to admire forty years later. The language attracted him first. As early as 1893 he delighted in Swift's 'plain and honest speaking';[38] in his preface to Synge's *Poems and Translations*, 1901, he includes among those 'simple sentences that will never die' Swift's epitaph, 'more immortal than his pamphlets, perhaps than his great allegory'.[39] In 1913 he reported to Lady Gregory the success at the Abbey Theatre of *The Dean of St Patrick's*, 'an effective, slightly melodramatic piece of commercial drama' by novelist G.S. Paternoster, but was more excited about the success of his own speech the next night on 'Home Rule and Religion' to a meeting of Irish Protestants. A second play about Swift, *The Drapier Letters* by Arthur Power, was produced at the Abbey in August 1927; it is perhaps to this play Yeats refers in an introduction to *The Midnight Court* when he speaks of the folklore concerning Swift's sexual exploits.[41] But by now Swift was one of Yeats's heroic figures, enscribed in the book of Irish Senate speeches: 'We are the people of Swift, the people of Emmet, the people of Parnell. We have created the most of the modern literature of this country. We have created the best of its political intelligence'.[42] Shortly after that memorable and arrogant speech, yet another play about Swift was published, this time by Lady Gregory's editor at John Murray Limited, Charles Edward Lawrence. Mary FitzGerald argues convincingly that Yeats was familiar with Lawrence's play *Swift and Stella*, and that, bad though it is, he recalled enough of it to use as a model for his own Swift play four years later.[43] Certainly in December 1928 he could write to Lady Gregory, 'I still read Swift' as if continuing a long conversation[44], and by 1930 he was studying Swift so thoroughly that he confided to his Diary, 'I know so much more about Swift than about the saints'.[45]

If not a saint, Swift had indeed become a possible saviour in Yeats's eyes. Looking back at the history of Ireland, he saw in the irascible Dean 'the last passion of the Renaissance'[46] and wrote in his Diary, 'In 1706 or 7 Irish intellect declared its separate identity ... Swift was their De Valera'.[47] Having himself just served six years as a Senator of the Irish Free State, he considered Swift's fourth *Drapier Letter* on the sovereignty of the Irish parliament the definitive statement of the Protestant aristocracy;

his age was 'that one Irish century that escaped from darkness and confusion'.[48] 'I want Protestant Ireland to base some vital part of its culture upon Burke, Swift and Berkeley,' he wrote to Joseph Hone in November 1930,[49] just after his play was completed. And during that year when the spectre of Swift was constantly beside him, while at Coole, for Yeats one of the last great houses still standing (he would dedicate his play to Lady Gregory), 'Swift's Epitaph' was completed:

> Swift has sailed into his rest;
> Savage indignation there
> Cannot lacerate his breast.
> Imitate him if you dare,
> World-besotted traveller; he
> Served human liberty.

Savage indignation, service, human liberty, and daring. But what was that liberty? 'There was something not himself that Swift served. He called it "freedom" but never defined it and thus his passion. Passion is to me the essential', Yeats wrote to Hone.[50] Elsewhere he interpreted Swift's meaning to be a perfect balance in the state between the One, the Few, and the Many.[51] 'The liberty he served was that of intellect, not liberty for the masses but for those who could make it visible'. 'All have "reason" but not all have "the means of exercising it and the materials, the facts and ideas upon which it is exercised", nor have all that have the means "power of attention".'[52] Casting the 'dice of arrogant intellect', Swift passionately committed himself to a life of service to the perfection of nature (the world of Gulliver's Houhynhms) and, like Gulliver,[53] retreated into isolation, stricken finally with the horror of a world—and a nation—ruined because of a counter-movement towards the 'common ivory dice' represented by Vanessa.

'History seems to me a human drama', Yeats confided to that 1930 Diary, 'keeping the classical unities by the clear division of its epochs, turning one way or the other because this man hates or that man loves'.[54] And thus it is Swift's passionate personality through which Yeats chooses to offer us this concept of Ireland's history. Obsessed by that 'passion ennobled by intensity, by endurance, by wisdom', as he was to describe Swift to Wyndham Lewis[55], Yeats sought in turn to exonerate while understanding the tragedy of his hero. 'We should see certain men and women as if at the edge of a cliff, time broken away from their feet'.[56] Even Swift's hatred of sex he saw as inherited, his tragedy and his genius the result of the dryness of his age.[57] In reply to John Corbet's question, then, the madness was of the age, not of the man.[58] But because of his great passion, Swift rose above the age and the threat of future ruin; it is that desperation Yeats celebrates. 'The one heroic sanction is that of the last battle of the Norse gods, of a gay struggle without hope,' he wrote to Sturge Moore in 1929.[59]

It was the expression of that indignation, that 'stringent eloquence' which, Yeats felt, created the political nationality of Ireland. And so in celebrating the spirit of Swift, he celebrates a certain style. 'One delights in his animation and clarity'; he 'wrote for men sitting at table or fireside—from that came his animation and his naturalness'.[60] In *The Battle of the Books* Swift condemned subjectivity; Yeats saw the same weakness in modern poetry; he had fought all his life against that fault in his own verse.[61] Swift thus became a model for the poet as well as for the nation. (Torchiana records a conversation with Oliver Edwards in which Yeats claimed he got his 'later manner from Swift'.[62]) When he came to write his last great prose work, *On the Boiler*, he had Swift's example clearly before him: 'I must lay aside the pleasant paths I have built up for years and seek the brutality, the ill breeding, the barbarism of truth'.[63] He would become the model for the young men of Ireland that Swift, belatedly, had become for him.[64]

Which leads us back, once more, to *The Words Upon the Window-Pane*: written in 'contemporary words and syntax', constructed with the directness and forcefulness that deny subjectivity, yet extending through the passionate image of Swift beyond realism to a greater truth still.[65] After watching a performance of Synge's *Well of the Saints*, Yeats had noted,

how can I help feeling that just as the actor's voice and form enlarge the written words, there are actions or thoughts, could I but find them, that would complete it all? . . . An abstract thinker when he has this relation to concrete reality passes on both the thought and the passion.[66]

He would strive for that same combination of thought and passion he had so long ago recognized in Synge. Now Yeats found himself in greater sympathy with Bernard Shaw than he had ever been before, admitting when he wrote his Roger Casement poems,

I am fighting in those ballads for what I have been fighting all my life, it is our Irish fight though it has nothing to do with this or that country. Bernard Shaw fights with the same object. When somebody talks of justice who knows that justice is accompanied by secret forgery, when an archbishop wants a man to go to the communion table when that man says he is not spiritually fit, then we remember our age-old quarrel against gold braid and ermine, and that our ancestor Swift has gone where 'fierce indignation can lacerate his heart no more', and we go stark, staring mad.[67]

'Why should not old men be mad?' Why not, indeed, for 'indignation is a kind of joy.'[68] We might even, without forcing interpretation, look back to the *Silver Tassie* controversy at the beginning of his Swiftian phase and recognize in his rejection of Sean O'Casey's play a more personal disappointment still. For in comparing this latest play to O'Casey's Dublin trilogy he wrote, 'you were exasperated almost beyond endurance by what you had seen or heard, as a man is by what happens under his window, and you moved us as Swift moved his contemporaries'.[69] In contrast, he felt *The Silver Tassie* was distant, subjective, a world created out of opinion—a far cry indeed from *The Plough and the Stars* which had, like Synge's *Playboy of the Western World*, incited riots. The new Swift had not yet appeared after all.

Was Yeats, then, in his last great period rejecting all that went before? I do not think so, for in this one-act prose play we can find many of the same preoccupations that inform his earlier dance plays. *The Words Upon the Window-Pane* can hardly be called a typical Noh play, even in a Yeatsian interpretation of that form, but it is possible to recognize the same emphasis on aristocratic culture, the climactic revelation of identity, the creation, as Hiro Ishibashi has pointed to, of 'its own time, its own reality', the 'discontinuity of personality', and 'the thought that can be conveyed through the senses'.[70] Just as a ghost in the Noh is often attached to a person or place, so Swift's spirit is drawn to Stella's words on the window; just as the central character in Noh speaks impersonally of himself, so Swift is at three removes from us, the audience; and, just as the appearance of a supernatural character brings spiritual enlightenment, so the agonies and passion of Swift's image satisfy John Corbet, the young seeker after knowledge, and, Yeats hopes, will increase awareness in his modern audience. Finally, as the Noh structure includes a chorus who do not participate in the action, so the séance attendants are helpless witnesses to the scene enacted through Mrs Henderson. 'I call to the eye of the mind' are the opening words of *At the Hawk's Well* (1916); the voices called forth out of a medium's mouth engage both eye and mind.

We might go back further still to two sets of 'First Principles' written before Yeats's first encounter with Noh. The first, published in *Samhain* in 1904, describes what early attracted him to drama: 'a moment of intense life. An action . . . taken out of all other actions . . . reduced to its simplest form, or at any rate as simple a form as it can be brought to without our losing the sense of its place in the world'.[71] The second set of principles was written eight years later but remained unpublished as a private directive to himself:

Not to find one's art by the analysis of language or amid the circumstances of dreams but to live a passionate life, and to express the emotions that find one thus in simple rhythmical language. The words should be the swift natural words that suggest the circumstances out of which they rose.

And he adjures himself to use 'a speech so natural and dramatic that the hearer would feel the presence of a man thinking and feeling'.[72] Surely what he was to recognize in Swift, what he was to find in the Noh drama, what he was to strive for in his translations of Sophocles, he had always sought. And, as the Japanese form freed his drama from all that had troubled him in modern theatre, so the 'half symbolic image of Swift' released him into further experiment, the joyful audacious creation of Crazy Jane (perhaps herself a borrowing from the eighteenth century[73]), the persona of the 'wild old wicked man' with 'an old man's frenzy'. Mischievously he wrote to Olivia Shakespear in 1927 of his latest poems, 'You will see that I am still of opinion that only two topics can be of the least interest to a serious and studious mind—sex and the dead';[74] and, to another friend, of *On the Boiler*, 'This is the proposition on which I write:' 'There is now overwhelming evidence that man stands between two eternities, that of his family and that of his soul''.[75]

But the joy and certainty are not unmixed with horror; *saevo indignatio* exacts it price. Charles Stewart Parnell must pass through 'Jonathan Swift's dark grove' and there pluck 'bitter wisdom' ('Parnell's Funeral'). The intellect demands purification, a moral frenzy that can itself turn immoral: we must remember the old man of *Purgatory*, who also deprives future generations of life. Swift, product of 'a dry age', denied in himself that which would have made him a whole being: Vanessa represents not only a concept of common democracy dragging the intellect and age down, she is also a woman, a product of the mire and blood of human veins, and in denying her, Swift denies a part of himself. The poem 'Blood and the Moon', written three years before his play about Swift, says it all:

> Swift beating on his breast in sibylline frenzy blind
> Because the heart in his blood-sodden breast had
>   dragged him down into mankind.

What then of Stella? She does not speak, nor is she present. We have only her words written on the window-pane—reflecting in their elegance and wit what she had learned from Swift until, in Yeats's opinion, she became the better poet. Through them only does Stella manifest herself.[76] There is irony in the spirit's recognition that Stella did not live to close his eyes as she had promised, and the mad old man watching his earlier self must know that sorrow and live again that isolation. A greater, more painful irony still, is ours to experience—for Stella's artistic creation is, finally, all there is or can be, the one monument of unchanging intellect; and if that is so, then the soul of Swift addresses, seeks comfort and confirmation of his choice of life, in a Void. If this be so, Swift's spirit will continue for generations to come in the incomplete, unforgiving, unknowledgeable state of the 'Return', much as the Old Man's mother is destined to do in *Purgatory*. If this be so, then *The Words Upon the Window-Pane* is Yeats's most tragic drama, echoing the grandeur and horror of the life of Oedipus, whose story just two years earlier Yeats finally succeeded in telling 'in the syntax and vocabulary of common personal speech'[77] for the modern theatre. Of the first performance of *Sophocles' King Oedipus* at the Abbey Theatre he reported to Olivia Shakespear, 'I had but one overwhelming emotion, a sense as of the actual presence in a terrible sacrament of the god.'[78] For Jonathan Swift, and for Ireland, the terrible sacrament is not yet over.

O BLISS! O POOP-POOP! O MY! O MY!

STEWART SANDERSON

Bibliographers love arcana. So do university examiners. Few things are better calculated to win a Ph.D. external's approving nod than the inclusion in the thesis bibliography of some pirated edition knocked out in defiance of copyright by an inexpert typist in Edgbaston and circulated in cyclostyled copies; or the notice of an early poem published in an obscure and short-lived magazine; or the citation of a polemic pamphlet appearing under an only once used *nom de plume et de guerre*. Such things bring simple joy to practitioners of the often useful, usually harmless, and, in academic thesis-land, always necessary exercise of bibliographical study.

It is characteristic of Derry Jeffares's generous temperament that in his own record of publication he has made it possible for one of his admirers to astonish the literary world by drawing scholarly attention to such a bibliographical rarity. Few critics familiar with his work on Yeats or on Restoration drama, one imagines, are conversant with his first published essay: yet its very title affirms the syzygy of two of his abiding passions, while the text embraces a third; for the essay is illustrated by an inset pencil drawing from the author's own hand. 'If Cars Could Write', by A. Norman Jeffares[1], may not have made the *Cambridge Bibliography of English Literature*, but at least it does not pass unnoticed in this volume of essays presented to him by his friends, pupils and colleagues.

A work of considerable imagination, the essay, narrative in mode, is an autobiographical piece written in the persona of a car competing in what I take to be an Irish Grand Prix race at the Phoenix Park circuit in Dublin. Somewhat breathless in pace, as befits the subject, and not always conforming to the prescriptions of Standard British English (a trait shared with other Anglo-Irish writers and, in the punctuational use of the

174

apostrophe, with as English an author as Evelyn Waugh[2]), it recounts the car's journey to the pits, towed by a Bugatti; the final preparations for the race; and in the course of the contest exciting duels with various cars including an Aston Martin and 'a red Italian', which I conjecture to be a supercharged Alfa-Romeo 1750cc, though whether it is indeed a Zagato-bodied two-seater or the larger engined *monoposto* Type B is not deducible from the text. These are all, at any rate, vehicles of marque and worthy opponents for the authorial car, which from iconographic evidence appears to be a rare model of Delage[3]. Driven with élan, sportsmanship and good manners (the author goes out of his way to comment on the courtesy displayed on different occasions by the competing drivers), the racing cars hurtle round the Gough and Mountjoy corners and accelerate exhilaratingly along the straights. But although the race ends sadly for the narrator, lying in second place when a feed-pipe fractures and a small fire breaks out (happily to be quickly extinguished), the essay does not terminate in dramatised self-pity. Instead it comes to rest on a note of philosophic resignation and phlegmatic good temper.

Was it Wordsworth who wrote something about the child being father of the man? One does not really need to be deeply versed in the kinds of critical theory that deal with text and sub-text, intention and execution, surface and deep structure, to recognise the characteristic and perennial qualities of the author in this somewhat neglected early work. And his artistic draughtsmanship is also clearly recognisable in the illustration, foreshadowing numerous later compositions interpolated in Senate minutes, British Council memoranda, and agenda papers for meetings of the Arts Council of Great Britain and the National Book League.

It seems legitimate to ask what formative influences may have lain behind this seminal *oeuvre*, apprentice piece though it be. They are, I suggest, twofold—the influence of literary experience and the influence of life in the Jeffares family ambience.

The latter, in Derry's early years, included amongst its appurtenances a torpedo-bodied Citroen, presage perhaps of the *traction-avant*, known to a younger TV-film-of-the-book nurtured generation as a Maigret-type, Citroen he was later to possess in South Australia. This taste for foreign vehicles, noted throughout his life, was no doubt reinforced by his family's peripheral interest in the agency for a Belgian brand of sparking plugs, yet another continuing strand in his personal predilections and Francophilia.

Along with these material domestic influences, however, there were the spiritual ones, not least the imaginative world entered through the portals of literature. A close re-reading of *The Wind in the Willows* reveals the extraordinary potential of this children's classic in the formation of character, ideals and attitudes. Mr Toad, destined to become an enthusiastic if wayward, not to say lapsarian, motorist, is before his conversion a paradigm of many of the qualities one would wish a boy to emulate: 'Early or late he's always the same fellow. Always good-tempered, always glad to see you, always sorry when you go.' And the apocalyptic vision Toad and his companions experienced on the highroad must surely have left an indelible impression on the sensibilities of the young Irish lad.

Glancing back, they saw a small cloud of dust, with a dark centre of energy, advancing on them at incredible speed, while from out the dust a faint 'Poop-poop!' wailed like an uneasy animal in pain. Hardly regarding it, they turned to resume their conversation, when in an instant (as it seemed) the peaceful scene was changed, and with a blast of wind and a whirl of sound that made them jump for the nearest ditch, It was on them! The 'poop-poop' rang with a brazen shout in their ears, they had a moment's glimpse of an interior of glittering plate-glass and rich morocco, and the magnificent motor-car, immense, breath-snatching, passionate, with its pilot tense and hugging his wheel, possessed all earth and air for the fraction of a second, flung an enveloping cloud of dust that blinded and enwrapped them utterly, and then dwindled to a speck in the far distance, changed back into a droning bee once more.[4]

Fortunately, however, this fictional introduction to the poetry of motion did not lead the youthful reader into the excesses and extravagances of the undisciplined Mr Toad. Nor was his good sense subverted by episodes in the detective adventures of Sexton Blake and Dixon Hawke, whose assistant, Tommy, was much habituated on the open road to giving his master's long grey car its head. Life encompassed letters; not the other way round. The flowery track which lay spread before the reader of *The Wind in the Willows* led on by way of classics at Trinity College, Dublin, to English Literature with the clever men at Oxford who know all that there is to be knowed; but whatever their eminence, one may justifiably misdoubt their ability to match the detailed and authoritative scholarship of which Derry Jeffares had already made himself master in a second field of learning.

It has sometimes struck the present writer that the literary response of those clever dons may have been impoverished, indeed in a new generation of dons may yet be so, by the limitations of their automobilistic experience and knowledge.

What subtleties of suspense may they not miss, in reading of Hannay's race northwards in his Bentley to the Island of Sheep, pursued by conspirators in a Stutz Bearcat, through sheer inability to appreciate comparisons of acceleration, road-holding, and refuelling delays calculated as a function of petrol consumption *vis-à-vis* tank capacity? What do they make of the yellow Rolls-Royces and Hispano-Suizas of Dornford Yates's novels? Do they clearly see their slightly raffish tincture and the implications of its reflection on the author's social cast (or caste) of mind? Have they any inkling of the time it took Lord Hovenden to reach sufficient speed in his 30/98 Vauxhall Velox to declare his love to Mrs Terebinth? And does the music of those magical names—Rover, Humber, Hupmobile—orchestrated amid the Surrey pines by the late Poet Laureate reverberate as richly for them as for those who have assiduously cultivated the fruits of a more liberal historical education?[5]

These are not in their implications altogether idle questions, though some may think them so.

What is however beyond dispute is that Derry Jeffares has both put a good deal more into, and taken a good deal more out of, motoring than motoring has taken out of him. The range of cars he has owned and driven is quite remarkable, from the Ford Y in which he and Jeanne travelled the West of Ireland when he was drawing the chapter tailpieces for his first book[6], to a Rolls 20 tourer, a Léon Bollet, an Alvis 12/50 equipped with twin cut-glass decanters, various Morrises, Austins and badge-engineered MGs, a succession of Simcas, Peugeots, Volvos and Volkswagens, to his current combination (at the time of writing, but for how long?) of a diesel-engined Peugeot 205 and a Passat with, unpredictably, an automatic gearbox. May the memory of these cars with their associations, and the anticipation of cars yet to come, continue to give him lasting pleasure.

When one reflects on all this, it seems in some ways a pity that he decided to go in for English Literature. With his wide and deep automotive scholarship, his eye for an object, and his ability with his hands, he would have made an excellent recruit to the museum profession. Where would such a career have taken him, one wonders. Doubtless from Keeperships of Engineering and Technology to the Directorship of the Science Museum, with, instead of an honorary doctorate and college fellowship, honorary curatorships at Beaulieu and of the Schlumpf collection of Bugattis in its heyday.

But that *is* idle speculation; and any potential loss to the museum profession is amply compensated by the gain to English studies in so many universities around the world. Besides, his passion for motor cars has been neither selfish nor wasted. Even if one sets aside all his other multifarious contributions in his chosen fields, there are duller and less effective ways of kindling the enthusiasm of literature students, and firing their imagination, than by enlivening one's lectures with metaphorical reference to revving up, wheelspin, and getting into overdrive. Particularly when the metaphors are deployed with intellectual precision.

WHO WAS PETER GRIMES?

JAMES SUTHERLAND

Not much is known about the sources of Crabbe's tales, but it is generally assumed that he made use of such incidents and situations as had come his way, either during his early years in Suffolk or in his later life as a parish priest. As he told Mrs Leadbeater, there was not one of his many characters 'of whom I had not in my mind the original'. As often as not, no doubt, the original would be someone he had known or known about; but in the preface to *Tales of the Hall* he notes that he owed the story of Lady Barbara to 'a fair friend', and that of Ellen to another friend whose conversation 'it is one of the greatest "pleasures of my memory" to recall' (i.e. Samuel Rogers). At all events, a firm basis of fact seems to have been essential for any human story that was to absorb his attention and give him the necessary impetus to write. 'I do not know that I could paint merely from my own fancy,' he told Mrs Leadbeater. But he had rarely presented his characters exactly as they were in real life. 'I was obliged in some cases to take them from their real situations, and in one or two instances to change even their sex, and, in many, the circumstances.'[1] . . . 'I wish to suggest that some such transformation may have occurred in the tale of 'Peter Grimes'.

The case for Peter Grimes being an Aldborough fisherman rests firmly enough on what can only be the poet's own testimony. In a note to the poem George Crabbe the younger states:

The original of Peter Grimes was an old fisherman of Aldborough, while Mr. Crabbe was practising there as a surgeon. He had a succession of apprentices from London, and a certain sum with each. As the boys all disappeared under circumstances of strong suspicion, the man was warned by some of the principal inhabitants, that if another followed in like manner, he should certainly be charged with murder.[2]

Although in *The Village* Crabbe characterised the inhabitants of eighteenth-century Aldborough as 'a bold, artful, surly, savage race', one might have thought that the death or disappearance of three boys in succession should have evoked from 'some of the principal inhabitants' rather more than a warning to the fisherman that one day he might go too far. Whether this is so or not, the man in question clearly existed, and was identified in a manuscript note made by Edward Fitzgerald as one Tom Brown. [3]

This may seem to settle the matter. But it is just possible that when Crabbe was writing his poem the misdeeds of another sadistic fisherman may have blended in his mind with the Aldborough original. Early in the year 1733 John Bennet of Hammersmith, fisherman, was indicted for the murder of his boy George Main, aged about 11, 'by beating him with a Stick called a Tiller, on the Head, Back, Shoulder and Arms, and thereby giving him several Mortal Wounds'. This happened 'on the High-Seas, near Sheerness', and the boy died of his wounds on 2 December, 1732, 'in the Hamlet of Hammersmith'. The trial was fully reported in *The Proceedings at the Sessions of the Peace, and Oyer and Terminer . . . Number II.*, 1733, taking up over four pages in double columns. [4] However rare those *Proceedings* are today, they were popular reading in the eighteenth century among high and low. Crabbe might have found copies or sets in the library of the Duke of Rutland when he was living at Belvoir, or he could equally well have read them in his father's house, or have come across them on a London bookstall. There is even some reason to believe that such reading had a special appeal for Crabbe. Replying in 1813 to a letter from Sir Walter Scott, who had said he was accustomed to 'fag as a clerk' in the Supreme Court at Edinburgh, Crabbe assured him: 'I have often thought I should like to read reports, that is, brief histories of extraordinary cases, with the judgments. If that is what is meant by reports, such reading must be pleasant. . . . ' [5] *The Proceedings of Oyer and Terminer*, with their verbatim reports of the evidence given by witnesses, certainly provided the kind of factual reading that would have pleased and interested this poet.

In the comparison that follows between the behaviour of Peter Grimes to his three apprentices and that of John Bennet to his eleven-year-old boy various resemblances will be found, some perhaps no more than incidental to such inhuman circumstances, but others in which the coincidence seems more unusual.

(1) Crabbe presents Peter Grimes to his readers as a confirmed

sadist, taking pleasure in the maltreatment of the three boys who came under his power:

> He wished for one to trouble and control;
> He wanted some obedient boy to stand
> And bear the blow of his outrageous hand.

His favourite punishment was to beat his boys with a rope. John Bennet was apparently made in the same mould. At his trial the first witness, George Sugg, described the brutal way in which the Hammersmith fisherman punished his feeble and half-starved apprentice for his mistakes. On one occasion, having caught some fish, Bennet decided to sell them at Feversham:

Sugg. We set the Boy on Shore with the Fish, and then put off again: but the Shore being very slippery the Boy let the Fish fall, upon which The Prisoner desir'd me to put to again; he went to the Boy, and beat him with a Rope, and return'd to the boat, when presently the Boy fell down again; the Prisoner again went a-shore and beat him, and so return'd a second time to the Boat; the Boy happen'd to fall a third time, upon which the Prisoner went a-shore once more, and he and the Boy went away together.

(2) Crabbe returns several times to the failure of Peter to give his boys adequate food. The first prentice found 'his efforts punished, and his food refused'. ('His efforts punished' calls up the picture of Bennet's boy slithering on the quay and spilling the fish.) Starved of food the first prentice was 'compelled ... by need to steal'. The third prentice lived as long as he did only because compassionate townspeople gave him the food that Peter denied him. Bennet's boy fared even worse. On Sugg's evidence he

threaten'd to beat the Boy for asking some Body at Feversham for a bit of Bread. Says the Boy, I hope there was no harm in asking for a little Bread when I was very hungry? Well, says the Prisoner, I won't beat you now, but I'll give it you by and by when we come into Queenborough-Grounds ... Then the Prisoner took a 2 Inch Rope, and splitting it into 7 Strands, he ty'd 3 Knots in each Strand, and stripping the Boy stark naked (except only his Shoes and Stockings) he whipt him with this Cat of Nine Tails for, I believe, full three Quarters of an Hour by the Clock.

(Peter Grimes, too, treated his third prentice in the same brutal fashion, enforcing his 'rude command' with 'knotted rope'.) Three days later Bennet 'beat the Boy again because the Boy had eat more Victuals than he intended to let him. '*Sirrah*!' says he, '*if you offer to eat a bit of Bread without asking my leave, I'll strip your Skin over your Shoulders*'. A later witness, John Dafforn, giving evidence about the final and fatal attack with the tiller, testified that on that November day, when there was a very hard frost, he saw the boy with nothing on but a serge waistcoat and breeches. The boy told him he had been working all night and all next day in the cold, and had had nothing to eat. Asked if he thought the boy's wounds had caused his death, Dafforn replied: 'Wounds and want of looking after ... for we must all dye if we have nothing to eat or keep us warm.'

(3) Crabbe goes out of his way to emphasise the muted response of Peter's neighbours to what was going on in his boat. None enquired 'how Peter used the rope', and some, on hearing cries, said calmly, 'Grimes is at his exercise'. The same tendency to leave ill alone, and not to become involved, appears in the report of Bennet's trial. The most painful example of this will be found in the evidence given by Sugg, some of which has already been quoted. Over a period of some weeks this man sat in Bennet's boat witnessing repeated beatings of his boy, but making no attempt to stop them. When the cat o'nine tails was being used on him at Queenborough Grounds, the boy's ordeal might have been even more prolonged if two fishermen had not pulled up alongside. According to Sugg, one of them asked, 'Why don't you kill the Boy outright? You had better hurl him over-board at once, and put him out of his Misery.' Upon that, Bennet 'left off Beating the Boy, and made him put on his Cloaths again.' Yet if this intervention by the two fishermen gave the boy a temporary respite, it may be too charitable to call them good Samaritans: the wording of their protest suggests rather that the commotion taking place in Bennet's boat, together with the cries of the victim, was distracting them from their fishing. Another witness, who had seen Bennet 'beat the Boy barbarously with a Tiller', told the court that he had protested. Going perhaps beyond the normal limits of his vocabulary, he claimed that he had 'ridicu'd' the prisoner. "You Villain! You Rascal you!" says I, "your Master never served you so!"' Yet from first to last the attitude of most of those who saw Bennet 'at *his* exercise' seems to have been one of cautious non-interference.

(4) The most cogent reason for supposing that Crabbe may have had the 1733 trial in mind when writing his poem is the explanation given by Peter of how his second apprentice met his death:

He climb'd the main-mast and then fell below.

When he spoke those words Peter was apparently on trial for his life, for Crabbe suddenly introduces 'the jury' who 'were long in doubt', but who finally dismissed him with a warning to keep his hatchway closed when he had boys who climbed:

> This hit the conscience, and he colour'd more
> Than for the closest questions put before.

Peter's claim that his boy died accidentally is similar to that made by Bennet when he returned to Hammersmith with a dead boy in *his* boat. At his trial, Robert Davis, a waterman, testified that on Friday, 2 December, about 2 a.m., he had met Bennet at the waterside near Hammersmith, and Bennet had asked him to carry some fish to Billingsgate for him.

> *Davis.* Says I, 'How came you to bring this Fish by Billingsgate last Night, and now want me to carry it back thither? "Why," says he, "something has happened."

What had happened was the death of his apprentice, and Bennet, presumably unwilling to tie up at Billingsgate with a dead body in his boat, had rowed on to Hammersmith. But one of the witnesses for the defence, Henry Savery, told the court about a conversation he had with Bennet about eleven o'clock that same morning:

> *Savery.* I met the Prisoner in his Boat by Greenwich, and says I, 'John, where's your Boy?' 'Why,' says he, 'I am come to a sad Misfortune, I sent him up the Mast at Old-Haven in Essex, and he fell off and killed himself.'

It would therefore appear that between 2 a.m. and 11 a.m. on that Friday morning Bennet had put together the story he was afterwards to repeat whenever he was asked what had happened to his boy. It did not satisfy everyone. Sugg, who was admittedly a hostile witness, told the court that it was impossible the boy could have been killed by falling from the mast-head since Bennet's mast was so low 'that a Man may stand upon his Boat's Head and reach the top of it'. Later the defence managed to produce a witness who said the mast was fifteen feet high, and that Sugg was a liar.

There is, then, a marked resemblance between the stories told by Bennet and Peter Grimes. Each returned with a dead boy in his boat, and each had to account for an ugly wound in his boy's head. Both offered the same explanation of a fall from the mast, and Peter backed up his by showing the corpse and pointing to the blow. It is worth recalling here that when Peter was lying delirious on his parish bed it was the death of his second apprentice that tortured his fevered brain. 'It was the fall . . . ', he kept muttering, 'I never struck a blow . . . On oath, he fell, it struck him to the brain.' Three of Peter's boys had died or disappeared. Is there then some significance in the fact that the one who preyed on his guilty mind was the one that he said had fallen from the mainmast? If so, was it because this boy's fate also preyed on Crabbe's mind, and did so because he had at some time read and never forgotten the grisly trial of John Bennet for the murder of *his* boy? There are, it is true, some minor differences in the two cases. Bennet asserted that he himself had sent his boy up the mast, and that he fell and killed himself, presumably on the hard deck: Peter claimed that his boy was skylarking and fell into the boat's well,

> Where fish were living kept, and where the boy
> (So reason'd men) could not himself destroy.

But the fall into the boat's well is clearly one of several adroit touches by which Crabbe seems willing to establish Peter's guilt in the mind of the reader. The poet, as we have seen, felt free to 'change the circumstances'.

(5) To dwell on more minute resemblances would only weaken a case that most readers may consider to be weak enough already, but I will end with another possible coninicidence. When Bennet's boy died Bennet was, as we have seen, on his way to Billingsgate to sell his fish, but arranged to have his catch taken down-river from Hammersmith to Billingsgate next day. When Peter's third apprentice died Peter had got such a heavy catch on board that he decided to sell the fish at 'London-mart', presumably Billingsgate. But on the way there the seas grew rough, 'the boat was leaky, and the time was long', and the boy expired. *If* (for the last time) Crabbe had in mind the report of the Bennet trial, that might account for a Suffolk fisherman going all the long way to Billingsgate to sell his fish.

Bennet, charged with murder, was convicted of manslaughter. That was no doubt the best a well-meaning jury could do on the evidence presented in court. The Hammersmith fisherman had clearly contributed to the death of his apprentice, and may actually have killed him as charged with a fatal blow from the tiller; but there was no positive proof that the boy had not fallen from the top of the mast. One can only hope that John Bennet was transported to one of the least pleasant of the American colonies.

METHOD AND DECORUM IN DON JUAN

ALASTAIR W. THOMSON

I

Much of Byron's poetry is intensely conscious of time. Sometimes it is the weight of ages, more often the movements of a creature caught in time: sardonic, or wistful, or anguished, but always with the fullest understanding of what time gives and takes. It is difficult to think of him, in fact, without thinking of him in time, or at particular periods of his life. The cancelled stanza of Canto I of *Don Juan*, 'I would to heaven that I were so much clay', which Thomas Moore used as a headpiece for the 1833 edition of the poem, is characteristic of this, and of much else: the despairing cry for insensitivity, the rapid detailing ('blood, bone, marrow, passion, feeling') of what makes him despair, then the past which will not pass away, and the future no sooner spoken of than swallowed up in what he calls elsewhere (XV. i) the interjection of the present. Moore's use of the stanza was appropriate, not only because it is a remarkable expression of weariness and self-disgust, but because one senses in it something of the mature judgment which he claims for himself in a notable passage at the end of Canto I. According to Medwin, he said his epic satire was 'an epic as much in the spirit of the day as the *Iliad* was in Homer's', and that love, religion, and politics formed the argument.[1] The world is that of Europe and Russia just before the revolution which would end in the Holy Alliance. He is writing of it a generation later, when France has failed, and when England, as he says in Canto X, has lost her chance of greatness, being only the false friend of liberty, the 'first of slaves', and a gaoler as much a victim of the lock as his prisoners. Elsewhere in Europe, there is a casual and vivid evocation, in Juan's journey through Poland and Prussia, of salt-mines and iron yokes, of dull enslaving metals, and cloudy useless philosophy. (The part played by Russia is significant, whether in the narrative's 'race of polish'd boors' under Catherine, or in the bullying Czar of one of his digressions. The European fear of Russia had been growing for many years; brought into Europe by the Napoleonic wars, she now began to think of herself as Europe's saviour, with all that that implies.) Byron seems to have looked forward to more revolution, by which power would pass from tyrants to enlightened aristocrats and responsible thinkers. But this optimism, such as it is, is qualified by that conviction of man's fallen state which is hardly ever absent from his poetry. The optimism and the pessimism, man's good and bad, mingle in *Don Juan* in a wry acceptance that things cannot be other than what he describes, in the *Detached Thoughts* of 1821, as a jar of atoms.

It is probably because of this that his hopes for the future tend to be more concrete than those of his great contemporaries. In Canto X Newton ('that proverb of the mind', as he calls him in VII) inaugurates the age of the machine, and is described as 'the sole mortal who could grapple, / Since Adam, with a fall, or with an apple'. 'Man fell with apples, and with apples rose': since man spends so much of himself on sexuality, the ironic reference to what confirms the fall is hardly gratuitous, and the stanza goes on to state the arrival of the new technological man, who may or may not repair something of the past. Wordsworth's description of Newton's statue at Cambridge is like a reflection of Wordsworth himself: 'Newton, with his prism and silent face, / The marble index of a mind for ever / Voyaging through strange seas of Thought, alone'. Byron's Newton suggests another type of modern man, and of what the future may hold for man, inspiring him now in his own task of poetry; a lesser task, as he admits in stanza iii, in which he yet 'would skim / The ocean of eternity', perhaps with a glance at Newton's famous remark, which he quotes in VII.v, that he 'felt only "like a youth / Picking up shells by the great ocean—Truth"'. It seems that poetry, though only mimetic, has its place in this world where man, condemned by the fall to be the creature of circumstance, struggles with or submits to his fate, his advances only a stage in another progress towards catastrophe. The struggling or submission; the hope that persists within a great process of regression ('even worlds miscarry, when too oft they pup, / And every new creation hath decreased / In size, from overworking the material', he remarks, in IX. xxxix); the images of the fall, and the necessary scepticism; the inability to *know* which he continually returns to: what sets Byron apart from so many of his contemporaries is not so much, as is sometimes assumed, his knowledge of the world, as his knowledge of himself and his own contradictions, his ability to hold these contradictions together in synthesis, and his refusal to be deceived either by himself or by others. The last action in Greece is part of the legend, but it is the mingling in him of act and dream, past and future (the wonder if man will war with comets, and leave to the next cycle a legend of Titans warring with gods, is typical) which makes him seem more substantial than his contemporaries. His descriptions of poetry have the same weight and substance: poetry as 'the feeling of a Former world and Future,' his poetry as 'the *dream* of my sleeping passions.'[2]

Perhaps it is no longer very easy for us to understand the authority of the epic satire which Byron revived in the age of subjectivity and sublimity, which may be why we have recently heard so much about *Don Juan* being in the tradition of the English novel. So far as the corrective of satire is concerned, the present age sometimes seems unable to go much farther than the absurd, as in the last image of the Buñuel film, of the ostrich looking closely and idiotically at the camera, and the camera looking as closely and idiotically at the ostrich. No doubt a predilection for the meaningless, as distinct from the recognition that we can know nothing, is a natural reaction from earlier insistences on meaning in and moral life given to every natural form, as in *The Prelude*. Some comparison with Wordsworth's near contemporary epic is hardly to be avoided. *The Prelude* is visionary and recreative. It is also in some sense the product of the eager reaching out to 'some work of glory' which Wordsworth describes in the first book. Byron's rejection of glory in *Don Juan* reflects a different purpose. But as epic *Don Juan*, like *The Prelude*, has a definable moral purpose; Medwin reports him as substantiating his claim for it as epic by referring not only to its argument, but to its moral. The world of Byron's poem, so far from being one of strange visitings and great unifying ideas, is a world where things fall out according to the laws of appetite, in which a hero, whose natural advantages enable him to triumph by following his natural instincts, figures in a corrupt society which (one supposes) will destroy him. The 'Fierce warres and faithful loues shall moralize my song' of *The Faerie Queene* is transformed.

> 'Fierce loves and faithless wars'—I am not sure
> If this be the right reading—'tis no matter;

The fact's about the same, I am secure;
I sing them both ... (VII.viii)

This is the conclusion to the short exordium to Canto VII, on the siege of Ismail, which begins 'O Love! O glory!', and goes on to describe the poem as 'A nondescript and ever-varying rhyme, / A versified Aurora Borealis, / Which flashes o'er a waste and icy clime', then to justify it before those who have accused him of mocking 'human power and virtue, and all that'. Byron quotes precedents, and scourges his detractors in some of the harshest words in the poem ('Dogs, or men!—for I flatter you in saying / That ye are dogs ... '), before recasting Spenser, and turning again to his narrative with insolent authority: 'I sing them both, and am about to batter / A town which did a famous siege endure'. It is the anger at the cant of his detractors, as well as the recognition of nothingness, that is the context of this description. The 'ever-varying rhyme' means nothingness and illusion, and the waste it shines over, as one commentator remarks, is the contemporary ice-age: an age of migratory wars, of slavery, and cant.[3]

The age has forgotten virtue and heroism, and has replaced them by verbal notions of virtue and sublimity; in some quarters, by ideas about the complacently solitary poet as hero. 'Human power and virtue, and all that' has to do, not so much with the growing evangelical spirit in England, as with the Rousseauistic *vertu* of the eighteenth century, which had been embraced by sympathisers like Robespierre. Byron remarked that the sentimental anatomy of Rousseau and Madame de Staël, with its pretensions to 'Optimism,' sapped the principles, and it is reasonably clear how the age of self-righteous abstracting sensibility became the age of political inhumanity. He rejects systematising, and the provincial sublime, with much else, as mere verbal decorum.[4] It is not surprising that in the 'Dedication' a reference in stanza iv to Wordsworth's 'new system' in his *Excursion* is followed six stanzas later by what amounts to a revalidation of the word 'sublime', with reference to Milton. (His 'fallen in evil days on evil tongues' is from *Paradise Lost* VII. 25–26; in the 'Prospectus' to *The Recluse* Wordsworth had quoted, with reference to his own poetry, the 'fit audience find, though few' of line 31.) Finding in Southey, Coleridge, and Wordsworth political trimming, and the arrogance which is the effect of provincial seclusion, he leaves to them 'the winged steed' of Pegasus, to wander with the 'pedestrian Muses' of Horace's satire.[5] He takes up the theme again in Canto III, after the trimming poet of the Cyclades, and after a 'let me to my story', turns back, almost compulsively, to Wordsworth and the *épopée* in several harsh stanzas, before the final curt 'T'our tale'. The names of the Lakers are 'the very Botany Bay in moral geography'; Wordsworth pretends new things, but his virgin birth is only a dropsy; he writes 'pedlar poems', which 'from the bathos' vast abyss / Float [ ] scumlike uppermost'. Readers of Wordsworth formed by the several *Preludes*, or by powerful reconsiderations of 'Simon Lee', or by scholarly ideas of Romantic apocalypse, tend to react angrily to this. (Some years earlier, though condemning 'the Pedlar's portion' of *The Excursion*, he had spoken to John Murray of Wordsworth's 'powers to do about any thing', and to Leigh Hunt of the natural talent spilt over *The Excursion*, but lying on rocks or sands.)[6] But our admiration for Wordsworth's greatest poetry sometimes makes us forget how much of it is dull, or eccentric. Byron was not the only contemporary of Wordsworth who regretted his egotism, and his perverseness. When he dismisses Wordsworth's system-making by describing him as 'that pedlar-praising son of a bitch', his comment is not really very different, except in style, from some of Coleridge's strictures: 'Is there any one word ... attributed to the pedlar ... characteristic of a *pedlar*?'[7] Obviously the Wordsworth of *The Excursion* and the Byron of *Don Juan* are nearly antithetical. But the real vulgarity, or absence of decorum, often seems to be in Wordsworth, not Byron.

II

The 'Prospectus' to *The Recluse* is spoken by 'the transitory Being that beheld / This Vision'; the narrator of *Don Juan* is the man who wishes us to believe that romance, the 'sole world' of the heart, has been replaced in him by judgment. Much of *The Prelude*, with its 'I was lost' and 'I am lost', is concerned with the visionary apprehension of truth. In its closing lines, Wordsworth looks forward to the redemption of mankind, and his own part in it; he and Coleridge will instruct men how 'the mind of man becomes / A thousand times more beautiful than the earth / On which he dwells'. Byron, while continually regretting that things are as they are, has only a qualified belief in what the mind of man may become, and the truth he is capable of perceiving. It seems to be the bedrock of his thinking in *Don Juan* that nothing

can be known, that 'still the spouseless virgin *Knowledge* flies'.
The rapid accumulation of similes that sometimes takes up most
of a stanza may represent a despair of knowledge or possession,
as much as a Lucretian delight in the forms of life. (His insistence
on accuracy is perhaps significant: Wordsworth, defending his
leech-gatherer to Sara Hutchinson, speaks of the single 'figure
presented in the most naked simplicity possible'; Byron, more
concerned with plurality and 'things', comments on Wordsworth's inaccurate descriptions in *The Excursion*.[8]) The con-
comitant is the difficulty of action, and the end of pleasure in
ennui: the woe of undressing after a rout or dinner, next only to
the woe of dressing for them; the dry reversal of *perdidi diem* in 'I
wish they'd state how many they have gain'd'.

> The evaporation of a joyous day
>   Is like the last glass of champagne, without
> The foam which made its virgin bumper gay;
>   Or like a system coupled with a doubt;
> Or like a soda bottle when its spray
>   Has sparkled and let half its spirit out;
> Or like a billow left by storms behind,
>   Without the animation of the wind;
>
> Or like an opiate, which brings troubled rest,
>   Or none; or like—like nothing that I know
> Except itself;—such is the human breast ...
>   (XVI. ix, x)

'Or like a system coupled with a doubt': the unexpected
'system', between the parallel images of champagne and soda,
suggests a mind working restlessly, and to no effect. After a rush
of similes, the *ennui* of the end of pleasure is indescribable; like
the ambrosial sin of first and passionate love in Canto I, it stands
alone.

The passage is from Canto XVI, where Juan, in some respects
the plaything of women, though a finished courtier, is soon to
become the lover of the Duchess of Fitz-Fulke, with the promise
of a more dangerous involvement to follow. Much of *Don Juan*
has to do with male helplessness, of which there is a continual
reminder in the dry use of the word 'gentlemen'. The gentlemen
of the poem are predestined to destruction. 'Single gentlemen
who would be double'; 'Thus gentlemen may run upon a shoal';
'Full many an eager gentleman oft rues / His haste'; 'An honest
gentleman on his return / May not have the good fortune of

Ulysses'; 'Gentlemen must sometimes risk their skin / For that sad tempter, a forbidden woman'; 'Gentlemen, whose ladies take / Leave to o'erstep the written rights of women. . . . ' The original instance is Juan's father, Don José: 'a mortal of the careless kind', who was 'Oft in the wrong, and never on his guard'.

> It was a trying moment that which found him
> Standing alone beside his desolate hearth,
>   Where all his household gods lay shiver'd round him:
> No choice was left his feelings or his pride,
> Save death or Doctors' Commons—so he died.

(I. xxxvi)

(How far 'trying' is a mockery of the polite usage which conceals the sense of *épreuve* is difficut to say: the experience was Byron's own, which may affect the usage here.) 'A better cavalier ne'er mounted horse, / Or, being mounted, e'er got down again' acts out the vacancy of 'cavalier' in the modern world, perhaps with a glance at the opening lines of the *Orlando Furioso* of Ariosto: 'Le Donne, i Cavalier'! l'arme, gli amori, / Le Cortesie, l'audaci imprese io canto.' In Canto I, as in much of what follows, the hapless gentleman or cavalier is directed by woman as the agent of nature. As Don José is the original instance of Byron's male, his wife Inez, Juan's mother, is that of the female. The principal actors in I are the unremarkable Alfonso and the sixteen-year-old Juan on the one hand, Inez and Alfonso's wife, the sentimental dishonest Julia, on the other. (So far as the minor characters are concerned, Julia's knowing maid is like a caricature, whereas the prying snub-nosed lawyer hardly qualifies as a man, far less a gentleman.) The impression we have is that gentlemen, whether of fifty or sixteen, are clay in women's hands. Inez desires 'perhaps to finish Juan's education, / Perhaps to open Don Alfonso's eyes'. The farce of the old husband and young wife is darkened beyond farce, not because it is Julia who takes the lead ('One hand on Juan's carelessly was thrown / Quite by mistake—she thought it was her own'), but because Juan's mother, having trained him up in the way he should go, by tutors and the expurgated classics, uses him to cuckold Alfonso, who rumour said had been her lover before he married the beautiful Julia. Under the mask of concerned and gossiping friend of the family, Byron frequently asks why Inez allowed Juan to see so much of Julia, and who could have told Alfonso, without being able (or willing) to suggest an answer. The effect of the repeated silences is to make Inez brood like an unholy providence over the action of I. The stanzas describing Julia's temptation, on the other hand, are an ironic delineation of self-deception, of desire born of boredom that continues to think of itself as innocent. 'Love, then, but love within its proper limits / Was Julia's innocent determination / In young Don Juan's favour': the irony of 'innocent' is that of the impersonality of 'then there were sighs, the deeper for suppression', or 'that night the Virgin was no further pray'd'. But the irony of Julia's dream of how Juan might serve seven years for his Rachel, when (being the same age as she is now) he would suit 'a widow of condition' (the sin of wishing Don Alfonso dead no doubt compounded by the virtue of a decent maturity for Juan) is only the harsher for the insistence on it as supposition: 'and in the interim (to pursue this vision) .... ' 'So much for Julia', is his valedictory comment on her struggle, which is not to be compared with that of Madame de Rênal in *Le Rouge et le Noir*: we cannot be other than what we are.[9]

The contrast between the treatment of Inez' manipulation of her son (either for revenge, or to drive out one scandal by another), and that of Julia, is of some significance. The mature viciousness of Inez is given in hints and silences, the youthful self-deceit of Julia is studied with some tolerance, and at length, before her dismissal from the poem. The range of treatment reflects the importance of the woman's role in the first canto, as well as the difference between hardened maturity and pliant youth. Men and women in *Don Juan* are different races, and that neither understands the other is made more palpable by the urge to mate, which brings them together only to separate them further. (The action of the canto virtually begins and ends with divorce proceedings.) Since we are not always much more than agents of procreation, the race is with the young, and it is the mental processes of Juan and Julia that Byron dwells on, after the sardonic account of the education Juan receives from Inez and his tutors. 'This was Don Juan's earliest scrape', he remarks, just after the description of Julia's seal, motto, jewel, and wax, and it sounds like a comment on her artifice. Earlier he has called him 'poor little fellow', or a sort of gentleman in embryo. The 'unutterable things' he thinks, the 'self-communion with his own high soul', the 'longings sublime, and aspirations high', arise from puberty, but the processes are never reductive. 'Silent and pensive, idle, restless, slow, / His home deserted for the lonely wood, / Tormented with a wound he could not know': the evocation of Petrarch (which is followed by a sharp comment on Campbell) relates the youthful sentiment at the outset to the human experience that Juan is heir to.[10] A few stanzas later he evokes the later Spanish Petrarchans in a passage which suggests a distinction between life and the imitation of life in poetry.

> Sometimes he turn'd to gaze upon his book,
>   Boscan, or Garcilasso;—by the wind
> Even as the page is rustled while we look,
>   So by the poesy of his own mind
> Over the mystic leaf his soul was shook ...
>
> (I.xcv)

The lovely formal inversions and parallels of this imitation both maintain the authority of the sixteenth century 'mystic leaf,' and support the sudden turn of 'by the wind' against those names, and the supremacy of the poesy of the mind over other men's poetry. It is at moments like these that one realises again Byron's humanity and artistry, the breadth and unhurrying ease of Canto I, and its fine decorum. It has not always been properly valued by critics, who tend to prefer the English cantos to the more Italianate first canto. He thought well of it, describing III and IV as 'very *decent*—but *dull*—damned dull', not written 'con amore', and lacking 'the Spirit of the first'.[11] That he seems to have added more to I than to the other cantos may suggest that he was feeling his way. It probably also suggests a recognition of what had been achieved, and some excitement over what was to come; the addition of Julia's letter to the first draft speaks for itself.

Lucretius, in the first book of *De Rerum Natura*, compares his poetry to the honey by which doctors try to make children drink restorative wormwood. Byron likens the amusement and the moral which he offers to a coral for children to cut their teeth on (I.ccix). That is, *Don Juan* will bring the public to maturity, and a sense of things as they are. (He has bribed the *British Review* (he says), and this 'holy new alliance' means the poem will not be attacked, and can be safely read.) The canto which first sets out the conflict of man and woman, youth and maturity, presents his own achievement of mature judgment. We are to understand that 'the freshness of the heart' has gone: 'I / Have spent my life, both interest and principal, / And deem not, what I deem'd, my soul invincible.'

> No more—no more—Oh! never more, my heart,

Canst thou be my sole world, my universe!
Once all in all, but now a thing apart,
  Thou canst not be my blessing or my curse:
The illusion's gone for ever, and thou art
  Insensible, I trust, but none the worse,
And in thy stead I've got a deal of judgment,
Though heaven knows how it ever found a lodgment ...

  ... 'You've pass'd your youth not so unpleasantly,
  And if you had it o'er again—'twould pass—
So thank your stars that matters are no worse,
And read your Bible, sir, and mind your purse.'

This a little resembles Pope's 'I pay my debts, believe, and say my prayers' in the 'Epistle to Dr Arbuthnot'; it is hardly the 'gear and grace' of 'Holy Willie's Prayer', or the 'sense' achieved by those who 'add the halfpence to the pence, / And prayer to shivering prayer' in Yeats's 'September 1913'. The Bible reading and purse minding are what the ordinary man associates with mature judgment, and youth comfortably if not gratefully over. From an early age Byron had been formed by the Bible, and in later life did more than mind his purse, developing a strong interest in money. As narrator, he often plays at being the confused plain gentleman ('I'm a philosopher; confound them all!'), and here he gives himself a counsel of ordinariness. It is partly a recognition of approaching age, of what has been taken away, partly a mask for the real judgment, which is not complacent, or detached; it is one of the greatest sources of authority in the satire, that Byron writes from the human condition, and not from some sphere above it. Whatever the tolerance of frailty, as distinct from corruption, *Don Juan*, as several critics have reminded us, is the product of bitterness and despair. In the third canto of *Childe Harold*, written two years before he began his epic satire, and notably darker than the preceding cantos, he speaks of how the absence of hope is accompanied by 'less of gloom', and of how vanity and the end of life 'had made Despair a Smilingness assume' (III.xvi); the slight clumsiness, and rather facile readiness of this, is that of a different context. The most succinct statement is in the fourth canto of his satire (IV.iv): 'And if I laugh at any mortal thing, / 'Tis that I may not weep; and if I weep, / 'Tis that our nature cannot always bring / Itself to apathy'. (The first part of this is classic, the second unexpected, and proportionately bitter.) The satirist, of course, is often required to be mature, even in *English*

Bards and Scotch Reviewers, where he is 'so callous grown, so changed from youth'. The character assumed in *Don Juan* is founded on self-knowledge, which helps him to the judgment which spares Julia, and lashes Castlereagh and Southey. The judgment, like the self-knowledge, commands respect, if only because 'insensible, I trust', so far from meaning insensible, resembles 'I would to heaven that I were so much clay'. Byron's projection of a persona is less complex, and more honest, than is sometimes supposed. (There is a tendency among critics to dismiss such projections for not being part of an alchemical process.) What is assumed, however incomplete, is always essential, and usually in control. The delight, of course, is not in himself, or in the world he depicts, but in what is being done. 'My poem's epic' ... ' "Longinus o'er a bottle"' ... 'The public approbation I expect' ... 'Gentle reader! and / Still gentler purchaser!': the closing stanzas of this brilliant canto are alive with it.

III

A reading of most episodes in *Don Juan* confirms Byron's own judgment (as distinct from what he assumes as narrator) in that understanding of what is appropriate, or rendering of what is due, which is decorum. His method has sometimes been misunderstood. Although the St Petersburg cantos, for example, may suffer from a comparison with other parts of the poem, there is no reason to suppose that they demonstrate a lack of interest or conviction about Russia, and that their only function is to give Juan enough poise to undertake his diplomatic mission in London. This seems unlikely, and comments on his 'immature fondness for gossip' in these cantos, and regrets that the historical Catherine remains little more than a royal harlot are beside the point. [12] That Byron knew England and the Levant, and did not know Russia, might suggest that he is turning a limitation to account, but it is more a matter of what is appropriate to the subject of autocracy, imperial whoring, and self-love. So far from being concerned to weigh the good and ill in Catherine the Great, he uses her as a type of tyrannous appetite, in a work which transcends history because it is a farther fiction, and part of a larger moral truth. We have to take account of the broad brush strokes used, and the reason for them. Juan is now on stage, his self-love making him an apt protagonist. The autocratic Russia of 'polish'd boors' is a show; St Petersburg is a place of painted snow (that is, painted over), and Juan lives

in a hurry
>Of waste, and haste, and glare, and gloss, and glitter,
>In this gay clime of bear-skins black and furry—
>   Which (though I hate to say a thing that's bitter)
>Peep out sometimes, when things are in a flurry,
>   Through all the 'purple and fine linen,' fitter
>For Babylon's than Russia's royal harlot—
>And neutralize her outward show of scarlet.

The issues are too clear, and Juan's success too immediate, for the intimacy of the southern or the English cantos. The harsh light first falls on Juan before Catherine's throne, 'made up by youth, fame, and an army tailor', wearing the uniform of the big guns, which are Catherine's other pastime, and seeming 'Love turn'd a lieutenant of artillery'. (Whether Byron means us to think of another lieutenant of artillery of the same generation is anyone's guess.) The brilliant vulgarity of the description is a product of the light itself.

The scandalous double meanings which accompany the brutal Russian masquerade have little to do with gossip or padding, and their real propriety should be obvious enough. Like gallows humour, such double meanings have always represented a defence. The *locus classicus* of near the knuckle as condemned mankind's defence is probably IX. xix.

>'But heaven,' as Cassio says, 'is above all—
>   No more of this, then, let us pray!' We have
>Souls to save, since Eve's slip and Adam's fall,
>   Which tumbled all mankind into the grave,
>Besides fish, beasts, and birds. 'The sparrow's fall
>   Is special providence,' though how *it* gave
>Offence, we know not; probably it perch'd
>Upon the tree which Eve so fondly search'd.

This stanza is part of the exordium to Canto IX, which (if the inclusion of three stanzas of narrative does not make what follows digression rather than induction) contains forty-one stanzas. The mask is that of the average thoughtful man who moralises, but, unlike the visionary man who would transform the world, writes 'what's uppermost, without delay', as he says in XIV. vii. Here, as elsewhere, he is haunted by meaninglessness: the end of this long induction on power and responsibility, fame and slaughter, the Fall and suffering mankind, being and knowing, the war with those who war with thought, is a mocking evocation of regressive catastrophism: of worlds hurled out of and back again to chaos, of the mammoth bulk of George IV dug up to make this age an age of giants, and of the new age slowly labouring towards the crowning arts of war and taxation. The outrageous nineteenth stanza rises from this like a gesture of despair. It moves from intellect to soul, from soul to body, as if the mind were only a disease or malfunctioning of the body. Man is in the toils, like Cassio drunkenly trusting to heaven, preoccupied with his soul, dominated by the flesh. Eve slipped; Adam fell; and the two of them 'tumbled', or fornicated, mankind and the animal kingdom into the grave. All have given offence, and God's mercy in regard to sparrows (the Bible, by way of *Hamlet* V. ii) is mockingly compounded with the old tradition of the lechery of sparrows. The ludicrous image in which the human protest of the stanza comes to rest is reasonably clear if we remember the vulgar meaning of 'tree' or 'branch', and also perhaps that other tradition, by which our first parents were giants.

Often the mockery is more of a grin than a gesture of despair, as in these lines on the seraglio in Canto VI. The Sultan, with the aid of guards and punishments,

> contrived to keep this den
> Of beauties cool as an Italian convent,
> Where all the passions have, alas! but one vent.

But in its own way this passage, and what follows it ('And what is that?'), is no more gratuitous than the lines about the sparrow, since it has to do with the innocence of a natural accommodation to a state of bondage. The simile is apt, incidentally, for the general picture of the seraglio is that of a place of girlish uproar and sentimental friendships. It is hardly what one would expect from an institution where the women, eager for promotion and wealth, contended with one another in pleasing the Sultan, with the result that some sultans died young, and others went mad. Byron gives us nothing of this, which is worth remembering if we are tempted to regret what he does not give us of the historical Catherine the Great. His confirming shadow falls in the tenderness of the stanzas on the sleeping girls ('the dream of some far shore / Beloved and deplored'), whose imagery modulates with the moving eye from the lovely garden of lxv to the statuary of lxviii. The simile is apt in another way, since it points to common ground between the Turkish seraglio and the Italian convent where girls are preserved for the marriage market, whose English equivalent is what he will describe as the Smithfield Show. It takes the cruel world of the Russian cantos, however, to produce such a passage as the address to the vulva, the perennial fountain which restocks the world for war, and which, so far from being merely a *blason du corps féminin*, resembles the *ennui* of the end of pleasure in being so much itself that it is a 'nondescript': that is, in natural historical terms, a species not easily described, or that has not so far been described. The passage (IX. lv-lvi) is a notable example of the 'rend'ring general' of what in other hands could easily have remained 'especial', a difficulty which he mentions, in another context, in XV. xxv.

If we had to single out one quality which would do justice to *Don Juan*, it would probably be its humanity, its sense of a human reality larger than any of the systematising abstractions or orthodoxies which seek to reduce mankind to somthing less than itself. One of the best of his interpreters, George Wilson Knight, has spoken of 'a certain optimistic universal' underlying the humour of the poem, and 'a basic and golden human centre' which we do not find in, say, Ben Jonson.[13] It is an accurate description of something which is as different as may be from the cloudy 'pretensions to Optimism' that Byron finds in the 'sentimental anatomy' of Rousseau and Madame de Staël. The despair over the 'jar of atoms', and over human action which might as well be inaction, outweighs the strong feeling in passages like the conclusion of Canto VIII, where he seems to look to a millennium. But the manner which qualifies the despair is nearly everything. It also qualifies such a statement of optimism as this.

> But heaven must be diverted; its diversion
> Is sometimes truculent—but never mind;
> The world upon the whole is worth the assertion
> (If but for comfort) that all things are kind.
>
> (XIII. xli)

The second sentence, with its accommodating reservations, does not quite negate what is sardonically accepted in the first; 'all things are kind' is a loaded phrase, despite the rejection of Manichaeism that follows. On the other hand, the mocking acceptance throughout by rhythm and rhyme is the reverse of mere stoicism. In IV.xc the captive Italian singers, invited 'back to their sad berths' by the pirate crew, look ruefully at the waves

Dancing all free and happy in the sun,
And then went down the hatchway one by one.

The cadence of the last line of the stanza is that of a mockery of
misfortune, which still has something kindly about it. (The
stanza ends a malicious description of his colleagues by the *buffo*
Raucocanti—he and the tenor to whom he will be chained 'hated
with a hate / Found only on the stage'—which suggests an
unquenchable spirit.) The seventy-first stanza of Canto VIII is a
notable instance of this poise. The narrative action of this stanza
is the rise and fall of Kutuzov and his grenadiers. Kutuzov
('follow'd in haste by various grenadiers') throws himself into a
ditch, then climbs up to the parapet, from which 'the Moslem
men / Threw them all down into the ditch again'. This is the
classic rise and fall of the human comedy, set off by the intrusion
of what sounds like the thin level voice of the Gazette: '('Mongst
other deaths the General Ribaupierre's / Was much regretted).'
Rising and falling are movements which recur throughout *Don
Juan*. But the mocking rise in the scrupulous observation of these
falls is the narrator's, and is born not only of the knowledge that
it has all happened before, and will happen and be endured
again, but of his own part in the instinctive struggle to reject
man's destiny, whether in the Europe of the Holy Alliance, or in
a world history of regressive catastrophism. 'The unforgiven /
Fire, which Prometheus filch'd for us from heaven': the human
'filch'd', which has the warmth of dirt about it, says it all.

The manner combines a maturity which has forgotten nothing,
and tests everything, with the 'mobility' which (speaking of
Lady Adeline, but thinking probably of himself) he describes as
'a thing of temperament, and not of art ... And false—though
true' (XVI. xcvii). In his note on the word he defines it as 'an
excessive susceptibility of immediate impressions—at the same
time without *losing* the past', and in his own case it has much to
do with variety, and comprehensiveness. It is worth remembering this quality of comprehensiveness when we find anything
in *Don Juan* which looks like coxcombry. There are occasional
moments of it, despite its absence in Juan when he gets to
England, where the recommendation, 'the absence of pretension
/ Will go much farther than there's need to mention', is not,
however, about writing poetry. He dropped from the second
canto two stanzas about a recent affair, which were rather
pretentious. There are also the five stanzas on rape at the end of
Canto VIII, which most readers agree are in bad taste. It is a truth

not quite universally acknowledged, that soldiers often rape because an outrage has been committed on them, but Byron has nothing to say about this, and the jocularity is unpleasant. The most unexpected piece of coxcombry is probably in the stanzas which present the pregnant girl in Canto XVI.

> There was a country girl in a close cap
>   And scarlet cloak (I hate the sight to see, since—
> Since—since—in youth, I had the sad mishap—
>   But luckily I have paid few parish fees since):
> That scarlet cloak, alas! unclosed with rigour
> Presents the problem of a double figure.
>
> (XVI.lxi)

The reference to his own adventures, and the grinning hesitations, strike us perhaps more unpleasantly than anything else in the poem. His human comedy, of course, includes himself; he does not only present and comment on folly, but will sometimes act it out within the commentary, as at the end of II (' "Stop!" so I stopp'd'). As with the sexual double meanings in the poem (or many of them), it is something of a protest from as well as at the human condition. Distant and aloof among people he was unsure of, he was ready enough to clown among his intimates, and the clowning in *Don Juan* is like the mobility of a comedian. It is perhaps significant that this passage occurs at a moment of anger; the Hogarth-like scene of the girl waiting for judgment in the great hall, with her red cloak and pale face, is followed by a bitter denunciation of Lord Henry and his patriotic occupation. (It is also possible that he was on his guard against hypocrisy.) In the conclusion to the exordium of Canto XIV, the process by which the poem itself is included in the comedy is more subtle. This long induction sweeps with superb aplomb from nature's abyss and man's through a dozen different themes to that of unfortunate if dangerous woman—'Poor thing of usages! coerced, compell'd, / Victim when wrong, and martyr oft when right' (XIV.xxiii). Having gone so far, it then contrives what looks like a perversely complacent reflux, by way of 'petticoat influence', in the petticoat itself ('A garment of a mystical sublimity, / No matter whether russet, silk, or dimity'), reaching a kind of climax in the sight of the petticoat on a windy day. That is, the last stanzas, in an exordium which from beginning to end is concerned with our fallen state, enact contented male sexuality ('that chaste and goodly veil, / Which holds a treasure'), with lovely woman, as in a bottle song, as the one thing which relieves the soul-destroying dullness, on a day of dust and wind that is like an image of the fallen world. (To which one should add that behind 'petticoat influence' lurks the idea of the gynocracy, and that even as man looks happily about him, his bondage is assured, at a deeper level than that of sad rakes tamed to sadder husbands.) The exordium introduces the poem's latest episode of *ennui* and sexuality, and says, in effect, that the male relief in the closing stanzas is only too much a part of the fallen world that it seems to relieve. After so much of reminiscence and observation, it is to this that Byron's thinking brings us, like a comedian acting out a human weakness.

In an uproarious letter to Hobhouse describing a bad stage performance, he says 'Damn me, if ever I saw such a scene in my life ... "Love a la mode" was damned, Coates was damned, every thing was damned & damnable.'[14] The exhilaration of this is like the characteristic sense of liberation which he describes in *Don Juan*: 'So now all things are damn'd one feels at ease' (VI. xxiii). That is, our mature judgment can go no farther than the recognition that (to invert Kipling), the worst is like the best. (Elsewhere – XI. xliii – he describes the national oath, with its shadowing of actuality, as 'rather Attic ... quite ethereal, though too daring— / Platonic blasphemy, the soul of swearing.') Our only resource is recognition of the truth, and moral judgment, which are the source of decorum. Since we have been speaking of Byron as comedian, it might be appropriate to end with the letter to Hobhouse of June 1818, announcing his death, and supposedly from his valet Fletcher. It is one of the most amusing of his letters; more to the point, it may illustrate, in a modest way, how Byron kept things in proportion. Fletcher is made to speak of how his master died of anxiety, sea-bathing, women, '& riding in the sun against my advice'. 'His nine whores are already provided for ... but what is to become of me?' And so down to the postscript, which asks for a character reference, similar to that Hobhouse gave his 'late Swiss servant', who supposedly produced this recommendation at his trial, when he was sent to the galleys for robbing an inn.[15] The interesting thing is that the spelling and punctuation are so much better than that of the letter Fletcher wrote to Hobhouse from Missolonghi six years later, announcing Byron's death, in which there are many more mistakes, and hardly any punctuation from beginning to end.[16] (Something must of course be allowed for the effect of Fletcher's distress, which he speaks of.) It would have been easy for Byron to write an illiterate as well as a revealing letter. (An example of this which comes to mind – which usually means that one cannot think of any other – is the uneducated letters to be found in the ghost stories of Montague Rhodes James, who was never done poking fun at unlettered people.) Did he feel that, since Fletcher was not a writing man (' "quel' illustre letterato" ', he called him in a letter to Teresa Guiccioli), to have written exactly as he did would have been in some sense to misrepresent him? It might be pushing things, not rather far, but beyond bounds, to say that in that case the bogus letter renders general that which is especial, or to relate it to Irving Babbitt's statement, in *Rousseau and Romanticism*: 'true decorum is only the pulling back and disciplining of impulse to the proportionateness that has been perceived with the aid of what one may term the ethical or generalising imagination.'[17] There is a moral there for commentators, as well as for poets. But it would not be too surprising if in more than one way the truth of that letter was to the spirit.

SENECA AND THE ENGLISH RENAISSANCE: THE OLD WORLD AND THE NEW

ROBERT WELCH

Seneca has, over the last one hundred years or so, tended to attract a very tedious kind of scholarship. It is as if a Stoic endurance has had to be practised by reading through interminable quantities of Elizabethan closet tragedies, picking out the lumps of Stoical wisdom embedded in the texts, and attaching them to phrases by Seneca from the Latin plays and essays.

There is value in all of this, of course, but very little of the scholarly work done on Seneca has answered to the feeling that somehow he is a very dominant presence in English literature, especially that of the late Renaissance period. This feeling, and for all his various writings on the subject it is no more than that, finds direct expression in T.S. Eliot's footnote in his Introduction to Newton's *Seneca his Tenne Tragedies* (1927), in which he says that 'in the most serious matters of life and death' Shakespeare's is the voice of his time and that this voice 'is the voice of Seneca'.

Again, a good deal has been made of this idea, not all of it satisfactory. G.K. Hunter has pooh-poohed the whole idea of a Senecan influence on English drama, but it seems to me that his notion of influence is limited and innocent. What do we mean when we say that a writer has an influence on others? It is not primarily at all what literary historians often assert: not the taking over of a set of ideas, or a repetition of certain types of formal pattern. If we think about how writers influence ourselves we may get some idea of what goes on when a great creative imagination clashes or engages with another. A writer influences us when he opens up pathways of seeing and knowing that maybe had been hoped for, guessed at, wondered about, thought of, but to which we had no access from our own store of memory, the activity of our own will. A writer who influences us opens. What he opens may be delightful or it may be fearful, but it will tend to be towards greater being, and deeper, and because deeper, more harmonious complexity. As it is for us, so it is for writers, except, of course, that a creative imagination accelerates and ramifies experience, broadens it and refines it, and makes it touch all the modes of knowing and perceiving.

If this is a valid theory of influence, then an influence should open. Harold Bloom, the American deconstructionist, maintains that influence carries with it anxiety, which is true, up to a point. But then, Bloom being a Freudian, he goes on to say that the strong poet kills his forebears, thereby liberating himself. This is limiting. Some writers want to kill some of their forebears, but there are others with whom they form the deepest most affective relationships. And I would think that a really great artist will hold all his relationships with all his forebears open, in a fine suspension, not of disbelief, but of loving terror. He will know that they are in his chromosomes anyway, and that if he tries to deny them he is denying constituent parts of himself, turning himself into a bitter half-corpse, rather than trying for the full open venture of exultant being that any writer, worthy of the name, wants to be. The Bloom picture of the strong poet is full of Bloom's own anxious gloom: metal faces tearing at each other, in a nightmare doggedness for survival. I am afraid that this only reflects the critic's anxiety about his own neglected creative powers, as he prowls the University precincts. Anxiety gives intensity, of a kind, but it is, by definition, incapable of depth.

Eliot argued for Seneca's influence on the Elizabethans and Jacobeans, and I am sure he is right. If he was an influence on them, using the kind of language I have been working with, Seneca will have opened something for them, something by means of which aspects of their own natures, their own conditions of being, were revealed to them. What did Seneca open for the Elizabethans?

He opened fear. And he opened the way of seeing that fear has. In Seneca's drama men can do the most terrible things, and Seneca's great power as a dramatist is the unflinching witness he bears to the ruthlessness and energy of human cruelty. The Elizabethans were right to admire the bloody barbarity of Senecan tragedy, because that is exactly its most serious claim to power. His moral aphorisms, his pithy pronouncements, his sonorous rhetoric—all these had their attraction for the Elizabethans, but essentially it was the obsessive attention

Seneca brings to the details of violence and cruelty that fascinated them. However, having said that, we cannot leave it there. This could make it sound as if they sought a sanction from Seneca for indulging a taste in blood and gore. It is not that simple, thought there are elements of bad taste, of what we would now call the gratuitous, in Senecan and in Elizabethan and Jacobean drama.

Underneath the bad taste, the sensationalism, of Seneca, there is a profound sense of shock at human suffering. This is why he cannot really be called a pornographer of violence. The shock is simple and the moral feeling strong: how can it be that men do such terrible things to each other? This sense of bafflement drives Senecan drama to expatiate endlessly on the details of human cruelty: the savage blows; the deep cuts; the ripping of flesh; the blood; the muscle; the tearing ligaments; the opened secrecies of the mutilated body. And it is the body that is at the centre of Seneca's vision of man: human flesh tortured and abused; divided and scorned; torn and opened up. This is the contrary of the typical Roman view of the gloriously physical being, strong and unsubduable, whole and beautiful. Nor does Seneca's view of human suffering compare in scope to that of the Greek dramatists, Sophocles for example. In Greek tragedy there is a pity for the frailty of the human body, but always we are aware of the dignity of man, of his power and energy, the terror that his nature holds in balance. In Seneca men are terrible because they do terrible things to each other and to themselves. Their lot is a terrifying one. The emotion is not really awe, as in Greek tragedy, but most often panic. The panic of fear at the cruelty of man, his inventiveness in torture, his obsession with hate. For a long time it was felt that Seneca no longer spoke to our condition and it was even a puzzle as to why the Elizabethans and Jacobeans were so drawn to him. But now, for obvious reasons, we are once again familiar with the world that Senecan drama opens up. Once again, his obsessive accuracy, his terrible fascination with the details of torture and cruelty, reflect our nightmares, nightmares begotten by what men have been (and still are) prepared to do to each other:

But Atreus fierce the sword in him at last
In deepe and deadly wound doth hide to hilts, and gryping fast
His throate in hand, he thrust him through. The sword then drawne away
When long the body had uphelde it selfe in doubtfull stay,

Which way to fall, at length upon the unckle downe it falles.
(Jasper Heywood's translation in Newton's *Tenne Tragedies*)

This is from *Thyestes*, describing how Atreus savages Tantalus, one of the sons of Thyestes, in the dark grove in the centre of the complex labyrinthine palace. This is where the horrible meal is to be prepared for Thyestes, using the flesh of his son.

Seneca is very good then, at conveying the sensation of panic and of fear. But this sensation rises out of the ground of his dramatic art, its moral, philosophical basis. And that can be stated fairly simply (unlike, say, the ground out of which Sophoclean drama arises). It is this: men are seen as creatures subject to inconsequence. Senecan drama, at its most critical moments (and it is these moments towards which the whole drive of the drama moves), contemplates a universe devoid of significance, a cosmos of clashing interests, with no sure sign to be discerned. Augury is to be defied, because the guts of the sacrificial beast only reveal the tangle of chaos, which is the one sure thing to come again. You will see that I am deliberately picking up the Shakespearean phrases, to show how deep Shakespeare's acquaintance was with the inner texture of the Senecan universe. Men will do things (and do and do and do) and certain results will follow. Cause and effect do exist; but the nature of the effect proceeding from the cause cannot be assured. To be is to be a machine, operating in a world of other machines, each one plugged into a different programme. ('As this machine is to him'—Hamlet's words to Ophelia.) The effect (to steal from pedantic old Polonius) is defective; the cause (to steal from distracted Othello, who knows about Chaos) is the cause, and there can be no coming to a clear judgment as to how it may issue. All that can be known about it is that it will proceed to an effect, and that procedure will have its own law, which it will make up as it goes along, accelerating as it goes. No one captures so well as Seneca does the sense of circumstances operating with their own pure logic of event and materiality. The individual in Seneca is a pathetic, evil thing, blasted by terror and suffering, his eyes wide with the fear of what may come next. And he has no idea of what that may be; nor any control over it. Again here we seem to be describing the contrary to Roman law and logic; the opposite of the Roman citizen, confident of his privilege and superiority. A Freudian might describe Seneca as performing a necessary therapeutic task for maintaining the security of Roman civilization, in expressing, formally, its discontents; but again, while there may be some truth in this, there is more to it than that.

Seneca's drama enacts discontinuity and breakdown, and the image most commonly used to express that is the human body abused and strangled. It contemplates man abandoned out of law and significance, and therefore deprived of all liberty and volition. Seneca's art is doing more than merely providing an opportunity for the dispersal of civilized tension. It bears witness to the need to tell a truth that is whole: all the broken bodies of Seneca's dramas are an imaging out of the absence of wholeness. He is speaking of a desire to be whole (and to be healed) in Roman, and in Western civilization of the time. The healing wholeness came in the life and death and mangled body of a Jew, at the periphery of the Empire, the centre of which was Rome and the depraved Imperial Court in which Seneca served.

If what has been said about the laws of causality and effect in Seneca has any truth in it, then we can take the argument one step further. If human life is subject to inconsequence and insignificance, then the human body itself becomes a source of immense and cruel humour. If there are no systems of valuation, if there is no form of protective love that can release man from himself, considered as pure material event, then the best attitude is a kind of wild inconsequence. Often in Senecan drama we find this kind of inconsequence erupting in what comes very close to bad taste; in, for example, the image of Thyestes belching after banquetting on the bodies of his sons:

> In glittering gold and purple seat he sits himself upright,
> And staying up his heavy head with wine, upon his hand,
> He belcheth out.

> (Jasper Heywood)

We are accustomed to thinking of Elizabethan comedy as deriving from native folk or medieval sources; from mystery plays; and from Ovid; but surely one of the deepest strains in Elizabethan and Jacobean comedy is this sense of the grotesque, when the human body is seen as a wretched, pitiable and absurd piece of machinery, negotiating the passages of fortune with varying degrees of clumsiness. The body is a ridiculous weight, fretted by ague and sickness, cramped by pain, and inflamed by lust. It will, if it can, swell up into the bloated gigantism of Sir Epicure Mammon or Falstaff or decline into the weak lankiness of Aguecheek.

What then did Seneca open for the Renaissance? A sense of fear at the cruelties of human outrage; an emotion, not of awe, but of panic; and a way of looking at the human body in a ludicrous light. Further, he opened a view of the gathering of human beings into cities as a thing fraught with precariousness. Savage emotions were still there, under the surface, all the more turbulent for the attempt civilization made to suppress them. When they surface, they do so all the more explosively. The Latin language itself, in all the pride of its clarity and coherence, becomes a vehicle for voicing the underworld of brutality and incoherence it is part of its function to keep subdued. Seneca opened up an old world; not the world of the Old Testament, where the covenant between God and man, through dark, is always to be counted upon; but an older one still, where the laws that determine human action and re-action conduct themselves under no sure sign. There is no unity, only the chaos of barbarism.

Though we say that this is an old world, or that it is a world unvisited by the new laws of love and faith and hope, we also can see that it is not the old world of tribalism or so-called primitive man. We know that primitive man had all sorts of codings that gave the tribe coherence. What we watch in Senecan drama is the breakdown of all codes and relationships; what we enjoy is the crack-up, the destruction of the body. So when we say it is an old world, we do not mean a primitive one; we mean one unknown to law, uncivilized by the gathering that the city represents, and which the family embodies.

But of course it is only when the city arrives, and when the family starts to refine itself out of the tribe, that the nightmare of their opposite forms, that of chaos old. All cities are precocious networks of relationships, all families hostages to fortune, in Bacon's words. What Seneca communicates is the doubt about the strength of civilization itself. How can it survive, in all its frail and delicate actions, when we know in ourselves such floods of anger, lust and cruelty, such strivings of contempt and malice? In itself, of course, it cannot. Cause will have its effect, as every dog will have its day. The pure logic of human greed will collapse all structures, outgo all love. A man must retire into himself; into the 'circle of his liberty' (as Samuel Daniel has it), a circle with an ever-contracting circumference and, as he grows older, he realises all the follies of friendship; the ludicrous expectancies of love; and the inherent injustice of all systems of law and order.

Seneca is probably the first voice of modern despair. This

despair is related to the apparent strength, vastness and essential unknowableness of the machinery human beings create to manipulate, frighten and subdue others. The law is so strong, the city so gleaming in its white colonnaded perfection, that the emotion most familiar to men is the one of fear. Those who do best in the system are those best able to disguise their panic by a calm surrender of themselves to the materiality of their function. Be detached and quiet and ferocious. Feel nothing. That is the Stoic advice. Carry yourself well when you go out in public. And go out as little as possible. All contact with humanity reduces and contaminates. Men in the mass are despicable. To console yourself, think of your insignificance. What agitation over so little:

All things human are short-lived and perishable, and fill not part of all of infinite time. The earth with all its cities and people, its rivers and the girdle of the sea, if measured by the universe, we may count a mere dot; our life if compared with all time, is relatively even less than a dot.

('De Consolatione', 1–2)

And later in the same epistle he says that prayers and struggles against what is laid down for us in this foreign and unknowable machinery of things are all in vain: 'Frustra vota ac studia sunt'.

A tradition exists of a connection between St Paul and Seneca. It has even been suggested that Seneca intervened in Paul's trial at Rome, and that it was because of conversations with Seneca that Paul went to Spain after his release, complying with the philosopher's wish that his homeland should be touched by the Gospel of Christ. A spurious correspondence has come down, and Augustine and Jerome saw letters that purported to have passed between them. Whatever we think about all of that the instinct that led to the invention of the letters is interesting. Seneca's world, agitated, as it is, by fear and panic, longs for coherence and gentleness. Senecan necessity, under which the human spirit trembles, and the inexorable claims of cause and effect in the universe, cry out for another kind of law, another sense of justice. Love is what is missing in Seneca, and it is what Paul is trying to call men towards. It is true, Paul says, that there is none righteous, not one: ' . . . all have sinned, and come short of the glory of God; being justified freely by his grace through the redemption that is in Christ Jesus: whom God hath set forth to be a propitiation through faith in his blood, to declare his righteousness for the remission of sins that are past, through the forbearance of God' (*Romans*, 3).

This is the new law, that leaps out of the despair of Seneca's continual melancholy. Happiness, in Seneca, is submission to what Nature can throw up, and readiness for the worst. But his darkness is an extreme that wants to realise the new departure in thought that the Pauline breakthrough brings about.

Paul says that the sins are past. A new time has come, a new way has broken through the hopeless repetitiveness of material action. There is a break, and time cannot be the same again. A new law emerges, the law of the spirit of life in Christ Jesus which makes the new man, reborn in Christ, 'free from the law of sin and death'.

This is not to argue that there was a meeting between Paul and Seneca, nor is it to make the obvious point that their thinking is very different. Seneca's view of the human condition, and the thinking that comes out of that view, takes us to an extreme of panic and despair when viewing the human enterprise, as one governed by cause and effect, passion, power, the survival of the fittest, and fortune. Reading Seneca, and believing him, provides a peculiarly sensual thrill of submission, a yielding to a powerful mind that speaks out in the curt self-confidence, the searing gravity, of the Latin rhetoric. He is dictatorial and totalitarian. But the Senecan law is the law of death. All his thought continually revolves around it, and in the end he was to justify his precepts by taking his own life 'when in disgrace with fortune and men's eyes'.

The line from Shakespeare helps us here, because it reminds us that at the extreme of Senecan thought there is only death, whereas in the sonnet, Shakespeare's poetry turns aside and goes for life, for the other; not for the old self, but for a new man reborn in love for the other. It is a turn for life, and it is Pauline:

> When in disgrace with Fortune and mens eyes,
> I all alone beweepe my out-cast state,
> And trouble deafe heaven with my bootlesse cries,
> And looke upon my selfe and curse my fate,
> Wishing me like to one more rich in hope,
> Featur'd like him, like him with friends possest,
> Desiring this mans art, and that mans skope,
> With what I most enjoy contented least,
> Yet in these thoughts my selfe almost despising,
> Haplye I thinke on thee, and then my state,
> (Like to the Larke at breake of day arising)
> From sullen earth sings himns at Heavens gate,

For thy sweet love remembred such welth brings,
That then I skorne to change my state with Kings.

Maybe it is not an accident that the woman who presides over the awakening of the classical statue of Hermione in *The Winter's Tale* is called Paulina.

When then does Seneca open for the Renaissance? In him they found a picture of the relentlessness of human fury; a vision of the universe as a shocking shackling of accident; and the idea that the best thing to be done, the world being what it is, is to relax into a mindless, passionless and conscienceless state. Be as absent as you can. When we consider that the Renaissance saw a powerful mobilisation of the human spirit we may wonder why Seneca held such an attraction for that period. There are two reasons, at least, for this attraction.

In the first place, Seneca is the conclusion of a certain kind of ordinary human wisdom, the kind expressed in the phrase, which you often hear: 'Your day is there, nothing to be done about it'. The day of your death is fixed, nothing you do can make the slightest difference to that; so it is pointless preoccupying yourself too much with anything. Get what you can, form no attachments. This line of thought leads to apathy, indifference; in a word, despair. And despair always threatens when a great shift is to take place. In a phase of opening and discovery (such as there was in the Rome of Paul and Seneca, and in the Europe of Shakespeare and Michelangelo) a great deal has to be learned, as if for the first time, and a great deal has to be unlearned. There is a new call into life, because the patterns and structures are altering; new laws are being opened up, new depths are being revealed. The temptation here is to listen to the voice which says: 'All you do makes no difference; all our yesterdays have lighted fools', and so on; nothing to be done.

It is with this inertia that we find Spenser's heroes continually in conflict. Their destiny is to *be*, to complete themselves in integrity, but all along the way they are beset by trial and difficulty and often the greatest temptation lies in yielding to a sense of their own powerlessness and insignificance. How can they matter in a world so full of energy and power and strength? What is the sum of all their actions but futility and emptiness?

In Book I of *The Faerie Queen*, Red Crosse Knight, having come free out of the foul 'dongeon' of Orgoglio, falls into despair. It happens like this: Despair has brought Sir Terwin (meaning exhaustion) to so great a sense of his own worthlessness that he takes his own life. When Red Crosse Knight sees the youth, lying in his blood, he demands that Despair pay for his crime with his own blood. He is appalled by the 'sight':

> What justice can but judge against thee right,
> With thine own bloud to price his bloud, here shed in sight?

(I.ix.37)

All the Knight sees is the sight, the 'spectacle', as he also calls it in the stanza. He does not see that what he has just said is a refutal of the Gospel of Matthew, which speaks of the 'blood of the New Testament, which is shed for many for the remission of sins'. He is ready to become the victim of Despair, who goes to work on him immediately. Despair argues in favour of suicide and speaks of life as a 'wearie wandering way', and death as a cold flood that has to be crossed to achieve the peace of non-being. What harm can there be, says Despair, in helping a man to kill himself when he feels he has had enough, and so speed him to the rest and silence of death? The Knight tries to argue back, but again he does not see that his argument is doomed to lose by virtue of the way it starts out, because he opens from a viewpoint that is pure Seneca:

> The terme of life is limited,
> Ne may a man prolong, nor shorten it . . .

(I.ix.41)

In other words, your day is there. He argues himself into the Senecan maze where he must lose himself: everything on earth is the will of God, so there is nothing for us to do but submit to that:

> . . . did not he all create
> To die again? all ends that was begonne,
> Their times in his eternal booke of fate
> Are written sure, and have their certain date.

The bathos and triviality of that rhyme, 'fate'/'date', shows the level on which the thought proceeds. But the Knight is mesmerised by the apparent logic of his own rhetoric. He becomes more trapped as the stanza goes on to discourse, inevitably, upon 'necessitie'. The language is pure Seneca:

> Who then can striue with strong necessitie
> That holds the world in his still chaunging state,
> Or shunne the death ordained by destinee?
> When houre of death is come, let none aske whence, nor
> why.

No point in questions, nor in action. There can be no striving against the limitless strength of what is ordained. We are as nothing. The next stanza opens:

> The lenger life, I wote the greater sin ...

This is the Knight speaking, but it might just as well be Despair, because to all intents and purposes the Knight has now lost himself in a Senecan maze of trivial thought, and has become Despair. When he looks back on all he has done it seems futile and worthless. The sooner the whole sorry affair is ended the better. When Despair (now called the 'miscreant' or bad creator) sees the Knight in this mood, he shows him a picture of the souls in Hell, to oppress his spirit further. He is drawing him into the sensuality of giving in, of surrender to the deliciousness of hopelessness, the pleasure of not trying any more. He is gone, really, save that Una, standing by all the time, is stricken by this:

> through every vaine
> The curdled cold ran to her well of life
> As in a swowne: but soon reliv'd again ...

> (ix. 52)

The innermost core of her spirit is frozen by shock, but comes to life again. The Knight has talked himself into this labyrinth (he is 'much enmoved with his speach'); and the state of mind, thought intense, is banal. Una's fear is great, but all she has to do is *not* share his mood of panic and isolation, for him to regain the strength to go on once again on the quest for the true self, the new man, in Christ. The 'well of life' in Una is the water of baptism into Christ, of which she is the keeper:

We are buried with him by baptism into death: that like as Christ was raised up from the dead by the glory of the Father, even so we also should walk in newness of life.

Thus Paul in *Romans* 6.4. This is not easy to grasp, but seems to be saying a kind of death is necessary to walk in the new life:

For if we have been planted together in the likeness of his death, we shall be also in the likeness of his resurrection: Knowing this, that our old man is crucified with him, that the body of sin be destroyed, that henceforth we should not serve sin.

The Senecan despair is a kind of death, in which, through the grace of God, the new man may start to rise. The excitement of the Spenser lies in the fact that we watch this process poetically imitated in the action. The turn for life is represented; in the Shakespeare sonnet it is embodied.

This then is the first thing that Seneca opened for the Renaissance: a view of man's being as inconsequential and insignificant, which needed a recovery of a living sense of the Gospel of Christ, and its interpretation by Paul, to counter it. The only answer, in Rome, in Renaissance Europe, and in the nuclear age, to the banal confidence of Senecan assurance, is the one of transformation. So Seneca opened a way of uncovering that very thing which is conspicuous by its absence in his writings, and this is love, and the change of being that issues in love, the Shakespearean turn (not the 'Shakespeherian rag'), that is like a 'Larke at breake of day arising'. This is the new thing, the new venture of spirit, that we see opening in the Shakespeare sonnets; the Spenser *Hymnes*; and the later plays of Shakespeare. It is not just simply a recurrence of Platonic idealism (that is itself a Senecan way of looking at the phenomenon, seeing it in cyclical terms); it is an opening into a new phase of possibility for being itself, carrying with it a new darkness, a new chaos, a new blackness.

And this leads to a consideration of the second thing that Seneca opened for the Renaissance, and that was a new sense of the bleak depths of self. This is not to say that they learned psychology from Seneca, but Seneca's brutal world of inescapable cause and effect, cruelty, fear and panic, offered an image for the mind's fear of its own interiors. Hamlet has 'bad dreams'.

With the new potential for being, there came a new sense of the abyss, of the unfathomability and depth of consciousness, a sense that our minds but tentatively negotiate between possibilities, the consequences of which are unknown to us. The Ghost of his father brings Hamlet to the edge of the precipice; the past infiltrates the present by throwing a complexion on the mind, and we can remain unaware of this until a chance encounter throws out the fault, and then the little state of man is put into confusion. All is awry. We did not know the old man had so much blood in him.

The Senecan themes of ghosts, descents, smoke, depth, confusion, fury ripping through a whole family, were not just attractive for a drama that wished to sensationalise and entertain. There was more to it than that. All this forlorn and dreary stuff provided a language for speaking of the mind's fear of itself, and of what will happen if it remains unknown. Andrea's account of his journey to the underworld at the beginning of *The Spanish Tragedy* is not just Senecan bombast: it opens a mental state of blackness and terror, and an excitement which we feel when something dark is beginning to be named, something that asks to be known, and if not known, will damage or impair.

The drama of the Renaissance, and the English drama in particular, is exciting because it is both unruly and at the same time looking for coherence. In this drama all kinds of different levels of the mind come into play, and not just of the individual mind, but of the mind of society as well.

There is a kind of literary history which tries to see English drama primarily in a moralistic light, in which the key to Faustus, for example, lies in the notion that he is the new man of the Renaissance, condemned and finally overwhelmed by the outmoded system of thought of the medieval church. However, Renaissance drama is much more interesting than that. Instead of bringing in our anarchic instincts, only to show us how reprehensible and unprofitable they are, this drama brings them into play; they are, in figures like Iago or Falstaff or Faustus or Angelo, allowed their life and weight, and the drama is the means of their weighing. In this way it reflects the scope of the mind for entertaining possibility. At its greatest moments there is a sense of exultance, because the opposite of repression is taking place. The shaping instincts of art are finding a way of talking with that which most wishes to remain hidden: the secret violence; the liking for darkness; the pleasure of wounding; the delight in rage; the love of violation; and the thrill of the exercise of arbitrary power. In Renaissance drama the imagery for much of this, and for a good deal of the atmosphere it evokes, comes from Seneca.

Countering this, and countering it fiercely, thereby drawing both elements in the antagonism into the full openness of play, was a sense of the vulnerability of human flesh, not just because it was so easy to hurt (although this is true); but because it was something of potential value in itself, not just the 'box of worm seed', that Bosola, against himself, despairingly, tries to convince the Duchess of Malfi that it is. The flesh (this 'too too, sullied flesh') had value, in that it was seen to compose a unity and relationship of a more intense and integrated kind than that inherited from the past. All families have corruption in them. They are Thyestean or Oedipal to one degree or another. But in this drama there is also the saying of the potential for another kind of family, another coherence, in which the flesh will discover a more integrated life. The family, gathering together around the cold statue, under the watchful eye of Paulina, brings the stone to life. If this be magic, says Leontes, let it be an art lawful as eating. But this is not the eating of the Thyestean banquet, but that other eating which we call communion, through which there is an entering into the body of the new man.

I am not trying to moralise Renaissance drama. I aim to show it as a venture of human consciousness for inclusiveness, and that it was driven to that inclusiveness by the challenge of the desolation the Senecan codes carried with them. Elizabethan and Jacobean drama is bloody, sensational, and is fascinated by the readiness of our species to dismember, uproot, and destroy. But where it surpasses the Roman drama is in its refusal, by and large, to retire into panic-stricken terror at this prospect. It does not mesmerise itself with the banal rhetoric of despair.

It makes a venture for the variety of human experience. It is an open place, and a place for opening. The language flourishes, not because the Elizabethans had some wonderful gift of language now lost to us, but because it was in touch with that which it most wished to say. And what it says, superbly, time and again, is how our being hangs in the balance between savagery and gentleness, hate and love. It takes into itself, and finds dialogue for, all the bleak fatalism of the Senecan universe. It engages with it, plays with it, mocks it (in *A Midsummer Night's Dream*), but mainly it *says* it, without becoming convinced that it has all the story.

There was a Senecan tragedy of blood, but there was another drama of blood, that took place not just through our fault, but *for* our fault, which pushed the Renaissance into the challenge of the encounter with Despair. That challenging drama of blood was not a tragedy or a tragi-comedy or anything else of that sort. It was life itself, turning to arise, like the 'Larke at breake of day'.

Let us return to that Eliot footnote where he says that when he comes to consider Shakespeare as the voice of his time, that voice in poetry is, in the most serious matters of life and death, most often the voice of Seneca. I think Eliot is half-right. I would say that in the most serious matters of life and death in the literature of the Renaissance the voice of Seneca is continually being challenged by another way of thinking, by another sense of the possibilities of consciousness. Where that other sense is lacking, or where it cannot open, the writing is threatened by sterility, monotony, and boredom. But where the mind will not luxuriate, art becomes a form of re-creation, of participation with being, that it may be extended into more and more life.

FASCINATION AND SCANDAL

ON JOHN GAY'S *BEGGAR'S OPERA* AND THE DOCTRINE OF POETIC JUSTICE

WOLFGANG ZACH

I

In the spring of 1728, a visitor to London from the North, somewhat disconcerted by the London theatre-going public's reaction to John Gay's *Beggar's Opera*, observed, 'It seems to me to be odd that what everybody condemns, everybody should countenance'.[1] In fact, the play's sensational and unprecedented theatrical success (in its first season, it enjoyed an uninterrupted run of 62 performances) was only parallelled by the extreme vehemence with which the critics simultaneously erupted against it. There was hardly a single play more popular—and certainly none more controversial—until late in the eighteenth century[2].

The intention of the following remarks is to focus on one of the play's most fascinating aspects: the aura of attractiveness which surrounds its hero, the robber Captain Macheath: and also—still more closely—on the critical responses which have been sparked off by this character. Furthermore, it will also be asked what specific norms, aesthetic and moral, governed the portrayal of violations of the accepted codes of conduct and morality in eighteenth-century literature, a question closely bound up with the above.[3] In this context, one factor which demands the fullest consideration is the penalty exacted for deviant conduct portrayed: one dimension of the literary doctrine of poetic justice, i.e. the just distribution of rewards and punishments in literature.[4] An attempt will here be made to assess the importance of this concept in the eighteenth century, and it will be accepted in the process that, in our excursion into that period, there will be much that may appear odd and bizarre.

As far as *The Beggar's Opera* is concerned, it should at the outset be stressed that we know from a number of documents how fascinated the public who crowded into the theatre was by the 'aristocratic' highwayman Macheath and by Polly, his moll. This is also apparent from the existence of numerous prints of various poems written 'To Polly', and of one real curiosity, an allegedly authentic biography of Macheath.[5] The depiction of Macheath as a gentleman rogue, with his code of honour among his gang, his victimization by his treacherous antagonist Peachum, the constancy of the love which he arouses in Polly and his love duets with her must have made a particularly marked impression. A central role, however, was indisputably played by the 'charisma' associated with Macheath's identity as a criminal, and by his attractiveness as a sexual partner, an aspect which the play's thematic emphasis renders quite inescapable. Here it should be remarked that James Boswell was in the habit of identifying himself with Macheath in his erotic adventures: and that, for this reason, Macheath virtually dominates Boswell's private *London Journal*.[6]

It was also of highest significance for the public at the time that Macheath, in *The Beggar's Opera*, finally escapes his punishment and is actually allowed to sing a triumphal closing song. Thus, many critics, neglecting all the other features of the play— especially the less appealing elements of Macheath's character and of his highwayman's existence as well as the satirical critique of the vices and virtues of 'polite society' which Gay intended— concentrated solely on its supposedly 'immoral' focus of sympathy and, above all, on the fact that poetic justice did not seem ultimately to be enforced.

Dr Thomas Herring, later Archbishop of York and Canterbury, gave the signal for the attack on Gay's plays with a sermon which he preached in March 1728, and which received much attention. He maintained that young people in particular would be tempted, by the seductive portrait of Macheath and by his final escape from the gallows, to imitate his conduct and become criminals themselves.[7] This was the general line of argument adopted by *The Beggar's Opera*'s opponents, which remained practically unaltered for the whole of the eighteenth century[8]. It is especially remarkable that to the chorus of voices which could be heard in support of this view was joined that of Daniel Defoe; indeed, Defoe, basing his case on the apparent absence of any penalty for Macheath, credits him with a virtually—or at least potentially—proteic effect. 'Every idle Fellow, weary of honest labour, need but fancy himself a Macheath ... and there's a Rogue made at once', he writes; and he even follows this up with, 'The Author, I think, is punishable for not punishing the Persons in his drama according to their deserts'.[9] Thus, Gay is held responsible—and not only by Defoe—for all the social consequences arising from the actions of those spectators who imitate his central figure, consequences which are themselves postulated as self-evident. According to Defoe, in fact, the author should himself be called to account for allowing a criminal to escape punishment in his play.

To us today these criticisms may seem strange, and yet they do correspond to what was at the time the dominant paradigm in regard to the moral and social effects ascribed to literature. According to this view, the distribution of rewards and punishments in a literary work was credited with a direct influence on the evaluative and behavioural norms of its recipients. Rewarded conduct, it was believed, would be imitated, penalized conduct would be avoided—literature was, as it were, viewed as a behaviouristic 'Skinner-Box' for mankind. It is this theoretical model which lies behind the moral and didactic dimension of 'poetic justice'. Moreover, the affirmation, internalisation and tradition of a uniform, 'ideal' social code of morality and conduct appeared to be of highest value to the predominantly static normative thinking of classicism and to be rendered possible by a 'just' distribution of punishments and rewards in literature. This at least partially explains both the great prestige which poetic justice then possessed[10] (as it certainly does not today) and the violent critical opposition which *The Beggar's Opera* provoked.

However, Gay's *Beggar's Opera* was not by any means the only play on the London stage in which infringements of the socially accepted norms went unpunished: but most of the time these only took the form of violations of the moral code, as they did, for example, in Restoration comedy. But in depicting Macheath—a highwayman who apparently has his origins in the London underworld of the period, who is portrayed as attractive, and who finally escapes punishment—John Gay had touched on one of the strictest taboos of those days, the one concerning property, and, through it, on the very structure of society. To be aware of the truth of the latter, one need only consider certain features and events of the time—the enormous discrepancy between rich and poor, the harshness of the laws which then protected property, the vast number of criminal acts as well as of executions and transportations for offences relating to property, and, also, the cheers with which the crowd accompanying Jack Sheppard to the gallows a few years before had fêted Macheath's real-life original as a hero. One then comes to realise clearly to what lengths the establishment went to uphold the rights of property and how great the sense of personal danger among the propertied classes must have been.[11] This social climate and, of course, the immense popularity of *The Beggar's Opera* may help to explain why this play found itself exposed to such ferocious criticism.

It should also be pointed out that, at this time, both fictional and real figures from the London underworld were among the most popular characters of narrative literature. To a certain extent, they even achieve heroic status; and they seem to have offered the reader the chance to escape from the repression of the established order, and give free rein to his innermost fears, hopes and aggressions. In such works, however, the criminals are inevitably punished, their punishment often being elevated to a religious level by being ascribed to the intervention of Providence. Thus, the order sanctioned by society is affirmed, and—this aspect must not be overlooked—the work is thus rendered immune to criticism on moral grounds.[12] Without poetic justice—which actually was at that time a mode of legitimizing the realistic portrayal of crime—*The Beggar's Opera*, however, was delivered up defenceless to its critics. One of Gay's contemporaries, James Ralph, already noted this 'immunising' function of poetic justice, observing that *The Beggar's Opera* lacked 'Justice, to countenance its Run and screen it from the Critics'.[13] On no other account could Gay's masterpiece have come under such heavy fire, probably serving, in the process, as a scapegoat.

As has already been mentioned, the specific artistic intentions which had motivated Gay to allow Macheath to escape scot-free were of no importance to *The Beggar's Opera's* opponents in this matter; they simply insisted on the execution of poetic justice. Incidentally, the much smaller number of literati who came to the defence of Gay's play, in particular Jonathan Swift, hardly emphasised anything other than Gay's satire on the vices of the nobility and the bourgeoisie in putting forward their case; from this they derived positive moral consequences for society, but did not further comment on the ending of the play itself.[14]

In the twentieth century when *The Beggar's Opera* has finally obtained a permanent place in the theatre—with, indeed, several highly successful runs to its credit—critics have, of course, also commented upon the play's conclusion. Some of them maintain that Gay's attitude towards the doctrine of poetic justice is one of fundamental critical detachment. Gerd Stratmann, for instance, claims that Gay, in *The Beggar's Opera*, explicitly calls the doctrine into question. [15] However, this view seems to me to be in need of some modification. To substantiate this claim, it is necessary to consider in more detail both the aesthetic context of the time and Gay's own authorial intentions.

Here, one should first mention that around 1700, particularly in the course of the 'Collier controversy', poetic justice in its punitive aspect was promoted to the status of a central axiom in the period's conception of both tragedy and comedy. [16] On this point, the most prominent critics of the eighteenth century, including Defoe and Swift, Dennis and Gildon, are at one [17]; and George Farquhar even writes: 'If they [= authors] have left vice unpunished, virtue unrewarded, folly unexposed, or prudence unsuccessful, the contrary of which is the *Utile* of comedy, let them be lashed to some purpose.' [18] After 1700 we hardly find a single literary critic who would still have dared to defend the Restoration comedies with their 'rewarded rakes', and in 1719 even an opponent of the theatre in the tradition of Jeremy Collier, Arthur Bredford, could not—though trying very hard—find one single contemporary comedy in which a rake was allowed to go unpunished. [19]

However, the poetic norm now came into fundamental conflict with the wishes of the theatre audiences, which began increasingly to turn away from those art forms which were viewed as 'moral' and 'legitimate' by the classicists (i.e. tragedy and comedy) and to develop a taste instead for 'amoral' and 'illegitimate' dramatic forms, such as farce, pantomime, or the Italian opera. In these genres, especially that of Italian opera, the dramatic norm of the time—as was obvious to all contemporaries—was not that of 'moral' poetic justice, but of an 'amoral' happy ending: and among the most prominent literary critics of the early eighteenth century these genres elicited fierce opposition [20]. A considerable number of authors of the period, therefore—and we are speaking here of writers of the prominence of Farquhar, Defoe and Swift—explicitly reproached theatre-goers with giving no consideration whatsoever to a character's moral qualities, and with being satisfied with a mere happy ending regardless of its moral implications, rather than demanding poetic justice. This was interpreted as a sign both of immorality and of artistic ignorance.[21] William Coward in 1709 voiced the opinion that it was the playwrights' dependence on popular taste and, indeed, on box office returns which kept them from doing their duty of instructing as well as entertaining their audiences; and he lamented the fact that they should be forced to prostitute their art as they did.[22] Alexander Pope refers to the theatre public, with great contempt, as 'a senseless, worthless, and unhonour'd crowd'[23] and memorably describes the authors' dilemma in *The Dunciad* (1728–43).

We should not, therefore, be too surprised that Gay, whose spiritual affinity with Pope was considerable, took a similar attitude. He is sharply critical of those farces and harlequinades which aim at nothing more than cheap entertainment, and expresses a fear that, the prevailing public taste being what it is, tragedy, with its ethical and artistic values, may no longer be able to compete with these other forms of entertainment, least of all with that most fashionable one, the opera, whose sole intent, he believes, is to arouse ecstatic sensual pleasure and irrational emotive effects. Furthermore, he reproaches the public with simply not being interested in moral instruction through dramatic poetry. And—most noticeably in the years around 1720—Gay's declared intention was to educate his audience to recognise the values of Christian humanism: the desired aim of his fables, according to him, was 'to make men moral, good and wise'.[24] Given the high status which poetic justice enjoyed at the time, we need hardly be surprised to find that, in the plays preceding *The Beggar's Opera*, Gay does in fact show it in operation.[25] In the introduction to his tragedy *The Captives* (1724) he gives special emphasis to the practice of such justice; and furthermore, in a letter dated 28 August, 1726, he expresses his satisfaction that Elkanah Settle's tragedy *The Siege of Troy* differs from its source in one respect—namely, in that Settle employs 'poetical Justice'.[26]

With his plays still denied success, his hopes of court patronage unfulfilled and financial ruin staring him in the face, only one escape from his predicament seemd to present itself to him—submission to the dictates of public taste.[27] However, Gay's fear was that this would strip him of both his moral and his artistic integrity, and among other similar statements, he writes, with bitter irony:

Why art thou poor; exert thy gifts to rise,
And banish tim'rous Virtue from thy eyes.[28]

Gay had already solved this dilemma in his farce *The What D'ye Call It* (1715), by actually making the consequences of the author's financial dependence and his enforced obedience to public taste the play's theme. Within the framing action of the play, the uncultivated squire Sir Roger orders his steward to write a play in complete accordance with his wishes; the result, naturally, is nothing but a vulgar farrago of different dramatic genres. *A Tragi-Comi-Pastoral Farce*, corresponding to the vulgar taste of its commissioner. The important point here is that the Squire, an unjust Justice of the Peace, insists on a happy ending to his steward's fictional play-within-a-play when it is finally performed; and precisely because of this, he finds—outwitted by his steward—that in the pseudo-reality of the play's frame he has to accept 'poetic' justice when it is turned against himself. Much against his will, he has to do justice himself and, at the end of the play, we hear the words 'It is good in law'[29]—justice finally triumphs through the cunning of the steward or, rather, through the artistry of the poet.

The audience—and Gay here, in essence, allies himself with Defoe, Swift and Farquhar in his reproaches—only craves a happy ending; the spectators do not want to see ideal ethical norms or justice realised, certainly not in their own lives, nor in society at large. It is also striking that Gay's conception of poetic justice is exceptional at this time: Gay does not attempt to obtain the didactic effect desired by emotionally involving the spectator in an action which is intended to demonstrate the utility of the conduct represented by meting out rewards and punishments accordingly. As a satirist, he prefers to operate via the intellect, making the spectator perceive the difference between the justice of the fictional world depicted by the artist and the injustice of social reality. In this play, however, Gay has also expressed his yearning that poetic justice and social reality should be one, just as the spectator is called upon not to adhere to the conventional, corrupt social norms, but rather to endeavour to change these, beginning in his own mind, so that they may finally become identical with the ideal ethical norms of art.

II

Turning to *The Beggar's Opera* itself, we now immediately recognise how relevant these considerations are to the play.[30] It becomes evident that Gay, here as previously in *The What D'ye*

Call It, has depicted the consequences of the author's servitude to his 'patrons'. This is particularly apparent in the fictional ironies of the scenes at the beginning and shortly before the end of the play, in the dialogues between the fictional Beggar-Author and the Actor ('Introduction' and III.xvi, pp.112 and 158ff.). By introducing a fictional beggar, who is unquestioningly dependent on his patrons, as the writer of his Opera, Gay makes the financial predicament of the poet manifest. He also makes it clear to the audience that it is being confronted with an emanation of its own corrupt moral values and poor literary taste. *The Beggar's Opera* even identifies itself as a 'pre-programmed' theoretical success, aiming at the widest possible impact; the opera as the basis for Gay's burlesque, the London underworld milieu, the gentleman bandit, the robber bride, the popular melodies, etc., all this belongs to Gay's 'success strategy'.[31]

When the fictional Beggar mentions at the beginning of the play that his opera has already been performed before, with the assistance of the inhabitants of St Giles and with great success, Gay implicitly insults the audience in the theatre; he identifies its taste with that of the London underworld, calling its critical ability and moral sense into fundamental question. We further hear that its author enjoys the patronage of the beggar's guild, which thus proves to be more generous than the English Court, which had degraded his real-life counterpart, Gay himself, to the level of a beggar, and forced him into economic dependence upon the whims of the public. It is here of especial significance that the Beggar is in some sense the *poet laureate* of his social group; his play, in other words, is to be understood as a panegyric to the London underworld. Thus, Gay makes it clear that he has been driven to flatter immorality; he draws the audience's attention to his mock-heroic technique and the resulting reversal of values in his play. Gay may have been prompted to adopt this strategy by applying Pope's formula for a successful panegyric, 'the Golden Rule of *Transformation*, which consists in converting Vices into their bordering *Virtues*'— Pope's '*Rule of Contraries*' for social and literary success.[32]

Thus, Gay gives his audience, to use Brecht's words, 'such aspects of life as it wishes to see in the theatre'[33]; but through the attached fictional plane of his ironic commentary, he hints at the author's enforced servitude and at the confrontation of the audience with its own poor taste and corrupt values. He has—as he had previously done in *The What D'ye Call It*—preserved his own integrity. Furthermore, the vices of the criminal world represented are, in *The Beggar's Opera*, constantly identified with those of the aristocracy and the bourgeoisie; so each member of the audience becomes the potential victim of Gay's satiric critique of the misdemeanours and vices portrayed. The spectator who overlooks the mock-heroic and ironic-satiric artistic principles of *The Beggar's Opera* may indeed have only himself to blame; he must, however, also feel that he is positively being invited to connive at the existence of the world which contains the 'bourgeois' Peachum's boundless lust for profit or the 'aristocratic' Macheath's uninhibited satisfaction of his desires—that world which is ostensibly the normal one, but for which Gay feels profound contempt. But as a beggar, Gay implies, he has no choice but to accept this possibility as well, and Colley Cibber even interpreted this as Gay's choice of a fitting revenge on the ignorance and low taste of the public which had disliked his earlier plays, thus forcing him into servitude to its poor literary taste; indeed, Cibber sees in this the greatest triumph of Gay's satiric art.[34]

We can now see, therefore, how well the conclusion of *The Beggar's Opera* (III. xvi, xvii, p.158ff.) fits into the context just described; it is the culminating point of Gay's satiric attack on his audience. Just as Macheath's fate seems finally to be sealed, the Beggar and the Player re-enter. Macheath, who has been betrayed by one of the members of his gang, is now about to meet his doom; he, for his part, has made sure that Peachum and Lockit, who have engineered his downfall, will also end on the gallows. A denouement seems inevitable in which the criminals in the play embodying the contending vices of the aristocracy and the bourgeoisie destroy one another.

But here, characteristically, the Player intervenes to prevent the Beggar-Author from employing poetic justice and letting Macheath hang—with his reference to the rule that operas have to have a happy ending. It is striking that, in so doing, the Player first addresses the author as 'honest friend', using an *epitheton ornans*, which was in fact indissolubly linked with Gay's name during his lifetime.[35] The Beggar, fearing for his success—after this point he is only addressed as 'friend'—now ceases to set any store by poetic justice. He now accepts the Player's objection as 'just', prostitutes his art in this respect as well (he had not wanted to make his Opera as unnatural as was customary—cf.'Introduction'), has the mob proclaim Macheath's pardon whilst appealing to the fact that the plots of operas are necessarily absurd in any case, and allows his hero to enter, surrounded by his wives and his whores. The Player also makes it quite clear who has decided what the texture of the play should be like—and especially how the play should end—when he says 'All this we must do to comply with the taste of the town' (III.xvi,p.158). This shortly follows the words 'Gold from law can take out the sting' (III. xiii p.157), and it appears that 'gold' here has also affected the very 'law' which prevailed in literature at the time—that of poetic justice.

We agree here with Martin Price's opinion when he says that 'the beggar's manipulation is, in one sense, a symbolic selling out in key with the world he has presented'.[36] The renunciation of poetic justice, the reference to this idea and the happy ending which is ultimately depicted, thus become for Gay—at least on one level—methods of satirizing the artistic and moral norms of the public. Here, it can only briefly be remarked that this does not exhaust the implications of this 'quotation' of poetic justice; as the 'moral' of the Beggar, placed at the end of the scene, makes particularly clear, Gay also employs the doctrine as a satiric weapon in the struggle against the social injustice which he had diagnosed. Consequently, he has here ascribed to the concept of poetic justice—in contrast to the way in which it was mostly understood at the time—a satiric function quite similar to that which we have already observed in *The What D'ye Call It*. In any case, it is my view that what we find in *The Beggar's Opera* is not Gay's rejection of the idea of poetic justice, but Gay's satirical critique of the public's rejection of it.[37]

Gay has, by the way, also ironically undermined the happy ending (III.xviii.p.159) which is in fact presented; and the allure with which he depicts Macheath in the closing scene, and the ostensibly highly entertaining nature of this finale, are accordingly only the last ironies in a play which is shot through with ironies in abundance. Unlike Gay's fictional audience and many of his critics, we should not miss the fact that the ending which he has given to his *Beggar's Opera* can be appropriately juxtaposed with that of Pope's *Dunciad*. The narrator of *The Dunciad*, it is true, takes a far stronger stand against the victory of Chaos over true poetry, morality and religion than does the Beggar-Author, but he is still finally forced to record it. And is not Macheath as he appears at the play's close—presented as a Turk, surrounded by prostitutes, respecting no law—practically a symbol of the artistic, moral and religious anarchy which both Pope and Gay detested, and which both saw rising out of the darkness to engulf society? And yet, given the ironic-satiric method which had, as it were, been imposed on him, Gay had to accept that the moralist would probably confuse the author with his protagonist, and that the conclusion of *The Beggar's Opera* could be interpreted as a denial of poetic justice *per se*, rather than as a critique of the public's literary and moral norms.

III

I should now like to deal more fully with the history of *The Beggar's Opera*'s public reception. First of all, it should once more be pointed out how vehement criticism of the refusal to punish Macheath already was in 1728, and how certain the critics were that this would inevitably lead to emulation of Macheath's example.[38] Gay was by no means indifferent to these rebukes, as we can deduce from his next play, *Polly. An Opera. Being the Second Part of the Beggar's Opera* (1728/29).[39] In the Prologue to this play, the poet enters *in propria persona*: now, as a successful dramatist, he has put aside the beggar's rags, and has slipped on instead the robes of the preacher. Again, there is a conversation between author and actor; but this time, the author refers to the stage as a pulpit, and he makes it clear that he now intends not to make any concessions to the audience's taste, but to castigate all vices openly with his satiric scourge. The successful author now knows that he is no longer the slave of the mob's whims. He rejects any idea of ironic self-distancing, allocates his sympathies to the characters according to his own moral norms and actually metes out poetic justice—Peachum has been hanged since the end of the previous play, and Macheath, along with other characters from *The Beggar's Opera*, has been transported to the West Indies to which the scene has shifted. Macheath has escaped and become a pirate captain; he is portrayed as despicable, brutal, and cowardly. As a result, he completely loses his previous heroic aura; and furthermore—and this is particularly curious—he commits his crimes disguised as a negro. Now, in my view, there are no textual reasons to suppose from this that Gay is mocking the critics of *The Beggar's Opera*, attractive though this idea undeniably is. We must rather assume, I believe, that Macheath's blackness is intended to reflect his character; moreover, it may even have been conceived as a distancing element, preventing the spectators from identifying with Macheath and thus disarming from the outset further accusations that he may be setting a bad example.

Unlike *The Beggar's Opera*, *Polly* also contains a dramatic foil to
the world of the European colonialists and of the European
pirates, who are seen as being fundamentally alike in their total
corruption by materialism and egoism. A contrast is achieved
through Gay's antithetical depiction of the Indians of the West
Indies as 'noble savages', or, rather, as truly civilized human
beings, who are distinguished by all the virtues of Christian
humanism so dear to Gay himself, i.e. integrity, industry,
honour, courage, loyalty, affection etc. Thus, Gay has modified
the perspective from which his characters are viewed, turning
away from ironical satire to moral allegory: he has made both his
social criticism and his intention to educate the public to an ideal
morality as obvious as possible. Finally, the 'noble savages'
defeat the pirates and, this time, Macheath's reprieve comes a
little too late: his execution has already been carried out and is
verbally justified by the king of the Indians, who is presented as
an ideal ruler. Not only is vice punished, however, but virtue also
receives its appropriate reward: Polly, who now appears as the
typical 'virtuous heroine' of sentimental drama, will possibly
marry an equally virtuous Indian prince. The play then closes
with a hymn to the triumph of virtue and justice, ending in the
refrain:

> Justice long forbearing,
> Power or riches never fearing,
> Slow yet persevering,
> Hunts the villain's pace. (III.xv,p.591)

In his earlier plays, Gay had been concerned that the audience
should not confuse poetic justice with social justice. In *Polly*, too,
justice is only practised in an unreal world whose artificiality is
deliberately stressed. In all this, however, the element of *apologia*
and the attempt to deprive criticism of *The Beggar's Opera* of some
of its force become as apparent as the weight which this criticism
evidently had at the time. We do not know whether *Polly* would
have been a success anyway, for the Walpole government, which
had been shocked by *The Beggar's Opera*—in which the criticism
of Sir Robert Walpole had been unmistakeably clear—refused to
licence the play for performance[40]. However, when *Polly* finally
received its first production in 1777, many literary critics saw it
not only as a kind of moral atonement for *The Beggar's Opera*, but
even as its missing conclusion,[41] and it should not be forgotten in
our evaluation of this view that John Gay had himself spoken of
Polly as the second part of *The Beggar's Opera*.

In now turning to the subsequent theatrical history of *The Beggar's Opera*, we will only take those points into account which seem especially relevant to Macheath's fate, on the one hand, and to the significance of fictional punishments in the eighteenth century, on the other. Here, one bizarre fact, which today may sound scarcely credible, should be mentioned first—the reason why *The Beggar's Opera* remained unperformed in France throughout the whole of the eighteenth century. This consisted in the refusal of its translator, A. Hallam, to allow Macheath actually to end on the gallows, as—if we are to believe the contemporary reports—was demanded, in all seriousness, by the Parisian theatre managers of around 1750.[42] This rejection of *The Beggar's Opera*—which, by the way, was frequently considered by French critics to represent the nadir of English bad taste, because of its lack of 'decorum'—indicates how deep-rooted the demand for a just distribution of rewards and punishments was in the French theatre, as late as the middle of the eighteenth century.[43]

The situation in England—at least as far as *The Beggar's Opera* is concerned—was completely different, however, and the play retained its immense popularity until towards the end of the eighteenth century. It also retained the continuous accompaniment of repetitive criticism of the kind which we have already described. According to the still dominant paradigm of literature's moral and didactic effect, anyone who saw the play was considered as a potential Don Quixote of the 'brotherhood of robbers'; and the critics would also frequently make quite concrete claims that Macheath's example had actually been followed. Gay's *Beggar's Opera* was also often compared with Lillo's *The London Merchant* and their social consequences were often described in antithetical terms: just as it was inferred from Macheath's escape from punishment that he would find imitators, so it was believed that the execution of George Barnwell could produce deterrent effects.[44]

However, attention must also be drawn to the decisive changes in literary axiomatics, as well as in the public taste, which took place in the years between 1720 and 1770. Whilst avant-garde critics began to dissociate themselves more and more from the dogma of poetic justice, the audiences came more and more to demand its practice, and the number of plays to appear on the stage which did not contain it became steadily fewer. By 1770, the 'moralisation' of the drama was to a large extent complete; the Restoration comedies in particular, with their rewarded rakes, were either adapted to fit the norm of poetic justice, or had disappeared completely from the London stage. At the same time, the 'moral' sentimental comedy became the dominant dramatic genre, and Gay's *Beggar's Opera* was then left in the repertory as, so to speak, a single remaining anomaly from an earlier age.[45]

So we can hardly be surprised by the fact that in the London of the 1770s several campaigns were conducted against *The Beggar's Opera* in journals and pamphlets, which were intended to force the theatre managers to withdraw the play from the repertoire.[46] *The Beggar's Opera* was especially at risk when, in 1773, Sir John Fielding, who had succeeded to his brother Henry's judicial office, approached the managers with this very suggestion, backed by support from all the justices of Middlesex. Sir John took this step because his notes indicated—to him at least—a direct connection between the series of performances which the play received and the number of robberies committed. In other words, he believed that he could actually give statistical proof that Macheath's bad precedent was responsible for the increase in robberies in and around London. As an alternative, Sir John Fielding demanded that, if nothing else, the managers should change the ending of *The Beggar's Opera*, letting Macheath hang, if they did not want to withdraw the play completely from the repertory.[47] One would like to regard this simply as the idiosyncratic dream of a paranoid fanatic with a passion for 'justice'; but when one considers the almost unbelievable ferocity of the criticism of the period, and the fact that the Parisian theatre managers had already made the same suggestion, this explanation does not seem to be sufficient.

For some time, Sir John's demand was ignored; but for the season of 1777/78 the Covent Garden Theatre commissioned Edward Thompson to write a new conclusion to the play. This involved the last two scenes, the dialogue between the Beggar and the Player and the finale (III. xvi, xvii).[48] Both were completely changed. Now, the Beggar has no desire at all to allow criminals to escape their just penalty. The theatre, he argues—rather similarly to Sir John Fielding—has to come to the assistance of the jurisdiction of the real world. However, Macheath is not condemned to execution, but to forced labour on a convict ship. The Player puts forward those objections that the managers expected to be raised by the audience, but he eventually agrees, and the Beggar now calls out: 'Let Poetical Justice take its course'. In the final scene, we are shown the ship 'Justitia', lying at anchor at Woolwich Warren harbour.

Macheath avers his repentance, hopes for a future reunion with Polly, appeals to the audience's compassion, and warns them against a similar fate. The play ends with the moralising maxim 'The wicked today shall be virtuous tomorrow'. Even in *The Beggar's Opera* itself, Macheath has now fallen victim to poetic justice. However ridiculous this altered ending may seem to us today, I believe that nothing else can illustrate quite so clearly the extent to which the authors of the period were pressured into punishing those of their protagonists who infringed the socal norms.

It is remarkable and indicative of the change in aesthetic attitudes that most of the literary critics condemned the new ending. The interest of the public, on the other hand, was at first considerable, chiefly perhaps because of the appeal of novelty and the publicity which the event was given.[49] However, the public's disapproval, which had evidently not been expected by the managers, must have prevailed, because the original ending was restored to the stage in later years. In this context, it must also be emphasised how firmly the audience at this time demanded that characters should be punished for their crimes in a play. When it once happened that Richard Cumberland, in fact one of the sternest advocates of poetic justice, allowed such a character to escape unpunished in his play *The Walloons* (1782), the audience protested so vociferously that Cumberland had to write a new concluding scene, which was performed from the second night onward.[50] Macheath's unique fascination, however, was apparently as much alive as ever, and Gay's *Beggar's Opera* had evidently become a classic.

Towards the end of the eighteenth century, therefore, *The Beggar's Opera* was again performed with its original conclusion; but at the same time—and this fact has scarcely been considered until now—the versions in which it was produced actually omitted more and more of the play as time went on. Finally, all that remained was a two-act skeleton of the original by Henry Bishop (1813), in which Macheath's gang and the whores no longer appear at all, whilst the plot, now almost completely deprived of any but the private dimension, serves only as drapery for the most popular songs.[51] Obviously, the fear had become wide-spread that the representation of deviant behaviour alone— with or without poetic justice—was sufficient to seduce recipients into imitation, and less and less of such behaviour was thus concretely shown on stage. It should also be mentioned that the dialogue of this stage version of what was formerly Gay's *Beggar's Opera* had been fully bowdlerized. Both these alterations also reflect the increasing spread of prudery and of the impetus which censorship had received from fear of revolution, as the revolutionary tendency of Gay's masterpiece could hardly be overlooked.[52] In addition, the Beggar/Player scene (III. xvi)—which, incidentally, had also been frequently cut earlier—had become increasingly less comprehensible to the public, and is here, of course, also missing. In this version, then, there was hardly any reason left to punish Macheath, whom it was now practically impossible to recognise as a highwayman at all. As Macheath's 'roaring' life and his charismatic criminality disappeared, however, so too did his fascination for the audiences. This 'revised' *Beggar's Opera*, a shadow of its former self, could not maintain its place upon the nineteenth-century stage for very much longer.

The theatre history of *The Beggar's Opera* in the eighteenth century, in any case, has shown us the continual struggle of the play with both the moral and the literary norms of the period, and in particular with the axiom of poetic justice. In literary criticism too, by the way—and even among the play's editors— moral considerations dominated until the end of the eighteenth century; even the myth of Macheath's role as a paradigm for real-life robbers lived on, as did the attempts to produce concrete evidence, in the form of individual cases, to substantiate it[53]. It should also be remembered that Dr Johnson was one of the very few writers in the late eighteenth century to condemn any speculation as to whether Macheath's example would indeed be imitated as totally futile.[54] All in all, one can however observe that the moral and didactic aspects of punishment in literature tend to recede increasingly into the background, at least in the criticism and works of the more prominent literary figures of the second half of the eighteenth century. Indeed, the very belief that literature can induce such effect was waning by this time.

In this process, a significant part was played by the fact that the dominant psychological paradigm of the early eighteenth century, which linked utility with hedonism and which ultimately lay at the core of this confidence in the didactic effect of fictional rewards and punishments, was superseded by other psychological paradigms.[55] Poetic justice, then, became increasingly to be looked upon as an unnecessary, undesirable or even positively suspect literary device. Here one need only mention William Hazlitt, who—almost as if anticipating the psychoanalysis of today—claimed that the imagining of freedom from all moral constraints could produce a positive, cathartic effect. This, he believed, could make the yoke of morality easier for man to bear in real life, whilst the punishment of deviant conduct when portrayed in literature, could, precisely because of its repressive effect, drive the reader or spectator to revolt against such crushingly oppressive norms in reality. Hazlitt accordingly reverses the estimation of the relative effects of *The Beggar's Opera* and *The London Merchant* which had been customary in the eighteenth century: of the two plays *The Beggar's Opera* is now considered the moral work, *The London Merchant* the immoral one.[56]

Furthermore, we begin at this point to hear another argument in the debate. It is now claimed, not only that the psychological mechanisms which come into play when fictional texts are concretized may obey other laws than those pertaining to actual human conduct, but also that this renders any moral-didactic effect of poetic justice and of literature impossible anyway. Jean-Jacques Rousseau had already put forward this view polemically, and his ideas, as their reception into English criticism illustrates, made a significant contribution towards literature's gaining of autonomy, to its liberation from previous subjection to moral and didactic concerns.[57]

The features of the new paradigm, then, were literature's didactic ineffectiveness and, additionally, the view that, in fiction, moral instruction was not in fact a desideratum. As a result of all this, the presentation of wickedness ceased to become problematic for the Romantics: many authors, indeed, actually saw it as valid *materia poetica*, and fictional punishment was denied any didactic significance whatsoever.[58] Thus, Macheath, for Lord Byron, Wilson Payne Knight and Sir Walter Scott, retained his fascination, but without any scandal attached.[59] In 1811, Lord Byron gave, and in no uncertain terms, his own view:

> Macheath's example—psha! no more!
> It form'd no thieves—the thief was form'd before;
> And, spite of puritans and Collier's curse.
> Plays make mankind no better, and no worse.[60]

Besides, during the Romantic period, the social implications of the work of art lost so much of the importance that had previously been ascribed to it that, to name just one example, George Daniel could write in 1828: 'We cannot afford to lose so much wit, for the bare possibility that Macheath ... may find imitators. ... Gay must not suffer to die, that rogues may live'.[61]

Thus, in the Romantic era, the question of whether the actions of characters in a fictional work might be imitated by individual members of the audience was completely irrelevant to the literary avant-garde; fictional punishments were considered to be didactically ineffectual; values were so reversed that it became scandalous to conform to received morality rather than to violate it in literary works; thus, 'poetic' justice, devalued, became 'unpoetic' justice. By this time, therefore, that view had become dominant which still prevails today according to which poetic justice is seen as the quintessence of inartistic triviality. This attitude finds particularly concise expression in the title of Dieter Wellershoff's essay 'Von der Moral erwischt. Analyse eines Trivialromans' ('Caught by Morality. Analysis of a Trivial Novel.')[62]

The title just quoted indicates, however, that the demand for the punishment of wrong-doing in literature has remained highly significant up to our own day: when we consider fiction of the lighter kind and the mass media, we realise that it is still very relevant even now. Incidentally, not only did the English censor insist that fictional offences in plays be punished before allowing them licences[63] as late as 1900, but the law of poetic justice can also still be found, for example, in the guidelines laid down for TV-programmes by the ARD and the ZDF in Germany in the 1960s—even if it is not necessarily complied with in practice. In the ZDF rules, for instance, it is stated that 'the representation of criminal actions, vice, violence and criminal milieus should not be so executed as to give these an exemplary effect, to incite to imitation, or to instruct people in the methods of pursuing illegal activities ... indications that such behaviour is being punished should not be missing in the representation.'[64]

The fear that epidemics of real crime could be the result of the depiction of crime in literature is, then, more than a curiosity from the past; it is also rife among us today. The old paradigm of poetic justice may have been devalued, but it is still with us. And it seems that today, as ever, fictional punishments are still accredited with a kind of immunising effect against the danger of possible imitation of misdemeanours and crimes represented in literature. The depiction of crime and its punishment is obviously believed to guarantee conformity to the dominant norms of value and behaviour.[65] Even today, the question as to what effects a 'Cautionary Tale for Adults' may have—or, indeed, whether is has any effect at all—has not been answered, even through empirical research; so finding an answer to it has certainly not been our task here. Instead, an attempt has been made to draw attention to the significance attributed to fictional punishments in the past, and to its parent, the paradigm of literature's moral and didactic function. In this, the fascination engendered by the robber-captain Macheath and the scandal produced by his missing punishment has been used as an illustration. As far as was possible within the limited space of this essay an attempt has been made to indicate the high prestige ascribed to this paradigm, its decline and eventual loss.

As was attempted here, today's literary studies should in my view focus more intently on the historicity of poetics and its doctrines. Taking notice of modern theoretical thinking in other fields,[66] literary critics should also feel called upon to examine the dogmatic premises of critical discourse over the centuries including their own. They should come to recognise the fact that the prestige of certain axioms of literary criticism is inescapably dependent on norms bound up with the historical period concerned, and dictated to a great extent by ideological considerations.[67] For all those who share this view, this brief excursion into the eighteenth century may perhaps have been, in the end, something more than a tour through the Old Curiosity Shop of literature and literary criticism.

A HAILING

earle birney

Derry dear Dubliner now doughty in Stirling
We send you saluyings sixty & five & a hailing
From Canada carings to the Keltical critic,
To Derry drystoner & drawer & thatcher.

Wondrous was it for Wailan, weary, & me
In Westermoss walls to be welcomed so royally
'With right rich revel & careless myrth'
& in joyful jestings with Queen Jeanne joinëd
& by beauteous Bo-daughter and boyfriend bewitched.
We knew then no Norman our noble host Jeffares,
His A must be Arthur & his Jeffares a Monmouth,
Kinross a new Camelot with a Keep by a Rumbling Bridge
Young-old but no Yochel, & Yeats-man of the best.
Derry, the Arthur whom young Gawain held dearest,
'Like a child so merry in mirth, but loving
Little to lie long or long to sit,
So busied him his young blood and his brain',
In your Commonwealth a thousand of Gawains
Grow old now remembering Arthur the host,
Hospitable and hamie by the hay in the hammil
A Derry D'Arthur dancing to the drone of the smallpipes,
Derry the undaunted world-faring professor
We, all your friends, wish you wealth of years yet to wander at will
        to criticize, to create
        to sketch or scolaye or be still
        to be merry with man and with mate
        and drink life's flask to the fill.

May 1985.

OUT OF THE TOWER

J.P. Clark

That air and light may come again
Clean and free into the chambers
Of my heart, I give up, perhaps
In folly, my tenure in a tower,
Built upon a place of swamp.
I had thought, standing in the cesspool,
Head, shoulders and trunk above
The stench, the rot around could not
Infect my life. But feet in boots
Over years of no reclamation
Grew fetid, and lungs that were clear
Before so much congested,
It would have been suicide
To stay any day longer,
Believing one might as well accept
The conditions, since they were
After all endemic to the country.

THREE POEMS
Dan Davin

THE IRISH

Our touch so gentle, voice so soft,
You'd think us seraphs up aloft,
Us savage men of Ireland.
But the past is there, deep down there.
Beware, beware, of your feeling for
The savage men of Ireland.

INFERNAL IDYLL

The devil kissed me lightly
And took me by the hand.
We danced where he danced nightly,
Upon the lip-wet sand.
He said, 'You dance delightfully,
Most devilishly well,
And you must join my band.
And when you burn most frightfully,
I hope you'll kiss my hand.'
Then he smiled serenely,
Above his flaming brand,
And laid me down most tenderly,
Upon that lip-warm sand.

DAY'S END

The hens are fed, the pigs are fed.
The cows are milked, and out for the night.
So are the stars.
The Building Society's bill is paid.
We haven't lost the land beneath us.
The night is light,
And so is the moon.
And down by our gorse-flamed hedges
You and I lie prone on the sky
And grow up at our edges.
That's the way it ought to be
And that's the way it was.
That is the way it will always be,
Because.

241

A BLESSING OF DOLPHINS

Geoffrey Dutton

Jim (he calls himself here), begins
By laughing, how he, a musician, was skippering
This boat from Vietnam to the Phillipines,
An old wooden boat, nine metres long,
With a compass made from a biscuit tin,
Swung on cooking oil, and a map
Of acquaintance stars. He told how it happened.

'I came with bare hands, like a baby.'
They were all like children, in a cockle-shell, bailing,
Jim and his boat people, they were just that,
People with no country but a boat.

The storm struck when they were nearly there,
A few hundred hungry kilometres away
From Manila. Waves grew higher
Than the boat was long. Just she might
Ride one shuddering, when sideways
A beam-on breaker rolled.
Ribs lost timbers, nails
Slipped their grip. Jim knelt and prayed
To any god who might kindly hear
Words folded in foam and fear.

But no winds listened, no waves
In their heaping-in of water obeyed.

Then the sea burst open, ten thousand
Dolphins erupted around them, rousing
The air, whacked down on the sea.
In arcs of joy they declared peace
On the warring waves. Their ring of calm
Around the boat eased it from harm,
While the storm outside the charmed
Circle still tore the tops off waves
And dug ten thousand angry graves.

Each dolphin in a shining somersault could crack
The clutch of tired old planks,
But only one came aboard, and flipped straight out,
One out of thousands of leaping thousands.

At last it was over, and the gentled sea
Rocked the sighing timbers to sleep.
The boat was blessed, guided home,
Wreaths of scud now garlands of foam,
While the dolphins circled the boat each day
To Manila harbour, then curved away
To the hot horizon in cool play.
Jim and his boat people were ferried
Ashore, and as they turned to wave farewell
To the old boat, it groaned at anchor,
Quietly opened up, and sank.

TEN POEMS IN THE GREEK ANTHOLOGY MODE

Nissim Ezekiel

1) From the age of 20 to 30
   She waited passively for a lover.
   From 30 to 40
   She tried actively to catch one.
   Now she is known
   As the lively virgin
   Of the National Centre for the Performing Arts.

2) He devoted his life to the defence of freedom.
   All who worked with him resented his tyrannical
   ways.

3) Radha says she longs for Krishna
   As the soul longs for union with God — Krishna
   likes the idea

4) Asked about his critics,
   The poet moaned: They crucify me
   Because I am creative.

   Asked about a contemporary,
   Sometimes admired, he played iconoclast
   And howled,
   'He's not a major poet by any standards.'

   Then he crawled back proudly to his Cross.

5) Bitten by bugs in her friendly bed,
   He sent her the next morning
   Instead of a bouquet of flowers
   A packet of the New Tick-20,
   Which was the more practical gift
   And less expensive.

6) Here lies a poet whose theme was human failure,
   For which he was praised in a dozen famous
   obituaries.

7)   'Is this a sign?'
      She asked when she
      First held my hands.
      'Does this mean acquiescence?'
      She asked when she
      Let me touch her breasts.
      'No, that is not a sign.
      This does not mean acquiescence,'
      I said, as our naked bodies
      Came together.

8)   When the female Railway Clerk
      Received an offer of marriage
      From her neighbour the Customs Clerk,
      She told him to apply in triplicate,
      And he did.

9)   She announced herself a painter
      Over and over again,
      Until she came to be known
      By the nickname 'I'm-a-painter'.
      Now she is dead
      Her lovers mourn for her,
      Who always kept silent
      When she talked about art.

10)   Why do so many of those
      Greek Anthology poets
      Says it's best not to be born,
      And being born, to die early?
      I disagree.
      It's best to be born,
      And being born,
      To write verses saying
      It's best not to be born.
      To live long
      And to write verses saying
      It's better to die early.
      Because if you're not born,
      What can you say?
      And if you die early,
      How well can you learn to say it?

TWO POEMS

Alastair Fowler

Love's Raptures Interpreted

I give up: it isn't any use;
There's no getting poems across to them.
So far as most reviewers go, you write
Literally, or lie. A verse of secret love
Proves you're untrue; a twinge of married lust
Means the affair has ended. An elegy, and I'm down:
A song lets out (to those with longest ears)
I've found new life.—Written the same day?
That only shows I couldn't sort it out.
As for the body thinking private thoughts.
If I so much as mention a middle leg
I'm a monster. Still, those keen biographers
Aren't so bad as this postmodern mob.
What ruptures may the joyless structuralists not
Find in our love (concealed from all but them)?
In the gaps I leave—the things I haven't said—
The words that fail to reach a mood of love
Beyond my forking tongue, what will they
Construct for me to have meant and given away
By never writing? Indeterminacies. Things
That you and I must read with a straight face.
They'll say there is a gap between us, in spite
Of what we know and all my poems mean:

Our love. But I'm caught between the literal devils
And these deep-sea-divers in system suits.
I'm interpreted. I'm done. I give up—
Which means (we know) there's more of this to come.

* * *

Untitled

Longevity is measured by
Activity.
The gnats that agitate the light
Rave ephemerally;
But we who love
Loll in immortal languor.

246

THE DARK WOOD
for Derry Jeffares

Seamus Heaney

In the middle of the journey of our life
I discovered myself in a dark wood
Where the straight road had been lost sight of.

Ah, it is hard to say how gnarled and strong
And full of thickets it was in that wood
I panic even now remembering.

It is bitter almost as the taste of death.
But to rehearse the good that came of it
For me, I will tell the other things I met with.

How I got into it I cannot clearly say
For I was moving like a sleepwalker
The moment I stepped out of the right way

But when I came to the foot of a hill
That stood at the far end of that valley
Where my heart had begun to fear and tremble

I looked up, and saw its shoulders glowed
Already in the rays of the planet
Which leads and keeps men straight on every road.

Then I sensed a quiet settling
Into those depths in me that had been rocked
And pitifully troubled all night long,

And as a survivor gasping on the sand
Turns his head back to study in a daze
The dangerous combers, so my mind

Turned back, although it was reeling still,
To inspect that gap no one ever entered
And came out again alive to tell the tale.

I rested a little then for I was tired
And began to climb up the waste slopes once more,
With my lower foot always my best support,

When suddenly the spotted fluent shape
Of a leopard crossed my path
Not far up from the bottom of the slope,

Harrying me, confronting my advance,
Loping round me, leaping in my face
So that I turned back downhill more than once.

The morning was beginning all above,
The sun was rising up among the stars
That rose with him when the Divine Love

First set those lovely things in motion,
So I was encouraged to face with better hope
The beast skipping in its merry skin

By the time of day, the sweetness of the season:
But not enough not to be frightened by
The sudden apparition of a lion

That came for me with his head in the air
And so maddened by hunger it seemed
The air itself was bristling with fear.

And a she-wolf, so thin she looked as if
All her appetites were gnawing at her.
She had already brought many to grief

And I was so scared at the sight of her
My courage broke and I lost heart
In climbing the mountain any farther.

And like somebody keyed up to win
Who, when the time comes round for him to lose,
Weeps, and is inconsolably cast down—

I was like that as I retreated from
The animal's turbulent head-on attack
Gradually, to where the sun is dumb.

While I was slipping back, about to sink
Back to the depths, I caught sight of one
Who seemed through a long silence indistinct.

When I saw him in that great waste land
I cried out to him, 'Pity me,
Whatever you are, shade or living man.'

He answered, 'No, I am not a living man
Though I was alive once, and had Lombards
For parents, both of them Mantuan.

Though I was born *sub Julio*, my prime
Was spent in the heyday of the false gods
When I lived in Rome, in good Augustus's time.

I was a poet, and I sang of that just son
Of Anchises who came out of Troy
After the burning of proud Illion.

But why do you face back into misery?
Why do you not keep on up the sweet hill,
The source and cause of all felicity?'

'O are you then Virgil, are you the fountainhead
Of that wide river of speech constantly brimming?'
I answered and for shame kept my head bowed.

'All other poets live by your honour and light.
Let me be enabled by the great love
That impelled me to your book and bound me to it.

You are my master, my authority.
I learned from you and from you alone
The illustrious style for which they honour me.

Look at the beast that has forced me to turn back.
O help me to confront her, famous sage,
For she makes my veins race and my pulses shake.'

'You will have to go another way around,'
He answered, when he saw me weeping,
'To escape the toils and thickets of this ground;

Because this animal you are troubled by
Lets no man pass but harasses him
Until she kills him by her savagery

And she is so consumed by viciousness
That nothing fills her, and so insatiable
That feeding only makes her ravenous.

There are many animals she couples with
And there will be more of them, until the Hound
Shall come and grind her in the jaws of death.

He will not feed on money or on earth,
But wisdom, virtue and love will sustain him
And between two bits of felt he will have his birth.

To humble Italy, for which the virgin
Camilla died bleeding, and Turnus died, and Nisus
And Euryalus, he will bring salvation.

He will hunt the wolf through every town
Until he has hounded her down to hell
Where envy first unleashed her and set her on.

Therefore, for your own good, I think the best course
Is to follow me and I will be your guide
And lead you from here through an eternal place

Where you will hear hopeless screams and see
The long-lost spirits suffering their pain,
Lamenting the second death they have to die.

And then you will see those who are not distressed
In the fire because they hope to come,
Whenever their time comes, among the blessed.

If you want to ascend among these, then you
Will be guided by a soul worthier than I
And I will leave you with her when I go;

For that Emperor above does not allow
Entry to me into His city
Because I was a rebel to His law.

His empire is everywhere but His high seat
And city are there, in His proper kingdom.
O happy is the man He calls to it.'

And I said to him, 'I ask you, poet,
In the name of that God you were ignorant of—
To prevent worse happening, to help me flee it—

Lead me to that place described by you
So that I may see St. Peter's Gate
And those other ones you spoke of in their sorrow.'

Then he set off and I began to follow.

Dante, *Inferno*, Canto I.

DERRY JEFFARES IN AUSTRALIA

A.D. Hope

He burst upon us like a shooting star,
A genial, lively Mercury of a man,
A mobile mentor, reading as he ran,
Bringing us inspiration from afar,
Scattering ideas we'd had no notion of,
Startling us to fresh action everywhere.
We never thought he 'occupied a chair'.
We christened him the Peripatetic Prof.

His greatest feat, however, and his best
Was to abolish the Antipodes.
'Down Under' had no meaning when the test
Was his. Rolling the Globe about with ease,
Although he very rarely seemed to stop,
Where Derry halted had to be the top.

LINES FOR DERRY JEFFARES

Brendan Kennelly

The first time I saw Derry Jeffares
Was in his winey room in Leeds:
'How would you like to go to Africa, Brendan?
Encounter different styles and creeds?'
And so, throughout the years. Something in him
Insists on treating men as brothers:
'Remember, if you bore yourself
It's likely you'll bore others.'

'There's a mighty pilot lost in you, young Jeffares.'
'Pilot? I'm a racing-driver, man!'
It's well I know. One summer day
He scorched six hundred miles through France
Yarning, humming, whistling, all alive
And vibrant as a springing Wexford day.
We passed crashed cars, smouldering; no lessening
Of speed for him who knew the way.

'Stay off the whiskey; no white; stick to the red;
Whiskey-drinkers feel they must finish the bottle;
White wine drives one nutty but red compels
One to return to Plato and Aristotle,
The fresh old fathers. Read the ancients well;
Write as if you were born and lived without fear;
Face your own confusion; think through that hell
And try to be clear.'

He serves a servant. Yeats served poetry well
And Jeffares' service to the poet is true
And long. His stamina inspires us all,
Helping us to do the best that we can do.
Everything he does, he does with the laughter
Of the serious mind, never the solemn or dull:
'You're getting bleary: a swim at the Pont du Gard,
And after that we'll build a wall.'

The indifferent demons are his only enemies
And what man could be a friend of these?
Writing, teaching, thinking, having fun,
Thanks be to Christ he never praises fleas.
Come over to Sligo; it is August there;
Midnight in the Imperial by the river;
Derry is into a story; a relaxed father
Laughs by the promising waters forever.

NOTES TOWARDS A.N.J.

Séan Lucy

I

Three strange things to find in a senior scholar:
the senses of a child;
the warm arrogance of an aristocrat;
the nightmares of a shaman.

II

Sayings I

The Renault protests a little
as he thrusts it round a redbrick curve in Leeds
on the way to the board:
'You see, some of the buggers have marking constipation,
compounded by the fact
that they simply can't believe that *anyone*
can be as good as they once were.'

III

Sayings 2

Puts down his wine in the sun
on a table by the river,
speaks seriously of a departmental wreck:
'You've *got* to give him time.
We all go off—deteriorate—
but it's often cyclical.
He was once fairly good:
he could well come back out of this mess.'
(After, this proves quite true.)

IV

Sayings 3

Watching a senior Oxbridge scholar
finally warm to an Irish party:
'You see he's really a good fellow.
It's just that like many Englishmen
he starts about one-and-a-half pints
below par.'

V

Abroad

Listens, really listens;
then shares his best stock of ideas,
the highish voice urging its Trinity tunes,
the head cocked, the quick eyes sly and friendly.

Departments spark

Patient with much waffle for a little wisdom's sake
he stokes the mutual fires.
All except bitter fools feel that they do better,
and many really do:
the academic garden flowers with brighter lectures,
                with livelier books.

VI

At Home

Those Jeffares places safe and adventurous,
Like big ships underway through time:
Leeds like a tall weighty Fastindiaman;
Westermoss more like a strong clipper in shrewder seas.

Good to be going in for work or talk.

Here he is gentler, lapses in warmer silence,
in a close family, but open to travellers, with
big pots of savory food,
gallons of wine,
truths, jokes,
songs, books,
paintings and parties,
cats,
and always talk.

VII

Paradox

Not a soft man. Watch his keen delight
as he giggles over inanities
                or insanities
                of
                (even)
                friends.

And against that, intelligent affection.
Listen. He can praise. He likes praising.
Also being honest he likes praising most
                his magic wife,
                his winged daughter,
                his Japanese son-in-law,
                his powerplant grandson,
                and his friends ('Who are, naturally, the best.')

VIII

Dusk,

a cold light on Dublin, an East wind.
The boy on the pavement stops to watch
the different movements of the ragged clouds
the stubborn march of the cold Liffey ripples
the way the trams swing under spilt sparks.

He is a little awkward and sometimes a lot lonely.
He is keen to find out how to be somebody who
will be who he wants to be.

He does not buy defeat, even though he's afraid.

This one will not melt in the puddles of sad imagination;
   this one will be glad to be human;
      this one will be somebody
         who is who he wants to be.

Jan.'85

HUSBANDRY

John Montague

Because you were barren,
male by male tree, or
one female by another,
I had to cut you down.
Near to earth as possible,
the gardening manual said:

A hard task, kneeling with
the saw's serrated blade
to scythe thick grass,
seek out your smothered side.
A neighbouring appletree
shook petals on my head,

A bird called and called,
balanced upon a thorn,
a slug crawled along
my sweating hand until
the foot was sawn, and
all your branching platform

Swayed: but still held on.
I had to put both arms
around your lean waist
to tug you finally down.
Damp pith spirted, but
that raw stump shone.

GATHERING SPEEDWELLS

Lorna Reynolds

In true academic style, 'The Extern Examiner',
Flatly they called him—this rosy bringer
Of airs from far places, this quick-going man,
Arriving in Galway, according to plan,
From the Cameroons, swinging hence
To the highlands, easy everywhere,
A seed-nurturer, a fanner of smoke to flame,
A turner of the earth, a beauty-acclaimer,
Who saw that all dues were acknowledged,
And all talents praised,
No matter whose eyebrows were raised;
A life-enhancer, knowing that to spend
Is to find oneself, that to pass gently on
Is to gather speedwells, that learning lightly worn
Is a princely robe;
That *sprezzatura* is the province, not of the courtier
Only, but may be any man's *modus operandi*.

What wonder then, though christened Alexander—
A name to suggest the highest endeavour—
He is known to all simply as Derry,
An abbreviation apt and homely,
Affectionate, genial and merry?

THE HAPPY WORRIER

James Simmons

'Professor Jeffares,' I said; but you were merry:
'Drop the bloody handle. Just call me Derry.'
I sat beside you listening to the same
lecture, inwardly giggling at that name,
my eyes fixed on your neat trousers, aware
that underneath would be blanched skin and hair,
that you were a forked animal like me.
That seemed to be true only in theory
for your power made me tremble, and I choked
with embarrassment and nerves the more you joked.
They were Professor's jokes. And so the stance
I took up waveringly was defiance,
though even at the time I was ashamed,
even in self-defence, to be unkind.
You didn't notice or you didn't mind.
You see you didn't have to justify
yourself. I felt I did. I felt some lie
involved your power and title.

I'm a grey-haired
lecturer now; but my students don't seem scared
of the power I have to judge them. They feel free.
I'd rather be scared of them than them of me.
They make or waste themselves. On *their* whim,
not at my invitation, they call me Jim.

* * *

I was the virtuous one in my own eyes
in that poem years ago. I apologise.
I was just lucky with students, I now see,
luckier, Derry, than you were with me.
In too much of a hurry to be at the top,
to survive myself, I measured you for the drop
and listened to gossip that made you shallow and bland,
less interested in poems than in command,
who must have felt some qualms, uncertainty,
filling the chair of Bonamy Dobrée.
Leaning on Wordsworth still the last verse stands,
a bright ideal shaped with dirty hands:

* * *

I am looking for teachers who need bluff less than nerve,
who don't solicit more than they deserve
of deference, who cultivate a sense
and faculty for storm and turbulence,
who won't stir trouble up, but will endure
and expect it, sustaining grace under pressure,
style and a sense of form under duress
although their master-bias leans to quietness.

EXTRACTS FROM *PASO DOBLE*

Michele Spina (translated by Robert Welch)

(An old, dying, parish priest is tended by a small boy.)

Enjoying the quiet of the evening the child could think a panoramic extension into the expanse of the countryside, with its small towns and orchards way beyond what the tiny window of the priest's room disclosed. Through the half-open window he could see a fig tree, its leaves shining in the sun, and beyond that a fragment of a hazel on the slope of the mountain. He could think the flat land beyond the mountain, and through it towards Battipaglia, and the straightness of the wires and poles of the new telegraph. Of such things one can think and talk, saying, for instance, that such a direct rectification as the wires added to the expanse of the plain gave it depth and clarity . . .

Battipaglia, the telegraph, and the priest. Priests telegraph to Battipaglia the death of the priest. That's good sense. Which priest telegraphs which priest? This is reason. It would be more diverting, however, to think of the subtile, linear rigidity of the telegraph wires with pendant priests looped by their necks. Perhaps without any great mechanical difficulty one could draw the wires to form loops, and then release them with the priests' necks caught in the snares. The wires would then, through a combination of natural elasticity and tautness, return to a harsh rigidity. Anyway this subtile and tense straightness of the wires, hardly visible by itself, would have been diversified by such an aerial arrangement of pendant priests, black and silent and solemn . . .

Sometimes when the silence took over, priest and child would look at each other through a curtain of opium as if through a window, one on each side, both mindless, vacant, in a great quietness.

A similar thing happens between chickens and scorpions. As the child had seen many times, the chicken would watch the scorpion, swivelling the left eye towards him, and the scorpion perhaps would watch the chicken above him, raising his little tail and his tiny trembling pincers towards the great shadow. So they would stand, still, or they would move relative to one another, each matching the other, in a paso doble, until with a sudden decision, *furore accensa et ira terribilis*, the chicken would snap the scorpion's little tail with an exact lunge of the beak. One could see the little black tail fly, and then from the most distant nooks and corners of the yard other chickens, two or three, in an intense flurry of excitement, would scurry to surround the maimed little creature and together contemplate him from above.

Why then did this rage of the chicken enter into the manic quiet of the paso doble with the scorpion; and why did the scorpion become the object of such fierce regard by the chickens? Sometimes he would find himself looking at his priest with a sudden access of rage when the old man, soporifically, with mouth agape, would release long bursts of foul wind. Violent emotions—Quintilian maintains—are usually brief and momentary . . .

While the child was going towards the lamp, like every other evening, the old man, stretching his arm out across the table, tried, stealthily, but not without scrabbling, to reach for the bottle of laudanum that the child always put well in sight, but at a safe distance, no more than a centimetre beyond the reach of the stretched arm and extended fingers of the priest. It was like every other evening.

'Leave that bottle alone, your worship', warned the boy as usual.

All was equal then: the lamp, the paraffin, the slight humidity of the evening impregnated with the smoke of burnt stubble. The moon, still pallid, althrough it had slightly shifted its position in the sky, and become fuller, could not be said to be very different. Or could it? How different? A little? Very different? How different was the priest's reach in trying to steal the laudanum, or was it identical? Absolutely identical? And at the same time absolutely different?

This slow, tranquil explanation, this, yes, this was a novelty, because the child never gave explanations, only warnings. This explanation was a prolix extension of what was necessry, a disentanglement of a totality, which, although contracted in that one single moment of the evening, comprehended much else; just as the room comprehended many pieces of furniture, books, the commode, the old man's long table—always the same things in the same room. These things now belonged together in a different manner, more relaxed and calm, with a greater distance and without those hateful interferences which made of the room and the hour an oppressive totality of time and place. Now, for instance, to go from the table to the lamp, obeying the prolix tempo of the explanation, was like the first strolling out for its own sake, so extensive as to include (hypothetically at least) the courtyard, and passing under its porch, the garden, and then the lovely laurel grove which, in the evening, beneath the rising moon, he knew to be thick with rigid leaves, dense with the nests of spiders with their swart clots of dried flies. And then one could go beyond, following allurement after allurement (obeying the same steadiness of mood)—the minute attractions of the world, the ample skies of the effulgent moon; the settlements, the countryside opening out . . .

'Well then, your worship, would you care for a spoonful of laudanum? Should I put it in the wine?'

'Eh-yes', said the old man with gluttonous assent. 'Eh-yes, Eh-yes', he continued to repeat, while the child poured the laudanum into the spoon, which he then, with pharmaceutical care, tilted into the glass, without spilling a drop. 'Eh-yes', said the priest, watching the straw-coloured wine clouding with amber tones, as it mingled with the maroon of the laudanum.

In this series of actions every minute detail was enjoyed. It proceeded slowly and with decorum, taking a certain length of time, that was a centre of attention to all those involved. Moreover it could be added that between the old man and the child there obtained a deliberate conjuration in the action, setting it apart from all else, enacting a selection from among the things of the world, setting aside all that is not utile, delegating them to exclusion beyond the space of the action, and drawing into that space the lamp for its light, the table for its level expanse, the spoon for its concave holding, the wine for its dispersions.

Everything then was happily ordained. Things that might interfere, books, old sausages, crusts of bread and bits of chicken, although all over the place, were held at bay by a magical circle, so that in the domain of the act, and in the time and place in which it was enacted, there was no superfluity.

In this gracious offering, the gratuitous and the necessary, fortune and what ought to be, imaginative freedom and technical discipline were reconciled in a balance so difficult as to be a delight. It was just as it had been when he and his brother, balancing on a narrow lip of a wall, their brushes already immersed in the bucket of pig's urine, measured the advance of the solemn procession by the growth in distinction and clarity of the recited litanies. Second by second, in the air lightened by the evening dew, they could see the growing celestial reflection of the candles. Even their increasing anticipation, before the aspersion of urine, was an integral part of their freedom for the dispersal of their blessing. Before belonging to after; after belonging to before. Although he shouted 'Come on, run', to his brother, the calm accuracy with which he moved along the top of the wall, balancing the bucket in his hand, saying: 'The whole lot on the priest's head', endured, increased, or evolved according to a necessity and rule of its own, exceptional to everything else, totally selective. It happened then that while the parish priest was agitating the standard and shouting and swearing at those who had broken rank, the brother, taking account of his movements and those of everybody else, found him on his own, at a point near the wall, and drenched him with the full bucket of urine all at once. The priest stopped, and was silent. In an instant the confused and vocal consternation of the crowd changed into a deep silence of calm and wonder.

'Does your worship remember last year's procession?' asked the child. This was not properly a question, rather a consolatory insinuation. He wanted to suggest that the flat ferocious logic of the universe had incidents, such as those described, which were objectively happy, and that they were not few.

Not all that is out there then is grey and indifferent, but maybe there is something (in natural history, in botany, in mineralogy, in the tribology of materials)—a moment, a passage, which can be extrapolated from the universal context, and enjoyed for a length of time as a thing in itself. This was now happening, possibly, in the biology of the priest. His drinking of laudanum and his feeling of happiness was like being relieved of his huge intestinal disorder. It was a closed moment ordained under rules of lucid calm, an episode of quiet, or maybe quiet itself.

Perhaps then in such moments of extravagance, within the inexorable uniqueness of the facts, there is an ingredient which refers to individual destiny; the ought no longer necessity in the total, indifferent and unmediated sense of the universal and the infinite, but reconciled with the particular and the singular . . .

This was how it was between himself and the priest. Between his pouring of the laudanum and the other's drinking of it, there was only a proceeding in accord, an arrangement, a specular going, from two remote points in a separate distance. Now the bottles were empty, the old man was sleeping and the boy was awake. But from both remotenesses they were going into a paso doble, perhaps not even looking at each other, having no need any longer, but looking instead at the sameness of another thing, that sameness containing the sameness of all other things, and, as well, their own likeness. Just as the boy, awake, could see, calmly, the same things: the books, the chairs, the lamp, the table, all the other small innumerable objects; so in that nerveless sleep the old man was seeing everything in tranquillity, the elegant successions from thing to thing without agitation and internal dissension. In quiet, in great quiet, in the luxury of interminable time, he could have counted all the stars in the heavens, all the leaves of the world, all the same leaves and stars and ideas, without fret, giving himself up to the slight rhythm of the child's embrace, as he was rocked to and fro in those small arms, that frail circle.

THIS DESIRABLE ANGLO-IRISH PROPERTY

for Derry Jeffares

Randolph Stow

An Irish mile of untrimmed rhododendrons
approaches, like a track in coastal Papua,
this manison of my dream, and Le Fanu's.

Before we reached this point were dry-stone walls
crumbling below the fuchsias' blood-red lampshades,
beyond which some unseen and long-dry cow
clanked, with a wooden sound, its fissured bell.
The grass was thin and sour; what flowers there were
would taint the milk if there were milk for tainting.
No soul was to be seen but one poor soul
weak in his intellect, who crossed himself.

And now the house, across its knee-high lawn:
a plain, a grand, a seemly nest for gentry;
and now, black as a rook, the chatelaine
who blocks the doorway, staring genocide.
Some bitter byblow of The Family this,
known by a barbarous nickname, Phib or Shibby,
pickled in unrelenting unforgetting,
with eyes like pikes, not half so mild as Maeve.

The parapet above is bright with grass
and stonecrop, thistles, moss; the pediment
sheds a large gobbet, as a column bends,
and with it cracks a window. Tinkling shards
fall inwards to some dusty marvellous roòm
unknown except to her; although the attics
teem with her humblest kinsfolk, whom she hates.
Them she ignores; she too moves in a dream,
of glamour, rancour and comeuppances.

But see the ghosts; ah, see the pretty ghosts.
Here's Beauty Kit, astride a handsome mare,
bending his handsome neck in crude flirtation
with jolly, crude Magnolia Macnamara.
Here is sweet Lilias; here Augusta Gregory,

under a deodar, dispensing tea.
While, farther off in their swan-haunted pleasance,
gazelles in silk kimonos play at croquet
and Violet Martin, using as a shield
young Yeats's out-held jacket, stoops to light
against his breast a naughty cigarette.
Ah see them, see them, quick; before the chimneys,
walls, roofbeams fall, to bury him and me.

This house of Le Fanu's recurring nightmare
to me is folklore, but for him was death.
Nightly he went there; nightly he woke screaming;
and when the end had come, as to all dreamers,
'I feared' (above the staring body) 'this,'
the doctor murmured: 'that house fell at last.'

REJOICE:

May Ziadah[1]

A Prose Poem translated from the Arabic
and edited by Suheil Bushrui

For Derry Jeffares on his 65th birthday, in return for the many gifts he
has generously bestowed on his friends, students and colleagues.

In the temple of human sorrows the Great Master stood to speak
to the people and I heard him say:-

'If you are rich, rejoice! Experience of weighty matters has served
you well, your good deeds are praised and generosity is expected
of you. You have become powerful and no one can harm you.
Prosperity has put up a shield round your domain, protecting
your independence and freedom.

If you are poor, rejoice! You have been spared the spiritual
stupor which overcomes the avaricious and you are safe from the
jealousy and hatred attracted by the rich. Men's hearts do not
burn with envy on account of your prosperity, nor do they gaze
at your possessions with jaundiced eyes.

If you are charitable, rejoice! You have filled empty hands,
clothed naked bodies and endowed those who have nothinig.
These achievements have brought you pleasure and you have
wished to share that singular pleasure with hundreds so that it
might be multiplied by the number of those whom it benefits.

If you cannot extend charity, rejoice! The hour will never
come when you witness ingratitude from the one you have
helped, who has fashioned your kindness into a weapon to
threaten you, thinking it courageous to be aggressive and clever
to be fickle. You will avoid that hour which must inevitably
come to the generous man, bringing tension to his nerves,
provoking his rage, hardening his feelings, drying up the
springs of his generosity and creating within him a hatred for
men and a despair of their reform. All this he must endure
before he can attain the peak of sublime forgiveness and
forbearance.

If you are young, rejoice! The sap is rising in the tree of your
desires. The goal of your aspirations lies far ahead. If you are

worthy of your dreams, their realisation can be easy.

If you are old, rejoice! You have striven with time and men and, because of your discretion and foresight, you have been entrusted with the management of affairs. Everything you have done can bear fruit at your command. The minutes of your life are equal to years so full are they of experience, wisdom and accurate judgement. It is as if those minutes were autumn fruit: fully mature, succulent, and imbued with perfection, plenitude and passion.

If you are a man, rejoice! In the vigour of manhood lies the greater meaning of life.

If you are a woman, rejoice! Woman is the desire of man; her nobility is his support, her sweetness the source of his consolation and her smile the reward for his labours.

If you are of noble birth, rejoice! You have gained the confidence of the multitude unaided by anyone's patronage.

If you are of low birth, rejoice! It is better to make a name for yourself than to bear a great name reluctantly and without having contributed to its fame.

If you have many friends, rejoice! You will find yourself present in every one of them. They will reflect the brilliance of your success or sweeten the bitterness of failure. To attract men's hearts you must have qualities and abilities rarely found except in those who are truly great. Of these the most important is the capacity to break out of the restrictions of selfishness to discover the nobility, compassion and intelligence that others possess.

If you have many enemies, rejoice! Your enemies are the ladder of your ascendancy and they are the surest proof of your importance. The more strongly they oppose and attack you, the more you will feel your greatness. The more various their slanderous criticisms, the more scope you will have to discern what truth there may be in their intended poison, which you can then imbibe as the greatest of tonics. The remainder of their libel you can see to be fallacious and that part you can gracefully ignore, for it is nothing more than the product of impotence and deception. Does the eagle soaring in the heights take any heed of the conspiracies hatched by the dung-beetles of the ground?

If you enjoy good health, rejoice! In you the universal law has found its balance and has qualified you to deal with difficulties and overcome impediments.

If you suffer from ill-health, rejoice! In you the two great forces of the universe have found a battlefield. It is for you to choose the victor and, if you choose correctly, you can be healed.

If you are a genius, rejoice! A resplendent ray from the most sublime realm has shone upon you. The glance of the Merciful is reflected in the thought radiating from your forehead; there is mystery in your eyes and enchantment in your voice. The expressions of others that are mere sounds, mere mutterings and syllables, have become, by your touch and on your lips, a fire and a light, stinging and illuminating, burning and soothing, humbling and exalting, humiliating and stimulating, hurting and healing, rebuking and bewildering. No sooner do you inspire the birth of meaning than it exists.

If you are not a genius, rejoice! Men's tongues are not sharp when they mention you nor are their eyes afire with carping and criticism when they turn towards you. The summit is there for you to attain if you can and, if you cannot, there is satisfaction in supporting others on their way up. For the luxurious mansion could not stand without small bricks. You will enjoy a comfort reserved only for those whose lips taste Life's waters while their souls bathe in the floods of inspiration.

If your friend is faithful, rejoice! The world has bestowed upon you its richest treasure.

If your friend is faithless, rejoice! He has not been ready to listen to the parable you have offered to teach him. None forsakes the mansion of love but to vacate it for another, worthier and better than himself.

If you are free, rejoice! In liberty strength finds its exercise; faculties are reinforced and opportunities increased.

If you are enslaved, rejoice! Slavery is the best school in which to learn the lessons of liberty and acquire the qualities to earn it.

If you live in surroundings that cherish and respond to you, rejoice! There you will find second youth and new strength; your spirit will grow to astonish you by its realm of wide oceans and towering heights.

If you live in primitive and inferior surroundings, rejoice! You are free to take wings to rise above them to a place where you can create from the shadows of yourself a world that can satisfy the hunger of your thought and quench the thirst of your soul.

If you are in love and are loved, rejoice! Life has indeed pampered you and has included you among its chosen sons. Divine Power has revealed to you its compassion contained in the exchange of hearts. Two halves wandering in the darkness of the unknown have at last become united and unto them the wonders of daybreak have been disclosed; the suns have gladdened their hearts with that which they had not yet found in their orbits among the planets. The Ether has divulged to them its very secrets and so they know the way when he who is empty of love can go astray; they are silent when he speaks, in jest when he is serious. They divine the lines of eternity where he cannot even see shadows.

If you are in love and are not loved, rejoice! He who has spurned you does, in his highest being, truly love you with a love that cannot be matched by his infatuation for the one he apparently loves. To be rejected in love is an experience full of meaning and mystery; it diminishes inflated desires and purifies polluted feelings, leaving the heart transparent, glittering and resplendent as the vessel from which the gods drink of immortality. You are bound to win the one you love, if not in his remote and worldly form then in another form. Be ready for love no matter how heavy the burden of your feelings, for love is unpredictable and you know not the hour of its passage. Be great so that you may be chosen by a great love and lest your lot be a love that feeds on dust and wallows in the mud, either leaving you unchanged or lowering you to its depths instead of raising you as high as the towers that are out of human sight, whose wonders are beyond our dreams. The edifice of our desires is founded on imaginary plans invented by our longing.

Rejoice! The doors of happiness are many in number, the gates of good fortune are countless and the paths of life are renewed minute by minute.

Rejoice always! However you may find yourself, rejoice!

A SELECT CHECKLIST OF THE WRITINGS OF ALEXANDER NORMAN JEFFARES

COLIN SMYTHE

The list that follows indicates the wide-ranging interests of Derry Jeffares, and particularly his long-standing preoccupation with W.B. Yeats: it is now over forty years since his first article on the poet was published.

The Bibliography is divided into six sections: a) works by Professor Jeffares; b) works edited by him; c) introductions and contributions to books; d) contributions to periodicals, including a selection of reviews; e) radio scripts, and f) series and journals of which Derry has been editor.

There are many hundreds of reviews that he has been a regular contributor. They include *Australian Book Review, Australian Letters, AUMLA, British Book News, English Studies, Hermathena, The Irish Times, The Journal of Commonwealth Literature, Levende Talen, The Literary Half-Yearly, The Literary Review, Museum, Notes and Queries, The Oxford Magazine, The Review of English Studies, Sewanee Review, Stand, Time and Tide, The Times, The Times Educational Supplement, The Times Higher Education Supplement, The Times Literary Supplement, Wascana Review, Wending, Western Humanities Review, World Language in English,* and the *Yorkshire Post.*

A few of the more important reviews are included in section D, but obviously I have been selective in my choice. As a bibliographer I would like to provide a much more complete listing, but it would have taken much more time than has been available, and I suspect this section would then have become an unacceptably dominant part of the book.

A. BOOKS BY A. NORMAN JEFFARES

Trinity College Dublin: Drawings and Descriptions. Dublin: Alex Thom,
1944. Reprinted 1944, 1945.
A Poet and a Theatre. Groningen and Batavia: J.B. Wolters, 1946.
W.B. Yeats: Man and Poet. London: Routledge & Kegan Paul, and New
Haven: Yale University Press, 1949.
2nd edition, London: Routledge & Kegan Paul, and New York: Barnes
& Noble, 1966.
Oliver Goldsmith (Writers and their Work Series). London: Longmans,
Green & Co., 1959. Revised and, together with the other titles in the
series, printed in I. Scott-Kilvert (ed.) *British Writers*, New York:
Charles Scribner's Sons, 8 vols., 1979–84.
Language [,] *Literature and Science*. Leeds: Leeds University Press, 1959.
Some Indian and African Novelists. Dortmund: Dortmunder Vortrage,
1963.
The Poetry of W.B. Yeats (Studies in English Literature Series 4). New
York: Manuel Barron, and, under the title *W.B. Yeats: The Poems*,
London: Edward Arnold, 1961.
Goldsmith: She Stoops to Conquer (critical commentaries). London:
Macmillan, 1964.
George Moore (Writers and their Work Series). London: Longmans,
Green & Co., 1965. Revised and, together with the other titles in the
series, printed in I. Scott-Kilvert (ed.) *British Writers*, New York:
Charles Scribner's Sons, 8 vols., 1979–84.
A Commentary on the Collected Poems of W.B. Yeats. London: Macmillan,
and Stanford (California): Standord University Press, 1968.
The Circus Animals. Essays: Mainly Anglo-Irish. London: Macmillan, and
Stanford (California): Stanford University Press, 1970.
W.B. Yeats (Profiles in Literature Series). London: Routledge & Kegan
Paul, 1972.
(with A.S. Knowland) *A Commentary on the Collected Plays of W.B. Yeats*.
London: Macmillan, and Stanford (California). Stanford University
Press, 1975.
Jonathan Swift (Writers and their Work Series). London: Longmans,
Green & Co., 1976. Revised and, together with the other titles in the
series, printed in I. Scott-Kilvert (ed.) *British Writers*, New York:
Charles Scribner's Sons, 8 vols., 1979–84.
Sheridan's *The Rivals* (York Notes). London: Longman, and Beirut: York
Press, 1981.
Goldsmith's *She Stoops to Conquer* (York Notes). London: Longman, and
Beirut: York Press, 1981.
A History of Anglo-Irish Literature. London: Macmillan, 1982.
*A New Commentary on the Poems of W.B. Yeats. London: Macmillan, and
Stanford (California). Stanford University Press, 1984.*
Poems of W.B. Yeats, A New Selection. London and Basingstoke:
Macmillan, 1984.

2nd edition, London & Basingstoke: Macmillan, 1987.
Yeats's Selected Poems (York Notes). London: Longman, and Beirut: York Press, 1985.
Brought up in Dublin. Gerrards Cross: Colin Smythe, 1987.
Brought up to Leave. Gerrards Cross: Colin Smythe, 1987.

B. BOOKS EDITED BY A. NORMAN JEFFARES

Maria Edgworth, *Castle Rackrent. Emile de Coulanges. The Birthday Present*. Edinburgh: Thomas Nelson & Sons, 1953.
Seven Centuries of Poetry. Chaucer to Dylan Thomas. London and Melbourne: Longmans, Green & Co., 1955.
2nd edition, London and Melbourne: Longmans, Green & Co., 1960.
(with M. Bryn Davies) *The Scientific Background: A Prose Anthology*. London: Pitman, 1958.
W.B. Yeats, *Selected Poems*. London: Macmillan, 1962.
(Selector) Poems of W.B. Yeats (The Scholar's Library). London: Macmillan, 1962.
Cowper: Selected Poems and Letters (New Oxford English Series). London: Oxford University Press, 1963.
A Goldsmith Selection. London: Macmillan, and New York: St. Martin's Press, 1963.
W.B. Yeats, *Selected Prose*. London: Macmillan, 1964.
W.B. Yeats, *Selected Plays*. London: Macmillan, 1964.
Eleven Plays of William Butler Yeats. New York: Collier Books, 1964.
W.B. Yeats, *Selected Criticism*. London: Macmillan, 1964.
(with K.G.W. Cross) *In Excited Reverie. A Centenary Tribute W.B. Yeats, 1865–1939*. London: Macmillan, and New York: St. Martin's Press, 1965.
Henry Handel Richardson, *Maurice Guest*. Melbourne, Victoria: Sun Books, 1965.
Oliver Goldsmith, *She Stoops to Conquer*. London: Macmillan, and New York: St. Martin's Press, 1965.
Whitman, Selected Poems and Prose. Oxford: Oxford University Press, 1966.
William Congreve, *Incognita* and *The Way of the World*. London: Edward Arnold, 1966.
Fair Liberty was All His Cry. A Tercentenary Tribute to Jonathan Swift 1667–1745. London Macmillan, 1967.
Richard Brinsley Sheridan, *The Rivals*. London: Macmillan, and New York: St. Martin's Press, 1967.
William Congreve, *Love for Love*. London: Macmillan, and New York: St. Martin's Press, 1967.
Richard Brinsley Sheridan, *The School for Scandal*. London: Macmillan, and New York: St. Martin's Press, 1967.
Swift (Modern Judgements Series). London: Macmillan, 1968, and Nashville, Tennessee: Aurora Publishers, 1970.

Scott's Mind and Art. Edinburgh: Oliver & Boyd, 1969.

George Farquhar, *The Beaux Stratagem* (The Fountainwell Drama Series). Edinburgh, Oliver & Boy, 1972.

Maria Edgeworth, *Ormond.* Dublin: Irish University Press, 1972.

George Farquhar, *The Recruiting Officer* (The Fountainwell Drama Series). Edinburgh: Oliver & Boyd, 1973.

Restoration Drama (4 vols.). London: The Folio Society, and Totowa (New Jersey): Rowman & Littlefield, 1974.

W.B. Yeats, *Selected Poems.* London: Pan Books, 1974.

W.B. Yeats, *Selected Plays.* London: Pan Books, 1974.

W.B. Yeats, *Selected Criticism.* London: Pan Books, 1974.

W.B. Yeats, *Selected Prose.* London: Pan Books, 1976.

W.B. Yeats, *The Critical Heritage.* London and Boston, Mass.: Routledge & Kegan Paul, 1977.

W.B. Yeats, *Selected Criticism and Prose.* London: Pan Books, 1980.

Yeats, Sligo and Ireland (Irish Literary Studies series 6). Gerrards Cross: Colin Smythe, and Totowa (New Jersey): Barnes & Noble Books, 1980.

C. INTRODUCTIONS AND CONTRIBUTIONS TO BOOKS

'Introduction' to Benjamin Disraeli, *Sybil.* Edinburgh: Thomas Nelson & Sons, 1954, pp.vii-xx.

'Introduction' to Benjamin Disraeli, *Lothair.* Edinburgh: Thomas Nelson & Sons, 1957, pp.vii-xi.

(with J.J. Auchmuty) 'Australian universities: the historical background' in *The Humanities in Australia* (ed. Grenfell Price). Sydney: Angus & Robertson, 1959, pp.14-34.

'Whitman: the barbaric yawp' in *The Great Experiment in American Fiction* (ed. Carl Bode). London: William Heinemann, and New York: Frederick Praeger, 1961, pp.29-52.

'The "Ern Malley" poems' in *The Literature of Australia* (ed. Geoffrey Dutton). Ringwood, Victoria: Penguin, 1964, pp.407-12.

'Die Commonwealth-Literaturen' in *Die Literaturen der Welt* (ed. W.V. Einseidel). Zurich: Kindler Verlag, 1964, pp.659-78.

'Was Clytemnestra a liar?' in *Of Books and Humankind* (ed. John Butt). London: Routledge & Kegan Paul, 1964, pp.3-24.

'*A Drama in Muslin*' in *Essays Presented to Amy C. Stock* (ed. R.K. Kaul). Jaipur, India: Rajasthan University Press, 1965, pp.137-54.

Revised and printed in *George Moore's Mind and Art* (ed. Graham Owens). Edinburgh: Oliver & Boyd, 1968, pp.1-20.

'Introduction' to *Commonwealth Literature* (ed. John Press). London: Heinemann Educational Books, 1965, pp.xi-xviii.

'John Butler Yeats' in *In Excited Reverie* (eds. A. Norman Jeffares and K.G.W. Cross). London: Macmillan, and New York: St. Martin's Press, 1965, pp.24-47.

Reprinted in part in *Dublin Magazine*, IV, 2, Summer 1965, pp.30-37.
Revised and printed in *The Circus Animals*, 1970, pp.117-46.
'The literary influence' in *W.B. Yeats, 1865–1965: A Centenary Tribute*.
Dublin: Irish Times, supplement to the issue of 10 June 1965, p.vi.
'Foreword' to *W.B. Yeats, 1865–1965: Centenary Essays on the Art of W.B. Yeats* (eds. D.E.S. Maxwell & S.B. Bushrui). Ibadan: Ibadan University Press, 1965, pp.ix-x.
'Women in Yeat's poetry' in *Homage to Yeats 1865–1965*. Los Angeles, California: William Andrew Clark Library, 1966, pp.41-74. Revised and printed in *The Circus Animals*, 1970, pp.78-102.
'Commonwealth literature and its wider horizons' in *1868–1968 Royal Commonwealth Society Souvenir*. London, 1968, pp.79-81.
'In one person many people: *King Richard the Second*' in *The Morality of Art* (ed. D.W. Jefferson). London: Routledge & Kegan Paul, 1969, pp.50-56.
'Die Moderne Englische Literatur' in *Englische Literatur der Gegenwart*. Dortmund: Stadtsbucherei, 1969, pp.iii-vii.
'Pallas Athene Gonne' in *Tributes in Prose and Verse to Shotaro Oshima*. Tokyo: The Hokuseido Press, 1970 pp.4-7.
'Introduction' to *National Identity* (ed. K.L. Goodwin). London: Heinemann Educational Books, 1970, pp.ix-xvi.
'The Anglo-Irish Temper' in *Essays by Diverse Hands*. New Series XXXVI, London: Oxford University Press, 1970, pp.84-112.
'Introduction' to *A Bibliography of Yeats Criticism 1887-1965* (K.G.W. Cross and R.T. Dunlop). London: Macmillan, 1971. pp.vii-ix.
'Eric Ambler', 'Nicholas Freeling', 'William Haggard', 'Margaret Laurence', 'Mary Lavin', 'Johy Le Carre' in *Contemporary Novelists*. London: St. James Press, 1972, pp.42-44, 428-31, 543-44, 740-42, 742-44, 746-58.
'Honoris causa' in *The Art of I. Compton Burnett* (ed. Charles Buckhart). London: Victor Gollancz, 1972, pp.15-18.
'Foreword' to *Sunshine and the Moon's Delight* (ed. Suheil Badi Bushrui). Gerrards Cross: Colin Smythe & New York: Barnes & Noble (where published as *A Centenary Tribute to J.M. Synge*), 1972, pp.9-15.
'Yeats' in *Irish Poets in English*, Thomas Davis Lectures (ed. Sean Lucy). Cork: Mercier Press, 1973, pp.105-17.
'Introductory note' to Richard Brinsley Sheridan, *The Rivals* (facsimile edition). London & Ilkley: The Scolar Press, 1973.
'Walt Whitman' in *Encyclopaedia Britannica*. London & New York, 1974, pp.819-21.
'[The literature of] Ireland' in *Literature of the World in English* (ed. Bruce King). London: Routledge & Kegan Paul, 1974, pp.98-115.
'George Farquhar', 'Richard Lovell Edgeworth' and 'Maria Edgeworth' in *The Reader's Encyclopaedia of English Literature* (ed. Edgar Johnson). New York: Thomas Y. Crowell Co., 1974.
'Lever's *Lord Kilgobbin*' in *Essays and Studies*, (ed. Robert Ellrodt). London: John Murray, 1975, pp.47-57.

'Commonwealth literature in the modern world' in *Commonwealth Literature and the Modern World* (ed. Hena Maes-Jelinek). Bruxelles: Marcel Didier, 1975, pp.9-14.

'Place, space and personality and the Irish writer' in *Place, Personality and the Irish Writer* (ed. Andrew Carpenter). Gerrards Cross: Colin Smythe, & New York: Barnes & Noble, 1977, pp.11-40.

'Foreword' to *The Emergence of African Fiction* (Charles R. Larson). London: Macmillan, 1978, pp.v-vii.

'William Cooper', 'William Butler Yeats' in *Great Writers of the English Language. Poets*. (London: Macmillan, 1979, pp.236-39, 1104-09.

'William Congreve', 'Richard Brinsley Sheridan', William Butler Yeats' in *Great Writers of the English Language. Dramatists*. London: Macmillan, 1979, pp.129-32, 531-33, 629-34.

'Joyce Cary', 'Charles Lever' in *Great Writers of the English Language. Novelists*. London: Macmillan, 1979, pp.234-37, 726-28.

'Eric Ambler', 'Erskine Childers', 'Nicholas Freeling', 'Bram Stoker' in *Crime and Mystery Writers* (ed. John M. Reilly). London: Macmillan, 1980, pp.30-33,303-04, 608-10, 1349-51.

'Introduction' to and 'Yeats and the wrong lever' in *Yeats, Sligo and Ireland* (ed. A. Norman Jeffares). Gerrards Cross: Colin Smythe, & New York: Barnes & Noble, 1980, pp.viii-x, 98-111.

'Jeunesse a Dublin' in *William Butler Yeats* (ed. Jacqueline Genet). Paris: Cahiers de l'Herne, 1981, pp.23-36.

'*The Vicar of Wakefield*' in *Goldsmith, The Gentle Master* (ed. Sean Lucy) (Thomas Davis Lectures). Cork: Cork University Press, 1984, pp.38-49.

'Yeats's birthplace' in *Yeats Annual*, 3. London: Macmillan, 1985, 175-78.

'Anglo-Irish literature: treatment for radio' in *Irish Writers and Society at Large* (ed. Masaru Sekine). Gerrards Cross: Colin Smythe, & Totowa (New Jersey): Barnes & Noble Books, 1985, pp.42-95.

'Torrens: an Irishman in South Australia' in *Australia and Ireland 1788-1988. Bicentenary Essays* (ed. Colm Kiernan). St. Lucia, Queensland: University of Queensland Press, and Dublin: Gill & Macmillan, 1986, pp.170-81.

'Anglo-Irish literature: some critical perspectives' in *Critical Essays: A Presentation Volume for Professor V.S. Seturaman (eds. S. Viswanathan, C.T. Indra, and T. Sriraman). Madras: Macmillan India, 1987, pp.87-104.*

D. CONTRIBUTIONS TO PERIODICALS

'"*Two Songs of a Gool*" and their explanation' in *English Studies*, XXVI, 6, December 1945, pp.169-71.

'The Byzantine poems of W.B. Yeats' in *Review of English Studies*, XXII, 85, January 1946, pp.44-52.

'W.B. Yeats and his methods of writing verse' in *Nineteenth Century and **After**, CXXXIX, 829, **March 1946, pp.123-28. Reprinted in** *The*

Permanence of Yeats (eds. James Hall and martin Steinmann).
'Gyres in the poetry of W.B. Yeats' in *English Studies*, XXVII, 3, June 1946, pp.65-74.
Revised and printed in *The Circus Animals*, 1970, pp.103-14.
'"The New Faces": a new explanation' in *Review of English Studies*, XXIII, 92, October 1947, pp.349-53.
'Thoor Ballylee' in *English Studies*, XXVIII, 6, December 1947, pp.161-68.
Revised as 'Poet's Tower', *Envoy*, V, 20, 1951, pp.45-55. A further revised version appears in *The Circus Animals*, 1970, pp.29-46.
[Review, in Dutch, of A.G. van Kranendonk, *Geschiedenis van de Americaanse Literatur*] in *Museum*, 4-5, April-May 1948, pp.80-81.
'An account of recent Yeatsiana' in *Hermathena*, LXXII, November 1948, pp.21-43.
'The source of Yeats's "A Meditation in Time of War"' in *Notes and Queries*, CXCIII, 24, 27 November 1948, p.522.
'Graham Greene' (in Dutch) in *Wending*, 3, 10, December 1948, pp.575-87.
'The last twelve years' Yeatsiana' in *Levende Talen*, February 1949, pp.109-13.
'Notes on Yeats' "Fragments"' in *Notes and Queries*, CXCIV, 25 June 1949, pp.279-80.
'Problems confronting British universities' in *Questiones Academiae Hodiernae*, 1949, pp.50-59.
'Yeats's mask' in *English Studies*, XXX, 6, December 1949, pp.289-98.
Revised and printed in *The Circus Animals*, 1970, pp.3-14.
'A Source for "A Woman Homer Sung"' in *Notes and Queries*, CXCV, 5, 4 March 1950, p.104.
'Notes on Yeats's "Lapis Lazuli"' in *Modern Language Notes*, LXV, 7, November 1950, pp.488-91.
'James Clarence Mangan' in *Envoy*, IV, 14, January 1951, pp.23-32.
'The sad glory of Clarence Mangan' in *Irish Digest*, XXXIV, 3, May 1951, pp.62-65.
'Education in Holland' in *University of Edinburgh Journal*, XVI, 1, Autumn 1951, pp.25-28.
'Yeats's "The Gyres": sources and symbolism' in *Huntingdon Library Quarterly*, XV, 1, November 1951, pp.87-97.
'Jeffares on Saul' in *Modern Language Notes*, LXVII, 7 November 1952, pp.501-02.
'Australian literature' in *Etudes Anglaises*, VI, 4, November 1953, pp.289-314.
'Stefan Zweig's "Kaleidoscope Two"' in *CAE Discussion Notes*, Victoria, 1953, pp.1-8.
'*The Horse's Mouth* by Joyce Cary' in *CAE Discussion Notes*, Victoria, 1953, pp. 1-9.
[Review of Birgit Bjersby, *The Interpretation of the Cuchulain Legend in the Works of W.B. Yeats*] in *Review of English Studies*, IV, 13, January 1953, pp.86-88.

'Irish Doctor: Oliver St. John Gogarty' in *The AMSS Review*, LXVI, 3, October −954, pp.5-12.
'Children and Books' in *Australian Quarterly*, XXVI, 4, December 1954, pp.94-101.
'Australian literature and the universities' in *Meanjin*, 3, 1954, pp.432-36.
'Fielding's *Joseph Andrews*' in *WEA Discussion Notes*, Adelaide, 1954, pp.1-11.
'Disraeli the novelist' in *WEA Discussion Notes*, Adelaide, 1954, pp.1ff.
'James Joyce's *Exiles*' in *CAE Discussion Notes*, Victoria, 1955, pp.1-10.
'William Butler Yeats: a mind Michael Angelo knew' [in part a review of W.B. Yeats, *Autobiographies*]cin *Meanjin*, XIV, 4, December 1955, pp.565-68.
'Australian retrospect' in *Australian Letters*, I, 2, November 1957, pp.51-53.
'The expanding frontiers of English Literature' in *University of Leeds Review*, V, 4, December 1957, pp.361-67.
'Robert Richard Torrens (1814−84)' in *Proceedings of the Leeds Philosophical and Litrary Society*, 1958, pp.275-300.
(with H.W. Piper) 'Charles Robert Maturin the innovator' in *Huntingdon Library Quarterly*, XXI, 3, May 1958, pp.261-84.
'Poetry in Britain since 1945: sketch for an extensive view' in *The London Magazine*, November 1959, pp.30-36.
'Maurice Guest' in *The Dubliner*, I, 1, 1960, pp.3-7.
'Editorials [32] in *A Review of English Literature*, I-VIII. London: Longmans, Green & Co., 1960-68.
'Milton: poet of conflict' in *Venture*, I, 2, June 1960, pp.98-111.
'Oliver St. John Gogarty' (Chatterton Lecture) in *Proceedings of the British Academy*, XLVI, 1960, pp.7 73-98.
Revised and printed in *The Circus Animals*, 1970, pp.147-74.
'The Importance of English as a world language' in *Proceedings of the Inaugural Meeting of the English Academic of Southern Africa*, Johannesburg, 1961.
Also printed in *Symposium*, Johannesburg, 1961.
[Review of W.B. Yeats, *Essays and Introductions*] in *Stand*, V, 2, 1961, pp. 55-57.
'Yeats as public man' in *Poetry* (Chicago), XCVIII, 4, July 1961, pp.253-63.
Revised as 'Yeats the public man' in *The Integrity of Yeats* (ed. D. Donoghue). Cork: Mercier Press, 1964, pp.21-32. A further revised and expanded version appears in *The Circus Animals*, 1970, pp.15-28.
'David Nichol Smith 1875-1962' (obituary), in *The Oxford Magazine*, n.s.II, 12, 15 February 1962, p.192.
'Yeats's Byzantine poems and the critics' in *English Studies in Africa*, V, 1, March 1962, pp.11-28.
[Review of Robin Skelton (ed.) *Six Irish Poets*; Thomas Kinsella, *Downstream*] in *Stand*, V, 3, [1962], pp.63-66.

'Some Indian and African novelists', in *Dortmunder Vorträge*, 1963, pp.1-43.

'Thinking on paper' [unsigned] review of in *Times Literary Supplement*, 29 March 1963, p. 218.

'Mary Ballard Duryee', in *Times Literary Supplement*, 5 July 1963, pp. 498–99. [unsigned]

'English at Leeds' in *The Critical Survey*, Autumn 1963, pp.183-85.

'The Yeats Country' [review of, among others, Sheelah Kirby, *The Yeats Country*; M.I. Seiden, *William Butler Yeats, The Poet as Mythmaker*; Jon Stallworthy, *Between the Lines*; H.H. Vendler, *Yeats's Vision and the Later Plays*] in *Modern Language Quarterly*, XXV, 2, June 1964, pp.218-22.

'Value of the interchange of Commonwealth Literature' in *The Indian P.E.N.*, XXX, 10, October 1964, pp.309-11.

'Developments in Commonwealth Literature' in *Commonwealth Journal*, December 1964, pp.285-88.

'W.B. Yeats: the gift of greatness' in *Daily Telegraph*, 34256, 12 June 1965, p.8

'Prose fed by experience' in *Western Mail*, 16 January 1965, p.5.

'Miscellaneous memories' in *TCD*, 1250, 29 January 1965, p.10. Yeats as Critic' in *English*, XV, 89, Summer 1965, pp.173-76. Revised as 'The Criticism of Yeats' in *Phoenix*, 10, Summer 1965, pp.27-45. Further expanded and revised, and printed in *The Circus Animals*, 1970, pp.47-77.

'Notes on pattern in the Byzantine poems of W.B. Yeats' in *Revue des Langes Vivantes*, XXXI, 4, 1965, pp.353-59.

'The study of Commonwealth writing' in *Journal of Royal Society of Arts*, December 1968, pp.16-33. Reprinted as supplement to *WLWE Newsletter*, April 1969, pp.1-15.

'Maria Edgeworth's *Ormond*' in *English*, XVIII, 102, 1969, pp.85-90.

'The Study of Commonwealth Writing' in *Commonwealth Journal*, 1969, pp.67-74.

'Richard Mahony, exile' in *The Journal of Commonwealth Literature*, VI, 1969, pp.106-19.

Reprinted in *Readings in Commonwealth Literature* (ed. William Walsh). Oxford: The Clarendon Press, 1973, pp.404-19.

'Yeats as modern poet' in *Mosaic*, II, Summer 1969, pp.53-58.

'*Shirley* — a Yorkshire novel' in *Bronte Society Transactions*, Keighley, XV, 4, 1969, pp.281-93.

'Some academic novels' in *Wascana Review*, V, 1, 1970, pp.5-27.

'Editorials' in *ARIEL: A Review of International English Literature*, Vols.I-III, Leeds: University of Calgary, 1970-72.

[Review of Harold Bloom, *Yeats*] in *Review of English Studies*, XXII, 88, November 1971, pp.514-17.

'Extra dimensions' in *Books*, Autumn 1971, pp.6-9.

'September, Leeds' (poem) in *Contemporary Review*, CCXIX, 1271, December 1971, p.311.

'Swift and the Ireland of his day' in *Irish University Review*, II, 2, Autumn 1972, pp.115-32.

'Early efforts of the Wild Irish Girl' in *Le Romantisme Anglo-Américain* (Etudes Anglaises, 39), Paris: Marcel Didier, 1972, pp.293-305.

'The great purple butterfly' [review of W.B. Yeats, *Memoirs*; W.B. Yeats (ed.), *Fairy and Folk Tales of Ireland*; B.A.S. Webster, *Yeats: A Psycholanalytical Study*; R.M. Snukal, *High Talk: The Philosophical Poetry of W.B. Yeats*], in *The Sewanee Review*, LXXXII, 1, Winter 1974, pp.108-18.

'African Sequence' (poems) in *Contemporary Review*, CCXXV, 1304, September 1974, pp.158-59.

'A great black ragged bird' in *Hermathena*, CXVIII, Winter 1974, pp.69-81.

'Lawson Memorial' in *The Journal of Commonwealth Literature*, X, 1, August 1975, pp.77-79.

'Goldsmith the good natured man' in *Hermathena*, CXIX, *1975, pp.5-19.*

'*On not throwing the nurse out with the bath water: English and Commonwealth literature*' in *The Round Table*, january 1976, pp.45-51.

'Literatures in English' in *Contemporary Review*, May 1976, pp.264-68.

'Coughing in ink' in *The Sewanee Review*, LXXXV, 1, Winter 1976, pp.157-67.

'Brooding about biography' in *The Sewanee Review*, LXXXV, 2, April-June 1977, pp.301-31.

'Ostale Knijizevnosti Na Engleskom Jeziku' in *Poviject Svjeste Knijizevnosti Knijiga*, 6, Zagreb: Mladost, 1976, pp.400-26.

[Review of *Uncollected Prose by W.B. Yeats Vol.II* (eds. John P. Frayne and Colton Johnson)] in *The Review of English Studies*, New Series XXVII I, 109, February 1977, p.114.

'Lines of Time' (poem) in *Contemporary Review*, CCXXX, 1336, May 1977, p.268.

'Three questions' (3 poems) in *Etudes Irlandaises*, New Series 2, December 1977. pp.13-16.

'Unnatural Planning Permission' (poem) in *Contemporary Review*, CCXXXII, 1349 ,June 1978, p.326.

[Review of James W. Flannery, *W.B. Yeats and the Idea of a Theatre*] in *Theatre Research International*, New Series IV, 1, October 1978, pp.68-69.

'*The Fortunes of Richard Mahony* reconsidered' in *The Sewanee Review*, LXXXVII, 1, Winter 1979, pp.158-64.

[Review of F.W. Bateson, ed., R.B. Sheridan, *The School for Scandal*] in *The Literary Review*, 3, 2-15 November 1979, p.30.

'Words' (poem) in *Ariel*, XI, 1, January 1980, p.30.

[Review of F.S.L. Lyons, *Culture and Anarchy in Ireland 1890–1939*] in *Hermathena*, CXXIX, Summer 1980, pp.73-74.

'Teaching Anglo-Irish literature' in *Hermathana*, CXXIX, Winter 1980, pp.17-22.

'Yeats, Allingham and the Western fiction' in *The canadian Journal of Irish Studies*, VI, 2, December 1980, pp.2-17. Reprinted in *Unaging Intellect*.

Essays on W.B. Yeats (eds. Kamta C. Srivastava and Ujjal Dutta). Delhi, 1982.

[Review of Alan Wilde, *Horizons of Assent*] in *Western Humanities Review*, XXXVI, 1, Spring 1982, pp.77-78.

[Review of O.B. Hardison, Jr., *Entering the Maze: Identity Change in Modern Culture*] in *Western Humanities Review*, XXXVI, 3, Autumn 1982, pp.285-87.

'Three plays by W.B. Yeats' in *Gaeliana*, 4, 1982, pp.57-79.

[Review of Robert Scholes, *Semiotics and Interpretation*] in *Western Humanities Review*, XXXVII, 2, Summer 1983, pp163-65.

[Review of Stevie Smith, *Me Again*] in *Western Humanities Review*, XXXVIII, 2, Summer 1984, pp.170-72.

'Foreword' to 'Beckett at eighty: A Trinity tribute' in *Hermathena*, CXLI, Winter 1986, pp.7-9.

E. RADIO SCRIPTS

'Yeats the public man'. Thomas Davis Lecture, RTE, Dublin, 1963.

'The pleasure of vintage cars'. ABC, Perth, 1954.

'Sir Robert Richard Torrens'. ABC, Adelaide, 1955.

'West African Writing'. BBC, London, 1965.

'Yeats'. Thomas Davis Lecture, RTE, Dublin, 1971. Printed in *Irish Poets in English* (ed. Sean Lucy), 1973, pp.105-17.

'Goldsmith's *The Vicar of Wakefield*'. Thomas Davis Lecture, RTE, Dublin, April 1978.

Printed in *Goldsmith, the Gentle Master* (ed. Sean Lucy), 1984, pp.38-49.

'Anglo-Irish Literature'. ABC (3 hours), Sydney, 1980. A revised version was published in Masaru Sekine, ed., *Irish Writers and the Theatre*, 1985.

'The modern Irish realist novel'. Thomas David Lecture, RTE Dublin, 1984.

'W.B. Yeats'. ABC (3 hours), Sydney, 1987.

'George Moore'. ABC, Sydney, 1987.

F. EDITOR OF SERIES AND JOURNALS

Founding Editor, *A Review of English Literature*, I-VIII, 1960-67.

Founding Editor, *ARIEL: A Review of International English Literature*, I-III, 1970-72.

General Editor, *Writers and Critics Series*, Edinburgh & London: Oliver & Boyd.

General Editor, *New Oxford English Series*, Oxford. The Clarendon Press.

Co-Editor, *Biography and Criticism Series*, Edinburgh & London: Oliver & Boyd.

Literary Editor, *The Fountainwell Drama Texts*, Edinburgh & London: **Oliver & Boyd.**

General Editor, *Irish Novels Series,* Dublin & Shannon: Irish University Press.

General Editor, *Macmillan Commonwealth Writers, London: Macmillan.*

General Editor, *Macmillan International College Edition,* London: Macmillan.

General Editor, *Macmillan New Literature Handbooks,* London: Macmillan.

Co-Editor, *York Notes Series,* London: Longman and Beirut: York Press.

General Editor, *Macmillan Histories of Literature,* London: Macmillan, and New York: Schocken Books.

Editor, *York Handbooks Series,* London: Longman and Beirut: York Press.

Co-Editor, *Macmillan Anthologies of English Literature,* London: Macmillan.

NOTES

CANON SHEEHAN AND THE CATHOLIC INTELLECTUAL
Terence Brown

1. Canon Sheehan, 'The Dawn of the Century', published in *Literary Life* (Dublin: the Phoenix Publishing Company Ltd., no date given), pp.145–6.
2. Cited in John A. Murphy, 'Priests and People in Modern Irish History', *Christus Rex*, Vol. XXIII, No. 4, 1969, p.251. I am indebted to this detailed study.
3. Sheehan, 'The Irish Priesthood and Politics', *Literary Life*, pp.112–13.
4. Quoted by Sheehan, *Irish Ecclesiastical Record*, August, 1886, p.690.
5. Sheehan, *Irish Ecclesiastical Record*, July, 1886, p.629.
6. See Herman J. Heuser, D.D., *Canon Sheehan of Doneraile* (London, 1917), pp.73–86.
7. In a letter of 1911 Sheehan told a friend 'I have a new novel completed; it deals with Socialism in Ireland and many other matters'. Heuser, *op.cit.*, p.258.
8. I was aided in my interpretation of this novel by the helpful reading Austen Corcoran supplied in his unpublished doctoral thesis *Violence and the Form of the Irish Novel* (University College, Dublin, 1981).

PANGUR BAN AND THE SCHOLAR CRITIC
Maurice Harmon

1. A talk given to the postgraduate seminar in Irish Studies at University College, Dublin.

LAFCADIO HEARN, W.B. YEATS AND JAPAN
Barbara Hayley

1. The most easily available brief biography is in the introduction to the Penguin Travel Library *Lafcadio Hearn: Writings from Japan*, edited, with an introduction, by Francis King (Harmondsworth,

1984). The biographical details in this differ in some respects from those of earlier biographers such as Miss Bisland (see note 2 below)

2. *The Life and Letters of Lafcadio Hearn*, edited by Elizabeth Bisland (London, 1911), p.400.
3. 'The Autumn of the Body', *Essays and Introductions* (New York, 1961), p.191.
4. 'The Cutting of an Agate', *Essays and Introductions*, p.228.
5. Letter to Shotaro Oshima, 19 August 1927, quoted in Shotaro Oshima, *W.B.Yeats and Japan* (Tokyo, 1965), p.6. This book considers Yeats's Japanese reading and contacts, and Japanese writings on Yeats.
6. *A Vision* (London and Basingstoke, 1978), p.301.
7. Letter to Kazumi Yano, January 1928, quoted in Shotaro Oshima, *W.B.Yeats and Japan*, p.23. Yeats never went to Japan, despite various plans for lecture tours.
8. 'Intuition', quoted in *The Life and Letters of Lafcadio Hearn*, Vol. I, p.41.
9. Hearn's letters up to 1890 were published in *The Life and Letters of Lafcadio Hearn*, 1911, in two volumes. His letters after 1890 were collected in *The Japanese Letters of Lafcadio Hearn*, edited by Elizabeth Bisland (London, Boston, New York, 1911).
10. The articles quoted from in this section are from the New Orleans *Times-Democrat*, collected in Lafcadio Hearn, *Essays in European and Oriental Literature* (London, 1923).
11. The variety and extent of Hearn's reading can be judged by the *Life and Letters*, *Japanese Letters* and the *Essays in European and Oriental Literature*.
12. Hearn's method of observing Japan is close to that which he praises in Loti: 'On visiting a new country he always used to take notes of every fresh and powerful impression ... Nor did such exquisite notework as this alone satisfy him; for mere description of external objects alone forms but a small part of the charm of his books;—he subjoined notes of the thoughts and fancies also which such impressions of sight, sound, or smell produced in the mind; and thus his work is as much introspective as it is retrospective'. ('The Most Original of Modern Novelists: Pierre Loti'. *Essays in European and Oriental Literature*, p.137.)
13. 'In a Japanese Garden', *Glimpses of Unfamiliar Japan* (Rutland, Vermont and Tokyo, 1976), p.384.
14. 'A Pilgrimage to Enoshima', *Glimpses of Unfamiliar Japan*, pp.94–5.
15. 'Bon-Odori', *Glimpses of Unfamiliar Japan*, p.123.
16. 'In the Cave of the Children's Ghosts', *Glimpses of Unfamiliar Japan*, p.229.
17. 'Kidnappers', *Mythologies* (London and Basingstoke, 1959), p.74.
18. 'Village Ghosts', *Mythologies*, p.20.
19. 'Of a Promise Broken', *A Japanese Miscellany*, p.29.

20. 'Chief City of the Province of the Gods', *Glimpses of Unfamiliar Japan*, p.166.
21. 'The Story of Kwashin Koji', *A Japanese Miscellany*, p.50.
22. 'Folklore Gleanings, I, Dragon flies', *A Japanese Miscellany*, pp.94–5, 99.
23. 'An Indian Monk', *Mythologies*.
24. 'Of Moon Desire', *The Buddhist Writings of Lafcadio Hearn*, edited by Kenneth Rexroth (London, 1981), pp.149–50.
25. 'Otokichi's Daruma', *Ibid.*, p.234.
26. 'Gaki', *Ibid.*, p.245.
27. 'Dust', *Ibid.*, pp.22–23.
28. 'The Stone Buddha', *Ibid.*, p.20.
29. 'The Higher Buddhism', *Ibid.*, p.281.
30. 'The Higher Buddhism, *Ibid.*, pp.281–2.
31. 'Nirvana', *Ibid.*, p.50.
32. Alex Zwerdling, *Yeats and the Heroic Ideal* (New York, 1965), p.151.
33. 'The Household Shrine', *Glimpses of Unfamiliar Japan*, pp.388–9.
34. 'Sayonara', *Glimpses of Unfamiliar Japan*, p.686.
35. 'Kitzuki: the Most Ancient Shrine of Japan', *Glimpses of Unfamiliar Japan*, p.202.
36. 'Of a Dancing-girl', *Ibid.*, pp.531–2.
37. 'Bon-Odori', *Ibid.*, p.134.
38. 'Rosa Alchemica', *Mythologies*, p.288.
39. *Ibid.*, p.290.
40. 'Bon-Odori', *Glimpses of Unfamiliar Japan*, p.137.
41. 'Certain Noble plays of Japan', *Essays and Introductions*, p.226.
42. 'A Pilgrimage to Enoshima', *Glimpses of Unfamiliar Japan*, p.102.

MY LIFE'S WORK, WITH A DISCUSSION OF FRANCIS BERRY'S POETRY
G. Wilson Knight

1. The matter is discussed fully in: my *Neglected Powers* (London, 1971), pp.384–7, 489–90; *Studies in Romanticism*, Boston University, Winter 1982; Philip L. Marcus, *Criticism* (U.S.A.), Winter 1967. See also John Bayley's review 'Soul' in *The London Review of Books*, 7 Aug.-6 Sept. 1984; and Ronald Bush, *T.S. Eliot* (London, 1984). Eliot gave me a copy of *Marina* inscribed to me as 'with, I hope, some appropriateness': it is lodged in the Shakespeare Section of the Birmingham Public Libraries.
2. In 'Pope's Waste Land: Reflections on Mock-Heroic' (in *Essays and Studies 1982*, 'The Poet's Power', collected by Suheil Bushrui), Professor Claude Rawson has discussed Pope's attitude to the higher, ideal, beyond-factual truth conveyed by ancient epic, and his toning down of Homeric cruelties in his translation of the *Iliad*.

3. See *The Road to Immortality* (London, 1932) and *Beyond Human Personality* (London, 1935, rev. 1952), purportedly from F.W.H. Myers, spirit-teachings transmitted through Geraldine Cummins; and *The Return of Arthur Conan Doyle*, edited by Ivan Cooke (The White Eagle Publishing Trust, Liss, Hants, 1956).

4. See also Peter Russell, *The Awakening Earth* (London, 1982 and 1984).

5. See Raymond Moody, *Life After Life* and *Reflections on Life After Life*, Bantam Books, 1975; also *Psychic News*, 4 February, 1984, p.5, reporting Margot Grey on near-death experience; and 5 January 1985, p.1, reporting on Bryce Bond's experience. These books by Moody, those by Geraldine Cummins and Peter Russell, and the numbers of *Psychic News*, can be had from the Psychic News Bookshop, 20 Earlham Street, London WC2.

6. John Masefield, *Lost Endeavour* (London, 1910), 2.XV. p.243, quoted by kind permission of The Society of Authors on behalf of the Estate of John Masefield.

DION BOUCICAULT'S 'AMERICAN' PLAYS
Heinz Kosok

1. The inclusion of Boucicault among the *American* dramatists was no exception. Arthur Hobson Quinn, in his influential *History of the American Drama: From the Beginning to the Civil War* (New York, 2nd ed. 1943), devoted a long chapter to him (pp.368–392). See also the detailed chapters on Boucicault in Montrose J. Moses, *The American Dramatist* (Boston, 1925), pp.146–170, and Jack A. Vaughn, *Early American Dramatists: From the Beginnings to 1900* (New York, 1981), pp.112–131 (note the programmatic titles of these studies). It is also interesting to note that Robert Hogan's book *Dion Boucicault* (New York, 1969) was published in Twayne's *United States* Authors Series.

2. Barrett H. Clark, 'General Preface', *America's Lost Plays*, Vol. I (Princeton, 1940), p.vi.

3. The best studies of Boucicault's life and works are Hogan, *op.cit.* and David Krause, 'The Theatre of Dion Boucicault: A Short View of His Life and Art', in: Krause (ed.), *The Dolmen Boucicault* (Dublin, 1964), pp.9–47. The standard biography is: Richard Fawkes, *Dion Boucicault: A Biography* (London, 1979). Biographical material is also contained in: Townsend Walsh, *The Career of Dion Boucicault* (New York, 1915, repr. 1967); Susan Peffer, 'Dion Boucicault', *Letters*, 2 (1929), 7–18; Albert Johnson, 'Fabulous Boucicault', *Theatre Arts*, 37 (March, 1953), 27–30, 90–93; *id.*, 'The Birth of Dion Boucicault', *Modern Drama*, 11 (1968/69), 157–163; Micheál Ó hAodha, 'The Quest for Boucicault', *Plays and Places* (Dublin, 1961), pp.1–12. Personal memories of Boucicault are contained in: Clement Scott,

The Drama of Yesterday & To-day (London, 1899), vol. I, pp.91–109; and William Winter, *Other Days: Being Chronicles and Memories of the Stage* (New York, 1908), pp.124–151. All biographical studies on Boucicault are incomplete, contradictory and, in many details, unreliable.

4. Quoted by Peffer, *op.cit.*, 7. Cf. Fawkes, *op.cit.*, p.210.

5 According to the survey in Fawkes, *op.cit.*, pp.260–266. Fawkes identifies 151 plays (including adaptations and short plays); 89 of them were first produced in England, 53 in the United States, one in Ireland; eight plays remained unproduced.

6. Dion Boucicault, *Jessie Brown; or, The Relief of Lucknow*, Lacy's Acting Edition no. 38 (London, n.d.), pp.6–7.

7. Dion Boucicault, *The Poor of New York: A Drama in Five Acts*, French's Standard Drama no. 189 (New York, n.d.). The title page states 'By the + + + + Club', but the title of the series, 'Boucicault's Dramatic Works No. 5', clearly identifies Boucicault as the author.

8. *Ibid.*, pp.44–45.

9. Fawkes, *op.cit.*, p.148; Hogan, *op.cit.*, pp.66, 129.

10. Hogan, *op.cit*, pp.66, 129.

11. *New York Herald* (Dec.10, 1857), as quoted in Barnard Hewitt, *Theatre U.S.A.* (New York, 1959), pp.183–185.

12. For this reason it was possible to use *The Poor of New York* for a demonstration of the typical elements of nineteenth-century melodrama: William Paul Steele, *The Character of Melodrama: An Examination Through Dion Boucicault's 'The Poor of New York'*, University of Maine Studies, no.87 (Orono, Maine, 1968).

13. The text is available in : Garrett H. Leverton (ed.), *Plays for the College Theatre* (New York, 1932), pp.129–147.

14. Dion Boucicault, *The Octoroon*, in: Arthur Hobson Quinn (ed.), *Representative American Plays: From 1767 to the Present Day* (New York, 7th ed. 1966), p. 389.

15. For details of the New York production see Seldon Faulkner, 'The Octoroon War', *Educational Theatre Journal*, 15 (1963), 33–38; and Fawkes, *op.cit.*, pp.106–111. That Boucicault designed his play to conform to his audience's expectations is confirmed by Frank S. Galassi, 'Slavery and Melodrama: Boucicault's *The Octoroon*, *Markham Review*, 6 (1977), 77–80.

16. The reasons for his decision are discussed by Nils Erik Enkvist, '*The Octoroon* and English Opinions of Slavery', *American Quarterly*, 8 (1956), 166–170. The relationship between the two versions is studied by John A. Degen, 'How to End *The Octoroon*', *Educational Theatre Journal*, 27 (1975), 170–178.

JULIA CAHILL, FATHER McTURNAN, AND THE GEOGRAPHY OF NOWHERE.
Augustine Martin

1. *The Untilled Field* by George Moore, London, (London, 1903), p.202. All quotations throughout this essay are from this edition.
2. Daniel Corkery, *A Munster Twilight* (Cork, Mercier Press, 1967), pp.86–92.

THE POET AND BARABBAS: KEATS, HIS PUBLISHERS AND EDITORS
J.E. Morpurgo

1. This essay is based upon the Keats Memorial Lecture given by the author at Guy's Hospital on Monday 25 February 1985 for the Royal College of Surgeons, Guy's Hospital and the Worshipped Society of Apothecaries.

SOUTH AFRICAN NOVELISTS AS PROPHETS
Arthur Ravenscroft

1. Karel Schoeman, *Na die Geliefde Land* (Cape Town, 1972); as *Promised Land*, translated into English by Marion V. Friedmann (London, 1978). For convenience, quotations are from the English translation, with page references in parenthesis to that version.
2. J.M. Coetzee, *Life and Times of Michael K* (London, 1983).
3. By contrast, Schoeman's attitude to nature is rather more austere. In *Na die Geliefde Land*, 'the troubles' drive a generation of thoroughly urbanized Afrikaners back to their family farms. That the children of the *Boerenasie*, or 'Nation of Farmers', of Afrikaner lore should find farm life uncongenial and strange is another neat Schoeman irony.
4. Sheila Fugard, *A Revolutionary Woman* (Johannesburg, 1983; London, 1984); the reference is to the London edition.
5. Nadine Gordimer, *July's People* (London, 1981).
6. Nadine Gordimer, *The Conservationist* (London, 1974); *Burger's Daughter* (London, 1979).
7. Sipho Sepamla, *A Ride on the Whirlwind* (Johannesburg, 1981; London 1984); the references are to the London edition.
8. Mongane Serote, *To Every Birth Its Blood* (Johannesburg, 1981; London, 1983); the references are to the London edition.

STONE PEOPLE IN A STONE COUNTRY: ALAN PATON'S *TOO LATE THE PHALAROPE*
Anna Rutherford

1. Wilson Harris, *Explorations* (Aarhus, 1980). This volume is a collection of Harris's critical essays.
2. Eric Williams, *Capitalism and Slavery* (London, 1967), p.7.
3. For a more detailed explication of Harris's ideas, see Kirsten Holst Petersen and Anna Rutherford, *Enigma of Values* (Aarhus, 1975).
4. Alan Paton, *Too Late the Phalarope* (Harmondswoth, 1979). All references are to this edition and will be included in the text.
5. W.A. De Klerk, *The Puritans in Africa* (Harmondsworth, 1976), pp.12–13. This description of the Afrikaner may not be valid today but I am suggesting that it was valid for the time in which Alan Paton set his novel.
6. Christine Bolt, *Victorian Attitudes to Race* (London, 1971), pp.131–2.
7. Patrick White, *A Fringe of Leaves* (Harmondsworth, 1977).
8. See G.D. Killam, *Africa in English Fiction* (Ibadan, 1968).
9. Joseph Conrad, *Heart of Darkness* (New York, 1960), p.42.
10. *Heart of Darkness*, p.85.
11. Doris Lessing, *The Four Gated City* (London, 1969), p.510.
12. *Heart of Darkness*, see pp.16–20.
13. See Simone de Beauvoir, 'The Social Construction of Woman: Western Mythic and Religious Stereotypes' in *Hecate*, Vol.I, No.1.
14. Athol Fugard, *The Blood Knot* (Harmondsworth, 1968), p.101.
15. Werner Heisenberg, 'Rationality in Science and Society' in *Can We Survive Our Future*, edited by G.R. Urban (London, 1972), p.84.
16. Mervyn Peake, *Gormenghast* (Harmondsworth, 1973), p.72.

It has been suggested that my conclusion is too negative and that a ray of hope for the society lies with women like the mother and the aunt. Both certainly possess the necessary compassion, and the opening of the front door and the rolling up of the blinds (p.199) are, of course, symbolic gestures expressing, no doubt, Paton's hope that there is a possibility for dialogue. This may be so if people such as these ruled South Africa. But they don't. South Africa is ruled by a white patriarchal society that rejects dialogue and refuses justice, and as a consequence I believe it is doomed to eventual destruction.

THE THEATRICAL VOICE: *THE WORDS UPON THE WINDOW-PANE*
Ann Saddlemyer

1. 'A People's Theatre', first published in the *Irish Statesman*, 29 November and 6 December 1919, printed in *Explorations* (London,

1962), pp.254–57. My essay derives from a paper read to the Yeats Society of Japan in September 1984 and I am pleased to record my gratitude to my Japanese colleagues for the invitation which initiated it.

2. 'Swedenborg, Mediums, and the Desolate Places' (1914), *Explorations*, pp.30–31.

3. The first Abbey Theatre play with a Dublin seting was W.F.Casey's *The Suburban Groove* (1908), but the most famous tenement plays are Sean O'Casey's *The Shadow of a Gunman* (1923), *Juno and the Paycock* (1924), and *The Plough and the Stars* (1926); in 1926 Lennox Robinson wrote of the decline of the gentry in *The Big House*.

4. Author of *Human Personality and its Survival of Bodily Death*, 2 vols (New York, 1954).

5. In his introduction to Percy Arland Ussher's translation of Brian Merriman's *The Midnight Court* (1926), *Explorations*, p.281, Yeats alludes to the view that the poem was founded upon Swift's *Cadenus and Vanessa*.

6. 'Pages from a Diary Written in 1930' (1944), *Explorations*, pp.319–20.

7. See Earl Roy Miner, 'A Poem by Swift and W.B. Yeats's *Words Upon the Window-Pane*', *Modern Language Notes* LXXII (April 1957), pp.273–75; Swift's verses are published under the title, 'Written upon windows at Inns, in England'.

8. All quotations from the play are from *The Collected Plays of W.B. Yeats* (London, 1952), and unless otherwise indicated, quotations from the Introduction are from *Explorations*.

9. 'Pages from a Diary', p.322.

10. Entry dated 18 September 1930, quoted by Mary FitzGerald, ' "Out of a medium's mouth": The Writing of *The Words upon the Window-Pane*', *Colby Library Quarterly*, 17, 2 (June 1981), p.70. On the same day Lady Gregory wrote to T.J. Kiernan, 'He is writing a play—and also studying Berkeley—will write on him' *Bulletin of Friends of the New York Public Library*, 72, 1 (January 1968), p.57.

11. All quotations from the poems are from *The Collected Poems of W.B. Yeats* (London, 1952).

12. *A Vision* (New York, 1961), p.19.

13. *The Letters of W.B. Yeats*, ed. Allan Wade (London, 1954), p.781.

14. Introduction to *A Vision*, pp.22–23.

15. 'Pages from a Diary', p.322.

16. 'The Soul in Judgment', *A Vision*, pp.224–26.

17. *A Vision*, p.228n.

18. *A Vision*, pp.226–28.

19. Peter Ure, *Yeats the Playwright* (London, 1963), pp.100–01. Most critics assume her presence, see below note 76.

20. In phase two of the period after death, the phase during which the 'Dreaming Back' and 'Return' take place, the dead being wears 'the form it had immediately before death' (*A Vision*, p.235).

21. Donald T. Torchiana, *W.B. Yeats and Georgian Ireland* (Evanston, 1966), p.139.
22. 'Ideas of Good and Evil' (1903), reprinted in *Essays* (London 1924), p.33
23. *Explorations*, pp.49–50 and 54–55.
24. Quoted by Virginia Moore, *The Unicorn: William Butler Yeats's Search for Reality* (New York, 1954), pp.378–79.
25. 'A Commentary', *The Dublin Magazine*, January-March, 1932.
26. *A Vision*, p.25.
27. John Rees Moore, *Masks of Love and Death: Yeats as Dramatist* (Ithaca, 1972), p.259.
28. David Clark, *W.B. Yeats and the Theatre of Desolate Reality* (Dublin, 1965), p.65. I am indebted to Clark's fine study in a number of ways, particularly to his analysis of the various levels of language in the play.
29. Miner, 'A Poem by Swift and W.B. Yeats's *Words Upon the Window-Pane*', p.274.
30. Cf. Ann Saddlemyer, 'The "Dwarf-Dramas" of the early Abbey Theatre', in *Yeats, Sligo and Ireland*, ed. A.N. Jeffares (Gerrards Cross, 1980), pp.197–215.
31. Cf. Douglas N. Archibald's excellent article '*The Words Upon the Window-Pane* and Yeats's Encounter with Jonathan Swift' in *Yeats and the Theatre*, eds. Robert O'Driscoll and Lorna Reynolds (Toronto, 1975), pp.176–214; and Yeats's poem 'Blood and the Moon'.
32. 'Introduction to Essays' (137), *Yeats on Yeats*, ed. Edward Callan (Dublin, 1981), p.79.
33. 'Pages from a Diary', pp.332, 301–302.
34. *Explorations*, p.345; the introduction was not written until a year after the play was produced.
35. Yeats's Introduction to Joseph Hone and M.M. Rossi, *Bishop Berkeley: His Life, Writings and Philosophy* (London, 1931), p.xvi.
36. Quoted by Richard Ellmann in *Yeats: The Man and the Masks* (London, 1949), p.110; a slightly different version appears in W.B. Yeats, *Memoirs*, ed. Denis Donoghue (London, 1972), p.68.
37. 'The New Irish Library', *The Bookman*, June 1896.
38. 'The Silenced Sister', *United Ireland*, December 30, 1893.
39. Reprinted in J.M. Synge, *Poems*, ed. Robin Skelton (Gerrards Cross, 1983)), p.xxxiii; in his chapters on Swift in *Yeats's Heroic Figures: Wilde, Parnell, Swift, Casement*. (Albany, 1983), Michael Steinman records most of Yeats's early references to Swift. I did not see this book until after my paper had been written, but as can be seen, my interpretation differs.
40. 'Letters from W.B. Yeats to Lady Gregory', ed. Donald T. Torchiana and Glenn O'Malley, *A Review of English Literature*, IV, 3 (July 1963), pp.20–23.
41. *Explorations*, pp.281–82.

42. 11 June 1925, *The Senate Speeches of W.B. Yeats*, ed. Donald R. Pearce (Bloomington, 1960), p.99.
43. ' "Out of a Medium's Mouth''; The Writing of *The Words Upon the Window-Pane'*, pp.65–73.
44. Quoted by Torchiana, *W.B. Yeats and Georgian Ireland*, p.133.
45. Quoted by Torchiana, p.131.
46. Letter to Lady Gregory, 7 April 1930, *Letters*, ed. Wade, p.773.
47. Quoted by Torchiana, p.154; this passage was later cancelled.
48. Introduction, *Explorations*, p.345.
49. *Letters*, ed. Wade, p.779. The same sentiment was expressed in conversation with Ramsay MacDonald and George Trevelyan, cf. William Rothenstein, *Since Fifty: Men and Memories 1922–1938* (London, 1939), p.242.
50. 14 February 1932, *Letters*, ed. Wade, p.791.
51. Yeats considered Swift's pamphlet *The Discourse of the Contests and Dissensions between the Nobles and Commons in Athens and Rome* his one 'philosophical work' and quoted it frequently. Cf. Introduction to the play; introduction to *The Resurrection*, and 'Pages from a Diary', pp.292–3, 313–17.
52. 'Pages from a Diary', p.315.
53. *A Vision*, p.28.
54. 'Pages from a Diary', p.290.
55. *Letters*, ed. Wade, p.776.
56. Introduction, p.360.
57. 'Pages from a Diary', p.334; letter to Rossi, *Letters*, ed. Wade, pp.616–19.
58. Introduction, pp.362–63; 'He [Corbet] imagines, though but for a moment, that the intellect of Swift's age, persuaded that the mechanicians mocked by Gulliver would prevail, that its moment of freedom could not last, so dreaded the historic process that it became in the half-mad mind of Swift a dread of parentage.'
59. Quoted by Joseph Hone, *W.B. Yeats* (London, 1942) p.405.
60. 'Pages from a Diary', pp.293–94.
61. Letter to Edmund Dulac, 15 July 1937, *Letters*, ed. Wade, p.405.
62. Torchiana, *W.B. Yeats and Georgian Ireland*, pp.128–29.
63. To Ethel Mannin, 17 December 1937, *Letters*, ed. Wade, p.903.
64. Cf. his letter to Olivia Shakespear, 9 February 1931, *Letters*, ed. Wade. p.781. 'I write very much for young men between twenty and thirty . . . '
65. Cf. letter to Dulac, 15 July 1937, *Letters*, ed. Wade, p.892.
66. 'Pages from a Diary', p.303.
67. Letter to Dorothy Wellesley, 23 December 1936, *Letters*, ed. Wade, p.876; cf. 'A General Introduction for my Work', *Yeats on Yeats*, p.63: 'Everything I love has come to me through English. My hatred tortures me with love, my love with hate. I am like the Tibetan monk who dreams at his initiation that he is eaten by a wild beast and learns on waking that he himself is eater and eaten. This is Irish

hatred and solitude, the hatred of human life that made Swift write *Gulliver* and the epitaph upon his tomb, that can still make us wag between extremes and doubt our sanity'.
68. Cf. letter to Dorothy Wellesley, 23 December 1936, *Letters*, ed. Wade, p.876: 'You say that we must not hate. You are right, but we may, and sometimes must, be indignant and speak it. Hate is a kind of "passive suffering", but indignation is a kind of joy'.
69. Yeats to Sean O'Casey, 20 April 1928, *Letters*, pp.740–42.
70. Hiro Ishibashi, *Yeats and the Noh: Types of Japanese Beauty and their Reflection in Yeats's PLays* (Dublin, 1965), pp.130, 143–50. See also Earl Miner, *The Japanese Tradition in British and American Literature* (Princeton, 1958), pp.262–263; Richard Taylor, *The Drama of W.B. Yeats: Irish Myth and the Japanese Nó* (New Haven, 1976), pp.170–73; and Yasuko Stucki, 'Yeats's Drama and the Nó. A Comparative Study in 'Dramatic Theories', *Modern Drama*, May 19, 1966, pp.101–22.
71. *Explorations*, p.153.
72. Quoted by Ellmann, *Yeats the Man and the Masks*, p.214.
73. See Horace Gregory, 'W.B. Yeats and the Mask of Jonathan Swift', *The Southern Review*, 7,3 (Winter 1941/2), pp.492–509.
74. 2 or 4 October 1927, *Letters*, ed. Wade, p.730.
75. To Dorothy Wellesley, 22 June 1938, *Letters*, ed. Wade, pp.910–11.
76. Although we do not agree in other particulars, my argument about Stella is similar to Peter Ure's *Yeats the Playwright*, p.100, but I do not think , as he does, that Swift is dreaming back all of the characters including himself at an earlier age; the thought of the Spirit is, as Yeats says, so fast, that both images almost co-exist. An interesting article by Joseph Brogunier, 'Expiation in Yeats's Late Plays', *Drama Survey* 5:1 (Spring 1966), pp. 24–28, also makes the point that 'Swift's peace is a temporary condition'.
77. Yeats actually applies the phrase to his later poetry in a letter to H.J.C. Grierson, 21 February 1926, *Letters*, ed. Wade, p.710: 'My own verse has more and more adopted—seemingly without any will of mine—the syntax and vocabulary of common personal speech.' Of his *Sophocles' Oedipus at Colonus* he wrote that he wanted to be 'less literal and more idiomatic and modern' even than his *Oedipus*; letter to Olivia Shakespear 6 December 1926, *Letters*, ed. Wade, p.721.
78. To Olivia Shakespear, December 1926, *Letters*, ed. Wade, p.720.

O BLISS! O POOP-POOP! O MY! O MY!
Stewart Sanderson

1. A. Norman Jeffares, 'If Cars Could Write', in Stephen King-Hall (ed.), *Young Authors and Artists of 1935*, Part II (Ages 12–14), (London, 1935), pp.98–101.

2. For pertinent testimony, see Mark Amory (ed.), *The Letters of Evelyn Waugh* (London, 1980), *passim*.
3. This is confirmed by the artist.
4. Kenneth Grahame, *The Wind in the Willows*, (London, 1908), Chapter 2.
5. The quest for the precise bibliographical references for the literary allusions in this paragraph, and for other notes towards a comprehensive bibliography of motoring in English Literature (Kipling, for instance; de la Mare's ghost story resolved, or rather escaped from, by repossession of the car's ignition key) may perhaps serve as an innocent recreation for the dedicatee of this essay.
6. A. Norman Jeffares, *Yeats: Man and Poet*, (London, 1949).

WHO WAS PETER GRIMES?
James Sutherland

1. René Huchon, *George Crabbe and his Times 1754–1832*, translated by Frederick Clarke, 1907 (reprinted 1968), pp. 308–9.
2. *The Works of the Rev. George Crabbe*, edited by George Crabbe (London, 1834), vol.IV, p.39n.
3. René Huchon, *op.cit.* p.310.
4. Since I came across this trial nearly forty years ago, when I was working through a good run of the *Proceedings* in the Harvard Law Library, I may be absolved from the charge of jumping to conclusions and rushing into print. Yet the possibility that the trial of John Bennet might be some sort of source for 'Peter Grimes' struck me at once, and I have been going around like the Ancient Mariner ever since, with a ghastly tale that must be told, but without much hope that anyone—let alone a wedding-guest— will listen.
5. Crabbe's letter to Scott, 5 March 1813, was printed in Arthur L. Humphreys, *Piccadilly Bookman: Memorials of the House of Hatchard* (London, 1893), pp.55–6. For Scott's letter to Crabbe, see *The Letters of Sir Walter Scott*, edited by H.J.C. Grierson, vol.III (1811–14), 1922, p.279n.

METHOD AND DECORUM IN *DON JUAN*
Alastair W. Thomson

1. See Thomas Medwin, *Journal of the Conversations of Lord Byron at Pisa* (London, 1824).
2. Leslie A. Marchand (editor), *Byron's Letters and Journals*, 12 vols.

(London, 1973–82): VIII, p.37; letter to John Murray, 2 January 1817, V, p.157. Hereafter referred to as *LJ*.

3. M.K. Joseph, *Byron The Poet* (London, 1964), pp.233–34. Hereafter referred to as L.J.

4. 'The sentimental anatomy of Rousseau and Made de S[taël] are far more formidable than any quantity of verse. They are so, because they sap the principles, by *reasoning* upon the *passions*; whereas poetry is in itself passion, and does not systematize. It assails, but does not argue; it may be wrong, but it does not assume pretensions to Optimism.' (*Second Letter to [John Murray], Esqre, on the Rev. W.L. Bowles's Strictures on the Life and Writings of Pope*, published 1835 (*Works*, edited by R.E. Prothero, 1901, Vol.V, Appendix III, p.582).) 'The truth is, that in these days the grand *"primum mobile"* of England is *cant*; cant political, cant poetical, cant religious, cant moral; but always cant ... I say *cant*, because it is a thing of words, without the smallest influence upon human actions; the English being no wiser, no better, and much poorer, and more divided among themselves, as well as far less moral, than they were before the prevalence of this verbal decorum.' (*Letter to [John Murray] Esqre*, etc., published March, 1821 (*ibid.*, p.542).

5. *Satires*, II, vi.17. The significance of the reference to Horace is discussed by George Ridenour, *The Style of 'Don Juan'* (New Haven, Connecticut), 1960.

6. Letter to John Murray, 7 September 1814 (*LJ* IV, p.167); letter to Leigh Hunt, 30 October 1815 (*LJ* IV, pp.324–25).

7. Moore's *Journal*, quoted *LJ* XI, p.198; *Biographia Literaria* I, ch. xxii.

8. Wordsworth, *Poetical Works*, edited by Ernest de Selincourt (Oxford, 1965), II, p.535; letter to Leigh Hunt, *op.cit.*, p.325.

9. Byron returns to this in the ironic yet gentle stanza (cxcviii) describing how Julia wrote her self-dramatising letter of farewell to Juan: ' "They tell me 'tis decided." ' (The letter begins with 'they,' and ends with 'you,' the implication being that among them she is nothing, except for her love.) The mingling of sincere feeling and self-indulgence is admirable, as is the valedictory stanza, which lingers over the gentle but undeluded observation of the seal, the motto, the jewel, and the coloured wax, which define her. One of the most amusing things about Julia's impudent harangue to Don Alfonso, incidentally, is the use she makes of the heroic formula 'was it for this?' In the first book of *The Prelude*, 'was it for this?' marks the moment when Wordsworth begins to turn defeat into triumph, as he considers what made him, and why. In Byron's epic satire it is the formula by which Julia catalogues her wrongs before the cuckolded Alfonso: ' "It was for this that I became a bride! / For this in silence I have suffer'd long" ... "Was it for this that no Cortejo e'er / I yet have chosen from out the youth of Seville?" ', and so to the shrewish modulation into ' "Was it for this you took your sudden journey, / Under pretence of business indispensable?" '

10. Ridenour, *op.cit.*, pp.101–2, describes this passage as 'a clear Petrarchan parody', and quotes *Rime* XXXIX: 'Solo e pensoso i più deserti campi / vo mesurando a passi tardi e lenti.'
11. Letter to Douglas Kinnaird, 10 December 1819 (*LJ* VI, p.256); letter to John Murray, 7 February 1820 (*LJ* VII, p.35).
12. T.G. Steffan, in *Don Juan*, edited by T.G. Steffan and W.W. Pratt, 4 vols. (Austin, Texas, and Edinburgh 1957), I, pp.237, 235.
13. G. Wilson Knight, *Poets of Action* (London, 1967), pp.257–59).
14. Letter to John Cam Hobhouse, 9 December 1811 (*LJ* II, pp.143–44).
15. *LJ* VI, pp.44–45.
16. Fletcher's letter is published in Peter Quennell, *Byron: A Self-Portrait. Letters and Diaries 1798 to 1824* (London, 1950), II, pp.428–29.
17. Irving Babbitt, *Rousseau and Romanticism*, 1919, p.201.

FASCINATION AND SCANDAL: ON JOHN GAY'S *BEGGAR'S OPERA* AND THE DOCTRINE OF POETIC JUSTICE
Wolfgang Zach

1. Quoted from Leo Hughes, *The Drama's Patrons: A Study of the 18-Century London Audience* (Austin and London, 1971), p.147.
2. Cf. William Eben Schultz, *Gay's Beggar's Opera: Its Content, History and Influence* (New Haven, 1923).
3. On this problem cf. *Literatur und Kriminalität: Die gesellschaftliche Erfahrung von Verbrechen und Strafverfolgung als Gegenstand des Erzählens*, edited by Joachim Linder and Jörg Schönert (Tübingen, 1983).
4. cf. Wolfgang Zach, *Poetic Justice: Begriff — Idee — Komödienkonzeption*, Buchreihe de Anglia, XXVI (Tübingen, 1986).
5. Cf. Schultz, *passim*; *Memoirs Concerning the Life and Manners of Captain Macheath* (London, 1728).
6. Cf. *Boswell's London Journal*, edited by Frederick Pottle (N.Y., 1950).
7. Cf. *Contexts 1: The Beggar's Opera*, edited by J.V. Guerinot and R.D. Jilg (Hamden, Conn., 1976), pp. 119ff., 150ff. Schultz, p.231.
8. Cf. Schultz, p.xxi: 'The Morality question'.
9. *Street-Robberies, Considered* (London, 1728), p.48; *Second Thoughts are Best* (London, 1729), p.3.
10. Joseph Addison's fundamental critique of the 'dogma' of poetic justice in *The Spectator*, 40 (1711), was a revolutionary act of 'heresy'. Yet he, too, held to the rule that offences against the moral norm should be punished in literature (see *The Spectator*, 548).
11. Cf. Michael Denning, 'Beggars and Thieves', *Literature and History*,1 VIII, 1 (1982), pp.41–55.
12. Cf. John J. Richetti, *Popular Fiction Before Richardson: Narrative Patterns 1700–1739* (Oxford, 1969), pp.23ff.
13. Cf. *The Touch-Stone* (London, 1728), p.56.

14. Cf. Schultz, pp.231ff.
15. Cf. Gerd Stratmann, 'John Gay: *The Beggar's Opera'*, in: *Das Englische Drama. Vom Mittelalter bis zur Gegenwart*, edited by Dieter Mehl, 2 vols. (Düsseldorf, 1970), II, 46–70, 55; cf. also Jörg Haslag, 'Poetische Gerechtigkeit und klassizistische Poetik in John Gay's *The Beggar's Opera'*, in *Studien zur englischen und amerikanischen Sprache und Literatur. Festschrift für Helmut Papajewski*, edited by P.G. Buchloh, I. Leimberg and H. Rauter (Neumünster, 1974), pp.195–223.
16. Cf. Joseph Wood Krutch, *Comedy and Conscience after the Restoration* (N.Y., 1924), pp.78ff., 101ff.
17. Cf. (Daniel Defoe), *Weekly Review*, III, No.129 (1706), pp.515ff.; Jonathan Swift, 'A Project for the Advancement of Religion, and the Reformation of Manners', in Swift, *Bickerstaff Papers and Pamphlets on the Church*, edited by Herbert Davis (Oxford, 1957), p.56; John Dennis, 'The Advancement and Reformation of Modern Poetry', in *The Critical Works of John Dennis*, edited by E.N. Hooker, 2 vols. (Baltimore and London, 1939–43), I, 225; Charles Gildon, *The Complete Art of Poetry*, 2 vols. (London, 1718), II, 263; *The Tatler*, 98, 182, 446; *The Spectator*, 51, 65, 75, 548; *The Lover*, No.5.
18. Georges Farquhar, 'A Discourse upon Comedy', in *Dramatic Essays of the Neoclassic Age*, edited by Henry H. Adams and Baxter Hathaway (N.Y., 1965), pp.211–233, 232.
19. Cf. Arthur Bedford, *A Serious Remonstrance in Behalf of the Christian Religion* (London, 1719).
20. Cf. Siegmund A. Betz, 'The Operatic Criticism of the *Tatler* and *Spectator'*, *The Musical Quarterly*, 31 (1945), 318–330; Jonathan Swift, *The Intelligencer*, III (1728); *Critical Works of John Dennis*, I, 382–393, II, 393–396; A.V. Berger, '*The Beggar's Opera*, the Burlesque, and Italian Opera', *Music and Letters*, 17 (1936), 93–105; Roger Fiske, *English Theatre Music in the 18th Century* (London, 1973), chapters I and III.
21. Cf. ' Preface' to *The Twin-Rivals'*, in: *Dramatic Works of Wycherley, Congreve, Vanbrugh, and Farquhar*, edited by Leigh Hunt (London, 1840), p.585; (Daniel Defoe), *Weekly Review*, II, No.26 (1705), 102; Jonathan Swift, 'Project for the Advancement of Religion', *op.cit.*
22. Cf. *Licentia Poetica Discuss'd* (London, 1709), pp.39,97.
23. 'Imitations of Horace. Epistle II.i. To Augustus', v.306., in Pope, *Horatian Satires and Epistles*, edited by H.H. Erskine-Hill (London, 1964), p.67.
24. Cf. *The Poetical Works of John Gay*, ed. G.C. Faber (1926, repr. N.Y., 1969), pp.236, 238, 265, 304ff., 435, 482; Patricia M. Spacks, *John Gay* (N.Y., 1965), pp.92ff.; Sven M. Armens, *John Gay—Social Critic* (1954, repr. N.Y., 1966), pp.217ff.
25. As is the case in Gay's farces *The Mohocks* (1712) and *The What D'Ye Call It* (1715) as well as in his tragedies *Dione* (1720) and *The Captives* (1724).

26. Cf. *Poetical Works of John Gay*, p.434; *The Letters of John Gay*, ed. C.F. Burgess (Oxford, 1966), p.53.
27. As Armens, pp.118f., has already suggested.
28. 'An Epistle to the Rght. Hon. Paul Methuen, Esq.', v.33ff.; cf. also *Poetical Works of John Gay*, pp.237, 289.
29. *Ibid.*, p.361.
30. Subsequently quoted from *The Beggar's Opera and other Eighteenth Century Plays*, edited by John Hampton, EL (London N.Y., 1928, repr. 1974), pp.107–159.
31. As Stratmann, *op.cit..*, has already demonstrated in some detail.
32. *The Art of Sinking in Poetry*, edited by Edna L. Steeves (N.Y., 1952, repr. 1968), p.78.
33. *Bertold Brechts Dreigroschenbuch* (Frankfurt, 1960), p.64; cf. also Stratmann, pp.65ff.
34. Cf. *An Apology for the Life of Colley Cibber. Written by Himself*, edited by B.R.S. Fone (Ann Arbor, Mich. 1968), p.135.
35. Cf. William H. Irving, *John Gay. Favorite of the Wits* (N.Y., 1962), pp.296ff., 308.
36. 'From *The Palace of Wisdom*', in *Twentieth Century Interpretations of the Beggar's Opera*, edited by Yvonne Noble (Englewood Cliffs, N.J., 1975), p.47.
37. As in Armens, p.141 ('The moral of the play is dismissed as the town in its ethical degradation dismisses morality',); and also in Harold G. Moss, '*The Beggar's Opera* as Christian Satire', in *Twentieth Century Interpretations*, p.63.
38. Cf. Schultz, p.209ff.
39. Printed in *Poetical Works of John Gay*, pp. 533–599. On the following cf. pp.537, 544, 591.
40. Cf. Schultz, pp.209ff.
41. George Colman toned down the social criticism in *his* adaptation of *Polly* (London, 1777). The play was only performed a few times. On the interpretation of *Polly* as the *Beggar's Opera*'s missing conclusion cf. *London Magazine* (June 1777); Schultz, p.238.
42. Cf. Schultz, p.244.
43. Cf. Sybil Goulding, '18th-Century French Taste and *The Beggar's Opera*', MLR, 24 (1929), 276–93.
44. Cf., for instance, Vicesimus Knox, *Essays Moral and Literary*, CXXI (1778), in *The Works of Vicesimus Knox*, 7 vols. (London, 1824), II, 19ff.
45. Cf. Hughes, pp.121ff.; Harry William Pedicord, *The Theatrical Public in the Time of Garrick* (N.Y., 1954), p.120ff.
46. Cf., above all, *The Rational Rosciad* (London, 1767), p.12; *The London Magazine* (1771), 483ff.
47. Cf. Schultz, pp.244–249; William Cooke, *Memoirs of Charles Macklin* (London, 1804), p.64; William A. Miles, *Letter to Sir John Fielding* (London, 1773), 'Postscript'.
48. This conclusion is not printed but is among the mss. in the collection of J. Larpent, the eighteenth-century English censor

(Larpent MS. 438). Cf. D. MacMillan, *Catalogue of the Larpent Plays in the Huntington Library* (San Marino, Cal., 1939).

49. Cf. Schultz, pp.74ff.; Hughes, pp.148ff.
50. Both closing scenes of *The Walloons* can be found in the Larpent MSS.
51. Cf. *The Beggar's Opera. Written by Mr. Gay. Compressed into Two Acts* (London, 1813).
52. Cf. L.W. Conolly, *The Censorship of English Drama 1737–1826* (San Marino, Cal., 1976), pp.137ff., 154ff.
53. Cf. Schultz, pp.256ff.
54. Cf. James Boswell, *Life of Johnson*, edited by R.W. Chapman and J.D. Fleeman (London, 1970), pp.628f. (18 April 1775); Samuel Johnson, *Lives of the English Poets*, edited by G.B. Hill (Oxford, 1905), II, 66.
55. 'Moral sense' psychology also played a significant role here. Cf. also Basil Willey, *The English Moralists* (London, 1955).
56. Cf. *The Complete Works of William Hazlitt*, edited by P.P. Howe, 21 vols. (London, 1930–34), IV, 153ff.; V, 1ff.; 324; VIII, 17ff.; XIX, 68ff.
57. Cf. Jean-Jacques Rousseau, 'Brief an d'Alembert über die Schauspiele', in *Theater der Aufklärung*, edited by R. Petermann and P.-V. Springborn (Munich and Vienna, 1979), pp.325–437; Hugh Murray, *The Morality of Fiction* (Edinburgh, 1805), pp.15ff.; Sir Walter Scott, *Lives of Eminent Novelists and Dramatists*, Chandos Classics (London, n.d.), p.32.
58. Cf. among others William Blake, *Complete Writings*, edited by Geoffrey Keynes (London, 1972), p.412; Wilson P. Knight, *An Analytical Inquiry into the Principles of Taste* (London, 1808), pp.457ff.; cf. also John Keats' letters (Feb. 3 and Oct. 27, 1818); Percy B. Shelley, 'A Defence of Poetry', in *English Critical Essays. 19th Century*, edited by Edmund D. Jones (London, 1968), pp.102–138, 116.
59. Cf. Scott, p.432; Knight, pp.430ff.; Byron, *Poetical Works*, edited by Frederick Page and John D. Jump (London, 1975), p.134.
60. Byron, *ibid.*
61. Quoted from Schultz, p.262.
62. In Dieter Wellershoff, *Literatur und Veränderung* (Berlin, 1969), pp.72–82.
63. Cf. Conolly, pp.155ff.; John R. Stephens, *The Censorship of English Drama 1824–1901* (Cambridge, 1980), pp.61ff., 78ff., 144ff.
64. Quoted from J. Scharrer, *Die publizistischen Mittel in christlicher Sicht* (Köln, 1965), pp.29ff.
65. Cf. also Günther Fetzer, *Wertungsprobleme in der Trivialliteraturforschung* (München, 1980), p.124.
66. Cf. Thomas S. Kuhn, *Die Struktur wissenschaftlicher Revolutionen* (Frankfurt, 1967).
67. Cf. also Jochen Schulte-Sasse, 'Autonomie als Wert', in *Literarische Wertung*, edited by Norbert Mecklenburg (Tübingen, 1977), pp.171ff.

REJOICE. A PROSE POEM
May Ziadah

1. May Ziadah, the foremost woman writer in Arabic literature of the first three decades of this century, was the only child of a Lebanese father and a Palestinian mother. Born on 11 February 1886, she was educated in her birthplace of Nazareth and in Lebanon before moving with her family to Cairo. After graduating from the Egyptian National University she became a writer, regularly contributing to several leading newspapers and periodicals, and in 1911 published her first major literary work, *Fleurs de Rêve*, written in French. Through her work as a reviewer she was introduced to the writings of Kahlil Gibran, whose influence on her thought and style can be found everywhere in her works, and with whom she corresponded intimately for twenty years. She also became closely involved with the Women's Emancipation Movement, led by the Egyptian suffragette Huda Sha'wari – a cause which developed into a consuming passion to the end of her life. She died in 1941.

The bulk of her published work consists of essays, articles, reviews, translations, two biographical studies, a few poems, a journal and letters. She is perhaps the most significant woman essayist in early 20th-century Arabic literature despite a style which now seems to suffer from a somewhat exaggerated emotional quality. At a time when few Arab women expressed themselves in writing, it is remarkable to find one able to put before us the deeper stirrings of her sex and generation with such honesty and force.

NOTES ON CONTRIBUTORS

Earle Birney was born, raised and semi-educated in Western Canada. Attempts at completion made in various universities (Toronto, California, London, etc.), and in the Canadian Army (Sussex, Ghent, Nijmegen, etc.). He taught ancient English to young Canadians and Americans until 1962. Since then he has written a lot of poems, some prose fiction, plays and the like, and avoided teaching anybody anything.

Terence Brown was educated at Sullivan Upper School, Holywood, Co. Down; Magee University College, Derry, and Trinity College, Dublin, from where he received the degrees of M.A. and Ph.D. He is Associate Professor in the Department of Modern English in T.C.D. and is also a Fellow of the College. He has lectured on Anglo-Irish literature in many parts of the world and was Secretary of the International Association for the Study of Anglo-Irish Literature (1976–79). Among his publications are *Time Was Away: The World of Louis MacNeice* (co-edited with Alec Reid, 1974); *Louis MacNeice: Sceptical Vision* (1975); *Northern Voices-Poets from Ulster* (1975); *The Irish Short Story* (co-edited with Patrick Rafroidi, 1979); *Ireland: A Social and Cultural History, 1922–79* (1981).

Suheil Badi Bushrui is Professor of English and Anglo-Irish Literature at the American University of Beirut, Lebanon, and is currently Distinguished Visiting Fellow and Kahlil Gibran Professor at the Center for International Development and Conflict Management, University of Maryland. From 1959 to 1962 he was British Council Scholar and Research Fellow at the University of Southampton, and in 1963 he was awarded the Una Ellis-Fermor Prize for literature. He recently spent a three-year period as Visiting Professor of English Literature at Oxford

305

University (1983–1986). Professor Bushrui is a distinguished author, poet, critic, translator and broadcaster, and is well known for his work on W.B. Yeats and on Kahlil Gibran, in both Arabic and English. He is also cultural and English language consultant to several Heads of State and Arab governments. Since 1985 Professor Bushrui has been Chairman of the International Association for the Study of Anglo-Irish Literature (IASAIL).

John Pepper Clark was born in Kiagbolo, Nigeria in 1935. He was educated at Warri Government College, at the University of Ibadan and Princeton. Head of features and editorial writer in the *Daily Express*, Lagos 1961–62. Since 1964 in the English Department, University of Lagos, where he is Professor. Founded *The Horn* magazine. He has published poetry: *A Reed in the Tide* (1965) and *Casualties* (1970); plays: *Song of a Goat* (1961) and *Ozidi* (1966); autobiography: *America, Their America* (1964); and criticism: *The Example of Shakespeare* (1970).

David Daiches is Director of the Institute for Advanced Studies in the University of Edinburgh and Professor Emeritus of the University of Sussex. Author of numerous critical, historical and biographical works, including *A Critical History of English Literature* and *God and the Poets*, he has taught at both Oxford and Cambridge and at a number of American universities.

Dan Davin was born in New Zealand in 1913, and educated at Otago University and Balliol College, Oxford (Rhodes Scholar, 1936–39). He served with the New Zealand Division in the Second World War (wounded in Crete, M.B.E., Mil., 1945), first as an Infantry Platoon Commander and, in the later stages of the war, as an Intelligence Officer. In 1945 he joined the staff of the Clarendon Press, Oxford. In 1978 he retired as Academic Publisher to Oxford University and Deputy Chief Executive of O.U.P. He is an Emeritus Fellow of Balliol College and has published seven novels and three volumes of short stories.

T.A. Dunn, a former student of Professor Jeffares when he was at Edinburgh, has been Professor of English in the Universities of Ghana and Lagos, Visiting Professor at U.W.O., London, Ontario, and is now founding Professor of English Literature in the University of Stirling. Author of a study of Philip Massinger.

Geoffrey Dutton was born at Anlaby, a sheep-station in South Australia, in 1922. He served as a pilot in the Royal Australian Air-Force 1941–45. After the war he read English at Magdalen College, Oxford (B.A. 1949). He lectured in English for some years at the University of Adelaide before retiring to work full time as writer, publisher and editor. He has published over forty books.

Nissim Ezekiel is the author of seven collections of verse, the latest being *Hymns in Darkness* and *Latter-Day Psalms* (Oxford University Press, New Delhi). He has edited *An Emerson Reader, A Martin Luther King Reader, Writing in India* and several other publications. He was Visiting Professor, University of Leeds, January—June 1964.

Alastair Fowler read English at Edinburgh University, where he was fortunate in having Derry Jeffares as tutor. Later a Fellow of Brasenose, and then Regius Professor of Rhetoric and English Literature at Edinburgh, he has published two volumes of verse, *Catacomb Suburb* (1975) and *From the Domain of Arnheim* (1982).

Maurice Harmon is Editor of *Irish University Review: A Journal of Irish Studies*, Director of the Postgraduate programme in Irish Studies at University College, Dublin where he is Professor, a member of the Royal Irish Academy, and former Chairman of the International Association for the Study of Anglo-Irish Literature. He has written a number of books on Irish Literature, including *Sean O'Faolain: a critical introduction* (1985) and has edited *The Irish Writer and the City* (1985).

Barbara Hayley is Professor of English at Saint Patrick's College, Maynooth. She was educated at Trinity College, Dublin, and the University of Kent at Canterbury. At the University of Cambridge she was a Gulbenkian Research Fellow and then a Fellow of Lucy Cavendish College. Her books include *Carleton's Traits and Stories of the Irish Peasantry and the Nineteenth Century Anglo-Irish Tradition; A Bibliography of William Carleton; Carleton's Traits and Stories: An Appendix*: she has co-edited *Irish Theatre Today*, and is at present writing *A History of Irish Periodicals, 1800–1870*.

Seamus Heaney was born in Co. Derry and educated at St Columb's College, Derry, and Queen's University, Belfast. He taught at Queen's University from 1966 to 1972. He moved to Co. Wicklow in 1972 to write full-time. He was appointed Boylston Professor of Rhetoric and Oratory at Harvard University in 1985 and teaches there in the spring term every year. His most recent books are *Station Island* (1984) and *Sweeney Astray* (1983). His translation of the Ugolino episode from the *Inferno* appeared in *Field Work* (1979).

Alec Derwent Hope was born in Cooma, New South Wales, in 1907. Poet, critic and university teacher (retired), he was educated at Sydney University and Oxford University. He has received numerous awards for poetry from England, Australia and the U.S.A. Awarded the O.B.E. and the Order of Australia. He has travelled widely in the British Isles, Canada, America, Europe, Asia and New Zealand. He is now living in retirement in Canberra, Australia.

John Horden is Professor of Bibliographical Studies at the University of Stirling. He has written extensively on Renaissance literature and bibliography. His books include: *Francis Quarles: A Bibliography* and *John Freeth: Political Ballad Writer*. At present he is engaged in editing *The Dictionary of Scottish Biography*.

Brendan Kennelly was born in Ballylongford, County Kerry. A Fellow and Professor of Trinity College, Dublin, he has published nearly thirty volumes of poetry, the most recent of which was *Cromwell* (1984). He is also a critic and an editor.

G. Wilson Knight, C.B.E., F.R.S.L. (1897–1985) was Chancellor's Professor of English at Trinity College, Toronto (1931–40) and Professor of English Literature at Leeds University, retiring in 1962. Novelist, playwright, poet, biographer and teacher, he is best known for his many original and illuminating interpretations of Shakespeare, from *Myth and Miracle* (1929) to *Shakespearian Dimensions* (1984). He also wrote seminal works on Milton, Pope, Byron especially, and other Romantic poets, as well as on contemporary writers, notably a pioneering study of John Cowper Powys, *The Saturnian Quest* (1964, 1978). His work in the theatre was as impressive. He both directed and acted leading roles in Shakespearian and other plays, and the last decade of his life was remarkable for his striking performances, in England, America and Canada, of his recital, 'Shakespeare's Dramatic Challenge'.

Heinz Kosok is Professor of English at the University of Wuppertal, Germany. He has published widely, both in German and in English, on eighteenth, nineteenth, and twentieth century literature in England, America and Ireland. From 1982 to 1985 he was Chairman of the International Association for the Study of Anglo-Irish Literature. His most recent book, *O'Casey the Dramatist*, was published by Colin Smythe and Barnes and Noble in 1985.

Seán Lucy is Professor of Modern English, University College, Cork. Has published two collections of poetry, and is preparing a third. Other works include: *T.S. Eliot and the Idea of Tradition*, *Love Poems of the Irish* (ed.), *Irish Poets in English* (ed.), and *How They Kidnapped Aoife*—a play.

Augustine Martin was born in Co. Leitrim in 1935, and educated at Cistercian College, Roscrea, and University College, Dublin (where he took the degrees of M.A. and Ph.D.), where he has been teaching since 1965. Among his publications are *James Stephens, a Critical Study* (1977), *Anglo-Irish Literature, A History* (1980), an edition of *Winter's Tales from Ireland* (1971) and of *The Charwoman's Daughter* (1972), articles on Yeats, Joyce, Synge, Behan, Mary Lavin, and Sean O'Casey. He was elected by the graduates of the National University to the Irish Senate in 1973 and 1977. He was Visiting Professor to Hofstra University (1974) and Scholar in Residence at Miami, Ohio (1980) and has been Professor of Anglo-Irish Literature and Drama at University College, Dublin, since 1979. He is engaged on a history of the Irish Short Story and a book on the politics of W.B. Yeats. He was Associate Director of the Yeats Summer School in 1977, and Director in 1979 and 1980.

John Montague was born in Brooklyn in 1929. He is the author of many books of poetry—*Poisoned Lands* (1961/76), *A Chosen Light* (1967), *Tides* (1970), *The Rough Field* (1972), *A Slow Dance* (1975), *The Great Cloak* (1978), *Selected Poems* (1982) and *The Dead Kingdom* (1984). He is working on a second collection of stories, the first being *Death of a Chieftain* (1964). Editor of *The Faber Book of Irish Verse*. He has taught at many universities in America and France, including Berkeley and the Sorbonne. He is currently an Associate Professor at University College, Cork. He has received many awards and is President of *Poetry Ireland* and Vice-President of the Irish Academy of Letters.

J.E. Morpurgo is Emeritus Professor of American Literature, University of Leeds, where he held the chair from 1969. He was Professor of American Literature at the University of Geneva 1969–70. Before that he was editor of Penguin Books and Director General of the National Book League. He is the author of numerous studies, histories and biographies, including *Last Days of Shelley and Byron* (1951), *Barnes Wallis: A Biography* (1972), and *Allen Lane, King Penguin: A Biography* (1979).

Arthur Ravenscroft has taught in the Universities of Cape Town, Stellenbosch, Zimbabwe, and Leeds. Editor (1965–1979) of *The Journal of Commonwealth Literature*, he has written extensively on African (e.g. *Chinua Achebe*, 1969) and other Third World literatures, as in Methuen's *Guide to Twentieth-Century Literature in English*, 1983.

Lorna Reynolds, who is at present co-editing with Professor O'Driscoll a series of books, the first of which will be *The Untold Story: The Irish in Canada*, is Professor Emeritus of University College, Galway, where she was formerly Professor of Modern English. Her book on Kate O'Brien has just appeared. She has written many critical articles, and many poems, published in various journals over the years.

Anna Rutherford is in charge of Commonwealth Studies at the University of Aarhus, Denmark. She is Chairperson of the European Branch of the Association for Commonwealth Literature and Language Studies, editor of *Kunapipi* and director of Dangaroo Press. Her published works include *Common Wealth*. She is co-editor, with Donald Hannah, of *Commonwealth Short Stories*; and, with Kirsten Holst Petersen, of *Enigma of Values*, a work of criticism on the Guyanese writer Wilson Harris, and of *Cowries and Kobos: the West African Oral Tale and Short Story*.

Ann Saddlemyer is Professor of English, Victoria College, and Director of the Graduate Centre for Study of Drama, University of Toronto. Author and editor of works on and by Yeats, Synge, Lady Gregory and other modern dramatists, co-editor of *Theatre History in Canada*. Former Chairman of the International Association for the Study of Anglo-Irish Literature; founding President of the Association for Canadian Theatre History. Most recent publication: *The Collected Plays of J.M. Synge* (2 vols.); now doing research towards a biography of George (Mrs W.B.) Yeats. Fellow of the Royal Society of Canada.

Stewart Sanderson, formerly Director, Institute of Dialect and Folk Life Studies and Chairman, School of English, is honorary Harold Orton Fellow, University of Leeds. Educated George Watson's College; the RNVR; University of Edinburgh. Corresponding Member, Royal Gustav Adolfs Academy; former President, Trustee, Folklore Society; Coote Lake Research Medal. Publications include: *Hemingway* (1961); *The Secret Common-wealth* (1976); *The Linguistic Atlas of England* (1978); *Studies in Linguistic Geography* (1985). British Library Advisory Committee on the National Sound Archive; Scottish Arts Council (Chairman, Literature Committee).

James Simmons was born in Londonderry in 1933. He has published eight collections of poetry, most recently *From the Irish* (Blackstaff Press, Belfast). Macmillan published his *Sean O'Casey* (1983). He founded *The Honest Ulsterman* in 1968. Two L.P.s of his songs have appeared. He taught English at the New Unversity of Ulster from 1968 until his retirement in 1983.

Colin Smythe, publisher and bibliographer, is general editor of the Coole Edition of Lady Gregory's works, co-general editor of the Collected Works of G.W. Russell (AE), editor of *Robert Gregory 1881–1918*, Lady Gregory's *Coole*, and *Seventy Years 1852–1922*, and author of *A Guide to Coole Park, Home of Lady Gregory*. He is presently working on the 4th edition of Allan Wade's *A Bibliography of the Writings of W.B. Yeats* and a bibliography of Lady Gregory's works. He is an Honorary Research Associate of Royal Holloway and Bedford New College, University of London.

Michele Spina was born in Messina on 9 June 1923. He studied first Architecture and later Literature in Milan. After the war he published articles and short stories in newspapers and periodicals, including *L'Avanti*, *Politecnico*, *Mondo Operaio*, *Domenica*, *Cosmopolita*, *The Kenyon Review*, *Letteratura*, *Il Caffe*. He has written art criticism and his articles, reviews and introductions for exhibitions have appeared in various newspapers and journals, among them *Prisma*, *Paese-Sera*, *Bimestre*. In 1967 he moved to England and taught art history at Leeds Polytechnic. In 1981 he published *Passo Doppio* (Scheiwiller, Milan). He now divides his time between London and Milan.

Randolph Stow was born in 1935 at Geraldton, Western Australia, and educated at Guildford Grammar School and the University of Western Australia. After graduation he worked on a Mission for Aborigines in the tropical north of Western Australia, studied anthropology, and for a while was attached to the Government Anthropologist of Papua New Guinea as his assistant. Has been lecturer in English Literature at the Universities of Leeds and Western Australia and a Harkness Fellow in the United States. Since 1969 has been a full-time writer, living in East Anglia. His publications include the novels *To The Islands, Tourmaline, The Merry-go-round in the Sea, Visitants, The Girl Green as Elderflower* and *The Suburbs of Hell*; the verse-collections *Outrider* and *A Counterfeit Silence*; the children's book *Midnite*; and the music-theatre works *Eight Songs for a Mad King* and *Miss Donnithorne's Maggot* devised for the composer Peter Maxwell Davies.

James Sutherland was educated at Aberdeen Grammar School, The University of Aberdeen, and Merton College, Oxford. Before going to Oxford he taught for two years at the University of Saskatchewan. Later he taught for some years at Glasgow University, and then for many years at the University of London, where he held in succession the Chair of English at Birkbeck College, Queen Mary College and University College, and was for some years Public Orator. From 1940–47 he edited *The Review of English Studies*, and in 1956 gave the Clark Lectures (*English Satire*) at Cambridge, and the Alexander Lectures (*On English Prose*) at Toronto. His books include: *Defoe* (1937), an edition of *The Dunciad* (1943), *A Preface to Eighteenth Century Poetry* (1948), and *English Literature of the Late Seventeenth Century* (1969). He is at present hoping to find a publisher for a book on *The Restoration Newspaper*.

Alastair Thomson has lectured at the Universities of Baghdad, Khartoum and Leeds and was Professor of English at the University of Ibadan, Nigeria, and at the New University of Ulster. He has published on Wordsworth, Valéry, and Tennyson.

Robert Welch is Professor of English at the University of Ulster. Before that he taught at Leeds, Ife and Cork. He has written *Irish Poetry from Moore to Yeats* (1980), *A History of Verse Translation from the Irish 1789–1897* (1988) and has edited various collections of essays. He is Vice-Chairman of the International Association for the Study of Anglo-Irish Literature, of which he was Secretary 1982–85. His *Companion to Irish Literature* is forthcoming.

Wolfgang Zach (M.A., Ph.D., Dr.habil.), teaches at Graz University, Austria. He has been the recipient of the Koerner Award; he has been Humboldt Fellow, and is Vice-Chairman of the International Association for the Study of Anglo-Irish Literature. Author of numerous studies in English and Anglo-Irish literature, literary theory and comparative literature (latest book on *Poetic Justice*, 1985). Co-editor of journals (*Irish Literary Supplement, Arbeiten aus Anglistik* und *Amerikanistik*), monograph series, bibliographies, and of the Proceedings of the Graz Conference of IASAIL, 1984.

INDEX